The Courts and the Colonies

Law and Society Series
W. Wesley Pue, General Editor

Alvin J. Esau

The Courts and the Colonies: The Litigation of Hutterite Church Disputes

UBCPress · Vancouver · Toronto

15 14 13 12 11 10 09 08 07 06 05 04   5 4 3 2 1

Printed in Canada on acid-free paper

Library and Archives Canada Cataloguing in Publication

Esau, Alvin A. J.
   The courts and the colonies : the litigation of Hutterite Church disputes /
Alvin J. Esau.

   (Law and society series, ISSN 1496-4953)
   Includes bibliographical references and index.
   ISBN 0-7748-1116-1

   1. Hutterite Brethren – Trials, Litigation, etc. 2. Hutterite Brethren – Manitoba –
Discipline. 3. Church and state – Manitoba. I. Title. II. Series.

BX8129.H8E83 2004   289.7'1   C2004-903152-X

Canadä

UBC Press gratefully acknowledges the financial support for our publishing program of the Government of Canada through the Book Publishing Industry Development Program (BPIDP), and of the Canada Council for the Arts, and the British Columbia Arts Council.

This book has been published with the help of a grant from the Canadian Federation for the Humanities and Social Sciences, through the Aid to Scholarly Publications Programme, using funds provided by the Social Sciences and Humanities Research Council of Canada.

UBC Press
The University of British Columbia
2029 West Mall
Vancouver, BC V6T 1Z2
604-822-5959 / Fax: 604-822-6083
www.ubcpress.ca

Contents

Acknowledgments

While I have drawn on a variety of scholarly works and journalistic accounts for this study, the primary sources are the voluminous court records at the pretrial stages, the transcripts of testimony and the documents introduced into evidence during the rounds of litigation in the *Lakeside* case, and the subsequent blizzard of litigation involving internal disputes at Hutterite colonies after the schism in the Schmiedeleut branch of the Hutterite church. Diane Rheault at the Manitoba Court of Queen's Bench Registry Office and Gordon Dodds of the Provincial Archives of Manitoba were particularly helpful to me in obtaining court records. Donald Douglas was the lawyer for the Hutterite defendants who were being sued by their own colony with the blessings of the leadership of the Schmiedeleut branch of the Hutterite church. I am most grateful to Mr. Douglas for not only providing documents but also kindly allowing me to sit at the counsel table during the second *Lakeside* trial. More recently, Michael Radcliffe, the lawyer who represented the plaintiffs, provided very helpful comments. Important unpublished materials were also provided to me by my now retired colleague, Prof. Burton Bass. I am also grateful to Dennis Stoesz at the Archives of the Mennonite Church at Goshen College for his help while I was researching the wider context of Anabaptist litigation.

Several Hutterite leaders allowed me to visit their colonies and were willing to share their perceptions with me and comment on aspects of the manuscript. I have learned a great deal from Rev. Samuel Kleinsasser of Concord Colony, both in our meetings and from his writings, which provide a particularly insightful overview of the causes and aftermath of the Schmiedeleut schism.[1] Rev. Michael Hofer of Sommerfeld Colony and Rev. John Hofer of James Valley Colony were both generous with their hospitality and insight. Finally, I want to thank the key players in the *Lakeside* case who were willing to meet with me, particularly Daniel Hofer and Paul Hofer, now of Heartland Colony, and Rev. Josh Hofer Jr. of Lakeside.

Dr. Leo Driedger, of the Sociology Department at the University of Manitoba, carefully read a much earlier draft of this book and provided useful directions. I have also benefited from the suggestions and encouraging comments provided by Dr. Ed Boldt, University of Manitoba; Dr. John Friesen, Canadian Mennonite University; and the late Dr. John Hostetler, then at Goshen College, Indiana. I am indebted to my colleague Dr. Wes Pue (now Nemetz Professor of Legal History at UBC), who first persuaded me to embark on this project many years ago, and also to Prof. John McLaren of the Faculty of Law, University of Victoria, who provided the intellectual leadership for a seminar on law and religion organized by the Centre for Studies in Religion and Society, where I was able to present a paper on the *Lakeside* case.[2] Prof. McLaren played the key role in organizing another conference where I again was provided an opportunity to present a paper.[3] Finally, my colleague Prof. Trevor Anderson provided considerable encouragement and reference material. Needless to say, if there are errors of fact remaining, they are the fault of the author and should not be attributed to those who have helped me.

Research assistance at early stages of the work was provided by Alexandra Lamont, Susan Waywood, and Michael Styczen, law students who worked for me on a variety of projects when I was the head of the Legal Research Institute at the University of Manitoba. The Institute has generously supported my work and the publication of this book. I would also like to acknowledge the stimulating and supportive work environment at the Faculty of Law, University of Victoria. I owe special thanks to Randy Schmidt, Darcy Cullen, and George Maddison at UBC Press, as well as the anonymous readers for their helpful comments. I am also grateful for the excellent work of my copy editor, Judy Phillips.

Like the litigation at Lakeside, which extended over a period of ten years, this book too has taken an extraordinarily long time to be completed. The work would not have been possible without Sandra Fowler Esau, who encouraged me and provided the support for me to take additional leave time. Leah, Rebecca, Benjamin, and Daniel Esau provided equal measures of diversion from the task and inspiration to continue it.

Introduction

The focus of this book is on Hutterite litigation generally and, more particularly, on the Manitoba case of *Lakeside Colony v. Hofer*, which went through two rounds of litigation, the first right up to the Supreme Court of Canada, and the second through a lengthy trial.[1] If ex-members of the Hutterite community had brought a lawsuit against the church to review the legality of their excommunication or to claim a share of the communal property, my interest in the case would not have been sparked. Indeed, such a case went all the way to the Supreme Court of Canada in 1970.[2] However, in *Lakeside* it was not the "apostates" but the leaders of the colony and conference who launched the lawsuit against another group of Hutterites who had allegedly been excommunicated but would not leave the colony. This sparked my interest because one central pillar of the Hutterite religion is nonresistance, the refusal to use violence against others. Initiating a civil lawsuit ultimately involves an aggressive act of getting court orders backed by the sword of the state, and the Hutterite leaders were willing to invoke this violence of the state to force those people who criticized and rebelled from their leadership off the colony. Was such action consistent with the historic nonresistance of Hutterites, or does it signal a fundamental change in Hutterite norms?

After the first round of litigation in the *Lakeside* case, the Schmiedeleut branch of the Hutterian Brethren Church split into two camps, partly as a result of the forces unleashed in the *Lakeside* litigation. The schism itself gave rise to a host of further litigation over membership and property issues between Hutterian factions at several Manitoba colonies, including Oak Bluff, Rock Lake, Huron, Cypress, Sprucewood, James Valley, and Concord, as well as at American colonies, such as Poinsett and Tschetter. I examine each of these court cases in this book.

Much of this book is descriptive. Reconstructing the historical events of this conflict within a colony and within the wider church serves in part as a case study of failure in conflict resolution. There may be many different perspectives that readers can bring to this narrative, and implications that they may draw from it. I hope that the narrative in and of itself has this purpose. My own limited analysis, however, involves a dual focus on what I call "inside law," on one hand, and "outside law," on the other hand. By inside law I mean Hutterite law: the fundamental ordinances of the Hutterite community that govern and structure it. For the Hutterite, the colony may be thought of as a communal ark of salvation that leads to eternal life in heaven, while the rest of the world is drowning in the flood of temporary selfish pride and pleasure leading to death. Life in the ark is based on ordinances which have a long tradition and which are legitimated as being divinely ordained. Nevertheless, Hutterite law is dynamic and subject to evolution as new circumstances and understandings arise. By outside law, I mean the law of the state, the official law of the host society, the law outside the ark. Thus Hutterite litigation, and the *Lakeside* case in particular, can be examined from the perspective of how the inside law and the outside law differ from and yet interact and affect each other.

Groups such as the Hutterites have a religious orientation that is comprehensive of all of life; thus the group potentially can generate and revise inside norms that apply to many areas of life over which the state also generates norms. The idea of inside and outside law may be misleading because the members of the religious group are also citizens of the state and so we may have various degrees of conformity or conflict between two legal systems that claim the same normative space. The concept of state law as outside law does not mean that it is foreign law or inapplicable to the religious group but only that it is generated from outside the particular group. The examination of Hutterite litigation raises questions as to how the outside law might deal with competing normative systems that claim their own jurisdiction; thus this work may have broader implications for studies on legal pluralism.

The Hutterites, operating large-scale agricultural and manufacturing enterprises, are frequent users of the outside law. Corporations are set up, land is purchased, contracts for the purchase and sale of products are entered into, and innumerable regulations are applied within the market economy in which Hutterites are integrated. But what are the inside law requirements as to the limitation on the use of the outside law? Did the Hutterite leaders violate their inside law by going to the outside law in the *Lakeside* case? To play with words, were they acting like outlaws by going to the outside law?

To shift the focus to the outside law, questions may be raised as to how the law should respond to what are essentially ecclesiastical disputes about church membership, discipline, and the division of communal church property in the face of a schism within a colony. Should the courts of the outside law even take jurisdiction to hear these cases and grant enforceable remedies to one or other of the parties? Should the outside law regulate the inside process of making decisions about expulsions from a colony? Should the outside law go even further and award shares of colony property to someone expelled from a colony?[3] Is the outside law premised on a normative culture of individual rights and autonomy that clashes with the communitarian norms of the inside law, or has the outside law accommodated the inside law? Should courts uphold the freedom of religious groups to act within their own normative space in ways that in other contexts would be considered violations of individual rights?[4]

There is obviously no neutral, unbiased perspective from which an author reconstructs historical events. From the outset it should be noted that I write as someone with roots in the larger Anabaptist community, and thus the tone of my comments will sometimes seem like that of an "insider" addressing Anabaptist readers. At the same time, however, my decision, about three decades ago, to become a lawyer was for me a conscious and often painful break with the more conservative Mennonite community I identified with. I write as an exile, living in the world of outside law, but deeply worried that outside law will eventually overwhelm and destroy the inside law of the Old Order Anabaptist communities. Furthermore, the story that I tell in this book, like all historical reconstruction, is shaped by the nature of the sources utilized. This is the story as found within the voluminous court records, involving dozens of cases, and I have attempted to put these cases into a comprehensive narrative with fairness to the arguments of both sides. Adversarial litigation may expose aspects of the story that would never have been available without it, but it also can distort and deflate other aspects. I expect there are many other stories that will in future be told utilizing other sources and perspectives.

Part One
Background

1
The Hutterites

Much has been written about the Hutterites in terms of their history and cultural practices.[1] In this chapter I provide only a very brief and broad overview of some matters so as to give a background understanding for the particularities of this case study.

Brief History

Like the Mennonites and Amish, the Hutterites trace their historical roots to the Anabaptist wing of the Reformation. Hutterites share with the Mennonites and Amish certain Anabaptist fundamentals, such as adult voluntary baptism, the separation of church and state, and the establishment of the church as a community that radically follows Jesus in all areas of life, including nonresistance – the refusal to use violence to protect the state or oneself.[2] However, what makes the Hutterites distinctive from other Anabaptist groups is that the communitarian view of the separated church includes the notion of community of property. Amish and Mennonites groups are known for having an ideology of, and organizations for, mutual aid to share property and resources within the group, but church members nevertheless individually own property.

In 1528 in Moravia (today a part of the Czech Republic), a group of Anabaptists who originally had fled from the Tyrol region of Austria decided to leave Nikolsburg, where the nobleman in charge was willing to use force to protect them from their enemies. Some Anabaptists did not want to be protected by force, even by those feudal nobles who were friendly to them.[3] This small group of two hundred or so people, at some stage in their journey from Nikolsburg to Austerlitz, so the story goes, placed all their personal belongings onto a cloak that had been put on the ground, and stewards were appointed to manage the property. When the group arrived in Austerlitz and lived on the estate of another nobleman sympathetic to Anabaptist views, the group continued to share all their possessions in common. Thus in addition to the central Anabaptist doctrine of non-violence, the Austerlitz group proclaimed a model of Christianity that included communal living and common ownership of all property. The concept of communal property simply means that all property within the group is church property. We can think of a Hutterite colony, including all the land, agricultural and manufacturing enterprises, housing units, common kitchen facility, machinery, and so forth as being a church, an "ark of salvation" set down in a "fallen" world. Hutterites live *in* a church, as compared with the modern secular-sacred division of life, where we go *to* church occasionally. This communal property regime is grounded in Hutterian religious belief, most notably from Acts 2:44: "And all that believed were together, and had all things common." It is noteworthy that this verse speaks of two matters: "being together" and "having all things common." We should not forget that communal property is just one foundational aspect of the larger concept of communal living. The central doctrine is that disciples of Jesus are called to live in community, yielding all of themselves to God and to each other, and that community property is a means to achieving this communal life. Without community of property, people tend not to really live together in a meaningful way. The rejection of private property is an act of loving the neighbour and surrendering individual self-will so as to live together as a community.[4]

During the group's first decade in Moravia, there were many difficulties in leadership, as well as severe persecution. The Hutterites eventually acquired their name from one of the early leaders of the group, Jacob Hutter, who was burned at the stake in 1536. Peter Riedemann, a subsequent leader, wrote a confession of faith while in jail in 1540; this work has nearly the authority of scripture for Hutterites to this day.[5] After an initial period of intense persecution, the Hutterites during approximately the last half of the 1500s had a golden period in Moravia and Slovakia, where approximately one hundred colonies were established under the protection of various nobles.[6] The Hutterites, perhaps numbering around 25,000, held all property in common at each colony, worked together at highly skilled crafts, sent out missionaries, and established many of the educational, religious, and cultural practices that they follow to this day. While the colonies (bruderhofs) were scattered throughout the region, they together constituted one brotherhood, with a senior elder (bishop) elected as head of the entire church, and with a minister in charge of spiritual affairs and a steward in charge of temporal affairs at each colony.

With the arrival of the Turkish War (1593-1606), the Thirty Years War (1618-48), and the persecutions of the Catholic Counter-Reformation, the colonies faced wave after wave of persecution and hardship. Hutterites were tortured and colonies plundered by marauding armies and bandits, and often men, women, and children were carried off into slavery. Finally, the remnant of Hutterites who survived was expelled from Moravia in 1622.

Some fled farther east to Transylvania (now Romania), while others found Slovakia (Upper Hungary) to be more peaceful, at least for some periods. However, the Hutterite colonies continued to experience severe persecution and decline. A remnant survived under the leadership of Andreas Ehrenpreis, the senior elder from about 1630 to 1662.[7] However, in the face of poverty, persecution, and loss of zeal, community of goods was abandoned in both Hungary and Transylvania in 1685-95, and many Hutterites were forcibly converted to Catholicism in the 1700s.

A tiny remnant of Hutterites could still be found in Transylvania in the late 1700s. This group traced its roots back to the expulsion from Moravia in 1622, though over the years it had dwindled down to only a handful of people. While the group had abandoned communal property, it still retained the Anabaptist religion. In 1755, a group of Lutherans who had been expelled from Catholic Carinthia in Austria came into contact with this tiny group of Hutterites. These Carinthian Lutherans, after reading the Hutterian literature, became convinced that the original Hutterian vision of community of goods should be reinstituted. These newcomers revitalized the movement. Many of the common Hutterian names of today, such as Hofer, Waldner, Kleinsasser, and Wurz, are derived from the Carinthians who helped revitalize Hutterianism. Community of goods was practised again, starting in 1762-63. The small group, under intense persecution, eventually found a short-lived haven at Walachia, near Bucharest. In 1770, in the face of renewed plundering and persecution, the group, by this time consisting of only about sixty people, fled to Russia.

A colony was established at Vishenka in the Ukraine and the old Hutterite pattern of life soon grew and thrived. In 1802 the colony moved to Radichev in the Ukraine. Although the Hutterites were not persecuted in Russia, they suffered a gradual loss of internal morale. A split developed between those led by Johannes Waldner, who wanted to stick to community of property, and those led by Jacob Walter, who wanted to abandon the concept. In 1819 community of goods was abandoned again, and the community rapidly declined. In 1842, in a state of utter poverty, the Hutterites moved to the Molotschna area of the Ukraine where the Mennonites lived. The Hutterites adopted the Mennonite village pattern of community life and, with the economic and educational help of the Mennonites, the community grew in prosperity. By 1868 there were five Hutterite villages within the larger Mennonite commonwealth.

It was here among the Mennonites that the second great return to community of property occurred. This was carried forward to North America, where it has thrived for more than a century. In 1859 Rev. Michael Waldner, a blacksmith by trade, reintroduced community of property in Russia and established a colony of seventeen families. Eventually this group grew into a branch of Hutterites calling themselves the Schmiedeleut (blacksmith people). In 1860 Rev. Darius Walter also managed to establish a colony with about the same number of families. This group eventually became known as the Dariusleut. When the Russian state threatened to remove military exemption and impose restrictions on education, these two colonies moved, in 1874-75, to what is now South Dakota. The Schmiedeleut established Bon Homme Colony and the Dariusleut established Wolf Creek Colony. It should be remembered that these two groups had already lived separately under a community of goods regime in Russia for about fifteen years before arriving in the United States. A third group, which had not practised community of property in Russia, moved to the Dakota Territory in 1877. This third group established Elmspring Colony and began practising community of property. Led by Rev. Jacob Wipf, a teacher, it eventually became known as the Lehrerleut (teacher people). Other Hutterites came to South Dakota at the same time; commonly referred to as "Prairieleut," they did not practice community of goods but, rather, homesteaded or purchased individual plots of land. Many of them later joined Mennonite congregations.[8]

Altogether, the three communal groups that established colonies in South Dakota numbered only about 450 adults and children. Yet, from these three original colonies established in 1874-77 grew the more than 400 Hutterite colonies currently in Western Canada and the United States, with approximately 40,000 members in total.[9] This growth is based on a high Hutterian birth rate (although more recently it has dropped), as well as the phenomenal economic success of the colonies.[10] The North American experience of the Hutterites has led to another golden period of prosperity, but there have also have been periods when the three Leuts experienced difficulties with the host society, and also, as I shall document in this book, internal conflicts that have led to severe hardships.

Discrimination and hostility toward the Hutterites in the United States arose during the First World War. According to John A. Hostetler, conscientious objectors were still required to join the army as non-combatants, and this meant registering for the draft, wearing the army uniform, and performing non-combatant tasks within the army.[11] Young Hutterite men arriving at induction centres would not wear army uniforms or do army duty. Persecution against them within the army became quite intense:

> At Camp Funston some of the men were brutally handled in the guardhouse. They were bayonetted, beaten, and tortured by various forms of water "cure" ... Men were often thrown out of a window and dragged along the ground by their hair and feet by soldiers who were waiting outside. Their beards were disfigured to make them appear ridiculous. One night, eighteen men were aroused from their sleep and held under cold showers until one of them became hysterical. Others were hung by their feet above tanks of water until they almost choked to death. On many days they were made

to stand at attention on the cold side of their barracks, in scant clothing, while those who passed by scoffed at them in abusive and foul language. They were chased across the fields by guards on motorcycles under the guise of taking exercise, until they dropped from sheer exhaustion. In the guard-house they were usually put on a diet of bread and water.[12]

At other camps, the treatment of the Hutterite men was similar, but the event that persuaded the Hutterites to move to Canada was the death of some of their men in prison camp. Four Hutterites who reported to Fort Lewis, Washington, refused to wear army uniforms or perform non-combatant service for the army. They were sentenced to thirty-seven years in prison and taken to the military prison at Alcatraz:

> They were taken to a "dungeon" of darkness, filth, and stench and put in solitary confinement out of earshot of each other. The guard placed a uniform in each cell and said, "There you will stay until you give up the ghost – just like the last four we carried out yesterday" ... For several days the young men slept on the cold, wet concrete floor wearing nothing but their light underwear. They received half a glass of water every twenty-four hours but no food. There were beaten with clubs and, with arms crossed, tied to the ceiling. After five days they were taken from the "hole" for a short time. Their wrists were so swollen from insect bites and skin eruptions that they could not put on their own jackets ... After four months at Alcatraz the men were transferred to Fort Leavenworth, Kansas, by six armed sergeants.[13]

At Fort Leavenworth, further persecution and hardship followed. Two of the Hutterite men collapsed and were taken to hospital. The other two were held in solitary confinement, placed on starvation diet, and "made to stand nine hours each day with hands tied and their feet barely touching the floor."[14] The two men in the hospital died. When the wife of one of them came to see his body, she found that the army had put a uniform on the dead corpse, finally accomplishing in death what it could not in life. This experience of persecution and death was pivotal to the mass exodus of the Hutterites from the United States to Canada. The Schmiedeleut moved to the Elie district of Manitoba, where they established six colonies in 1918. Today there are more than one hundred Schmiedeleut colonies in Manitoba. The Dariusleut and Lehrerleut moved to southwestern Alberta, later expanding into Saskatchewan.

As a more hospitable climate developed in the United States, the Hutterites again established colonies there. In addition to their more than 100 colonies in Manitoba, there are about 70 Schmiedeleut colonies in South Dakota, North Dakota, and Minnesota. The Dariusleut have about 150 colonies, mostly in Alberta and Saskatchewan, but also in Washington and Montana, and the Lehrerleut about 125 colonies, mostly in Alberta, Saskatchewan, and Montana. The movement back to the United States was partly because of the discriminatory legislation and governmental policy restricting Hutterian land purchases that arose in Canada in the wake of the Second World War.[15]

Cultural Practice

While the three Hutterite Leuts have much in common, they have retained distinctions in terms of customs, and there is little intermarriage between the three tribes. However, the three groups constitute a wider church in a formal sense. In 1950 the three groups came together and formalized a *Constitution of the Hutterian Brethren Church and Rules as to Community of Property*.[16] The colonies of all three Leuts (until the schism I will be dealing with) were affiliated by this constitution, which served as a kind of articles of association for the wider church. In Canada there was also an incorporation of the church at the highest level by federal legislation.[17] The primary motivation for both the transnational constitution and the Canadian incorporation was the need for the three groups of Hutterites to cooperate on common issues involving the host society. Thus, we have three levels of the Hutterian Brethren Church: the colony level, the conference (Leut) level, and what might be called the constitutional level, which includes all three conferences.

While colonies, once established, have economic independence, each is associated with the larger Leut for various temporal and spiritual matters. Each colony has two representatives (usually the first and second minister), who sit on the Leut council. There may be a number of common Leut financial enterprises, and a colony cannot establish a daughter colony without Leut approval. Furthermore, the minister who heads the colony is chosen by a process that involves nomination by ministers from throughout the Leut, followed by a choice by lot from the shortlist of nominees. The Leut itself is headed by an elected senior elder, and there is a conference-level council of ministers that has certain powers and responsibilities for establishing the norms for the Leut. Details of Hutterian life, particularly the formal structures at the different levels of the church, will be dealt with further in the narrative of the dispute at Lakeside and within the Schmiedeleut.

Turning to the colony level, in our dominant culture, saturated with what Hutterites would view as excessive individualism, the Hutterite colony may look quaintly attractive to us as a model of primitive communal solidarity. However, most of us would probably find it quite impossible to live in such a restrictive community, which has a host of internal community rules (Ordnung) that have developed over the centuries.[18] While dealing with the outside world according to the law of the host society, the Hutterite colonies have their own internal legal system, including degrees of shunning for those who have violated the norms.

While some forms of property, such as radios, television sets, and cars, are prohibited on colonies, and many matters of personal dress and personal consumption are regulated, generally the Hutterites embrace modern technology in their economic enterprises. This is in contrast to the Amish, for example, who often reject technological innovations.[19] In theory, aside from a few personal mementos that might fit into a hope chest, the individual Hutterite does not own anything. This renunciation of personal property should not be confused with personal deprivation, however. Some Christians may stress the renunciation of acquisitive impulses and embrace a lifestyle of material deprivation. Frugality and self-denial in consumer consumption may well be part of Hutterian practice, but property is held in common so as to support a secure and healthy community life and build up the assets necessary to form a daughter colony. Hutterite colonies may be labelled Christian "communistic" societies, but they are also multimillion-dollar capitalist enterprises where the needs of the colonists are looked after from cradle to grave, and where the continual establishment of new colonies provides for the needs of the next generation.

Hutterite colonies are usually large-scale, highly mechanized, mixed-agricultural producers. Grain crops, hogs, dairy, eggs, ducks, geese, and turkey production are common. While the colonies may occupy only about one percent of the agricultural land of the prairie provinces, they produce a vastly disproportionate amount of agricultural product.[20] In Manitoba this is particularly true in terms of hog production and ducks, geese, and turkeys. Increasingly, the Schmiedeleut colonies are diversifying by adding manufacturing enterprise alongside traditional agricultural production.

One of the central ideologies of Hutterianism involves "gelassenheit," roughly translated as "giving up" or "giving in." This means that persons give up and surrender their individual selves to God and the community. A common analogy used to portray the surrender of the self to the community is the picture of grapes being crushed to make wine. Individualist grapes that refuse to be crushed do not fit into the communal wine. However, in reality, the managers of enterprises at a Hutterite colony may take a great deal of personal pride in and psychic identification with the facilities and profits of the enterprise they head. All the property belongs to God, but stewardship involves expanding God's ark and even competing with other stewards to demonstrate your worthiness.

One of the first concepts that law students learn is that property as a legal category is not the physical thing but a metaphysical bundle of rights associated with the thing. This bundle can be divided up. Someone may have the right of possession and use, while someone else may have the right of ownership. Just because Hutterites may not personally own property does not mean that they do not have property interests. So long as they are members, they may have a rich bundle of usufructuary rights to colony property that makes them in actuality wealthier than many people in the host society.

Unlike the Doukhobors and Mennonites, who were originally granted a large exclusive block of land for community settlement and then ran into internal and external conflict when those communitarian blocks of land reverted to individual ownership or when the exclusive area was opened up to other landowners outside the religious group,[21] the Hutterites simply bought blocks of land on the private market and held title to the land by way of trustees for the community or, more commonly, by setting up ownership of the land by a corporation. Furthermore, while there was convenience in having Hutterite colonies close to each other, unlike the Mennonites who at one stage in Russia had a "country within a country"[22] and wanted to replicate the model in Canada, the fundamental Hutterite unit was the colony of approximately one hundred individuals, and these colonies could be spread out over many municipalities.

After a Hutterite colony is established, assets are built up so that the colony can split and establish a new colony. Both the mother colony and the new daughter colony will then build up assets for the time when both of them will establish new colonies again. This constant creation of new colonies, given the high birth rates among Hutterites, controls the size of a colony to allow for meaningful relationships and work opportunities. Generally colonies are composed of about 100 to 150 people.

It would appear that while a few colonies may undergo economic hardship from time to time, the model of collective ownership and labour, continual technological innovation, and diversity of agricultural and, now, manufacturing product has produced a collective prosperity. However, while this prosperity may provide security for those who are members, the inside law grants no right to a share of church property to those who leave the colony or are expelled from it. As we will see in the examination of lawsuits that follows, one of the pervasive potential sources of tension between the inside law and the outside law is whether the outside law will continue to support the notion that people who may have worked all their lives within a colony should nevertheless have no right to any compensation or shares in the community property but must leave with but their shirts on their back if expelled.

At the colony level, the minister is the head; a number of other men form the executive committee, or "witness brothers." A second minister is often appointed at some stage so that when the colony splits a minister is at hand for each. After the first minister, the next most important position is the secretary or steward. While women are expected to be baptized and join the colony as members, they may not vote on issues at formal colony meetings; here too is a fundamental tension between the norms of the host society and the norms of the religious group.

Colony land is usually held by a colony corporation, and the economic affairs of the colony will also usually be transacted through a corporation. The colony itself, however, is usually an unincorporated association of members affiliated through formal articles of association, which serve as a kind of contract between members and constitution of the social group. These articles of association commonly outline the basic principles of membership, voting rights, procedures for discipline, rules of property, and so forth. To a degree, the inside law of the group is accommodated by the outside law, because the group can use the vehicles or tools of outside law, such as contract, corporate, and trust law, in an attempt to translate inside law into outside law categories.

Children attend a colony kindergarten from the age of about three until they start public school. Unlike some conservative Mennonite groups, the Hutterites allow English public schooling for their children.[23] However, they insist that this schooling take place on the colony. The colony constructs a schoolhouse and then the public-school board hires and pays teachers to teach at the colony. The Hutterites send their children to school only for the minimum period required by law – usually to the age of fifteen – after which the young person formally enters the colony workforce. (The education issue, examined later in this book, is one of the numerous points of contention in the Schmiedeleut schism.) The practice of having their children attend classes through to grade 12, and even an openness to university training for some Hutterites to become public schoolteachers on the colonies, has been affirmed by some Manitoba colonies.[24] The colony also provides a private German school, the classes of which are held before and after public-school hours and taught by a colony member.

While no reported litigation over this accommodation of the public school system to the needs of the Hutterites has arisen in Canada thus far, in South Dakota the Federal Trial Court has denied the claim of Hutterite colonies that they have a free exercise of religion right to have a publicly funded school on the colony, if the school board decides that the children should be bussed to town.[25] Since Hutterites would never bus their children to town, the result of the decision is to force the colonies to create private schools at their own expense if public-school boards do not accommodate them.

Young men and women are expected to become baptized and join the church. It is at the point of baptism that the person makes vows to follow the Hutterian way and formally signs the articles of association of the colony. Young people cannot be married in the church without first being baptized and joining it. Upon being married, a woman leaves her colony and joins the colony of her husband. After marriage, the Hutterite man grows a beard.

Families live in housing units assigned to them, but all meals are eaten together in a communal dining hall. Women eat at a separate table from the men. There is (or is supposed to be) a church service every day, where sermons are read and hymns sung.

The growth in the numbers of Hutterites is now almost completely a matter of people being born Hutterite and eventually being baptized into formal membership. The number of people who were not born Hutterite but joined a colony as adults is minuscule. Despite that the sixteenth-century Hutterites supported missionaries, many of whom died at the stake for their efforts, the Hutterites of today just want to be left alone, and they do not proselytize for converts in the host society. Furthermore, there is defection, particularly among young unbaptized males who leave a colony and go into the host society for a time. However, studies indicate that the vast majority of these defectors return to the colony.[26] Most defectors want to taste the freedom in the "evil" world, but some defectors leave because they find a more vital personal spirituality in evangelical and other groups. These people are unlikely to return to the Hutterite colonies.[27]

Dr. Karl Peter makes the point that Hutterite society is not static. He claims that the world view of Hutterites shifted fundamentally at some point from the early version where community of goods and living in community was a context in which the individual would struggle with selfish tendencies and achieve the psychological state of "gellassenheit," the overcoming of the flesh in a complete surrender of the self to God. The new version that developed was that salvation was not an individual struggle of the conscience but a gift, a guarantee that salvation was yours simply by your faithful living within the community of goods model. The colony was itself a portal of heaven where upon your death you passed through the door into eternal life. Living in the world, in contrast to the colony, was living in an evil realm destined for eternal death. Thus, at the colony level, salvation is secure and individuals have a "culture of work performance," where the performance of work is a major source of individual pride and satisfaction. Religion has become ritualized, while the survival of the colonies depends at the same time on a high level of economic rationality.[28]

Even with a continuation of economic prosperity, and even in the absence of the kind of community-destroying conflicts portrayed in this book, one may well wonder how the Hutterites have survived so long and will continue to survive if their religion has become merely ritualized, as Dr. Peter suggests. Unless there is a vital and living stream of faith flowing from the hearts and minds of the leaders and the flock, motivating the daily struggle to follow Jesus in living in community, surely there will be no foundation to hold up a healthy colony in the face of increased exposure to the relativistic individualized culture of the host society.

2
The Bruderhof

There has been a series of on again, off again relationships between the three main branches of the traditional Hutterites and a smaller fourth group of communitarians calling themselves "The Bruderhof" or "Society of Brothers."[1] Within the traditional Hutterites, this fourth group is sometimes referred to as the "Arnoldleut," named after its founder, Dr. Eberhard Arnold. This group consists of about 2,500 people living in a number of colonies in New York, Connecticut, Pennsylvania, England, and Australia.

The history and practice of this fourth group is significant, because one of the main points of tension at the heart of many of the conflicts to be examined in this book was the special relationship between the Schmiedeleut and the Bruderhof that was fostered by the senior elder of the Schmiedeleut, Rev. Jacob Kleinsasser of Crystal Spring Colony in Manitoba. This relationship was instrumental in leading to the reunification of the Bruderhof with the wider Hutterite community in 1974, and also ultimately to the repudiation of that relationship in 1990 by the Darius and Lehrer groups, followed by a schism in 1992 within the Schmiedeleut over the leadership of the senior elder, who maintained the Bruderhof relationship while the other two Leuts rejected it.

Dr. Eberhard Arnold

In 1920 Dr. Eberhard Arnold, a German theologian who had been the general secretary of the Evangelical Student Christian Movement, moved with his family and a small group of friends from Berlin to a rented farm in Sannerz, Germany. There he founded a Christian community based on community of property and nonresistance. Many young people were seeking more meaningful spiritual experiences in the wake of the First World War, and soon this little community in Sannerz could not accommodate all the new members and visitors. In 1926 a large farm was purchased in the Rhön Mountains; this became known as the Rhön Bruderhof. Despite severe economic problems and internal divisions, the community continued to attract many visitors and converts.

The charismatic Arnold never intended to found a new sect but, rather, sought to unite his group with others that followed the principles of Christian love and discipleship. He read the old Hutterian literature available to him and, after corresponding with the North American Hutterites, embarked on a trip in 1930 to visit those Hutterites, with the view to uniting his group with them, gather for purposes of publication Hutterian literature available at the colonies, and seek financial aid for the struggling Rhön community. This trip turned into a year-long enterprise, as he visited all thirty-five colonies existing in North America at the time.[2]

His resolve to unite with the Hutterites was reinforced by Arnold's reception among them. Writing about his first colony visit, Arnold notes: "The brothers and sisters of Bon Homme are very, very loving to me and to all of you ... The spirit and truth of today's Hutterianism, also here and now, surpass by far our expectations. An intimate relationship with God is living here, as also the belief in the Holy Spirit and in the redemption of Christ. There is here the deepest and strongest awareness that we need the constant coming of the Holy Spirit to stimulate and speak to us in the church."[3]

As Arnold visited more colonies, he maintained these positive comments about the deep spiritual vitality of the Hutterites, in sharp contrast to contemporary accounts of the ritualization of their religion. For example, he wrote. "The Hutterian religious faith is real and genuine. It is deeply rooted in the hearts of all. They do not wish to live, nor can they, in any other way than in community. The practical self-forgetfulness in the service of the community is much stronger than it is with us. The seriousness of the divine witness of the truth is strong, also in the simplest members."[4]

Arnold was also able to see the faults in the group he so desperately wanted to join. His correspondence back to the Bruderhof in Germany contained numerous references to these. One common theme was that the division of the Hutterites into three separate groups was sinful. He believed that the three Leuts should be united under the overall strong leadership of one elder, and he urged the three current elders to at least meet with each other to consult about common problems. At this time the relationship between the Lehrerleut and the Dariusleut was particularly strained, with the Lehrer judging some of the Darius colonies as spiritually cold and undisciplined. Arnold, although strongly supported by many Darius ministers, largely agreed with this assessment, stating on his return to Germany that "[c]ertainly there is great danger in the Manitoba communities (Schmied) that the spirit of the world and present-day life may creep in here and there. But there seems to me a still greater danger among the Darius communities of love growing cold, injustice increasing, and unity being extinguished."[5]

A second concern expressed by Arnold related to community of property. He did not like the idea that each colony was economically independent, which resulted in rich colonies and poor colonies. Arnold would have preferred that all colonies be owned collectively by the whole church, and members of the church could be moved from colony to colony whenever the leadership felt it was necessary to do so in the face of economic need or to prevent problems such as family factions or conflicts. A person should not think of a particular colony as his or her home or collective property but, rather, identify completely with the wider Hutterite church as his or her home. The economic independence of colonies not only led to inequality of resources but fundamentally threatened the core of the spiritual principle of giving up private property. Arnold observed that sometimes a colony was dominated by particular families. He called this the sin of "collective egoism," which was just as bad as "individual egoism." Writing to an elder in confidence, he stated: "Today the devil is using a much more cunning way to take you in. Instead of tempting you with individual property, he is getting you through collective property and its democratic majority, acting in the interests of the families 'owning' the hof. Only one thing can help you: families claiming to 'own' a hof must completely and forever give up any rights of ownership to the whole body as to the church of God, under one spirit-filled elder."[6]

There were other weaknesses that Arnold noted, but at bottom the strengths of the Hutterite church far outweighed the weaknesses, and Arnold achieved the uniting with the Hutterites that he sought. After receiving the consent of the elders of all three Leuts, the formal affiliation of the Bruderhof with the Hutterites took place at Stand Off Colony in Alberta in December 1930. The elders of both the Dariusleut and Lehrerleut were present, and Arnold was confirmed as a minister in the Hutterite church. Arnold wrote in jubilation that "[w]e are now the first Bruderhof belonging at the same time to the Dariusleut, Schmiedeleut, and Lehrerleut."[7] Arnold then went on a second tour of the North American colonies seeking financial aid for what was now the new Hutterian mission colony in Germany. Arnold was apparently not particularly successful in getting funds from the Hutterites, but it is unclear as to whether the principle of economic independence or the financial state of the Canadian colonies in the depression era was at the root of the difficulty.[8] Interestingly, in the establishment of various Bruderhof colonies, financial aid was usually provided by Quaker friends rather than by Hutterite brothers.[9]

The Rhön community struggled with the imposition of the many ancient and seemingly arbitrary Hutterian regulations on its previously more bohemian lifestyle. The rise of the Nazis to power led to the raiding and closing of the Rhön Bruderhof after much of the community had already fled to

Liechtenstein and then ultimately to England. Eberhard Arnold died in 1935 while having an operation on his leg. There is speculation that the Nazi doctor performing the operation may have intentionally killed him.[10] In England the new Cotswold Bruderhof attracted many converts, and a second bruderhof was soon established at Oaksey.

After the death of Arnold, numerous leadership struggles took place between members of the Arnold family. One of the ministers (Servants of the Word) for the community was Hans Zumpe, who had married the Arnold's oldest daughter, Emmy-Margaret. Zumpe, who stood in as leader while Arnold was away visiting the Hutterites in North America, had a great appreciation for the Hutterites but apparently resisted accepting the entire bundle of Hutterian ordinances for the newer community.[11] Georg Barth, Eberhard Arnold's brother-in-law, was another community leader. Eberhard Arnold also had three sons, Hardi, Heini, and Hans-Herman; after a visit by two Hutterite elders in 1937, Hardi and Heini were also ordained as ministers. Hans-Herman was ordained eventually, as was Balz Trumpi, who married the youngest daughter of Eberhard and Emmy Arnold. Thus, despite the family factions that Eberhard saw as destructive of true community, the history of the Bruderhof itself was characterized by leadership devolving within one family and feuds between them for leadership positions.

Hans Zumpe was placed under church discipline and excluded for a year in England in 1938 as Hardi Arnold took over the leadership position. Hardi was a gifted evangelist and many new converts joined the community. However, as the Second World War got underway, English authorities, motivated by anti-German sentiment, notified the Bruderhof that German members would be interned. The Bruderhof decided to move en masse to Paraguay in 1940-41 after being refused admission into Canada and the United States. At this stage the community consisted of about 350 people. The Bruderhof sold the community property in England and bought a twenty-thousand-acre "ranch" called Primavera, in the jungles of Paraguay. A few members stayed behind in England, establishing the Wheathill Bruderhof, while the main branch established itself in Paraguay.

Primavera and Breaking Away from the Hutterites

Under incredibly harsh jungle conditions, the Bruderhof finally carved out three colonies (Isla Margarita, Loma Hoby, and Ibate) on the Primavera property. It also established a communal house in Asunción as a base for business in the city and as a home for young people from the community who were taking higher educational training. The Bruderhof consisted of people with diverse ethnic backgrounds and, unlike the traditional Hutterites, included many members with considerable educational achievements. An English lawyer joined the group and used his skills negotiating purchases of land and handling inheritances and legal transactions on behalf of the

Bruderhof. Several medical doctors joined the Bruderhof and established a thriving hospital that served not only the Bruderhof but also neighbouring Native people. The openness to higher education and diversity of backgrounds continues to this day. A sociologist who studied the group in the 1960s noted that the membership at that time included a former millionaire steel tycoon, a former Philadelphia lawyer, and several doctors.[12]

During the first few years in Paraguay, the leadership struggles continued. Hardi Arnold was placed under church discipline and his younger brother Heini took the leadership position. However, Heini Arnold got very sick and, on what he believed to be his deathbed, he reconfirmed his brother-in-law Hans Zumpe, his brother Hardi Arnold, and his uncle, Georg Barth, as Servants of the Word. After Heini recovered, the leadership tensions continued as Zumpe and Barth gained control. In 1944, all three Arnold sons – Hardi, Heini, and Hans-Herman – as well as several others associated with them, were sent away into exclusion, some for several years. The Bruderhof concluded that the Arnolds, including the wife of the founder, were unjustifiably demanding a privileged position in leadership.[13] Roger Allain, who was at one time a minister but later left the community, subsequently wrote about this exclusion using fictional names:

A joint Brotherhood meeting was suddenly called and a report given about a plot hatched to overthrow the leaders. The chief culprits, we were told, were Loni, Andy, Donald, and Ernst. They had met secretly to vent their grievances and written to the Hutterian Elders in Canada for their support. It was an attack against our most cherished principle, the unity of the Church – it was high treason! The accused acknowledged the main facts and recognized their responsibility. Short work was made of them. They were condemned to the Great Exclusion, away from the commune, while their respective wives and a few brothers who had been approached but not dared to join were condemned to the Small Exclusion for having failed to report the plot.

... [W]e didn't question the reports we heard, nor did we consider giving the accused brothers a really fair hearing, or to stop and think of the harm to their children who would be separated from their parents for months or years. Conditioned to obedience as we were, we blindly followed the leaders, fearful of the split in the commune which they said would have arisen out of the rebels' action. We didn't see that our canon of unanimity excluded the possibility of any loyal opposition and doomed any criticism or dissent to go underground and be treated as high treason, just as in any totalitarian state.[14]

The excluded former leaders later reconciled with the community. Heini Arnold, upon his readmittance into Primavera, spent many years working in the horse stables in the morning and teaching school in the afternoon. Eventually he was again made a minister and sent on a mission to North America, where he built a base from which he would emerge as the elder of all the Bruderhof. Hans-Herman, the younger brother, became a minister for a time but was excluded from the community after being accused of impropriety when he told a young woman that the man whom she loved had chosen a different life partner. As Elizabeth Bohlken-Zumpe recalls it, "[a]fter a few days, Hans-Herman asked for a personal talk with that girl. He tried to convey to her that the boy was no longer available to share her future. She was terribly upset. Hans-Herman tried to comfort her as he would have comforted his own daughter. What happened after that was incredible! The girl went to the other Servants and accused Hans-Herman of becoming too intimate, too personal. All the Servants of the Word and Witness Brothers convened at the Loma Hoby Bruderhof and put Hans-Herman into the Great Exclusion as though he had committed a terrible sin!"[15] After a year, Hans-Herman was back in the community but was later excluded for many years when his brother Heini was the leader.

Two Hutterite leaders travelled to the Primavera colonies in 1953, staying for a couple of months. At this stage the community had grown to about six to seven hundred people.[16] As a result of the visit, the formal incorporation of the Bruderhof into the Hutterian Brethren Church, which had lasted for twenty years, was revoked by mutual consent. One version of the event is that the Hutterite elders were not treated with the love and respect they felt they deserved. From inside the Bruderhof, Merrill Mow would later write: "These brothers [from North America] sensed that there was something missing in the community ... So in 1950 they asked that we take on certain 'points' that are traditional amongst the Western colonies ... The brothers had a series of these points from their rules of church order. The next day our brothers brought an equal number of points and said, 'We'll accept yours if you will accept ours.' Now this was a very disrespectful response, and not in a spirit of seeking unity."[17] Another insight into the event is provided by Hans Zumpe's daughter: "We acceded to their customs in order not to hurt their feelings, but this was not genuine. Many brothers and sisters were burdened by this and talked to my father. They felt it would have been more honest to tell these brothers from the very start of our differences. Our brothers smoked, we loved folk dancing, but we remained in complete unity about the beliefs and community rules written down by Peter Riedemann in the 16th Century ... Finally we held an honest talk with the two elders to address the differences."[18] Professor John Hostetler provides considerable detail as to the numerous points of disagreement between the Hutterite elders and the Bruderhof and then concludes: "The delegates returned home, sharing their frank discussions and their findings. The differences seemed so great as to be irreconcilable. There were exchanges of letters and admonitions, but both sides drifted apart. The Paraguayans were charged with worldliness, and financial support was terminated. The Hutterites were told that they had lost their missionary zeal, which, in part, they admitted."[19]

After the break with the Hutterites, the Bruderhof was free to pursue its own vision of communal life. Dr. Zablocki in a sociological study of the bruderhofs in the mid-1960s noted the intense emphasis on the spiritual inner life of giving up the self and being filled with the Holy Spirit. Unlike the Hutterites, the Bruderhof community affirmed the arts – music, painting, dancing, and poetry – and the community often had "love meals," where certain events were celebrated with songs and skits.[20] While the Hutterites looked at a person's outward behaviour in terms of applying church discipline, the Bruderhof had a great concern for the proper attitude that a person had in the community. People might be disciplined, not for anything they did wrong, but for not having "the right spirit."[21]

The Bruderhof movement now experienced a rapid expansion. New bruderhofs were established in England, the United States, Germany, and Uruguay. Primavera remained the mother colony. By 1957 there were nine bruderhofs. The Woodcrest Bruderhof in Rifton, New York, was established in 1954 with the aid of an existing communitarian group (the Macedonian community) that had an industry called Community Playthings. This business was taken over by the bruderhof. In 1995, it was reported that the bruderhof business generated about $20 million per year.[22] Under the Community Playthings trademark and Rifton Equipment for the Handicapped, furniture for nurseries and schools is manufactured, as well as equipment for children with disabilities and sturdy wooden toys.[23] One journalist notes that "[m]ore than 25,000 school systems, nurseries and pre-school programs are regular customers of the Hutterians, who say they send out four truckloads of merchandise each week from their headquarters in Rifton, N.Y. About 300,000 catalogues are distributed each year."[24]

The 1955 Forest River Conflict

During the establishment of Woodcrest Bruderhof, a number of young Hutterites made lengthy visits to it and became devoted to the spiritual vitality of the community, which stood in contrast to the perceived lifelessness of Hutterian ritual. As a result of these contacts, one Hutterite colony actually became a Bruderhof colony for a couple of years. Forest River was a new Schmiedeleut colony established in North Dakota in 1950 as a daughter colony of New Rosedale, Manitoba. Even though the formal relationship between the Bruderhof and the Hutterites had ended, a majority at Forest River invited the Bruderhof to visit Forest River in 1955, just as Forest River members had visited Woodcrest. For doing this, Forest River Colony was excommunicated by the Schmiedeleut. The many Bruderhof visitors to

Forest River included Heini Arnold and his wife, and even Emmy Arnold, the widow of Eberhard Arnold. In a clash of cultures, the colony was in effect taken over by the Bruderhof against the objections of the minority of the Hutterite members. Ruth Baer-Lambach, a resident of Forest River at the time, recalls the situation:

> This varied group bust into our 16th century farming village like a hurricane, upsetting our set way of life and changing it forever ... Their arrival and departure were full of unbelievable tension, anger, hate and bitterness and the results of that attempt at unification are evident to this day. The Hutterites live their lives without asking questions, but with the arrival of the Bruderhof, everything was put into question; the women stopped wearing the apron, shortened their skirts, gave up the traditional black and white spotted kerchief, and even cut their hair ... The Bruderhof put a stop to use of the children's dining room and we all ate together in the main dining room, in family groups. Twelve of us went to school at the local high school.[25]

Sixty percent of the original Forest River Hutterites voted to join the Bruderhof, while the 40 percent who objected, including the minister of the colony, were in essence forced to leave the colony and go back to New Rosedale.[26]

The Schmiedeleut sent ministers to the colony to persuade the Bruderhof to leave and to persuade the Hutterites to return to the fold. Being unsuccessful at this, the Schmiedeleut formally excommunicated the Bruderhof (in case there was doubt as to the effect of the earlier visits in Primavera), and also excommunicated the Hutterite members who had joined the Bruderhof. With Forest River now a base for the Bruderhof "evangelization" of other colonies, the Schmiedeleut elders wrote a letter that threatened excommunication on any Hutterite who had further contact with the Bruderhof. The senior elder stated:

> They will not be tolerated on any of our hofs. The reason is because of their shameless and arrogant behavior. They have brought division and confusion amongst us ... They have tried to undermine our foundations ... They behave like wolves and do not have compassion for anyone and mislead the herd. They impose on us and take our people away from us. They misuse the teachings and with that see to it that nobody will admit that they are in the wrong. We do not want anything more to do with them ... Within the span of one week they revealed themselves as liars, as hypocrites ... Their goal is to ruin us. If anyone who belongs to us speaks to them or listens to them, they will be treated as unfaithful members.[27]

The mess left by the Bruderhof at Forest River was made even worse when the Bruderhof abandoned Forest River in 1957 and established a new colony (later called New Meadow Run) in Pennsylvania. Forest River was left in the hands of three perplexed Hutterite families. What remained troubling for the Schmiedeleut was that the Bruderhof had "taken" thirty-six ethnic Hutterites, including fifteen baptized members, away from Forest River to their own community.[28]

Heini Arnold and the Great Exclusions

The expansion in the number of bruderhofs in the 1950s changed the dynamics of the community. Earlier, the group had been centralized in three colonies in the relatively isolated jungles of Paraguay, with just one additional colony in England. The American colonies in particular experienced rapid growth, both in numbers and financially. A number of conferences involving all the ministers and other leaders took place, giving rise to a mass exclusionary movement that would result in the closing down of all the colonies in South America, England, and Germany, and the consolidation of the Bruderhof at three colonies in the United States, under the primary leadership of Heini Arnold. In this process about half of the members were sent away or left the movement, and Heini Arnold was confirmed as senior elder. Previously there had been collective leadership, although Hans Zumpe was the main leader in Primavera and later in England. However, in 1959 Hans Zumpe admitted to having an adulterous relationship with his secretary and was expelled. After being sent away, apparently without being able to even say goodbye to his family, he sent a letter to his wife, a daughter of Eberhard Arnold, expressing his deep remorse for what had happened and pleading for forgiveness. This letter was apparently intercepted by the Bruderhof leaders and never shown to Zumpe's wife.[29] Other letters from Zumpe allegedly met a similar fate, and letters from his wife were never forwarded to him. Zumpe, cut off from his wife and children, tried to get back into the Bruderhof but was denied. He died in 1973 without ever seeing his wife and children again.

The issue of the earlier exclusions of 1944, and the Bruderhof attitude toward the Arnold family, came back to haunt the community. Heini Arnold, along with four of his leaders from the United States, swept into Primavera and started "house cleaning." Mass confrontations and individual and collective examinations of the inner life would lead to the disbanding of that particular bruderhof, followed by the start of a new bruderhof with a small circle of those deemed to have the "right heart." This circle would then choose those that would be in or out of the bruderhof. Those who were still in would be moved to the American colonies, while those who were excluded would be set adrift in the world. Roger Allain notes:

> There followed almost daily meetings of the "New Brotherhood." A few people would be called in to "take a stand," two or three accepted into their

ranks and two or three more sent away. Since we all had agreed to dissolve the old Brotherhood there was no more talk of formal exclusion or church discipline. People just were asked to leave the Bruderhof and were sent back to Europe or North America or Paraguay or Uruguay or from wherever they had come. Several people were simply called before the Servants and one or two of the Five, and then asked to leave without ever appearing before the "New Brotherhood." Single people and whole families were banished to face a world from which they had been estranged for twenty years or more. Parents were sent away without their adolescent children if the latter were already novices or had been induced to stay. In some cases, the family father was sent away and the mother and children stayed behind. Some of these families have remained disrupted ever since. It was distressing to see everyone torn apart and scattered, often without even a chance to say goodbye, after we had lived so closely together for so long. The people who were sent away left in a daze, while in the hearts of those who were still left, there remained the gnawing fear that they might be the next to be banished.[30]

The same process took place at the European bruderhofs and, in the end, the bruderhof was reduced from over fifteen hundred people in eleven communities to between five and six hundred people in three communities, now in the leadership control of Heini Arnold.[31] This process of the great exclusion left many people in crisis. Some even took their own lives. The "loving community" was seen as having been purified by one side, and as having been betrayed by the other. Dr. Julius Rubin states: "The Bruderhof showed extreme indifference to the material welfare of the apostates by providing little or no economic assistance. After years of hard work and service to the commune, many were cast out without passports, with uncertain immigration status, without money for travel or resettlement, without references, marketable job skills or sponsors."[32]

Reconnecting with the Hutterites
In 1964 Heini Arnold started to make overtures to the Hutterites in an attempt to reunite with them again. He travelled to Manitoba to meet with Schmiedeleut leaders and made many apologies for the Forest River debacle.[33] At this stage Arnold was apparently personally forgiven, but any reuniting with the Hutterites would have involved a formal exclusion ceremony before former Hutterite members would be accepted back into the fold. While this condition was unacceptable to the Bruderhof, the relationship between the two groups was fostered when several Hutterite elders visited with Arnold in the spring of 1973, and particularly after Rev. Jacob Kleinsasser visited the Woodcrest community the same year.[34] Kleinsasser was impressed with the Bruderhof and he worked actively to bring them back into the Hutterite fold. He invited Arnold and a group of Bruderhof ministers to visit Crystal

Spring, where a meeting of the leaders of all three Hutterite Leuts was being held in January of 1974. There was a great deal of discussion between the Bruderhof ministers and the elders of the Leuts. The discussion continued the next day at Sturgeon Creek Colony, where, after deliberating late into the night, Arnold's apology for the Forest River mess was accepted and the Bruderhof reunited with the Hutterite church. The Hutterite members who had left Forest River, however, would still have to go through a formal exclusion ritual at Woodcrest for a period before being accepted back into the church.[35]

The Bruderhof proceeded to adopt the Hutterian dress. Traditional "western" Schmiedeleut Hutterites now married "eastern" Hutterites and moved one way or the other on the colonies with the permission of the Schmiedeleut. One of Jacob Kleinsasser's daughters married a Bruderhof member. The influence was not just one way. Many Hutterites would later charge that Kleinsasser as senior elder of the Schmiedeleut was so much influenced by the Bruderhof culture as to adopt a centralizing and dictatorial style of leadership, which led to massive conflicts within the church and culminated in the schisms at colonies and within the conference.[36]

Heini Arnold died in 1982 and a renewed struggle over leadership took place. Kleinsasser advised that an elder be appointed as soon as possible, but the community wrestled with the issue until 1984, when Christoph Arnold, the son of Heini Arnold, was appointed senior elder. Thus the Arnold family remained in the leadership position. Kleinsasser was particularly influential in the Woodcrest community. He accompanied Christoph Arnold on mission trips around the world. At one stage Arnold summarized the relationship as follows:

> We have celebrated 22 marriages between our groups. We have sent young people to help out at various western colonies and they have sent many of their young people to help us. Most importantly, we have gone on many mission journeys together. My wife Verena and I traveled with Hutterite elder Jacob Kleinsasser and his wife Maria to Germany, England, New Zealand, Hawaii and Nigeria. We also made two other journeys to Nigeria and one to Israel ... In 1988, together with the western Hutterites, we started a Bruderhof [Michaelshof] in Germany. More recently, we joined forces to build up Palmgrove, our community in Nigeria, and baptized our first African members.[37]

Complex financial transactions involving loans and gifts flowed between east and west. More than one hundred Western Hutterites ended up living in the east. A decade or so after the great expulsions, the community started to expand its number of colonies again. By 1992 there were eight bruderhofs with a population of about two thousand.[38]

Breaking from the Hutterites Again

The unification of the Western Hutterites and the Bruderhof has always been an uneasy alliance, given the cultural differences between the two groups. Even their shared fundamental doctrines, such as community of goods and nonresistance, take a different shape. For example, although the Western Hutterites have a long tradition of mutual aid from colony to colony, each colony is economically independent of the others, whereas the Bruderhof holds all property at the larger Leut level. While the Bruderhof, like the Hutterites, reject television and other consumer frills, there are obvious differences in their property rules. The Bruderhof, for example, has fleets of cars whereas traditional Hutterites can use only vans or trucks. The Bruderhof also own several multimillion-dollar luxurious jets, which transport various members from place to place and also are chartered to rock stars and movie celebrities.[39]

The stance toward the host society is also different. Like the Hutterites, the Bruderhof colonies each have a school that runs up to grade nine, but unlike the Hutterites, Bruderhof children are bussed to public high schools in neighbouring towns or cities. Thereafter many young people are allowed to leave the colony for a time to pursue higher education at state colleges and vocational institutions before deciding whether to join the Bruderhof or not. (Indeed, an English report on religious beliefs among college students focused on a twenty-year-old female member of the Darvell Bruderhof in England who was a medical student.[40])

The Bruderhof has been much less isolationist on social issues. For example, in 1988 the community held a series of conferences at each colony, with many speakers and visitors from outside the colony. Conference topics included child abuse, prison conditions, homelessness, drug addiction, and abortion.[41] For many years the Bruderhof have been involved in anti-war rallies and demonstrations against the death penalty. The evangelical and social thrust of the Bruderhof was noted by a journalist in writing about the Deer Spring Bruderhof in Connecticut: "They draw new members from prisons, blood banks, soup kitchens, shelters for the homeless. Two months ago, they invited a woman and her baby, both with AIDS, to join them. Many members also come from the ranks of disgruntled social workers. By taking care not to proselytize, and by serving on local ambulance and fire squads and in other civic projects, the [Bruderhof] have earned a reputation as good neighbors, say several Norfolk citizens – although they admit concern about the group's 'communistic' ideas."[42]

Differences between the Western Hutterian mainstream and the Eastern Bruderhof also include theological fundamentals as noted by Dr. Hostetler:

> The Hutterites are to a large extent word-oriented rather than spirit-oriented. Hutterite sermons are impossible to separate from texts of scripture.

The word for sermon is the same as the term for Scripture (Schrift). A knowledge of the Scripture is pervasive in the education of children. It is not uncommon for 14-year-old children to be able to recite 250 bible verses. Adults retain a reservoir of biblical passages from their early training.

The Society of Brothers, by contrast, attempts to be spirit-oriented. Children's education is almost totally devoid of biblical memory work and recitation. Eberhard pointed out that the Word of God is a living word ... When a group is primarily spirit-led instead of scripture-led, authority tends to become centered on personal authority instead of textually interpretive authority.[43]

Given the many differences, it is not surprising, as we will see, that the Bruderhof was divorced again by the Darius and Lehrer branches in 1990, and that the Schmiedeleut split into two groups, partly because of the Bruderhof affiliation, and that finally, in 1994, even the Kleinsasser-led group broke all relations with the Bruderhof. Details as to these events will emerge in this book as the conflicts at certain colonies and within the wider church are examined.

KIT and the Bruderhof Apostates

From the many positive press accounts, the Bruderhof seems to be as close to a Christian utopia as one will find anywhere, and it continues to attract many visitors and new members. A recent article, for example, mentions Dr. Diane Fox and Dr. Paul Fox and their four children, who joined the Bruderhof after being weary and burdened by the hectic materialistic pace of their lives in the world:

> "My first response when I visited [the Bruderhof] was excitement and joy," Diane Fox says. "My second response was, paradoxically, one of dismay. It became more and more clear to me that in order to attain the freedom that Christ was offering me in community, I would have to give up all the false freedoms that I had worked so hard to acquire: all the money, all the status, and the apparent security."
>
> Yet the family has adjusted to the simple lifestyle. "My service is small: I practice medicine, I take my turn at preparing a meal or watching the children, I run an errand, answer the phone occasionally," Diane Fox says. "The miracle is that we receive a hundred fold for the small service that we do. The cars are maintained, the meals prepared, the laundry and cleaning done, the daycare provided, the gardens tended, the children taught, the elderly cared for. All for love, and all for free."[44]

But another side of the story is given by the many people who have been expelled or have left the Bruderhof. Many of these individuals have joined

together and formed a vibrant association, which publishes a monthly news-
letter and sponsors a yearly conference in the United States and in Europe.
The catalyst for the organization of ex-members was Ramon Sender. Dr.
Timothy Miller notes:

> Sender and his wife, intrigued with the prospect of communal living, had
> joined the Bruderhof as novices in the late 1950s. Sender soon found it not
> to his liking and left it in less than a year, but his wife disagreed and
> stayed behind, keeping their daughter with her. Given the hostility with
> which apostates were even then viewed by the community, communica-
> tions between Ramon and Xaverie [daughter] (he and his wife were later
> divorced) were virtually nonexistent, with visits and even letters disallowed
> by the Bruderhof leadership. Sender's quiet toleration of that unpleasant
> situation ended, however, when he learned that his daughter had died in
> 1988 of cancer at the Woodcrest Bruderhof in New York state; he had not
> been informed that she had been ill and thus had no chance to visit her
> during her terminal illness; he was not informed of her death until a month
> afterwards.[45]

Ramon Sender also did not know that his daughter had married and that
he was a grandfather.[46] After her death, Sender decided to research her life
story. The Bruderhof, however, would not allow him to interview members,
so he turned to ex-members, and within several months had contacted more
than sixty of them. Finding that ex-members were eager for news about
other ex-members, he started a monthly newsletter, called *KIT*, for "Keep in
Touch." From modest beginnings in 1989, the newsletter soon attracted
hundreds of readers. *KIT Newsletter* features ex-members' recollections, some
full of anger at how they had been treated within the Bruderhof, and accounts of the devastating effect of exclusions within and from the Bruderhof,
as well as of the continuing difficulties in maintaining a relationship with
relatives still inside the Bruderhof. The newsletter is available on the
Internet.[47]

The growth of *KIT* led to yearly conferences in both the United States and
Europe where ex-members could meet face to face and share their stories.
John Hostetler, the leading scholar on Anabaptist communities, attended
the first conference and reported:

> Story after story was told of crises and severe recriminations which the ex-
> pellees had experienced both as children and as adults. There were groups
> who talked late into the night, and after two days of sharing, there were
> groups who wanted to talk longer. Descriptions of childhood deprivation
> and punishments brought tears to the listeners. Of special concern was the
> treatment of children within the closed communities. There were reports of

young people who underwent deep depression and some who had been taught, even as children, that they were harboring an "evil spirit."

Conference attendees drafted an "open letter" which was sent to all eight communities. The letter asked for "serious dialogue" on important concerns. There are elderly ex-members living in poverty and with no access to Social Security payments because the Society of Brothers did not pay into the system. They asked that visiting privileges be allowed for those who wish to see their relatives, and that the practice of keeping secret the whereabouts of excluded members be stopped. The letter also stated that the threat of intimidation and expulsion gives rise to community-wide fear, that children who wish to leave the community must be given genuine choices, and that censorship and opening of mail must be stopped.[48]

The *KIT* network was established under a foundation that included the creation of a fund to aid those expelled from the Bruderhof or who left the group, and a publishing wing, which has resulted in several books written by ex-members.[49]

In her book, Nadine Pleil points out the harsh treatment of those kicked out of the community. Unbaptized young people would be sent away with but the clothes on their back, and cut off from their parents and from the community in which they had grown up.[50] Even more troubling was the treatment afforded members who had spent many years contributing to the community and who had given the community everything they owned when they joined. Pleil tells the story of her elderly in-laws' exclusion in Paraguay. They were ordered to leave the Bruderhof within three hours, and then taken to Asunción and dumped on the street. Mr. Pleil was seventy years old with a heart condition. Allegedly the Pleils were not even allowed to stay at a Bruderhof house in the city for the first night. They had to walk the streets in the pouring rain until they found a sympathetic Paraguayan man who took them in for the night.[51] Many years later, when Nadine Pleil and her family were excluded, they were given $500 and driven to the town of Washington, Pennsylvania, where a rundown shack had been found for them to rent. There were ten people in the family, and after the $500 ran out, they were told by the Bruderhof leaders to go on welfare.[52] It was a struggle for the family to find jobs for the adult members and survive in the world.

The shunning of ex-members means that the family relationships between those within the Bruderhof and those outside it are distorted. Pleil writes about the death of her foster mother within the community in 1993. Pleil was not told about the death of her mother until the funeral was over; the Bruderhof leadership did not want her on the colony to attend her mother's funeral. She wrote to the leadership: "It's almost three weeks since my mother died and I realize more and more how shocking and cold your attitude is toward me. The fact that you did not notify me of my mother's passing is absolutely despicable and disgraceful, apart from the fact that it is unloving, unchristian and cold. You who profess to be so loving can earn a prize for being cold and unfeeling."[53]

There appears to have been initial attempts at reconciliation between the Bruderhof and the critics of the community,[54] but the leadership of the Bruderhof took an increasingly harsh stand against them. Indeed, while the leadership of the Bruderhof might well counter criticism as unfair or inaccurate, the most obvious sign that perhaps the movement has derailed from the Anabaptist tracks is the recent host of lawsuits that the Bruderhof has threatened or initiated against its critics. (These developments are noted later in this book.) This willingness to sue your enemy rather than love your enemy was already manifest in the *Lakeside* case when the leaders of the Bruderhof and the Schmiedeleut were still in a happy relationship.

Part Two
The Inside Law on Going to Outside Law: Hutterite Litigation before the *Lakeside* Case

3

The Inside Law against Going to Outside Law

One of the rules (Ordnung) of traditional Anabaptist groups is that it is wrong for Christians to engage in litigation. Going to outside courts and appealing to outside law is a violation of inside law that can lead to expulsion from the community. However, as we will see in the next chapters, the Hutterites have in fact participated in, and sometimes initiated, a considerable amount of litigation, even before the recent cases that are examined in this book. This then raises the question of whether the inside law against going to outside law needs to be expressed in a more refined way so as to explain the existence of this Hutterite litigation, or whether the principle has actually lost its validity among Hutterites. In this chapter I attempt to outline the background justifications and the developing tensions involving the traditional prohibition on litigation, before surveying the cases.

The Separation of Two Kingdoms

The traditional Anabaptist position that disputes should not be litigated in outside courts may be viewed as a particular consequence of the more general doctrine of the separation of two kingdoms: the Kingdom of God and the Kingdom of this World. While original Anabaptist thought and practice was quite diverse, the two-kingdom model emerged as the dominant paradigm.[1] It must be emphasized that the modern liberal conception of the separation of church and state is not the same as the traditional Anabaptist conception. The modern liberal might posit a separation of subject matter jurisdiction between private life and public life, or between secular and sacred realms. Religion, narrowly confined to a set of beliefs and activities having to do with worship or private moral conduct, is relegated to a private sphere where the citizen should be free from any state coercion. Conversely, religion should not be the basis for norm generation in the public sphere. The price of religious freedom in this model of liberalism is the privatization of religion by the reduction of religion to modes of worship and abstract beliefs, and the reduction of religious communities to mere voluntary associations in the private sphere. In contrast to this, however, the Anabaptist separation of church and state is based on a rejection of the sacred and secular division. The Anabaptist separation of church and state must be linked to the Anabaptist refusal to separate Sunday and Monday.[2] The inside law of the church is comprehensive and applies to the whole life of the disciple. What you have is a separation of normative communities rather than subject matters. You have the church community, which is supposed to live all of life according to the law and love of Christ within the redeemed Kingdom of God, and you have the "world" community, which is not yet redeemed and in which the state must use norms of public justice backed by violence to ensure a minimum social structure of peace and order.

If the Anabaptists had pioneered only a jurisdictional separation of authority over different subject matters between different organizations in society, they might not have been tortured and killed for their "dangerous" beliefs. The significant point is not the separation, and therefore limitation, of jurisdictions between church and state but the integration *for church members* of all of their life into the jurisdiction of the church, and therefore the radical totalistic sovereign jurisdiction of the church as opposed to the state in regard to the members of the church. The Anabaptists called for a radical discipleship where the true followers of Jesus applied the ethics of Jesus, as best they understood them, to all of life. For the Anabaptist Christian, then, there were not two sovereigns with separate jurisdictions over different areas of life but only one sovereign Lord who took the whole pie.

It should be remembered that the nonresistant love ethic as a foundational inside law of the church was conceived by the Anabaptists as attainable only by those who had been converted and transformed by the grace of God and had entered into the new covenant community of the church. The state, acting through its officials, was not expected to act with nonresistant love. In 1527, two years after the birth of the Anabaptist movement, a synod of Anabaptists met at Schleitheim, Switzerland; seven articles were finally agreed upon. In regard to the law and the state, the Schleitheim Confession stated: "The sword is an ordering of God outside the perfection of Christ. It punishes and kills the wicked and guards and protects the good. In the law the sword is established over the wicked for punishment and for death and the secular rulers are established to wield the same. But within the perfection of Christ only the ban is used for the admonition and exclusion of the one who has sinned, without the death of the flesh, simply the warning and the command to sin no more."[3] The confession went on to claim that a Christian may not use the sword, even "against the wicked for the protection and defence of the good, or for the sake of love,'" and that Christians may not be magistrates or "pass sentence in disputes and strife about worldly matters."[4]

Thus, with their own form of ethical dualism, the Anabaptists affirmed the legitimacy of the state sword within certain boundaries as used by non-Christians in the Kingdom of this World, and yet renounced the use of it by Christians, who were citizens of Christ's Kingdom, even while residing in the territory of the old Kingdom. Membership in the church involved a new citizenship in a new social order of redemption. Citizenship in the church involved a border crossing, a change of passport, a movement from one Kingdom to another, not in terms of geography but in terms of ultimate loyalty and ethics. The Christian now was a member of the Cross-bearing church, and that membership was incompatible with full participation in the sword-bearing state.

Within this framework of the separation of two kingdoms, it is possible to understand how going to the law courts of the state would have been viewed as a violation of church citizenship. Quite apart from the issue of the violence of the law, it was clearly wrong for Christians to take their disputes with each other to foreign courts.[5] However, even when a Christian had a dispute with a non-Christian, the Anabaptist separationist model of two kingdoms would suggest that the Christian should not cross back over the border and invoke the courts of the old Kingdom.

In addition to this issue of jurisdictional loyalty to the Kingdom of Christ, going to court involved the invocation of violence. Suing someone in court at bottom involved calling on the violence of the state to uphold a court order in your favour. Thus, the assertion that Christians could not be soldiers, police officers, or magistrates, and that they could not use the law courts was grounded in this Anabaptist belief that membership in the church constituted a new and higher citizenship in a divine social order of redemption that was superior to the temporary God-ordained social order of preservation. Anabaptist Christians withdrew from positions involving state management. The job of the church was not to manage fallen society but to model the new order of redemption, the way of the Cross.

The radical priority the Anabaptists gave to their citizenship in the church as the Kingdom of God did not therefore mean that those who governed in the realities of the present social order were engaged in an illegitimate activity. The majority of Anabaptists asserted that the governmental authorities were ordained by God to use the power of the sword to maintain order and justice in a sinful world. Until the ultimate realization of the Kingdom of God and the victory of Christ over all the powers, civil authorities, including the courts of the state, had a God-mandated duty to keep the peace and promote the welfare of society. While governmental authorities themselves could turn lawless and pervert their God-given mandate, the Anabaptist position generally affirmed that the violent police power of the state was absolutely necessary as a kind of "divine accommodation to human frailty."[6]

Yet at the same time, the Anabaptists were clearly implying that all governmental positions involving the sword were filled by non-Christians, and supposedly if everyone were a Christian, properly so called, government, at least in terms of violent coercion, would be altogether unnecessary. Needless to say, in a context where governmental agents overwhelmingly viewed themselves as Christians, the Anabaptist position infuriated the authorities.[7] Today people still scratch their heads over the assertion that some measure of state violence is God-ordained in the context of a fallen world but that the Christian citizen must be more righteous and have nothing to do with it.

This full-bodied separation of church and state and the effect of having such a gulf between the nonresistance ethic of the church member on one hand and the necessity of violence by the state on the other fed logically over time not just to the withdrawal of Anabaptists from positions involving the management of governmental affairs but also to the increased separation and noninvolvement of Anabaptist groups with the rest of society generally. While to a significant degree the Hutterites remain within this two-kingdom mentality, it should be noted that many Anabaptist groups have rejected the separationist withdrawal model of church and society, adopting a much more activist, transformationist model, one in which the church prophetically witnesses to the state and to society, and where church members are fully engaged in working for peace and justice and serving the material and social needs of the wider community, while still affirming non-violence.[8] This shift in the Anabaptist model impacts on the particular issue of engaging in litigation.

The activist model is in part a response to the limitations of the separationist model. When engaging with Christians of different persuasions, it is inevitable that the following sort of charge will be made: "[n]onresistant communities face the charge of being moral freeloaders, because they benefit from the protections society provides but they refuse to share in the work of protecting. Although this difficulty can be overcome, to some degree, by alternative service, it can appear hypocritical to declare oneself too pure to participate in the use of force while significantly benefiting from the willingness of others to participate."[9]

But the shift to social and political activism is not just a reaction to charges of irresponsibility. More fundamentally, the new model reflects a reconsideration of the rift between the ethics of Jesus and the ethics of governmental power. While Jesus did not take up the sword to establish social change, a new generation of scholars argued that Jesus was fully engaged in the struggle for peace and justice in the sociopolitical context in which he lived.[10] More than four and a half centuries after the early Anabaptist confessions, one of the leading contemporary Mennonite confessions reaffirms the principle of non-violence as an ethic for the church, but also extends that principle as an ideal to all of society:

As followers of Jesus, we participate in his ministry of peace and justice ... As disciples of Christ, we do not prepare for war, or participate in war or military service. The same Spirit that empowered Jesus also empowers us to love enemies, to forgive rather than to seek revenge, to practice right relationships, to rely on the community of faith to settle disputes, and to resist evil without violence ...

Led by the Spirit, and beginning in the church, we witness to all people that violence is not the will of God. We witness against all forms of violence, including war among nations, hostility among races and classes, abuse of children and women, violence between men and women, abortion, and capital punishment.[11]

While new models of activism may narrow the gap, they do not necessarily replace the dualism of the two-kingdom model.[12] The dualistic tension can be removed only by revising the absolutist prohibition on all violence in all circumstances as the ethic for Christians on one hand, or by replacing the conception that it is necessary for the state at some level to use violence. Replacing non-violence as a requirement of Christian ethics would simply bring the Anabaptists into the mainstream and eliminate them as a distinct group. If Anabaptists take up the sword as police officers, soldiers, and executioners and argue that this is compatible with membership in the church, arguably they are now Calvinists or Lutherans and not Anabaptists. On the other hand, while the argument can be made that the state should and could function in a far less violent way, and that using alternative non-violent approaches in many areas of domestic and international affairs would be far more effective in securing peace and justice,[13] the claim that the state could function without at some point invoking the violence of police power to prevent harm to others seems impossible short of the eschaton. If one approach is no longer Anabaptist, the other approach is arguably no longer sane.[14] The activist confession that Mennonites "witness against all forms of violence" is still moderated, even in recent Anabaptist confessions, by some recognition of necessity:

In contrast to the church, governing authorities of the world have been instituted by God for maintaining order in societies. Such governments and other human institutions as servants of God are called to act justly and provide order ... Even at its best, a government cannot act completely according to the justice of God because no nation, except the church, confesses Christ's rule as its foundation ...

Territorial nations and their governments are limited in their ability to fulfill the will of God because of their reliance on violence, at least as a last resort ... However, a government that acts with relative justice and provides order is better than anarchy or an unjust, oppressive government ... Christians are responsible to witness to governments not only because of their citizenship in a particular country, but also in order to reflect Christ's compassion for all people and to proclaim Christ's lordship over all human institutions.[15]

Thus, as we examine the Anabaptist inside law on going to outside law courts, we may acknowledge activist concerns, but nevertheless our discussion is premised on the fundamental conflict between the voice of Jesus and the violence of the law.

Going to Court: The Violence of the Law and the Voice of Jesus

Taking a dispute to court is often expensive, time-consuming, involves an adversary process that is manipulative and hurtful to participants, and offers remedies that may be unresponsive to the real needs or interests of the parties.[16] This opinion that litigation is problematic is widespread, but the idea that it is actually wrongful would surely strike most people as strange. Indeed, while affirming the advantages of consensual alternative processes such as mediation and arbitration, most people would likely accept the view that going to court is sometimes necessary and even desirable. The reasons seem obvious. As a last resort when consent fails, we turn to coercion, so that legal rights will be vindicated. There must be a process of enforcement to get a remedy for breaches of law or else law fails as a method of social control. Sometimes those who do not fulfill their legal duties voluntarily must be held accountable so as to prevent them from harming others. To the extent that alternative dispute resolution processes are increasingly used within the framework of the governmental court system, such dispute processes also become part of the coercive nature of the formal legal system.[17]

In some instances, the government itself takes the initiative in directly enforcing the law. For example, with criminal matters or with most regulatory offences, police or law enforcement officers investigate and lay charges that are then prosecuted in court by government agents. However, in most areas of the law, its enforcement is initially left to those individuals who are directly affected by the alleged breach of the law. If someone breaks a legal obligation under a contract or causes damage through a negligent act, it is the victim who must seek redress for the violation. Unless a crime has been committed, complaining to the police or other government official will usually get you nowhere. Rather, you will be pointed to the courthouse door. If you want a remedy for a violation of your legal rights, you must bring an action in court. The vast majority of such claims will be settled without resort to further proceedings, because the facts and the law are so clearly in favour of one side or the other that it would be pointless and costly to continue to pursue or resist further. But, whether for tactical reasons or for reasons of disputed facts or law, many cases are litigated in court, and settlements are negotiated in other cases within the shadow cast by the courts, as lawyers predict what a court would decide if the case went to adjudication.

The coercive violence of the law is necessary. If a person refuses to acknowledge the complaint made against them or denies liability, there must be a process that is backed up by the force of the state that offers an avenue to adjudicate the matter. While the techniques and tactics of litigation can amount to a ritualized war and the violence of the state is used to enforce court rulings, litigation, ironically, is on one level actually a process of "keeping the peace" by creating a forum where disputes are "peacefully" resolved by the application of legal norms to the facts and by the making of an authoritative and enforceable pronouncement of duties and rights between the parties. If there were no state-sanctioned and -enforced court system of dispute resolution, we might well have a much higher degree of personal violence in society as aggrieved parties would take self-help action.

We do not often think of the law as fundamentally linked to state violence. To be sure, the system would collapse if people obeyed the law or court orders only because they were backed by the violence of the state. It is also true that law is much more about the avoidance of violence and the prevention of disputes by structuring transactions and ordering activities so that expectations are clarified and needs met. But we should not forget that while law is not legitimated by state coercion, at bottom the law of the state is still backed by the violence of the state.[18] When the court orders you to hand over property to someone, or orders you to do something or refrain from doing something, you obey the order of the court or the judgment of the court. The law has spoken. But while we do not see the exercise of the violence of the state in most cases, behind this obedience stands the reality that the violence of the police, sheriffs, bailiffs, or other state officials will be brought to bear if you do not obey the order of the court.

Thus, as has already been noted, initiating an action in court may be wrongful from an Anabaptist point of view because it is contrary to the Anabaptist non-violence principle. The bringing of an action in court usually involves invoking the threat of, or actual use of, coercive violence by the state to enforce a judgment in your favour. While that violence may not be personal to you, in civil cases it is the parties who are initiating and controlling the application of state violence between private parties, in a way that is very different from the state control exercised over court proceedings in criminal cases and other regulatory proceedings. Furthermore, while the public violence of the state may serve to provide the framework for the peaceful settlement of disputes between private parties, the process of court adjudication does not appear to be particularly about peacemaking but quite the opposite. The adversarial system of court proceedings often appears to be a process of verbal and psychological warfare, and if "peace" emerges at all, it is achieved only by the winning party destroying the losing party in a process that places might over right, process over substance, and tactics over truth.[19] Even when litigation proceeds on a much more civilized level compared with the pathological level of nastiness that it can be reduced to, parties often develop higher levels of antagonism toward each other simply because the process is adversarial. Reconciliation between the parties seems unlikely in a process designed for producing winners and losers.

That litigation is linked to violence is confirmed in a recent book that provides a compelling and challenging vision for Christian lawyers.[20] When the author turned to the ethics of litigation, he elegantly outlined all the arguments against it from a Christian point of view, and then concluded by turning to the principles used in the just war theory, using those same principles by analogy as a test to determine those circumstances where litigation might be justified.[21] Limiting but not eliminating litigation by applying a just war framework is telling because it properly recognizes the link between litigation and violence, and the difference between those Christians who accept the just war theory and thus litigation and traditional Anabaptists who do not accept either.

During the Roman phase of his trial, Jesus said, "Everyone who belongs to the truth, hears my voice." Pilate then asked Jesus, "What is truth?"[22] It would appear that Pilate was interpreting Jesus to say that those who already know or already belong to the truth will recognize and acknowledge the voice of Jesus. However, a more radical, disturbing, and even seditious interpretation is that we belong to the truth by hearing the voice of Jesus. Rather than being one of a number of potential witnesses to a pre-existent truth, Jesus is himself the truth. The early Hutterites, alongside other Anabaptists, proclaimed the Lordship of Jesus in this more exclusivist and radical sense. The question was not Pilate's "What is truth?" but the disciple's "What is the voice of Jesus on this issue?"

What was the voice of Jesus on the litigation issue? For the early Anabaptists, the voice of Jesus was heard from reading Scripture, particularly the New Testament. For example, the following passages quoting Jesus, or giving Paul's understanding of the way of Jesus, would at minimum lead to a heavy presumption that the disciples of Jesus should not take disputes to court:[23]

> You have heard that it was said, "An eye for an eye and a tooth for a tooth." But I say to you, Do not resist one who is evil. But if any one strikes you on the right cheek, turn to him the other also. (Matthew 5:38-39)

> And if any one would sue you and take your coat, let him have your cloak as well; and if any one forces you to go one mile, go with him two miles. (Matthew 5:40-41)

If your brother sins against you, go and tell him his fault, between you and him alone. If he listens to you, you have gained your brother. But if he does not listen, take one or two others along with you, that every word may be confirmed by the evidence of two or three witnesses. If he refuses to listen to them, tell it to the church; and if he refuses to listen even to the church, let him be to you as a Gentile and a tax collector. Truly, I say to you, whatever you bind on earth shall be bound in heaven, and whatever you loose on earth shall be loosed in heaven. (Matthew 18:15-18)

"Do you wish to go to Jerusalem, and there be tried on these charges before me?" But Paul said, "I am standing before Caesar's tribunal, where I ought to be tried; to the Jews I have done no wrong, as you know very well. If then I am a wrongdoer, and have committed anything for which I deserve to die, I do not seek to escape death; but if there is nothing in their charges against me, no one can give me up to them. I appeal to Caesar." (Acts 25:9-11)

When one of you has a grievance against a brother, does he dare go to law before the unrighteous instead of the saints? Do you not know that the saints will judge the world? And if the world is to be judged by you, are you incompetent to try trivial cases? Do you not know that we are to judge angels? How much more, matters pertaining to this life! If then you have such cases, why do you lay them before those who are least esteemed by the church? I say this to your shame. Can it be that there is no man among you wise enough to decide between members of the brotherhood, but brother goes to law against brother, and that before unbelievers? To have lawsuits at all with one another is defeat for you. Why not rather suffer wrong? Why not rather be defrauded? But you yourselves wrong and defraud, and that even your own brethren. (1 Corinthians 6:1-8)

Therefore, if any one is in Christ, he is a new creation; the old has passed away, behold, the new has come. All this is from God, who through Christ reconciled us to himself and gave us the ministry of reconciliation. (2 Corinthians 5:17-18)

While the Matthew 18 and 1 Corinthians 6 passages can be interpreted at a superficial level as dealing with disputes and lawsuits between Christians as opposed to dealing with lawsuits by Christians against non-Christians, there is no implication that just because litigation between Christians is explicitly prohibited, other litigation is allowed. It is not some specific text in isolation but, rather, the basic framework of the ethics of nonretaliation, reconciliation, and righteous suffering that informs the Anabaptist position on litigation. To be a disciple of Jesus is to be a witness in the world for Jesus' way of peace and reconciliation. To take an aggressive lawsuit against an individual, seeking the police power of coercion, even when you are in the legal right and an injustice has been done to you, is inconsistent with the suffering love of Jesus for those who had enmity toward you.

Traditional Absolutist Anabaptist Doctrine on Litigation

To the early Hutterites, the voice of Jesus was interpreted in an absolutist way. While in prison in the early 1540s, Peter Riedemann wrote his *Confession of Faith*, which to this day still serves as the foundational confession for Hutterites. Under the subtitle "Whether a Christian Can Go to Law or Sit in Judgment," Riedemann states:

> As we have explained, temporal things do not belong to us. Therefore, a Christian cannot quarrel or go to court because of them. On the contrary, if a person's heart is turned from the world and set upon that which is of God, that person should prefer to suffer injustice. Paul says, "You fail completely because you have lawsuits with one another. Why not rather let wrong be done to you? Why not rather let yourselves be harmed and defrauded?" (1 Cor. 6:7) If Christians should not sue one another, then going to court and sitting in judgment are completely eradicated among Christians (Matt. 5:39-42) ...
>
> Christ shows that Christians may not go to court when he says, "If any one will sue you and take away your coat, let him have your cloak also." (Matt. 5:40-41) In effect, Jesus is saying, "It is better to let people take everything than to quarrel with them, and find yourself in a strange court." Christ wants us to show that we seek what is heavenly and belongs to us, (Col. 3:1-2) and not what is temporal or alien to us. (Luke 16:19-25) Thus, it is evident that a Christian can neither go to court nor be a judge.[24]

It is interesting that Riedemann, while noting other precepts, links litigation with concerns over "temporal things." Thus, aside from issues involving the violence of the law and the jurisdictional disloyalty of going to foreign courts, in the Hutterite context there is the additional focus on the way in which litigation seems inconsistent with the Hutterian renunciation of private property. The subject of litigation is often property, and in many other cases what is sought as a remedy is property (monetary awards). Thus, litigation may be viewed as a manifestation of greed and covetousness. The temptation to sue is certainly lessened when a person owns nothing and cannot personally own any property awarded in a court judgment. But this should not obscure the reality that the temptation to sue, and the danger of greed, might still exist at the collective level. If colony property is lost through the wrongful act of someone, the colony itself may wish to sue, just as an individual would.

Around 1647, a century or so after Riedemann's statement on litigation, another great Hutterian leader, Andreas Ehrenpreis, wrote an account that defended the ideal of community of goods as a normative standard for realizing Christian community.[25] Interestingly, at the end of his work he notes that the Hutterites were having a problem with inheritance issues. After an appropriate period, a convert to the Hutterite community would formally bring all of his or her privately owned possessions to the community and hand them over to the community. Just as it might be said that the person had been converted and joined the church, so the private property of the person had been converted into common property. Once that conversion took place, the individual was forever renouncing any personal claim to those goods. However, sometimes the individual Hutterite might subsequently be entitled to more goods when his or her non-Hutterite parent or relative died, leaving an inheritance. Of course, any inheritance could not be claimed for the individual use of the Hutterite in question, but it would certainly be helpful to the colony if that inheritance could be brought in and converted to the community pot to be used by all. According to Ehrenpreis, non-Hutterite siblings or relatives often used every means available, including court actions, to prevent Hutterites from converting private inheritances into community property.[26] There was at least one case in which a Hutterite leader took "legal action" through an agent in an attempt to claim his inheritance for the benefit of the group, but on the information available to me, it is unclear whether the agent simply attempted to negotiate the claim or broke the absolutist rule against litigation and took the issue to a tribunal that we would recognize as functioning like a court.[27]

More than a century after Ehrenpreis, the absolutist prohibition on litigation still appeared to be solid. In 1783 a Mennonite elder in Prussia wrote about the Hutterites as follows:

> Legal disputes and lawsuits are unknown among them. That is why Joseph Muller [a Hutterite minister], on hearing us use the expression "lawsuit," asked me what kind of word this was, and what it meant. When it was explained to him and he was asked if they never had disputes which needed to be decided by a legal verdict, he told me, "No, because 'mine and thine' no longer exist nor have any place among us, and so such disputes do not arise. If something occurs we settle it ourselves in accordance with the teaching in 1 Corinthians 6:1-6. So we have nothing to do with magistrates except for paying our taxes. Any brother who went to the magistrates asking to have his rights protected would no longer be considered a member of our church."[28]

Consistent with this absolutist position on litigation, the internal historical record of the Hutterites appears to be free of any Hutterite-initiated litigation until the cases in the twentieth century that I will examine in the next chapters. This does not mean that Hutterites never found themselves in front of a court. In the periods of intense persecution, at least some of the many Hutterites who were executed for their faith would have first received a hearing of sorts before tribunals or officials for allegations that they were breaching particular laws dealing with religious belief. In addition there are a few, more detailed, stories of how Hutterites were dragged into court in circumstances that today might be classified as partly civil, rather than purely criminal, matters.

The history of the Hutterites includes stories of horrific violence by government authorities torturing and executing Anabaptists, and by marauding armies murdering, raping, and plundering the colonies. Yet these acts are suffered without any retaliation by the Hutterites. However, there is one case, recorded with shame, where a wrongful act by a manorial lord led to violent retaliation by some colony members, which then led to a lawsuit against one of the Hutterite communities.[29] In the 1630s, the Hutterian communities at Sabatisch (Hungary) lived under the jurisdiction of thirteen manorial lords. The Hutterites had made a contract with their lords to pay additional rents so as to be exempt from a variety of mandatory duties that would otherwise by owed to the lords. In 1632 one of the lords requested that the Hutterites give him horses and men to accompany him on a trip. The Hutterites, citing the contract, refused, but the lord came with his hussars to seize horses. Perhaps because the steward of the colony had just died and the minister was sick in bed, and the other members of the colony did not recognize that it was their lord and his men, rather than a band of robbers, seizing the horses, crowds of Hutterites came rushing from the fields with hoes, sticks, and flails as several of the Hutterites in charge of the horses were being assaulted.[30] While no blows were struck by the Hutterites, the lord and his men rode off in a fury after this show of force by the Hutterites, and in retaliation the lord sent back his men to seize the Hutterites' pigs. When the pigs were seized, several Hutterites gave chase and with violence wounded some of the hussars and rescued the pigs.[31] This show and use of violence was of course a gross violation of Hutterian norms, and those involved in the incident were placed under church punishment. The lord, however, argued that the show of force was an attempt to kill him and so brought legal action against the Hutterites. Against the wishes of many of the other lords, a manorial court was assembled with judges and twelve members of the nobility as jurors.[32]

Consistent with their absolutist position on litigation, the Hutterites refused to attend court. As the minister stated, "We and our brotherhood do not go to law as the world does."[33] Nevertheless, the Hutterite minister of the particular colony and four other members were taken by armed hussars to attend the trial. At the trial, the minister denied that there was any attempt to kill the lord and said that the lord had provoked the situation by enforcing a request that was contrary to the contract the Hutterites had made with all the lords. At the end of the case before the jurors rendered a verdict, they offered the opportunity for the Hutterites to make a settlement with the lord. After discussion with other lords who believed the lawsuit should never have been brought in the first place, the Hutterites offered forty imperial talers, but this was refused by the offended lord.[34] Settlement having been refused, the jurors rendered the following judgment: "According to present impartial judgment, it is understood that the brothers wanted, in their community, to strike their manorial lord dead, and therefore it is decided that all of them – men, women, and children – are liable to the death penalty. However, the court will show them mercy by having only twelve leading brothers beheaded. Alternatively it will be yet more merciful and grant the twelve brothers their lives on the sole condition of a payment of forty gulden from each male person over twelve years of age."[35] The minister of the community and the four brothers attending the trial were immediately taken into custody. The exact amount due based on males over twelve years of age is not given, but the amount was apparently substantial or impossible to pay, and in any event, the minister refused to pay it. The five men suffered a variety of hardships and indignities as prisoners during the time that other lords and Hutterite elders sought to have the judgment reversed and the jailed Hutterites freed.[36] After several months, a settlement with the lord was negotiated. The amount of that settlement is not recorded in the chronicles.

Another lawsuit took place in 1764 during a period of intense persecution of the Hutterite community in Alwinz, Transylvania.[37] A Jesuit by the name of Delphini was intent on forcing the Anabaptists to recant, and he found an opportunity to pressure the Hutterian leader, Joseph Kuhr, by bringing a lawsuit against him. Some years earlier the Hutterites, and Kuhr in particular, had pulled down a colony house that an excommunicated member had refused to vacate after joining the Catholic Church. Delphini now succeeded in dragging Kuhr and other brothers into court on the grounds that they were responsible for paying for the house they had pulled down. We are given no information as to why the excommunicated man had any legal claim to the community-owned building, but in any event, a bishop's court ordered the Hutterites to pay sixty gulden to the man for "his" house.[38] Kuhr refused to pay, was taken prisoner, and the case was sent to a "higher court judge at Wairwaitz."[39] In an attempt to free its leader, the community paid the sixty gulden, but Kuhr was still imprisoned for several years on the order of the higher court judge. He suffered many trials in prison before being exiled from the country. He eventually rejoined the Hutterian community.[40]

These two cases illustrate that while holding what might be considered an absolutist position against litigation, the Hutterites nevertheless defended themselves when dragged before a court.

Developing a More Particularized Inside Law on Going to Outside Law

Liberal separation of church and state was a considerable stride forward in ending persecution of people for simply having a faith different from a religion enforced by the state. However, the increasing jurisdiction of the state over activities that might previously have been left to the private sphere or to the church brought new conflicts between the inside law of the church and the outside law of the state. While all Anabaptist groups struggled with the issue of litigation in the context of the growing pervasiveness and complexity of the law and the legal system in the second half of the twentieth century, it was the Mennonite Church (MC) in particular that studied the issue, held conferences, and produced statements that moved away from absolutism to a more particularized application of Anabaptist ethics to litigation.[41] I deal with the details of these developments elsewhere.[42] The Mennonite Church discussion is important for understanding the actual practice of Hutterite litigation, because to a significant degree, as will be illustrated in the next chapters, Hutterite litigation implicitly fit within the categories created explicitly by the Mennonite Church branch of Mennonites, at least before that church itself moved to a more liberal statement as to the inside law that dealt with going to outside law.

In 1956 a Mennonite Church conference on nonresistance and political responsibility was held in Laurelville, Pennsylvania.[43] At this conference, Guy Hershberger, the leading Anabaptist social ethicist of the time, made a fundamental distinction between the parties to a lawsuit: there was a difference between initiating a lawsuit (taking someone to court) and defending a lawsuit (being dragged into court). Usually the party who initiates a lawsuit is called the plaintiff, in distinction to the defendant. For Hershberger, taking someone to court was almost always an aggressive action inconsistent with the "law of love," whereas defending a case in court might be acceptable. Hershberger summarized his position:

> (1) When the Christian is summoned to court charged with a violation of law, he may use the services of an attorney to establish his innocence or to show that the law is in conflict with his Christian conscience, as the case may be. (2) In case of a civil suit brought against a Christian by a non-Christian it is not necessarily inconsistent with the principle of nonresistance to defend the case in court by legal means, although every effort should be made in the spirit of love to make a settlement out of court even with an unjust and unchristian plaintiff. (3) It is inconsistent for the

Christian to be the aggressive party to any lawsuit, even when the legal justice is on his side. (4) Members of the Christian brotherhood may never settle differences among themselves by means of litigation in the civil courts. (5) Purely routine legal actions, such as suits to quiet title to real estate or to clear the records of estates or descendants, or to determine tax responsibilities, so-called friendly suits, are allowable.[44]

Hershberger's distinction between the ethical position of the plaintiff and that of the defendant in civil cases, or the accused in criminal cases, may be directly related to the violence of the law. A person bringing a matter to court was calling upon the police power of the state to coerce the other party to do something, pay something, or stop doing something, while the defendant was not calling on state coercion but, rather, seeking to avoid the application of it. Hershberger's position was also in tune with the separationist model of the church. While you could defend a case brought against you by the government or by a non-Christian, you could not defend yourself in a case brought by a fellow Christian, except for those "loving lawsuits" over matters requiring court application but which don't have adversarial motivation. Logically the Christian who initiated the lawsuit against a brother would be most at fault, but it was even wrongful for a brother to defend such cases in an outside court when the jurisdiction was supposed to be within the church community.

At the conference in 1956, Samuel Wenger, a Mennonite lawyer,[45] made a further distinction between governmental and non-governmental litigation. While discussing a case of seeking compensation for expropriation of land by the government, he said: "It is my opinion that a Mennonite can file such a claim without violating our historic stand against litigation because he is not taking an aggressive act against an individual. The 'state' is the party against whom he claims, and this is an impersonal sort of an entity against which it seems logically impossible to commit an 'offense.'"[46]

The Mennonite Church continued to refine a draft statement of the inside law as to the use of outside law at the Consultation on Litigation Problems, sponsored by Mennonite Mutual Aid at Goshen, Indiana, in July 1961.[47] Numerous issues were discussed, including the bringing of counterclaims and making appeals by the defendant and the problem of insurance litigation. After considering the numerous pressures to accommodate to the new legal complexities of the modern economy, the participants at the 1961 consultations essentially affirmed the Hershberger position against aggressive lawsuits and court involvement between Christians. A statement of findings was circulated.[48] A few years later, in 1963, a new statement, "Litigation and the Use of the Law," was published and circulated widely for comment.[49] Over the next few years the 1963 statement underwent revisions. However, as far as I am able to determine, the attempt to articulate a formal position on litigation was abandoned by 1965. Another attempt to formalize a Mennonite inside law on going to outside law was made in 1976, when the Mennonite Church established its Task Force on Litigation.[50] J. Richard Burkholder surveyed the Mennonite position to that point in time.[51] There was wide consultation with interested groups and several drafts were circulated and revised before the task force ultimately produced a statement on "The Use of the Law" that was adopted by the Mennonite Church in 1981.[52] This most recent statement reflected the shift that was taking place away from separationist nonresistance to activist peacemaking and justice concerns.[53]

In dealing with the issue of whether a particular litigation matter is or is not in conformity with the ethics of the Kingdom, the 1981 statement refused to make any categorical claims; instead of focusing on *what* the decision should be, it focused on *how* such decisions should be made. It was up to the church congregation to apply the Scriptures and discern the will of God in each situation. Whatever the intent, the statement might be seen as marking a fundamental shift in the official position of this branch of the Anabaptist church, from a rejection of all "aggressive" litigation to an openness to the possibility that in some circumstances going to law would be acceptable, so long as the permission came from the congregation after deliberation. The statement asserted that in the deliberation at the congregational level, alternatives to litigation would have to be given priority and "approval can only be for cases that do not share those elements which New Testament examples clearly advise against."[54] It is interesting to note that included in the questions for congregational consideration were the following:

(1) If a lawsuit has been filed against a believer, should he or she make the best defense possible and will this include a counter suit?
(2) If a Christian has acted negligently and then encounters unrealistic demands from the injured party, is litigation appropriate to establish the extent of the Christian's responsibility?
(3) Is litigation necessary to protect children, the aged, the poor, or other persons with limited power?
(4) Is a lawsuit the best way of dealing with a government agency or public institution that will not acknowledge questionable behavior or liability until such a proceeding is initiated?
(5) If a fairly negotiated business contract is broken, should it be enforced by a court?
(6) Is litigation an appropriate method of involving a party who refuses to acknowledge any responsibility?[55]

These questions reflect a considerable movement away from the blanket prohibition on lawsuits. One of the limitations to the exclusive use of consensual alternative dispute resolution processes is that, unlike the formal court system, such processes do not make law. In our common law system, while the courts adjudicate disputes between parties, they also at the same time make law for all of society, because the earlier decisions of courts, particularly appeal courts, give rise to legal rules and principles that form part of the law of the community. A great deal of the law is not found in legislation but in the precedents of court cases. Even the operation and application of legislation is contingent on judicial interpretations of that legislation arising from litigation. What this means is that engaging in litigation may well be motivated by concerns going beyond the seeking of redress for the particular party in a particular case. Instead, litigation can be a process of political engagement with issues of justice not just for the person involved but for the community as a whole. Litigation does not only deal with the vindication of clearly established legal rights and duties but also involves engaging in a process of arguing for what the law ought to be.

Somewhat related to the use of litigation for precedent setting is the use of litigation for public accountability through publicity. Generally, subject to protecting the identity of particularly vulnerable parties or witnesses, formal court proceedings and documents are open to the public. Courts are public institutions, and even though the disputes in civil litigation may involve two private parties, as opposed to any government entity as a party, those so-called private disputes nevertheless become public when litigated. While this may be seen as a disadvantage for the parties, it may be a real advantage in that it puts pressure on one side or the other to settle the matter should the parties not be willing to face the accountability of public opinion. Quite apart from what the judge will determine and enforce as to the merits of the positions of the parties, in litigating a matter, the parties are bringing their dispute out of the backroom and into the public square in front of the community, which is also potentially making judgments about the parties and the issues. In this sense, a party might win a lawsuit on a technicality or even substantively but completely lose a case in terms of public opinion. For some entities, the loss of public confidence may be a far greater loss than any monetary award against which they have successfully defended.[56]

The 1981 statement on the use of the law appears to be the latest Mennonite formulation on the issue. While this statement may capture the evolution of more liberal Mennonite practice from a more formal legislative set of prohibitions and permissions to a process-oriented approach within a set of broader principles, I would argue that the statement is out of step with a more legalistic and separationist Old Order Hutterite, Amish, and Mennonite culture. In my opinion, the earlier, more particularized statements from the late 1950s and early 1960s that distinguished between plaintiffs and defendants, and between governmental and non-governmental litigation, but prohibited the initiation of lawsuits against individuals best captures the traditional Hutterite inside law on going to outside law. This will be confirmed by the examination in the next chapters of the actual practice of litigation by Hutterites in North America, at least before the *Lakeside* case.

Classifying Hutterite Litigation

Having looked at some of the distinctions made in the Mennonite debate over litigation, a distinction between governmental or "public" litigation on one hand, and individual or "private" litigation on the other, needs to be made.[57] That is, bringing a lawsuit against a fellow citizen of the state may be contrasted with bringing a lawsuit against the government of the state. In the next chapter I first identify briefly the reported cases where Hutterites have defended themselves in court in lawsuits brought against them by a branch or agency of the government, or where Hutterites have taken cases to court against governmental authorities when an issue of fundamental importance to their religious freedom was at stake. Given the large number of these cases, one can only conclude that the Hutterites no longer consider engaging in governmental litigation a violation of the religious norm against the use of law courts.

Moving away from governmental litigation and turning to individual litigation, I make a further distinction between those cases that involve "external" disputes with individuals or corporations in the host society, and litigation connected to internal disputes between Hutterites. Given the multiple business enterprises of Hutterite colonies, accelerated by the movement into manufacturing, it is not surprising that colonies from time to time have been sued by non-governmental parties alleging breach of contract or claiming damages due to negligence, to take just two examples. It is not particularly surprising that in some circumstances the Hutterite colony, having been taken to court, has defended some of these claims. However, in this category of cases the more problematic development for our purposes is the more recent willingness of Hutterites to initiate lawsuits against outsiders. We may conclude that the historic religious norm against the use of law courts was already starting to unravel, paving the way for even more radical departures.

The most problematic cases of individual or private litigation are those related to internal disputes rather than external relations. The boundaries of this category may be difficult to draw, but clearly if one colony is suing another colony, or if one Hutterite or group of Hutterites is suing its own colony or another colony, it is in the category of litigation that most clearly violates the historic religious norm against the use of law courts to settle disputes between Christians. This category includes those cases where a colony is sued by a person or group of people the colony considers to be ex-members. Even if the individuals are now treated as outsiders by the majority, the dispute in question still deals with internal matters, that is, with events that took place on the colony. As we will see, an examination of the historical patterns of Hutterite litigation in this category indicates that Hutterites have defended claims brought against them by ex-members, but they did not initiate lawsuits against so-called apostates. The point to make here is that, despite the developing instability of the religious norm against litigation, the *Lakeside* litigation was unprecedented. That the church itself would go to outside law and sue ex-members in an attempt to get the state to kick the dissenters off the colony and force them to turn over property allegedly belonging to the colony seems to me a clear violation of the traditional inside law of the Hutterites.

4
Hutterite Litigation before *Lakeside*

Hutterite Governmental Litigation

There are approximately thirty reported cases in Canada and the United States involving Hutterites and governmental litigation. Approximately twenty of these cases involve litigation initiated by Hutterites; the remaining cases involve litigation where Hutterites defended against or appealed claims brought against them by the government. While these cases often raise important issues dealing with freedom of religion, I am mentioning them here simply to establish the amount and pattern of litigation, rather than to deal with the substantive content of the litigation.[1]

The American cases include extremely hostile court action brought against the Hutterites in South Dakota in the wake of the First World War attacking the Hutterite way of life and successfully annulling their incorporation as religious corporations.[2] Decades later, South Dakota passed legislation allowing for the incorporation of communalist societies, but then, in a new wave of hostility, legislation was passed prohibiting the incorporation of new colonies and limiting the expansion of existing incorporated colonies. Another hostile lawsuit was commenced against a South Dakota Hutterite colony, and while the colony was successful on the narrow point that it had not expanded its landholding, and thus had not violated the legislation, the courts upheld the hostile restrictive legislation as being constitutional.[3] However, while the intent of the discriminatory legislation may have been to control the establishment of new Hutterite colonies, in effect, such colonies could still be established on the basis of holding land in trust, rather than by incorporation.

In two cases, Hutterites in the United States went to court appealing income tax assessments by asserting that the colonies were religious organizations or corporations exempt under certain provisions of tax legislation as then existing.[4] In both cases the Hutterites lost the litigation, as courts refused to accept the proposition that the profits from the highly successful farming operations of the colony were exclusively used for religious or charitable purposes. There have been a couple of other reported tax cases in the United States on narrower points of valuation of assets, or investment tax credits.[5] There was also a case dealing with the proper classification of a colony under bankruptcy legislation.[6]

Finally, in regard to governmental litigation in the United States, a Hutterite colony was successful in establishing federal court jurisdiction to hear a challenge to a school board decision to bus Hutterite children to a public school in town, rather than establish a public school on the colony,[7] but when the case was heard, the court rejected the argument that Hutterites had any constitutional right to a publicly funded school on a colony.[8]

If we look at the results of governmental litigation involving Hutterites in the United States, we may conclude, at least as measured by the judicial opinions, that such litigation has been quite unsuccessful in advancing the interests of the Hutterites. It would appear that negotiating with governments to receive accommodations, and maintaining a good reputation in the host society as to honesty and charity, rather than bringing litigation against governments, has been the key to Hutterite survival. That the Hutterites are willing to go to court and challenge governmental action can be a bargaining tool of some importance, however, regardless of what appears to be at this point a very poor batting average in terms of litigation success.

With some exceptions, Hutterite governmental litigation in Canada has not been very successful either, even though there has been much more of it in comparison with the United States. Indeed, three cases were taken all the way to the Supreme Court of Canada. In the first case, a colony was successful in getting the court to characterize the colony as a "farmer" rather than as a "religious organization" for purposes of debt-relief legislation.[9] While successful, the case arguably set a bad precedent for when colonies later wanted to be classified, for other purposes, as religious organizations. For example, the Dariusleut challenged the payment of income tax by arguing that the colonies should be characterized as religious orders. This group of Hutterites litigated through four levels of court, all the way to the Supreme Court of Canada.[10] Again, while finally successful in challenging deemed individual taxation of overall colony profits, the victory was actually hollow, as the colonies were then taxed at a corporate rate, rather than being tax exempt as religious charities. The corporate rate, given that colonies paid no wages to members of the colony so as to be able to deduct these amounts from profits, turned out to be much higher than the scheme that the Hutterites had challenged.[11] A second series of court cases was then launched by the Dariusleut, again unsuccessfully,[12] and finally litigation was dropped in favour of a negotiated agreement with the government as to taxation on a deemed individual basis. More recently, a few more cases have dealt with taxation matters, again with mixed results.[13]

Probably the most important case, also taken all the way to the Supreme Court of Canada, dealt with challenging the hostile legislation in Alberta that restricted the ability of Hutterite colonies to purchase land.[14] However, the Hutterites were again unsuccessful in their litigation challenging the constitutionality of this legislation.[15]

There is some indication that litigation has been more successful when challenging particular zoning decisions by municipal officials and boards. A couple of cases from Saskatchewan have struck down zoning restrictions directly aimed at preventing colonies from being established.[16] There was also a series of cases in Alberta where a colony successfully went through at least four rounds of litigation in trying to establish a new colony in the face of hostile action by the municipal district. The Hutterites were successful three times before the Alberta Court of Appeal, and also in further litigation brought by the municipality.[17] There has been litigation involving zoning issues in Manitoba as well.[18]

To complete the list, there are a few other cases of governmental litigation involving Hutterites,[19] or featuring issues involving Hutterites.[20] It should be noted that I have not attempted to identify criminal cases, which are obviously governmental cases. There may be cases where a member or resident of a colony is charged with an offence. It is difficult to identify in the few cases that are reported whether the individual has left the colony and is thus hiring his or her own lawyer to defend against the charges, or whether the individual is a member or resident where the colony leadership or membership has agreed to engage legal counsel. In the course of my research, I came across cases dealing with speeding,[21] and impaired driving,[22] but the Hutterite crime rate in the past was so minuscule that it was hardly detectible. As we will see, the dispute at Lakeside blackened this good reputation, as Hutterites on both sides of the dispute were frequently charged with assault or breaches of court orders.

On the issue of criminal charges, a great deal of publicity was given to the criminal proceedings brought in May of 1998 against ten Hutterites, mostly youths, alleging a host of sexual offences that had taken place at an Alberta Lehrerleut colony and subsequently at the daughter colony as well.[23] The charges were laid after a teenage girl told a teacher about the sexual abuses she had experienced.[24] The teenager was removed from the colony and placed in foster care. The worst of the subsequent criminal cases involved her father, who was convicted and sentenced to four years in jail for offences committed against her.[25] The father represented himself in court. In another case, an elderly great uncle of the same victim was sentenced to thirty months in jail for sexual assault.[26] When the charges were first laid, it was reported that all the Hutterites "refused legal counsel because it is against their belief system."[27] However, lawyers eventually did act informally as advisors to the court.[28]

Based on the cases mentioned, it is clear that the Hutterites do resort to litigation when negotiation has failed to resolve the conflict between the demands of the state and the norms of the church community. Despite assertions to the contrary,[29] this record of governmental litigation may also be duplicated by an examination of Amish[30] and Mennonite litigation.[31]

The participation in governmental litigation by Anabaptist groups raises the question of why such litigation might be justified. Probably the most obvious answer is that in the vast majority of circumstances, when we turn to court adjudication of conflicts between religious belief and the apparent demands of the law of the host society, we are seeking to restrain state coercion, rather than apply state coercion of law enforcement onto a third party. The religious believer is usually trying to get an exemption from the coercive law because of a claim that the law is incompatible with his or her religious belief, but sometimes a person may be seeking a favourable interpretation of the law or a benefit under the law, rather than an exemption to it. In any case, governmental litigation seems easier to square with a pacifist position. At most, if the violence of the state sword is exercised at all, it is in the context of one part of the state coercing another part of the state to abide by the rule of law.

As noted in the last chapter, participation in governmental litigation may also be extended by more activist Anabaptist groups beyond the narrow self-interest of the group to preserve its own religious norms in the face of hostile regulation from the host society. Given the reality that courts lay down precedents that affect all of society, religious groups may seek standing to bring matters to court or intervene in cases that raise particular justice issues.[32]

The justifications for governmental litigation should not blind us to other problematic dimensions. To invoke the "government" as a party to a lawsuit involves abstract and fictional discourse not unlike having a "corporation" as a party to a lawsuit. Behind every governmental or corporate mask are real people who act for these institutional entities. The Anabaptist litigant will have to be careful, particularly in the context of adversarial procedures, that engaging in governmental litigation does not become itself a licence for aggression.

Non-governmental Litigation Involving External Relations: Hutterite Defence in Court to Lawsuits Initiated by Others

Turning to cases involving lawsuits with non-governmental parties, it should be noted that Hutterites, despite nonresistant religious ideology, do not necessarily accept and settle every claim made against them. There are at least ten reported cases in the United States, and about the same number in Canada that I have identified, where the Hutterite colony has gone to court to *defend* against court actions initiated by members of the host society.[33]

The first of these reported decisions arose in South Dakota in 1910 when the Hutterites were sued for having raised the height of their milldam in 1904, which allegedly led to flooding and damage to the land of an upstream neighbour. The case went to trial and the Hutterites were ordered to reduce the height of the dam to its original height when constructed by the Hutterites in 1895. The Hutterites unsuccessfully appealed the case.[34] However, in a second case brought by a flooded neighbour, the Hutterites were successful, both at the trial level and on appeal by the upstream landowner, because the plaintiff had missed the two-year limitation period to bring suit for damages against milldam construction.[35] I do not know if the Hutterites made reasonable offers to settle these claims brought against them but, in any event, there is still something troubling about the aggressiveness of appealing the first negative verdict, and the use of a technical defence such as a limitation period to defeat what otherwise might be a valid complaint.

Several more lawsuits dealing with land transactions were brought against the Hutterites during the great period of upheaval as the Hutterite colonies moved to Canada.[36] In one case a real estate broker successfully appealed trial court decisions denying his claim for commissions for an alleged cancellation of a contract for sale of Hutterite lands.[37] Another case involved action by the purchaser of Hutterite land against a colony that had a lease-back arrangement with the new owner. The courts upheld the terms of the lease in favour of the Hutterite colony.[38]

For a long period there were apparently no further reported cases of defending against non-governmental litigation in either the United States or Canada. A reported case finally arose out of a claim for damages against a Montana colony as a result of an accident in 1951 between the plaintiff driver and a Hutterite driving a truck. It turned out that the Hutterite was a visitor from a colony in Alberta. Upon receiving the court papers initiating the lawsuit, the leaders of the Montana colony visited the lawyer for the plaintiff and informed him that the truck driver was a visitor, that the truck was not owned by the colony, nor was the driver doing any work for the colony, and the driver had never been a member of the colony. Despite having this knowledge, and leaving the impression with the Hutterites that they could ignore the complaint, given that they were the wrong party, the law firm acting for the plaintiff proceeded to get a default judgment against the colony. A sum of money was then seized from the colony bank account and held by the law firm for the plaintiff. On appeal to the Supreme Court in 1953, the colony got the default judgment set aside. A dispute then arose over the return of sums that had been taken under the default judgment, including sums for legal fees. Eventually the court ordered the return of fees taken by the law firm for the plaintiff out of the colony bank account.[39] To a degree, this case might also be classified as one involving Hutterites going beyond simply defending a suit in court to actually taking court action and invoking the power of the state to rectify what appears to have been a theft of their property. Other more recent cases of American litigation include lawsuits against a Hutterite school board for wrongful dismissal,[40] a land dispute,[41] and a conflict over insurance coverage for damages caused by seeping sewage.[42]

It is of interest perhaps that despite Canada having the greater population of Hutterites as compared with the United States, there were no reported cases of Hutterites defending against non-governmental litigation filed against them in Canada until recently.[43] Furthermore, out of the ten or so recently reported cases, all but two probably involve defences brought by the insurance company of the colony. While most claims of damage resulting from an accident involving a Hutterite colony vehicle will be settled within the context of insurance negotiations, some of these cases have given rise to claims in court against individuals from Hutterite colonies.[44] It is doubtful that these cases should be counted as examples of Hutterites defending themselves in court, as opposed to insurance companies doing so. The same can be said for a few claims involving fires, or chemical spills that allegedly have damaged a neighbouring property.[45] Again it may be that the insurance companies are behind bringing a defence to court in these cases. Thus, there are just a few Canadian reported cases involving contractual or tort liability where clearly the colony is hiring a lawyer and defending against a claim.[46]

However, when one stops counting reported judicial decisions and starts examining court files, one discovers that, at least in Manitoba, there have been quite a number of cases brought against Hutterite colonies in the last couple of decades, particularly contract claims for unpaid debts.[47] By 2000 at least fifty court claims had been made against colonies in Manitoba, though the vast majority were against a handful of colonies which were sued repeatedly, indicating that these colonies were or are in financial difficulty. What is important to note is that in all but a few of these court cases, the matter was settled or discontinued without any filing of defences or counterclaims by the Hutterite colony. A few cases, however, were defended against. We may conclude that, while the numbers are not many, there is enough evidence to support the proposition that Hutterites have sometimes gone to court to defend against claims made against them by individuals in the host society. The greater challenge to the anti-litigation norm comes from taking aggressive action in court, rather than attempting to avoid the imposition of court judgments backed by the violence of the state.

Hutterite Initiation of Lawsuits against Others

I will examine with considerable detail in this book the rash of lawsuits in the last two decades initiated by one group of Hutterites, both against other Hutterites and against outsiders. That this embrace of aggressive litigation violates what used to be the inside law of Hutterites may be established not only by doctrinal writings on prohibitions on going to law but also by establishing the absence of any previous cases of such litigation. However, I will now note that there were indeed a few previous reported cases before the recent explosion. Even though there were only five cases in the United States and about the same number in Canada, the existence of any cases at all raises the question of whether the norm against litigation was still stable (and these few cases were anomalous) or whether the norm was actually somewhat unstable, or included exceptions within it. Given the multiple business transactions the Hutterites have engaged in with individuals and entities in the host society, and the extremely small number of lawsuits filed by Hutterites until recently, it is reasonable to conclude that historically if wrongs could not be dealt with short of going to court, the Hutterites suffered the wrong rather than take the person to court. Some of the anomalous cases in this period were probably due to insurance subrogation, whereas others may have been justified by the Hutterites as actions of resistance to prejudice against them in land-purchase deals.

The first anomalous cases of what might be called aggressive, rather than defensive, litigation were American. In the 1930s some Hutterites brought a claim to court to settle a dispute over the title to a patch of land which previously had been part of an island but had been submerged and then, because of accretion and changed river flow, had become attached to the land owned by someone else. The Hutterites brought action to quiet title to the land and also to recover for the destruction of trees on the land. The trial court found for the Hutterites, but the defendant appealed and won at the higher court level.[48]

Land was again the theme in a case brought to court in Montana in 1953.[49] A colony in Alberta bought land in Montana in 1947 by using an agent who did not disclose to the vendor that he was acting for a Hutterite colony. The contract for the sale of the land was assigned to the colony and the colony moved onto the land and began operations, but the vendor did not convey the land to the Hutterite colony, presumably because of prejudice against Hutterites. The vendor finally sued in state court to have the contract cancelled. The colony then sued in Federal Court for specific performance of the contract. It is unclear on the record available to me which side sued first. In any event, to avoid the contract, the vendor argued that the colony was a foreign corporation that had failed to comply with licensing provisions of state law before doing business in the state. According to state law, contracts made by foreign unlicensed corporations could be voided.

The Federal Court found that, indeed, the Hutterite colony had not registered in Montana for the first five years of being in the United States and had not paid the corporation licence tax or filed annual reports, the effect of which by Montana law might void the contract. The court also found, however, that the Hutterite colony by this failure to comply with corporate requirements did not have standing to sue in Federal Court, and the case was thus remanded back to the state court. I do not know what legal proceedings transpired thereafter, but it appears that the Hutterites received title to the lands that they had bought and were living on.[50]

Though I could find no reported court decision, in 1962 the newly arrived Hutterites in the state of Washington purportedly sued a newspaper for defamation.[51] The ability of the Hutterites to pay more for land than could the local farmers caused deep resentment of the new foreigners who established a colony in the Spokane area. Demands were made for restrictive legislation against communal property, and derogatory literature and rumours began to appear against the Hutterites. The *Spokesman-Review* newspaper published a number of negative articles, and the colony, on the urging of a lawyer, sued and won a modest settlement for defamation, as well as a public apology in the newspaper.[52]

A fourth American case where Hutterites sued involved the issue of another cancelled land deal. In 1968 Sand Lake Colony made a contract with a North Dakota company to buy over two thousand acres of land in South Dakota owned by the company. The colony paid a $50,000 down payment for the property and expected to take possession at the beginning of 1969. However, the colony discovered that portions of the land were subject to oral leases and they were unable to take possession when they needed to, so they rescinded the contract. The litigation arose by way of the colony claiming a return of the $50,000 that had been paid to the defendant vendor. At trial the Hutterites were unsuccessful, but on appeal (with one dissent) they got their money back.[53] The law in relationship to liquidated damages and penalties for failure to perform a contract are not important for our purposes. What is significant is that the colony sued.

A fifth American case involved a colony that lost a huge amount of money to an individual operating a classic pyramid Ponzi scheme. There were issues as to the way certain banks dealt with the accounts and the cheques that were returned for lack of funds. The colony sued the banks but was unsuccessful.[54]

Not surprisingly, the first reported cases where Hutterites in Canada took cases to court against individuals involved issues arising from land transactions. In 1962 an Alberta colony successfully sued a real estate agent in Saskatchewan who refused to return money left in trust with him.[55] Then, in 1982, a Saskatchewan colony sued for specific performance of a land transaction.[56] The colony claimed it had bought the land for $672,000 and wanted title to it, but the defendant claimed that the sale was subject to an option to buy from another party, an option which was exercised. The court found that the colony did have notice of the prior option to purchase, so the Hutterites lost the lawsuit.

There are also a few recent cases involving property insurance where the decision to sue was probably taken by the insurance company, with the colony being the nominal plaintiff.[57] However, what complicates matters is that the Schmiedeleut Hutterites at some stage formed their own insurance company. This company has commenced litigation against others, and it might be argued that the Hutterites, through this corporate front, are collectively violating their own anti-litigation norms. For example, there was a protracted litigation over the loss by fire of a feed elevator on a colony, allegedly caused by negligent advice given by the agent of the feed company. The case was settled on the eve of trial.[58] In another case, the Hutterite insurance company disputed the amount of loss and also brought a cross-claim against an insurance agency in a case of a power outage leading to a loss of hogs.[59]

Finally, there was the case where two Hutterite men were helping load concrete slabs that their colony had purchased from Barkman Concrete in Steinbach, Manitoba. One of the slabs slipped off the forklift operated by a Barkman employee and injured the two Hutterite customers. One of the men was hospitalized for a month and suffered permanent disability. The other man suffered less severe injuries. Assuming there was evidence of negligence on the part of the employee, the two men might have a good claim to receive compensation for the injuries, and presumably Barkman would have liability insurance to cover just such claims. But could the two Hutterite men sue to recover damages? If they were members of a colony, any recovery would be given over to the colony, since they could not have individual entitlement to property. What is interesting in this case is that the two men assigned their claim to a third Hutterite (it is unclear as to whether he was also a member of the colony or was living off a colony) and this person then filed a statement of claim.[60] No statement of defence was filed and the case was soon discontinued.[61] Presumably there was a settlement, but we have no information on the matter.

Despite a handful of cases such as just noted, it is my contention that the traditional approach of not bringing cases to court against individuals or private entities was until recently a solid part of the inside law of Hutterites. It must be said that more recently in Manitoba the traditional approach has broken down. There is a new willingness of Hutterites in Manitoba to launch court actions rather than suffer wrong to be done to them. In addition to all the litigation arising from the schism in the Schmiedeleut, without even attempting to be exhaustive, I can list at least a dozen more cases from the court files where Hutterites have launched lawsuits against outside individuals or entities.[62] As the Hutterites move into manufacturing and marketing of products outside the traditional agricultural products sector, it will be increasingly difficult to turn the other cheek when products are delivered and never paid for, or purchased supplies turn out to be faulty, or warranty disputes arise over manufactured goods. If it became generally known that the Hutterites never sued in court, there might be opportunity for the unscrupulous to take advantage of them. While these pressures to litigate are understandable, the willingness to sue outsiders can also be traced directly to the willingness of Hutterite leaders to sue *insiders* and litigate ecclesiastical disputes. How can the church now claim to have a prohibition on aggressive lawsuits against outsiders when the church leaders are willing to go to law against their own members?

Litigation Involving Internal Relations
While the prohibition against bringing aggressive litigation against outsiders is breaking down, at the epicentre of the Anabaptist anti-litigation doctrine is the concept that ecclesiastical disputes within the church community should not be taken to external courts. Other Christian groups who disagree with the Anabaptists on the issue of violence may nevertheless join with the Anabaptists in affirming the wrongfulness of going to court in these kinds of cases. Thus, the prohibition in these matters goes beyond the issue of the violence of the law. It is also a matter of the church's jurisdictional autonomy, competence, and witness. When the church is dealing with lawsuits involving outsiders or the government, it is usually dealing with the interpretation and application of the outside law. However, when a member or ex-member sues the church, raising issues of rights to be a member, damages for wrongful expulsion, or entitlement to church property, it will almost always be the case that the inside law of the church will be a key aspect of the litigation, risking the danger not only that the outside court will be incompetent to understand the inside law but also that the inside law will be transformed or even overturned, as it is measured by the additional requirements of the outside law, which may take precedence over inside law.

When we turn to the Hutterite cases in this category, we find that, until the *Lakeside* litigation, the previous five cases have all dealt with individuals or groups making a claim for a portion of colony assets. A subsidiary issue in some of these cases was the legality of the excommunication of members. Often with regrets about the unfairness of the inside law of Hutterites, the courts in these cases have refused to privatize communal property. It is also noteworthy that in every case the action was initiated by individual Hutterites who had left the colony or had been excommunicated, and not by the colony itself, as was the case in *Lakeside*. Because these cases are relevant to *Lakeside*, treatment of them needs to be expanded.

The *Raley* Case: Privatization Rejected but Division Ordered
The first case dealing with a claim for colony assets was decided on 13 December 1920 before Mr. Justice Walsh of the Supreme Court of Alberta, Trial

Division.[63] The information in the reported decision is sketchy at best. Apparently the Dariusleut's Foster Colony and Lake Byron Colony were about twenty miles apart from each other in South Dakota. It is not stated whether these were two separate colonies established out of the original Darius colony of Wolf Creek, or whether, because of a problem getting contiguous land, there was really only one colony that resided in two locations. At any rate, the trial judge accepted the argument that there were two separate colonies, except that Foster Colony did not have its own minister to head the colony. Instead, the minister of Lake Byron Colony, a Mr. Waldner, also served as minister of Foster Colony. In addition, while the two colonies were separate for most purposes, the land of both colonies was held in trust under the name of the Hutterite Society of Wolf Creek. In 1918, under the leadership of Waldner, both Foster Colony and Lake Byron Colony were sold, and land was bought in Alberta. It was alleged that there was an agreement that two colonies would be established in Alberta. However, instead of establishing two colonies in Alberta, the assets were consolidated and one colony, Raley Colony, was established. Thus, the Foster people and the Lake Byron people were brought together in one colony under the leadership of Waldner.

It is interesting to compare this information taken from the judicial decision with the genealogical maps of Hutterite colonies. The maps do not show a Foster Colony or a Lake Byron Colony but, rather, that a colony called Beadle was established in South Dakota in 1905 as a daughter colony of Wolf Creek and that this colony moved in 1918 to a colony in Alberta that was called Raley, according to one map,[64] and West Raley according to another.[65] Perhaps this casts doubt on the judicial conclusion that there were two separate colonies.

The few facts given in the reported decision do not really provide any details of the disputes that subsequently arose when the colony or colonies moved to Canada. What is clear, however, is that certain members of the so-called Foster Colony were placed under some form of church discipline and by the time of the court action they had left the colony. From what little can be gleaned from the court decision, it seems that at least three of the four adult men on the Foster side did not like Waldner's leadership. These three men and their wives sued Waldner as trustee for the rest of the colony at Raley, Alberta. The plaintiffs claimed their share in the assets of the Raley colony. That these individuals would bring a lawsuit against their minister and former community was a gross violation of traditional Hutterian norms.

Mr. Justice Walsh firmly rejected the plaintiffs attempt to privatize some portion of the community property of the colony. Walsh affirmed the basic principle that the plaintiffs were not entitled to any personal share of the colony:

When they joined the church they did so upon the distinct understanding that they would have no individual interest in the property which was common to them and all other members of it. They knew and they agreed that so long as they lived and remained members of the church they and their families would be fed and clothed and cared for in sickness and otherwise provided for to the extent of their actual needs and that upon their death those whom they left behind them would be similarly cared for, but they also knew that no property in the community holdings would ever vest in them and that if they left the church they would go out empty handed. This was a solemn compact between them and those who in like spirit and under the same pledge formed with them the church.[66]

Here we see that the court was upholding the inside law of Hutterites partly by fitting it into an existing outside law concept of contract or covenant. The plaintiffs had made a contract with each other and the defendants not to ever privatize the common property of the group, and the court was holding them to the bargain.

While rejecting the plaintiffs' claim to privatize the colony, the court did accept one exception. One of the plaintiffs, John B. Hofer, had married a Prairieleut (non-colony) widow, Barbara Wipf, who had two young sons. When her first husband had died, he left property to Barbara and the two sons in equal shares, and when Barbara married Hofer, she brought the proceeds of the sale of her former husband's lands and goods and gave them to the colony. Mr. Justice Walsh stated that a convert who brings private property and by contract puts it into the collective pot cannot later take it back out of the collective pot. But the two young sons never had the capacity to agree that the one-third interest that each of them had in their father's estate should now be collective Hutterite church property. Thus, Raley Colony was responsible to pay out to these two infant plaintiffs whatever value of their father's estate plus interest was due to them.

Walsh J. also found a way to give the adult plaintiffs what they wanted. During the trial, the plaintiffs were allowed to amend their claim. Instead of characterizing the claim as one involving individual ex-Hutterites suing for a share of the collective after expulsion, it was recharacterized as one involving a contract between members to divide the common property between two colonies rather than giving it to only one. The court was being asked to enforce a contract for the division of community property between Hutterites rather than to break a contract prohibiting the privatization of communal property when leaving the Hutterite fold. Walsh J. found as a fact that an oral agreement to sell the two colonies in South Dakota and move to Alberta was premised on the understanding that two colonies would again be established in Alberta. However, Waldner, as trustee for the assets of both colonies, had established only one colony in Alberta. Thus, the plaintiffs were really claiming a breach of trust. The court could grant specific performance of the original agreement. This was not a case of turning communal property into individual privatized shares but a case in which communal property remained communal property but was being illegally handled by those entrusted with it. In making this finding, the court claimed that it was not interfering with the doctrine of the church. It was not interfering with the principle of community of property by enforcing the understanding that there would be two colonies instead of one. On the point that the court should not intervene in what was essentially an ecclesiastical matter, Walsh stated: "It is not an interference with a matter of purely domestic concern which the authorities of the church should be left to deal with, but one involving property rights which this Court has, I think, jurisdiction to deal with."[67]

The remedy to enforce the trust consisted of a court-ordered division of the assets of Raley Colony into two parts, proportional to the assets derived from Foster Colony and Lake Byron Colony. Since one of the original Foster Colony men sided with Waldner, he could choose within a month which of the two groups he would go with. If he stayed with the Waldner group, the proportion of the Foster group would be reduced by one-fourth. While here colony division was based on a contract to divide, the argument could be developed that, in future cases, even without a contract to divide, a court might order the division of colony property in disputes between one group of Hutterites in schism with another group, as opposed to a dispute involving Hutterites simply leaving the colony or being expelled on grounds clearly indicating a departure from the faith. Put another way, it is very different for a court to divide community property into two or more community pots than it is for it to change community property into private property. But once the property is divided, what happens if one of the groups, having claimed in court that it would be establishing a new colony, then promptly privatizes that pot?

It was noteworthy that Mr. Justice Walsh emphasized that the division of the colony did not mean the privatization of the colony. While the moveable property that the Foster group was now in control of would be held by John B. Hofer, the leader of the plaintiffs, in trust for that group, Walsh J. noted as to the land that "I do not think that I should compel the transfer to him of the lands which will be assigned to him as trustee for himself and the others in the same interest. All that they are entitled to is the use and occupation of these lands and the defendant Waldner's title will be subject to these rights."[68] The implication here is that a second separate colony would be established within the territory of the present Raley Colony rather than at a separate location.

Thus far, the Raley decision, upholding both a contract not to privatize and a contract to divide, seems quite justified, assuming the facts as found by the court. It is at the membership stage that difficulty arises. If the plaintiffs were excommunicated from the church and colony, even if there was a contract to divide, they would have no rights to the use of the divided colony property. Walsh J. did not give many factual details about the process of discipline in the Hutterite church and specifically the process used in this case. Walsh treated the plaintiffs as members of the church, even though the defendants considered them to be excommunicated. Walsh J. stated:

> The impression left upon my mind by it was that though the plaintiffs had by their conduct in this matter broken the rules of the church and laid themselves open to exclusion from membership in it, nothing to accomplish that end had been done by the authorities and the plaintiffs, though offenders against the discipline of the church, were still regarded as having interests which the authorities always had, and were still willing to, recognize. The frequent form of the expression was that they had not been put out of the church but had put themselves out. I do not think that the forfeiture of all rights incidental to their membership followed automatically upon their commission of this offence, but that some action to that end was necessary on the part of the proper authorities and that action has never been taken. Furthermore their rights as members are expressly recognized and admitted by the statement of defence.[69]

By "offence," Walsh may have been referring to the bringing of the lawsuit, but it is not clear. In any case, this raises questions. Because the case treated the plaintiffs as still members of the church, the court could uphold the contract to divide the colony, and give the appearance that it was not interfering with the doctrinal autonomy of the church in regard to the rules of common property. But at the same time, by sliding over the fundamental questions of membership and excommunication, one might surmise that the effect of the judgment was to overrule the disciplinary process of the church. If the plaintiffs were in fact non-members, as they were viewed from within the church, the effect of the case came back full circle to a violation of the common property doctrine that held that expelled members have no legal right to receive a share of colony assets. Perhaps Raley Colony could have subsequently taken whatever formal steps were necessary to excommunicate the plaintiffs and then brought action in court to reclaim the Foster Colony assets, but the Hutterites, consistent with the anti-litigation norm, never initiated such a lawsuit.

Did the plaintiffs establish a Hutterite colony, or did they privatize the common pot that the court gave them? Was a new colony established by the Foster plaintiffs on the Raley land, or elsewhere with assets from the Raley colony? A current list of colonies indicates that a colony now called West Raley was established in 1918 and is still in existence today.[70] According to one genealogical map, another colony was established out of this colony in 1922; it later became extinct.[71] If the Foster plaintiffs established this now extinct colony, we might well conclude that the common pot was indeed eventually privatized. On the other hand, the evidence is ambiguous, because another map suggests that the Raley colony split into the New York colony in 1924, which is an existing colony today, and then Raley became extinct when the remaining members moved to West Raley Colony in 1929.[72]

More recently, insight on this situation was shed by Rod Janzen, who outlined a few situations in which non-colony Prairieleut individuals had joined Hutterite colonies. One such case involved Barbara Wipf, who, as mentioned above, married a Hutterite, John B. Hofer. Janzen states:

> In 1918, Barbara and John had accompanied their colony to Raley, Alberta (near Cardston), to escape World War I-era persecution. Personal and ideological conflicts there led John, his brother David, and their families to move to Grassrange, Montana, in 1919, however, in an effort to establish a new colony. Unsuccessful, they had moved back to the Raley area in 1922. John and David Hofer then formed their own independent "Hofer Colony" which functioned much like traditional colonies but had never been officially recognized by the Hutterites.
>
> ... In 1944, the Hofer Colony relocated to the Stirling area because of the construction of a dam near the Raley property. They began to call themselves "Stirling Colony." ... Stirling, like its predecessor, the Hofer Colony, was never recognized by the Hutterites, even though numerous attempts were made to establish some form of affiliation. The communal structure itself became optional in 1947. Members ate in the community kitchen and dining hall until 1962, however, and farmed collectively until 1990 ... In 1964 the Stirling congregation affiliated with the Western Conservation Mennonite Fellowship.[73]

The meaning of the subsequent history is ambiguous. On one hand, the fact that these people were never accepted by the Hutterian church indicates the probability that they had been excommunicated and the court was probably wrong in dividing Raley and entrusting them with a portion of it. On the other hand, while Janzen does not mention the lawsuit brought by John B. Hofer and others, further details about the members who joined this group and their activities indicate that this group of people retained a great deal of the communal and Anabaptist norms of the Hutterites, even if never officially recognized by the wider Hutterian church. There certainly was not a quick privatization of the collective pot. Despite the violation of Anabaptist norms in going to law, the plaintiffs did not thereafter obviously fall off the Anabaptist wagon. Thus, in granting the plaintiffs common property, the court perhaps legitimately facilitated another group of Hutterites to establish its own brand of the faith, however isolated from the mainstream.

The *Felger* and *Big Bend* Cases: Privatization or Division?

Although I have been able to find very little information about them, there were at least two other Alberta cases in which Hutterites launched lawsuits in an attempt to get a portion of the assets of the colony they were leaving. It is entirely possible that the precedent set by Mr. Justice Walsh in 1920 provided the plaintiffs with the leverage they needed. In both cases the plaintiffs received assets, but I do not have any judicial records as to the basis for the awards. For example, a Hutterite family left Felger Colony (Darius) in 1938 and commenced an action for compensation. Under a court settlement approved by Mr. Justice Tweedie of the Supreme Court of Alberta on 1 March 1938, George Hofer received $6,000 and his wife Susanna Hofer received $9,000 for herself and her six children from Felger Colony.[74] While Felger Colony itself was ultimately excommunicated from the church and privatized, we do not know if George and Susanna took their settlement funds into another Hutterite colony that they joined, or whether this situation essentially amounted to the wrongful conversion of community property into private property, and Felger Colony decided not to contest the matter.

Shortly after the Felger settlement, there was apparently another lawsuit launched in Alberta, this time against Big Bend Colony. Again, information is limited. Michael Holzach, a young German news reporter and freelance writer who in the late 1970s arrived uninvited to a Hutterite colony in Alberta and proceeded to stay with the Hutterites for a year, wrote a fascinating book on the Hutterites and his experiences on a number of colonies.[75] Holzach tells this story about the Monarch colony, a colony which was never accepted into the wider Hutterite church:

> The stories that I have heard about the Monarch community are colourful and contradictory. Only one thing seems to be clear: On November 22 in the year 1938, the first preacher of the Big Ben[d] colony, Jakob Mendel, was taken out of office by the conference of the [Lehrerleut] preachers for bearing "false witness." They accused him of having registered and then sold for 600 dollars the patent for a rock-gathering machine which he had constructed himself. Mendel, who believed in acting in his brethren's community's interest, did not accept the judgment but continued to preach to part of the colony, namely his relatives. This constituted a schism within

the community. The adversaries did not talk to each other any longer, they ate their meals in separate places, and their children were taught in two different classrooms. Neighbourly love was dead, and the community went to hell. In 1942 Jakob Mendel declared his willingness to split the community's property and to leave with his followers. The other party, however, did not want to give any "heavenly wealth" to the banned preacher. So the ex-preacher went before a worldly court and won: He built the new farm of Monarch next to the road to Lethbridge with 30,000 dollars from the colony's treasury.[76]

I can find no record of a "worldly court" dealing with this, but here again, if the Holzach story is taken as historically accurate, even though there is here a violation of the anti-litigation norm, there is a plaintiff who is seeking assets, allegedly not to privatize them but to establish another Hutterite colony. Perhaps, as in the *Felger* litigation, a settlement was made in the light of the precedent set by Mr. Justice Walsh in 1920. If the Hutterites thought of the Raley plaintiffs as having been excommunicated and yet successfully getting a portion of the colony when they sued, a belief may have developed among Hutterites that the courts would award property to departing members, so long as they established colonies rather than privatized the property. It is quite possible that Hutterite leaders would not know that the *Raley* case, even if it mischaracterized the status of the plaintiffs, was grounded on the finding of a pre-existing agreement to divide.

Returning to the Felger situation, many decades later, in the 1980s, a dispute arose over entitlement and valuation of shares in a corporate farm in Alberta.[77] This farm, valued at $5,700,000 at the time of the dispute, had at one time been the Felger Hutterite colony. Felger Colony near Lethbridge, Alberta, was established in 1926 and then, in 1927, Felger established Pincher Creek Colony. Those who remained at Felger gradually rejected their religious heritage. At some stage in the 1940s, the colony had been excommunicated from the Hutterian Brethren Church. The minutes of the first meeting of managers of the newly incorporated Hutterian Brethren Church held at Wilson Colony in Alberta in November 1951 read: "The matter of the Felger Colony was discussed and it was duly resolved that the Felger Colony be not at present admitted as a Congregation of the Church, but that the Darius-leut Conference endeavour to have the Felger Colony fit themselves for membership at a later date."[78] The colony never did come back into the fold.

Disputes had broken out on the colony between the members of the extended family of Darius Walter I. As noted previously, one daughter and her husband had already left the colony in 1938, and then had sued the colony for a share of assets, and money had been paid to the departing family. After the death of the patriarch in 1943, two sons and most of their families left the colony and moved to Spring Creek Colony in Montana. The last remaining son, Darius Walter II, became the head of the colony, and all assets were held by him as a sole trustee. The colony eventually became a partnership of nine members. Much of the business and management of the colony seems to have devolved to a grandson, Jacob Walter Jr., who remained behind when his parents and siblings left for Spring Creek. One of the issues in the subsequent winding-up litigation was whether Jacob Walter Jr. (who died in 1984) had over the years diverted funds from Felger Colony to Spring Creek Colony without the permission of the other members of the Felger partnership.

On application of Darius Walter II for directions as to entitlements to shares and the values of shares, the court determined first that certain former members who had left the colony or had received compensation settlements were not entitled to current shares. As to the nine people who had remained at the privatized "colony," the court determined that the shares should not be valued on an equal pro rata basis between the nine individuals, nor on the basis of splitting assets in three parts between the three extended families of Darius Walter I who had remained at Felger. Rather, the court held that the values should reflect the number of years each person had lived and contributed to the colony-farm. In addition, as to the share going to the estate of Jacob Walter Jr., the amount would be reduced by about $163,000 because of the diversion of assets to Spring Creek. The estate of Jacob Walter Jr. appealed this ruling, but it was upheld by the Court of Appeal.[79]

It is ironic that the payment of funds to Spring Creek Colony was treated by the court as "conversion," when more properly the real conversion occurred when Felger Colony was allowed to privatize church communal property. Although the Walter family members who remained at Felger and worked the land for many years after leaving the church were surely entitled to reap the financial rewards of their labour, why should some excommunicated Hutterites gain very substantial economic rewards, as indicated by the millions of dollars in the Felger case, while other Hutterites who are excommunicated have to leave without a penny in their pocket after a lifetime of labour? Hutterite colonies are established by the sweat and capital of the mother colony that gives birth to them, and the mother colony in turn was produced by the sweat and capital of an earlier colony, and so on. That the members of any colony could simply renounce their faith and then divide the millions of dollars of assets between them seems to be a betrayal of the trust of bygone generations. Is it fair that a group of Hutterites having control over a particular congregation can act together to leave the church or be excommunicated and retain the assets, but when an individual Hutterite or minority group at a colony leaves or is excommunicated it takes nothing with it?

To guard against such conversion, the *Constitution of the Hutterite Church* as formulated in 1950 required that "no congregation or community shall be dissolved without the consent of all of its members."[80] But it would be relatively easy for a majority of members bent on the privatization of a colony to first take away membership from the dissenting minority and then achieve a unanimous vote to privatize. Thus, when the Hutterite church adopted a new constitution in 1993, the provisions were tightened to state:

44. No Colony shall be dissolved without the consent of all the members and in the event of dissolution no individual member shall be entitled to any of the assets of the Colony but such assets shall be distributed and transferred to the Church or as otherwise provided for in the by-laws, rules and regulations of that Colony.[81]

Thus, if a Felger type of situation arose today on a colony, even by a unanimous vote to privatize, subject to the inside law on whether the church should litigate, it would be probable that the wider Hutterian church would have a claim on the assets, even though the titles to colony property are not formally held by the higher branch of the church. Because the more recent *Felger* case essentially dealt with disputes over what had long since become private property, the case is not particularly useful as any sort of precedent dealing with true communal property.

The *Bon Homme* Case: Privatization Refused

In 1961 the South Dakota Supreme Court decided the case of *Hofer v. Bon Homme Hutterian Brethren*.[82] The plaintiff was born at Bon Homme Colony in 1920 and grew up as a Hutterite. However, at the age of twenty-two he left the colony, returning in 1948 at the age of twenty-eight. He remained at the colony for the next twelve years. However, despite indicating in the early period that he wanted to become a member of the colony, he never did apply to be baptized into the church to become a formal member. During the dozen years that he was on the colony he had a two-room apartment of his own in a house where his parents and other members of his family lived. He was given work to do and treated like other members. When he finally left, he claimed that the colony owed him about $200 a month for his labour, amounting to about $28,000. He sued the colony on the ground that an implied contract of employment had existed between him and the colony. The court rejected this argument. While in theory a colony could hire someone and pay a salary, there was no evidence here that Hofer asked or expected to be treated outside the traditional rule, which is that no residents or members of the colony receive individual pay for services rendered. To that degree, this case may be seen as an example of the outside court upholding the inside law of the Hutterites.

The *Interlake* Case: Both Privatization and Division Refused

The *Interlake* case, not to be confused with the subsequent *Lakeside* case, serves as the most important past precedent for the *Lakeside* and other litigation examined in this book. Given the importance of the *Interlake* case, a more detailed examination is necessary. The case went to trial before Dickson J. of the Manitoba Queen's Bench in 1966,[83] was appealed to the Manitoba Court of Appeal,[84] and then went all the way to the Supreme Court of Canada, in 1970.[85] Although the court refused to allow church property to be privatized, the inside law was nevertheless destabilized in the process, as several judges expressed deep regrets at the harshness of the rule, even calling for legislation to overturn it. Furthermore, because the case dealt with a clear example of ex-members joining a church radically different from the Hutterite church, it did not necessarily close the door to the possibility that courts would divide assets in the future when there is a schism between Hutterites, as opposed to a situation where Hutterites clearly change their religion and leave colony life.

In 1960 Rock Lake Colony in Manitoba established a daughter colony called Interlake Colony near Teulon, Manitoba. The new colony was dominated by the extended families of the siblings of one Hofer family. In the *Interlake* case, four brothers sued as plaintiffs, and they brought the case against their other four brothers, two of whom were the main leaders of the colony, and two of whom were not as yet voting members. Another defendant was a cousin of the plaintiffs. At this time the Interlake Colony had seven male voting members, six of whom were brothers. All of the seven male voting members had wives and children. At the time of the dispute there were eighty-four people on the colony.

One of the plaintiffs, Benjamin Hofer, was the prime player in the scenario: He began to read the magazine *The Plain Truth* back in 1952 while still a member of Rock Lake. His brother David began to study the magazine in 1960. That these two brothers were studying the magazine of the Radio Church of God headed by Herbert Armstrong of Pasadena, California, did not go unnoticed within the wider Schmiedeleut conference of Hutterian Brethren. On several occasions in 1963 and 1964 Schmiedeleut ministers met with these two men to counsel them. After an earlier lengthy meeting with twenty ministers, and a grace period of ten days in which the men were to recant, twenty-four ministers from various colonies of the Schmiedeleut conference converged on Interlake Colony to talk with the two Hofer brothers. After much discussion of doctrinal matters, the brothers were asked if they would accept the punishment of "Unfrieden," which is a level of shunning. They stated that they would not accept the punishment, but the ministers voted to impose it. A minority of the ministers wanted an even more severe punishment. As stated by Mr. Justice Dickson at trial,

[t]he purpose of the punishment of unfrieden, through the pressure of shun-ning, is to cause the deviant to repent. When a member is in unfrieden he is not to associate with any other member, including his wife, nor eat in the public dining room; he is required to sleep alone; he must not leave the farm on business or on visiting trips; he is expected to attend church but to sit by the door and not with the congregation; he is expected to work. It is assumed that if the offender is a brother in spirit the initiative will be taken by him and that he will ask for his penalty and, having served it, which in the case of the shunning experienced in unfrieden may continue for two or three weeks, he will return to the fold.[86]

Since in this case the Unfrieden was not accepted by the two brothers, a meeting of senior ministers was held, and it was decided that two senior ministers should visit the brothers at Interlake again, and if they were still not persuaded to come back into the fold, they would be expelled from the church. This was the penalty of "Ausschluss," which was clearly of much greater severity than Unfrieden. The senior ministers called a meeting of the voting members of Interlake on 13 June 1964. The two brothers were allowed to attend the meeting, but being in unfrieden had to stand by the door. The impact of the meeting was outlined by Dickson J.:

I find that after lengthy discussion they were warned that they could no longer be members unless they changed their minds, to which plaintiff Ben Hofer, after saying that he was getting stronger every day in his religion, added, addressing the Rev. Jacob Kleinsasser, "Jake, it is no use. Do not waste time. I have my conviction. You just prove me otherwise." The Rev. Kleinsasser then said something to the effect, "We have tried so much. We have not been able to change you. But do you know you cannot stay mem-bers with us. Consider it." Plaintiffs Ben Hofer and David Hofer would not change. The Rev. Kleinsasser said, "Well, you are making your own deci-sion, you do as you please, and we will have to proceed further."[87]

Thereafter the two dissenting brothers left the meeting and the remain-ing five male voting members of Interlake voted to expel the two men from membership in the colony. Since the wives of the two men also supported the Church of God, they also would be expelled.

The two dissenting families had been given the penalty of Ausschluss, but they did not leave the colony. While living at Interlake, they were baptized in Winnipeg, formally joining the Church of God. Later in 1964, the two brothers travelled to California to visit Ambassador College, where *The Plain Truth* was published. Of greater significance, however, was that the two dis-senters managed to persuade two more of their brothers to read the maga-zine. John and Joseph Hofer began to read the magazine, and although they had originally agreed to put their brothers Ben and David under Ausschluss, they were now joining the other side.

The process of disciplining John and Joseph started in 1965. Again visits to Interlake by senior ministers took place. It culminated in a meeting of the five remaining voting members of Interlake on 17 March 1965. Joseph chose not to be present, but at this meeting Joseph and John were also expelled from membership, as Ben and David had been the previous year. Joseph and John were also subsequently baptized into the Church of God.

Not surprisingly, the dissenters demanded a share of the colony assets before they would be induced to leave the colony, and this demand was strengthened by the fact that the Church of God faction constituted the majority group at Interlake in terms of voting males, even though as a result of differential dates of affiliation they had been excommunicated by majority vote. After the Hutterian leaders refused any sort of compensation whatsoever, the four Hofer brothers who had renounced their Hutterite religion in favour of Armstrong's Church of God initiated a lawsuit against the colony. The lawsuit was particularly threatening to the Hutterite church because of the way the plaintiffs framed the case. They wanted the colony to be conceptualized as having two components: a church component from which they had been excommunicated, and a business component in which they had existing partnership rights alongside the other members. Thus, they sought a court order to place the colony as a business enterprise into receivership and wind it up so they would receive their proportionate shares. One might argue that, by asking the courts to adopt this conception of the colony, they in essence sought the privatization of all Hutterite colonies in Canada.

The colony might have chosen to simply defend the suit under the theory that the court would uphold the principle that the plaintiffs had no right to colony assets and that the plaintiffs would then voluntarily leave the colony. But instead of this, the colony brought a counterclaim for a declaration that the plaintiffs had been validly expelled, and that they should therefore vacate the colony and deliver up any property belonging to the colony. Technically – and I do not know to what degree legal counsel for the colony clarified the meaning of a counterclaim with the colony and church leaders of the Schmiedeleut – the bringing of a counterclaim meant that the church itself was now countersuing and calling on the violence of the state to throw the dissenters off the colony if they did not obey the court order to vacate.

After presiding at the trial, Mr. Justice Dickson's judgment was released in November 1966. He emphatically rejected the idea that the colony should be viewed as a business enterprise: "To a Hutterian the whole life is the Church. The colony is a congregation of people in spiritual brotherhood ... I find that the [colony] is a congregation of the Hutterian Brethren Church ... The Articles must not be construed in a vacuum but rather in the light of

Hutterianism. What is being dealt with here is a church, not a business enterprise. This is clear from the Articles and from the entire evidence. The signatories are not partners. There are no partnership assets, only church assets."[88]

As to the excommunication from the church, Dickson J. reviewed the requirements as outlined in the articles of association of the colony: "Any member of the Colony may be expelled or dismissed from the Colony at any General or Special Meeting of the Colony upon a majority vote of all the members thereof."[89] Mr. Justice Dickson also pointed out that the men had notice of the meetings and had the right to make their views known. More fundamentally, while the articles of association of the colony provided for expulsion by majority vote, this was subject to a prior requirement of the articles of association, namely that members of the colony had to be members of the Hutterian Brethren Church.[90] Suppose that a majority of the colony left the Hutterian church and then voted out the minority who remained faithful to the church. In this case a majority had in fact been expelled from membership by a minority. Even though a majority at each meeting – five to two at the first, and three to two (in effect) at the second – voted to expel, cumulatively the dissidents outnumbered the traditionalists four to three.

In answer to this, following the leading precedent from the House of Lords,[91] Dickson J. reasserted the basic principle that, absent a formal church charter or constitution that allows for amending religious doctrine or determining membership by majority vote alone, the property of a religious organization is normally impressed with a trust that requires that the property can be used only for the original purpose for which the organization was established. This may mean, of course, that a small minority of the organization will get all the assets of the organization if a court determines that the vast majority has fundamentally departed from the theology that is explicit in the constitution of the organization, or implicit in the founding of the organization. Those that dissent are free to leave and form a new congregation, but they are not free to take over the property of the old congregation, even if they are in the majority in terms of a doctrinal schism. As stated in a famous American case, "[t]he guarantee of religious freedom has nothing to do with the property. It does not guarantee freedom to steal churches. It secures to individuals the right of withdrawing, forming a new society, with such creed and government as they please, raising from their own means another fund and building another house of worship; but it does not confer upon them the right of taking the property consecrated to other uses by those who may be sleeping in their graves."[92]

Indeed, Mr. Justice Dickson went so far as to consider what would happen if all seven members of Interlake joined the Church of God and renounced the Hutterian Brethren Church. Unlike the Felger situation, which occurred

before this case, Dickson concluded that even though the articles of association stated that the colony could be dissolved only by unanimous vote,[93]
in the circumstances where the members were changing religious affiliation, the colony should not be allowed to privatize the assets: "In my view,
even if all seven of the signatories to the Articles of Association were to
abandon the Hutterian faith and unanimously attempt to dissolve the Colony
and divide the assets among themselves it would be repugnant to principle
and authority to allow this. It appears to me that no other conclusion is
possible than that the Rock Lake Colony of Hutterian Brethren established
the Interlake Colony of Hutterian Brethren and endowed it with the implied understanding that the Interlake Colony would constitute and continue as a congregation of the Hutterian Brethren Church."[94]

Mr. Justice Dickson pointed out the fundamental differences in the beliefs of the Hutterites and the beliefs of the Church of God. These included
the Church of God's views on Saturday observance, not eating pork, keeping religious festivals following Old Testament formulations, and not believing in community of property. Mr. Justice Dickson pointed out that it
was not for the court to decide who was right or wrong as a matter of theological truth, but it was perfectly obvious in this case as a matter of fact that
the beliefs of the plaintiffs departed substantially from the historic beliefs
of the Hutterian Brethren Church. He even noted that "[a]ll four plaintiffs
appeared in court clean shaven, contrary to the custom of the Hutterian
men who wear beards. All four plaintiffs appeared in Court in modern dress,
contrary to the custom of Hutterian men to wear plain black jackets but-
toned to the neck and wide black pants."[95]

Given the earlier *Raley* precedent from Alberta,[96] the plaintiffs at one stage
in the trial suggested that they wanted to establish a new colony and practise
community of goods even if that aspect was not required by the Church of
God, but this assertion did nothing to detract from Dickson's conclusion that
the plaintiffs had left the Hutterite faith. An attempt to argue division of common property, as opposed to privatization of common property, will equally
fail when the group seeking the division has adopted a contrary religion.

As Mr. Walsh did in the *Raley* case, Dickson grounded the refusal to privatize on a contract or compact or constitution that the members had made
with each other. Dickson pointed out that the articles of association, signed
by the members, explicitly rejected the plaintiffs' claim to be given a share
of the assets.[97] Denying that these principles were void as being contrary to
public policy, Dickson ruled against the plaintiffs' claim and granted to the
defendants the counterclaim sought – an order that the plaintiffs leave the
colony with no assets. He did note, however, that "[c]ounsel for defendants
have stated that defendants are willing to assist plaintiffs to move from the
Colony, and are prepared to permit their wives and children to remain at
the Colony until plaintiffs have established themselves elsewhere."[98]

The plaintiffs appealed to the Manitoba Court of Appeal. About a year later, in November 1967, a unanimous five-justice panel of the Manitoba Court of Appeal affirmed the judgment of Dickson J.[99] The opinion for the court was authored by Justice Freedman. A point that the plaintiffs particularly emphasized on appeal involved a direct assault on the community property regime. They argued that the covenants in the articles of association that in effect called for expelled members to leave a colony with only the shirt on their backs after a lifetime of labour were contrary to public policy and should be held by the court to be unenforceable. To this, Freedman J.A. stated: "It may be well to add that the position of the plaintiffs is one that excites some sympathy. They are obliged to leave the colony without a right to any share of its property. But if this result appears harsh, it is the consequence of their own voluntary and deliberate acts."[100]

The plaintiffs appealed to the Supreme Court of Canada and, about three years later, the final judicial determination in this matter was delivered. In May of 1970 a seven-member bench upheld the trial decision and the appeal court decision, six to one.[101] While the result in this case was nearly unanimous, a number of judges made comments that might yet come back to haunt the church.

The majority judgment was authored by Mr. Justice Ritchie, with Justices Martland, Judson, and Hall concurring, though Hall added separate comments. This four-person majority judgment upheld the decision of Dickson J. at trial, and the Manitoba Court of Appeal. After affirming that the appellants had been validly expelled according to the colony's articles of association, the majority decision turned to the issue of whether these articles should be declared void as contrary to public policy. On this point, Ritchie J.A. was emphatic:

> There is no doubt that the Hutterian way of life is not that of the vast majority of Canadians, but it makes manifest a form of religious philosophy to which any Canadian can subscribe and it appears to me that if any individual either through birth within the community or by choice wishes to subscribe to such a rigid form of life and to subject himself to the harsh disciplines of the Hutterian Church, he is free to do so. I can see nothing contrary to public policy in the continued existence of these communities, living as they do in accordance with their own rules and beliefs.[102]

It was this public policy argument that caused Mr. Justice Hall to add a few words to his concurrence. Hall was obviously uneasy with this "freedom to make a harsh contract" argument. In addition to raising questions about the treatment of children and others at the colony who were not yet formal members, Hall J. turned to the property issue and stated:

While agreeing that this appeal fails, I must, however, express my abhorrence at the treatment accorded the appellants by their erstwhile co-religionists. The insults and gross indignities inflicted on these men and their families as disclosed in the evidence is foreign to the whole concept of life in Canada, whether lived in a community or not. The rigidity of the law ... which deprives a dissident group, whether large or small, of all rights in the property and assets of a religious community should, I think, be softened by appropriate legislation under which a formula might be devised so as to permit a dissenter and his family to leave a community such as this one in dignity and with a severance adjustment corresponding in some degree to the contribution made by the dissident member in his years of service to the community. As it is, the dissenter, as my brother Pigeon points out, cannot even claim ownership to the clothes he is wearing as he departs.[103]

The second main judgment was written by Chief Justice Cartwright and concurred in by Spence J. While agreeing with the result and much of Ritchie's judgment, the basic disagreement dealt with the nature of the Hutterite colony. In the courts below, and in Ritchie's judgment, the colony as a whole, as a totality, was considered to be a church. However, Cartwright and Spence joined Pigeon in dissent in forming the minority opinion that at the colony level there existed a congregation of the Hutterian Brethren Church, though the colony as a totality was not a church but a business enterprise made up of a communal farm.

This different characterization of the colony meant that Cartwright and Spence disagreed with the majority that church excommunication alone would translate into automatic removal of membership in the business enterprise, and loss of claims for business assets. Rather, the plaintiffs would have to be validly expelled from the colony as a business entity in accordance with the articles of association, which acted as a kind of partnership agreement on these points. For Cartwright and Spence this different characterization made no difference to the final result in this case. The articles of association, viewed in part as a business contract, nevertheless included the provision that a member of the business organization could be expelled from membership with no claim on the assets when he or she changed religious affiliation. These provisions were not contrary to public policy. So even if the colony was a business organization rather than a church, such an organization could require its members to have a particular faith.

Cartwright's judgment also noted the harshness of the communal property regime for expelled members: "It is, I think, a matter of regret that the appellants, whose efforts have no doubt made a large contribution to the assets of the Colony, receive no compensation for their life's work and the learned trial Judge was not guilty of over-statement when he referred to the mistreatment of them and members of their families as strange, repellant [sic] and excessive; but the task of the courts is to deal with the rights of the parties according to law."[104]

The third judgment, and the longest, was authored by Mr. Justice Pigeon in dissent. In terms of the legal characterization of the colony and the scope of religion, Pigeon concluded that the colony was not a church but a commercial undertaking. He drew an anaemic picture of what legally could constitute religion: "Of course, some small part of the land is used for a place of worship but it is clear that, looking at the matter according to ordinary principles, this is only an extremely minor part."[105] This reduction of religion to beliefs one has in one's head and to worship practices, rather than the totality of life as encompassed by Anabaptist theology, grants little protection for religious individuals and collectivities in the face of laws that impose burdens on or violate religious faith.

Now that the case was recharacterized as a fight over business assets rather than over the property of a church, Mr. Justice Pigeon, like Cartwright, turned to contract law. The difference was that Pigeon, unlike Cartwright, concluded that this contract should be declared void as contrary to public policy. Cartwright thought that business partnerships could still be formed around exclusive religious beliefs and lifestyle codes, but Pigeon did not think so. Pigeon got to this point by turning the tables, as it were, on the religious freedom arguments in the case. Rather than affirming the religious freedom of Hutterites to hold and enforce their communal property regime, he focused on the alleged religious freedom of the individual plaintiffs to change religions. The shunning and other "indignities" associated with Hutterian discipline, and the harsh consequences of having to leave a colony without a penny of assets, meant that the freedom of religion of Hutterites was being denied by their own church. As a matter of striking down the inside law of the Hutterites denying individual property entitlements as being contrary to public policy, Pigeon seemed to conflate freedom *of* religion, as a matter of protection from governmental action that interferes with religion, with freedom *within* religion, which is quite a different matter.

At this level it appears that Pigeon's brand of religious freedom would involve state regulation of religion, at least in terms of striking down provisions that interfere with freedom to change religion. But at another level the argument could be made that Pigeon was calling for state regulation only in those areas outside church activities, narrowly defined. A member of a church, for example, might well be denied a share in the church property if he or she is expelled from membership in the church, even if that member had contributed to the church for many years. But at the same time, the member of a church might own a business and insist on hiring only co-religionists. This might be deemed contrary to public policy. For example, human rights legislation prohibiting discrimination on the basis of religion might be applied in the commercial sphere of business, as opposed to the sphere of employment within religious organizations. So the central point for Pigeon in dissent was that the colony and its assets were not a church, as he narrowly defined it, but a commercial organization. Thus, as to the requirement that membership in the commercial enterprise was contingent on membership in the church, Pigeon concluded: "I am of the opinion that such a provision would be unenforceable as contrary to freedom of religion and also contrary to public policy in the context of such an association or partnership as these colonies existing for commercial purposes, as opposed to Church bodies or other religious or charitable organizations that may be subject to the rules applicable to Churches and as to which no opinion is expressed."[106]

While this is a dissenting judgment, it illustrates the danger of litigating ecclesiastical disputes. In essence, Pigeon was of the view that the inside religious law of the Hutterites should be overruled by the outside law of the host society. If Pigeon's decision had formed the majority, the effect would have been to privatize every Hutterite colony in Canada but for the little area of the colony used for worship services. Instead of communal church property, the property of a Hutterite colony would be subject to the rules of business partnerships. Furthermore, even though this was not the view of the majority, many of the judges who sided with the majority nevertheless expressed regrets and disapproval of the content of the inside religious law of the Hutterites. Such disapproval may well lead to further challenges of the inside law.

In any event, as a result of the majority judgments in the *Interlake* case, the brothers who joined the Radio Church of God were unsuccessful at getting any assets of the colony, and the four families, amounting to thirty-four people, left Interlake.[107] But as I have just pointed out, this was not necessarily a great legal victory for the Hutterite church. About a decade later, when Mr. Justice Dickson had been elevated to the Supreme Court of Canada, he gave a lecture at the University of Toronto where, among other topics, he reflected on the *Interlake* case. He concluded: "So ended a long, hotly contested, and, in many respects tragic, piece of litigation."[108]

The *Berry Creek* Case: Retroactive Privatization by Loophole?
Just for the sake of completeness, although occurring subsequent to the *Lakeside* litigation and other cases we will examine arising from the schism within the Schmiedeleut, three families left Berry Creek Colony in Alberta (Darius) and then brought an action against the federal government and also their former colony, claiming they were entitled to family allowance

cheques and GST credits that had been sent to them while they were members of the colony. They had handed these cheques over to the colony without endorsing them, which was the common practice at the colony, but now the ex-members argued that the lack of endorsement meant that the funds had been improperly paid into the colony account, even though at the time they were handed over, they were duty-bound by Hutterian religious practice to hand all possessions to their colony, and if they had been asked to endorse them, they would have done so. Reportedly the amounts handed to the colony over the years without the formality of endorsement amounted to about $55,000.[109] The only reported decision in this matter deals with a preliminary issue denying summary judgment in favour of the ex-members.[110] Does it seem fair that the ex-members be allowed to retroactively impeach their covenant to divest themselves of personal entitlements to governmental benefits in favour of the colony by arguing that a technical loophole existed in the execution of their covenant? But as has been seen in all these cases, the church's decision of whether to fight such cases involves balancing the danger of setting a bad precedent within the church by settling with claimants out of court, thereby creating an expectation that the same will be done for the next claimant, with the danger of setting a bad precedent within the world by going to court and once again, even if it wins, focusing attention on the unhappy plight of ex-Hutterites tossed into the world with nothing.

Conclusion

While the Hutterites have not enjoyed any great success in governmental litigation, they have enjoyed some success in defending against claims that would threaten the inside law on community of goods. The Supreme Court has upheld the Hutterian inside law based on a covenant that members have made with each other when they joined the church. Although I will not debate the point at this stage, there is some question as to whether this success will continue in the face of developing outside law doctrines that allow people to escape improvident bargains, or to claim restitution in circumstances where it appears that the group is being unjustly enriched. It may be that the courts will have to move beyond dealing with the matter within a contract law framework and deal with it more directly as an aspect of religious freedom.

Another related issue in this line of cases is the judicial review by the courts of the process of discipline within the colony. Neither *Raley* nor *Interlake* dealt with this in any great detail, but it would become the central feature of the *Lakeside* case. If the courts are going to uphold the principle that the expelled members get no colony property, the process of getting to the decision to expel has enormous implications, arguably much greater than church discipline in other contexts. People kicked out of a typical religious association may feel deeply wounded in spirit, but rarely will their temporal livelihoods be at stake in quite the way it is for people who are excluded from a colony that has provided economic security to them all their lives, and has in some respects severely limited their educational and vocational options. In the process of denying a claim for a share of the communal property, or as will be seen in the *Lakeside* dispute, in the process of enforcing the expulsion of so-called ex-members, the court is again looking at the inside law of the Hutterites in terms of the process of shunning and excommunication. The effect of the *Lakeside* litigation was to impose on the inside law of the church the outside law concept of natural justice. By taking the case to court, the church subjected itself to outside law control over its own ecclesiastical procedure.

Finally, in terms of the issue of taking cases to court, all five of the cases mentioned here were initiated by individuals or dissenting groups, but not by the ministers or managers or majority who spoke in the name of the church. Once taken to court by its own members or ex-members, the colony might well defend against the claim, but what makes the *Lakeside* case so interesting is that it was the colony that initiated the lawsuit. That dissenting Hutterites would bring a case against other Hutterites to court might be one indication in and of itself that the plaintiffs are no longer Hutterites properly so called. However, when the Hutterite church itself brings such claims, what are we supposed to believe as to the nature of Hutterian commitment to nonresistance?

Part Three
The *Lakeside* Litigation: Round One

5

Daniel Hofer, Hog Feeders, and Excommunication

Lakeside Colony

Lakeside Colony, near Headingley, Manitoba, just a few miles west of Winnipeg, was established in 1946 as a daughter of Maxwell Colony, also near Headingley.[1] Like most colonies, Lakeside grew and produced new colonies of its own, including Homewood in 1962 and Broad Valley in 1974. Hutterite colonies develop their own personalities as a result of the particular relationships that develop between members, the leadership dynamics, and the economic and other circumstances that confront each colony, particularly after a colony division. Lakeside Colony has had a long history of economic and spiritual difficulties.[2] Indeed, the dysfunction at the colony gave rise to a kind of warning within Hutterite circles not to adopt "a Lakeside mentality."[3] In the face of management difficulties, the wider church supervised Lakeside in the early 1970s, and the creation of Broad Valley in 1974 was actually a premature division as a result of colony conflict. The senior minister, Rev. George Wipf, was moved to Broad Valley, while Rev. Joseph Hofer became the minister of Lakeside. However, the unresolved conflicts continued to boil to the point that the larger Schmiedeleut conference again felt it necessary to intervene if the colony was to be saved.

On 4 April 1979 a special meeting was held at Lakeside Colony. The senior elder of the Schmiedeleut, Jacob Kleinsasser, chaired the meeting and forty-six ministers from other colonies were present. A resolution was unanimously passed that for the time being all the members of Lakeside be suspended from membership and considered only as "house members," and that all the directors and officers of the colony be removed. Outside overseers were appointed to manage the colony. Rev. Michael Wollmann from Spring Hill Colony, Rev. Jacob Hofer of James Valley Colony, and David Waldner of Milltown Colony were appointed as president, vice-president, and secretary. The senior elder then proposed that Rev. Joseph Hofer move to another colony of his choosing but not be removed from office as a minister of the church. This motion was passed twenty-nine to seventeen.[4] Rev. Joseph Hofer left Lakeside for a period but later was allowed to return, although the management of the colony continued to be in the hands of the overseers.[5]

The litigation that arose at Lakeside about a decade after this takeover must be put into the context of this unusual situation of having "outside" overseers from other colonies manage the colony for an extended period. Normally, while Hutterite colonies would receive help in a number of ways from other colonies in times of difficulty, each colony is an independent entity in an economic sense, with its own internal management. But at Lakeside, the wider church was managing a particular congregation. Michael Wollmann, the outside president, compared the situation with being in "church receivership."[6] The effect of the 1979 meeting was that the ordinary "members" of Lakeside were excommunicated from the church for the time being.[7] Even though they were readmitted into membership in 1981 after renewing their baptismal vows and signing new articles of association, the colony remained under the management of the overseers under the authority of the Schmiedeleut conference. The outside managers fixed up a trailer and moved it onto Lakeside. They used the trailer as their office, even sleeping there when they had to stay at Lakeside overnight.

The "receivership" was successful for a time. Mr. Justice Ferg, in giving his reasons for judgment at the first trial in the *Lakeside* case, pointed out the condition of the colony in 1979 and the subsequent good leadership of the overseers:

> It [the colony] had no cattle, no hogs, no geese, no turkeys, only a few chickens, had lost its turkey quota, had no cows for milk for the children, the buildings were run down, the waterworks were not functioning and there was no treasury. Reverend Hofer [overseer] described the condition of the Colony with tears in his eyes, saying they were "spiritually and temporally broke." They got them some cattle and cows for milk, some geese on credit, built a big hog complex, got the turkey quota back, fixed the old barn, rebuilt some dwellings, renovated the kitchen, arranged for purchase of machinery, built a killing-plant, designed and built a whole water complex, dug four wells, and finally got the Colony, after some years, in a commercially viable condition.[8]

The spiritual state of the colony in terms of relationships between the members and obedience to Hutterian norms also was stabilized to a degree. Things were apparently going well and the overseers claimed that they wanted to pull out, but on the urging of members of Lakeside, including Daniel Hofer and Paul Hofer, who would ultimately be involved in the rebellion to follow, they were asked to stay on.[9]

When Lakeside was established in 1946, the colony had a variety of families, with typical Hutterite names such as Wipf, Wollmann, Gross, and Hofer, but after the establishment of Homewood and Broad Valley, Lakeside by 1984 had eleven families, all with the last name of Hofer. The overall population in 1984 was sixty-four, and by 1987, when the first litigation commenced, there were seventy-seven people living at Lakeside.[10] Essentially the population of Lakeside could be broken down into two extended families. The majority group was composed of the Rev. Joseph Hofer clan, while the minority group was composed of the extended families of two brothers from the John Hofer clan. For the convenience of readers, I have included a male genealogy of Lakeside families as an appendix to this book.

Rev. Joseph Hofer was the elder patriarch of the colony. Born in 1907, he was by this time an elderly widower. All of his thirteen children were married. Typically daughters leave the colony when married to join their husband's colony, while sons remain at their home colony when married. Rev. Joseph Hofer had four sons. His oldest son, Joseph Jr. (nicknamed K.O.), born in 1932, had a prolonged history of church discipline and had left the colony. For most of the conflict and litigation that will be outlined in this book, K.O. was not involved because he was living away from the colony. However, his wife and children remained at Lakeside, including five sons, most of whom were already baptized, married, and raising large families at Lakeside during the course of the dispute. The second son of Rev. Joseph Hofer, Joshua Hofer Sr., born in 1933, remained on the colony. He was married with ten children. Two sons died tragically in accidents in their youth; the other three eventually married and raised large families at Lakeside. Joshua Hofer Sr. was very much involved in the disputes to follow, as was his son Joshua Jr., who became the inside leader of the colony. Benjamin, born in 1935, was the third son of Rev. Joseph Hofer. Benjamin was married with twelve children, including nine sons, some of whom had married and established families at Lakeside. Finally, the fourth son of Rev. Joseph Hofer, Paul K., born in 1941, was married with four children – three daughters and a son – but like his oldest brother, K.O., Paul K. was also disciplined by the church and left the colony, thus he was living away from the colony during many of events to be outlined here, although his wife and children remained behind.

The other group at Lakeside consisted of the families of the two brothers, Daniel Hofer, born 1936, and Rev. Paul Hofer, born 1937. These were two sons of the John Hofer clan, which consisted of eight sons and two daughters. Except for Daniel and Paul, the John Hofer clan had moved from Lakeside over to Homewood when it was established in 1962. The blood relationship between the two families of Daniel and Paul was particularly close, because the two brothers had married two sisters, daughters of the Rev. George Wipf, who later moved to Broad Valley. Daniel Hofer and his wife, Sarah, had ten children: six sons and four daughters. Daniel Hofer's oldest

sons, twins Daniel Jr. and David, both married in 1984 and established families at Lakeside. Rev. Paul Hofer and his wife, Rachel, had eight children: six
sons and two daughters. At some stage Paul Hofer had been appointed as a
second minister at Lakeside. The married and unmarried sons of both Paul
and Daniel would be heavily involved in the dispute that developed.

As we will see, the schism that developed at Lakeside essentially followed
blood ties, although the Paul K. family (fourth family of the Joseph clan)
ultimately joined the so-called renegades, as did a son of Ben Hofer. Aside
from these exceptions, one Hofer family at Lakeside, which just happened
to be the larger family, sided with the overseers, while the other family
constituted the renegades. The conflict itself illustrates that it is probably
unhealthy to have colonies narrowly drawn on family lines rather than having a wider diversity of families. What makes the dispute at Lakeside even
more tragic is that the two clans were closely related at another level because
Joseph (Lakeside) and John (Homewood) were brothers. This means that
Rev. Joseph was an uncle to Daniel and Paul, and that the shunning, harassment, and violence at Lakeside often involved first and second cousins.
Deep animosity developed between first cousins who had grown up since
birth as brothers and sisters at the colony. In addition, some of the women
must have had a horrible time as a consequence of marriage between the
two clans, caught as they were in the lines of fire between a husband on one
side of the dispute and parents on the other. For example, the wife of Daniel
Hofer Jr. was a daughter of Benjamin Hofer, and the wife of Mike Hofer, a
son of Benjamin, was a daughter of Rev. Paul Hofer.

After the initial period of intensive activity by the overseers to get the
colony back on its feet, most of the day-to-day work of being an overseer
fell on David Waldner from Milltown, and while he was secretary, the colony
appeared to flourish and be at peace with itself. David Waldner consulted
and included the ordinary resident voting members in the important decisions to be made, but once he was gone, the renegades would allege that the
management of the colony by Mike Wollmann and Jake Hofer involved a
more dictatorial style.[11] David Waldner became very ill and was replaced to
a limited degree by a young inside member of Lakeside, Josh Hofer Jr., a
grandson of Rev. Joseph Hofer, but the president and vice-president continued to be Mike Wollmann from Spring Hill and Jake Hofer of James Valley.[12]

That Lakeside was under the authority of the larger Schmiedeleut conference, and particularly the senior elder, was illustrated during the transfer of
the secretarial post from the ailing outside officer, Dave Waldner, to the
young insider, Josh Hofer Jr. Jacob Kleinsasser, the senior elder of the
Schmiedeleut, wrote on 30 December 1985:

> Regarding the Lakeside situation, and because David Waldner ... is ill ...
> their accounts should be overseen by Joshua Hofer Jr. who should do this as

well as his task as work distributor until it can be reconsidered at a later time.

However, he should not have any more authority than in the past. It should all be done under the supervision of Michael Wollmann and Jacob Hofer and with their permission.

Because Joshua Hofer Sr. has remained stubborn until now, he shall from now on be shunned. He shall no longer be allowed to use the colony's vehicles to drive off the Hof. All visiting with him shall be stopped, and all colonies will soon be informed of this by a circular letter.[13]

It can thus be seen that the senior elder was very much in control of what was going on at Lakeside, appointing a secretary with limited authority and imposing church discipline on the father of the new secretary. Ordinarily the secretary would be appointed by a vote of the members of the colony, and discipline of a member also would be done by a vote of members, not by an order of the senior elder. As the colony stabilized, the overseers, while still in control, spent less time at the colony. Many matters could be dealt with by phone calls, and at Lakeside the day-to-day management fell on the shoulders of the young Josh Hofer Jr. and the two resident ministers, Rev. Joseph Hofer and Rev. Paul Hofer. However, increasingly some ordinary members of Lakeside were upset at a host of decisions that were made by the outside overseers, allegedly without consultation with the ordinary members.[14]

Daniel S. Hofer, the key player in the rebellion at Lakeside against the overseers, and a severe critic of Jacob Kleinsasser, the senior elder, had been the secretary of Lakeside before being removed from office and replaced by Joshua Hofer Sr., just before the overseers were appointed and Joshua Hofer Sr. in turn removed. Not only was Daniel Hofer removed from office but, according to him, false charges had been made against him.[15] Once the new overseer managers were in place, Daniel Hofer was assigned the job of German schoolteacher at Lakeside. It is also noteworthy that Daniel Hofer was not returned to the position of secretary when David Waldner was ill, but neither was Joshua Hofer Sr. offered the job. Moreover, when Daniel Hofer thereafter challenged the authority of the overseers to make a major expenditure without the consent of the voting members, he was disciplined and removed from his leadership position as German schoolteacher, becoming the head of the stainless steel shop instead.[16]

Thus, in the conflict and litigation to follow, the plaintiff overseers would suggest that Daniel Hofer, rather than acting out of principle, had wrongful motives in his rebellion. He had been removed from power in his colony and he was only seeking to gain that power back. As Michael Radcliffe, lawyer for the overseer group, stated, "[t]hey in fact pleaded with Danny Hofer on any number of different occasions to reconcile and cooperate with the majority of the members of the colony."[17] Daniel Hofer had a very different story to tell. He reacted to what he perceived as violations of Hutterian norms and unjust treatment by the leadership of the Schmiedeleut, particularly the senior elder. The actual dispute that triggered the litigation and ultimately helped unleash a broader conflict that split the whole church into two had its unlikely source in the circumstances surrounding Daniel Hofer's invention and manufacturing of hog feeders.

Daniel Hofer and Hog Feeders

In March 1984 Daniel Hofer, on behalf of Lakeside Colony and with the permission of David Waldner, then secretary of Lakeside, contacted Ade and Company, patent agents in Winnipeg, about the possibility of patenting a hog feeder that he was working on in the stainless steel shop. On behalf of Lakeside, Hofer paid a $300 retainer for a search to be done to see whether his preliminary design was already patented. On 9 June 1984 Daniel Hofer sent a drawing of a "wet feeder" to Ade and Co. He stated in typical Hutterian fashion that "*we* may be considering a patent for this design after we have tried out and tested it." He concluded, "Please file same. We'll be in touch."[18]

Ade and Co. completed a patent search in Canada and the United States on hog feeders and returned these to Daniel Hofer on 15 June 1984, and outlined the cost and process of filing a patent application.[19] Of great significance in the mind of Daniel Hofer was Ade and Co.'s information that he had up to two years from the first publication or use of a device to file a patent application. Several months later, the patent agents inquired as to whether Lakeside was ready to proceed.[20] Daniel Hofer replied in late October 1984 that the colony was working on a "new model" that seemed to work better and that in due course it might proceed with a patent application.[21]

In retrospect, it is unfortunate that he did not explain in detail, at least within the next few months, what this new model involved. At the end of November 1984, Lakeside installed into its own hog barns feeders that Daniel had built in Lakeside's shop. Daniel Hofer noticed that hogs could manipulate the device by shaking off the removable covers on one side of the feeder and eat dry feed from an upper ledge or eat wet feed from the trough. In other words, hogs were choosing to eat feed with water or eat feed dry.[22] It appears that Daniel Hofer had not set out to create a wet and dry hog feeder, but he discovered through this experimental use that the device could be used in that way and thus he started to perfect it. In January of 1985 Ade and Co. again inquired whether Lakeside was ready to proceed with a patent application.[23]

About four months later, on 6 May 1985, Ade and Co. submitted a crude sketch of a wet and dry hog feeder to agents in Ottawa for purposes of running a search. However, the sketch did not come from Lakeside but from

Jonathan and Daniel Kleinsasser of Crystal Spring Colony, near St. Agathe, Manitoba.[24] Jonathan and Daniel were brothers of Rev. Jacob Kleinsasser, the minister and head of Crystal Spring Colony and also the senior elder of the Schmiedeleut conference. When Daniel Hofer subsequently saw the Kleinsasser model, he noted that it was just the same as the feeders installed at Lakeside in late November 1984, minus removable covers that he claimed were unimportant.[25] Daniel Hofer was convinced that another Hutterite colony, the senior elder's colony no less, was taking and manufacturing Lakeside's invention and trying to get a patent for it.

Indeed, an application for the Crystal Spring patent was filed on 10 June 1985 and, on 1 August, Crystal Spring filed an application for a special order to have the application dealt with as soon as possible because, it claimed, a competitor was manufacturing "effectively an exact copy of the product."[26] Crystal Spring Colony was informed that its special order had been success-ful and that the patent application had been referred to the examiner for immediate consideration.[27] When Daniel Hofer found out that Crystal Spring was applying for a patent using the same agents as he had hired on behalf of Lakeside, he met with Mr. Battison of Ade and Co. at the company's offices, on 17 December 1985.[28]

On 2 January 1986 Daniel Hofer wrote to Ade and Co., including with his letter drawings dated 20 December 1985 entitled "wet and/or dry feeder and waterer"[29] and the following assertion: "It's been distressing to find that your office has gone ahead with patent *of our feeder* to another party, which (as you were aware) we were in the process of obtaining patent last 12 months or more. We were advised by you that it was fine to make sure feeder was functioning satisfactorily before completion of patent. Two years if need be. It was also brought to your attention Mr. Battison, that we have had much costly experiments inventing feeder, like labour, non-function-ing parts, remodelling etc. etc. out of which has evolved said feeder. Hope-fully by this time you've put a stop to patent of other party of our feeder."[30] Further arguments by Daniel Hofer that the feeder was invented at Lakeside and not at Crystal Spring included the assertion that Lakeside had been manufacturing and selling just such a device a year earlier, before Crystal Spring ever came on the scene, and that he could provide the sales invoices to prove it.

In reply to Daniel Hofer, Ade and Co. argued that the Crystal Spring de-vice was different from that illustrated in the drawings submitted by Hofer on behalf of Lakeside.[31] Daniel Hofer denied this allegation[32] and also wrote to the commissioner of patents in both Canada and the United States in an attempt to stop Crystal Spring from getting a patent.[33] Hofer wrote:

Two years or more ago we started development of a model wet and dry hog feeder, after many trials and errors, we finally surfaced with a model that seemed satisfactory ... We did however send Ade and Co plans of changes as we progressed, (not always complete in detail, but enough to know how we were progressing with apparatus.) We were advised by letter by Ade and Co we have two years to file a patent application of first date of public use, therefore felt no urgency to haste application. So it was our desire to test feeder extensively over a period of time before resuming with patent application. In the meantime Crystal Spring Colony copied our invention of our feeder minus two removable covers, (some of our feeders had said covers, some didn't) and applied for patent for himself at no experimental cost whatsoever ... We wish to advise your office at this time not to proceed with our patent to Crystal Spring Colony re our feeder.[34]

Ade and Co. wrote to Hofer again on 22 February 1986, repeating that the Crystal Spring patent involved unique features not contained in any drawing submitted by Lakeside and that, given the position taken by Daniel Hofer that the Crystal Spring application infringed Lakeside's invention, Ade and Co. could not act for Lakeside any longer.[35] Daniel Hofer replied that Ade and Co. should withdraw from representing Crystal Spring, rather than refusing service to Lakeside.[36] The patent to Crystal Spring Colony was granted on 8 April 1986.

Crystal Spring Colony began to aggressively market the hog feeder it was manufacturing. On 25 April 1986 Crystal signed a contract with C. and J. Jones Company granting to that company the right to be an exclusive distributor of the wet and dry hog feeders manufactured at the colony and also assigning the patent to C. and J. Jones. The contract stipulated that C. and J. Jones and Crystal Spring Colony would share equally in income derived from patent infringement claims. In addition, the contract stipulated that Crystal Spring could revoke the agreement with C. and J. Jones at any time.[37]

C. and J. Jones then proceeded to take action against a number of Hutterite colonies, including Lakeside, for patent infringement. On 21 October 1986 Grand Colony paid C. and J. Jones $25,000 in damages for infringement of the patent.[38] After legal expenses, Crystal Spring Colony received about $11,000.[39] Crystal Spring eventually also took out a patent for the hog feeder in the United States and made an arrangement with Gro Master for distribution and patent infringement claims.[40] Gro Master then proceeded to sue Hutterite colonies in the United States for patent infringement. Aside from the questionable competition between colonies over intellectual property within the context of a religion dedicated to communal property, the patent controversy raised serious questions in the minds of some Hutterites as to the character and conduct of their senior elder, Jacob Kleinsasser, as president of Crystal Spring.

First, the position of Crystal Spring was that Daniel Hofer had copied its design rather than the other way round. Lawyer Michael Radcliffe asserted that at some stage Daniel Hofer had "sent one of his helpers from the steel shop at Lakeside ... to James Valley prior to any dispute arising to purchase Crystal Spring manufactured hog feeders which he had heard about. Dan Hofer then proceeded to copy the Crystal Spring design ... Jonathan and Dan Kleinsasser at Crystal Spring Colony had effected a modification on the self-feeding hog feeder which was in fact unique. The self-feeding hog feeder was a well known invention, but the unique angle of the feeding shelf was in fact the modification which he copied."[41] However, given the claim by Daniel Hofer alleging the opposite, the head of the church appeared to be in a conflict of interest in trying to deal with a dispute involving his own colony, and apparently he did not institute any internal investigation of Hofer's claim by other more disinterested members of the church, who might have investigated whether the Crystal Spring design really did have any connection with the Lakeside developments. This might have settled the matter before it escalated out of control. The claims and counterclaims as to the invention of the hog feeder surely could have been investigated within the church and the facts established to the satisfaction of all parties.

Second, Hutterite colonies were being sued by C. and J. Jones Co., apparently without knowing that Jones had a contract to share infringement proceeds with Crystal Spring in these lawsuits, threatened or actual. Colonies would know that C. and J. Jones was marketing the feeders built at Crystal Spring, and that the patent had been assigned to it, but did they know that Crystal got a share of the patent infringement proceeds, and did they know that Crystal had the right to revoke the agreement with C. and J. Jones at any time? The senior elder, Jacob Kleinsasser, admitted that when he discussed the matter with colonies that were having claims made against them, he did not inform the managers of these colonies of the arrangement Crystal Spring had with C. and J. Jones.[42] Indeed, it was not until the Lakeside trial, which took place more than three years later, that Josh Hofer Jr. and other "faithful" members of Lakeside had knowledge of this. Daniel Hofer, in his objection to the actions of Crystal Spring, would have been even more incensed had he known at the time that Crystal Spring was in effect bringing lawsuits against other colonies through the "worldly" front of C. and J. Jones – that, even though in law C. and J. Jones was a separate corporate entity, the senior elder's colony was in effect suing its own brethren in other colonies.

In any event, Crystal Spring Colony now had a very profitable manufacturing activity protected by patent. The wet and dry feeder was seen to be economically advantageous in bringing hogs to market faster than more conventional feeders. Profits for the colony were made both manufacturing and selling the hog feeders and also in sharing revenues from patent infringement claims. According to its own recent report,

Crystal Spring Hog Equipment is a multi-million dollar, state-of-the-art manufacturing facility. The factory contains a full line of computerized metal fabricating machines such as brakes, shears, punch-presses, and robotic welders ... We manufacture a whole line of stainless steel hog feeder[s] based on a patented design called the Wet/Dry Feeder. Besides the stainless steel feeders, Crystal Spring Hog Equipment also manufactures hog penning, stalls and crates for confining hogs. We sell all over North America, including Mexico. We have also begun expanding into overseas markets such as Germany, Spain, Poland, Chile, Bolivia and Malaysia. Our business has been expanding tremendously in recent years and we now outsource to six other Hutterian Communities in order to be able to keep up with customer demands.[43]

The movement away from exclusive agricultural production on Hutterite colonies to the addition of small- or large-scale manufacturing enterprises involves serious risks in terms of how these new activities will impact on fundamental norms. While competition between colonies over market quotas for farm produce might produce undesirable conflict, and while colonies are independent economic units, good ideas about how to grow grain or raise cattle would traditionally have been shared within the wider Hutterite community. Furthermore, colonies often come to the aid of each other, reflecting the concept of sharing of goods and mutual aid, particularly within the Leut. With the movement to manufacturing comes the new development of a colony producing and owning intellectual property and not sharing it with other colonies. Should intellectual property be owned by a colony in the same way that a particular colony owns a certain number of hogs to sell in the market?

It might be asked, however, in what way Daniel Hofer's attempt to get a patent for Lakeside was any less problematic than Crystal's patent application. Daniel Hofer, in defending the lawsuit brought against him, claimed that his intention was to protect the manufacturing potential of Hutterite colonies against non-Hutterite manufacturing firms. This was admitted by the overseers when one of them confirmed that Daniel Hofer had wanted a patent so that "Henrich [a non-Hutterite firm] doesn't mass manufacture the thing."[44] Daniel Hofer claimed that if Lakeside had the patent, it would never have sued other colonies that used the invention in their own internal manufacturing endeavour.[45]

Lakeside Threatened with Litigation

Lakeside was one of the first targets of threatened litigation for patent infringement. Daniel Hofer received a letter on 9 May 1986 from Ade and Co. as agent of C. and J. Jones, stating: "It is our understanding that you have already manufactured or are proposing to manufacture feeders of this type whether for sale or for your own use. We must inform you that any such manufacture of a feeder of this type, even solely for your own use and even if including minor modifications in construction detail, is an infringement of the patent and it is our client's clear and firmly decided intention to take legal action through the Federal Court of Canada against any such infringement."[46] Daniel Hofer's reply on 21 May included the following: "We wish to advise you at this time, we will continue to manufacture and sell and use as we please the feeder we've invented and are in the process of patenting. You stated in your letter your clients have full ownership of patent, your clients probably aren't as much at fault re this matter as Ade and Co. When your client applied for patent of our feeder, Ade and Co. should have advised your client a patent is already in process for this feeder."[47]

Despite all the allegations that it was Ade and Co. that had failed to protect his invention, and despite Ade and Co.'s own withdrawal notice, Daniel Hofer sent another drawing to Ade and Co. on 2 July 1986 with a request to proceed with the Lakeside patent application.[48] Ade and Co. wrote back again advising Daniel Hofer that it could no longer act for him given that Ade and Co. was representing Crystal Spring.[49]

The Canadian Patent Office in Ottawa eventually embarked on an inquiry into the complaints of Daniel Hofer. Ade and Co. expressed its position that the original discussion with Daniel Hofer involved a hog feeder that had an actuator the hog could move to dispense a measured dose of feed. After recounting the various contacts and correspondence with Hofer, Ade and Co. stated:

> In 1985 we were approached by Mr. Kleinsasser concerning a hog feeder in which the feature of novelty was an arrangement in which a shelf is positioned beneath a hopper and above a trough so that the feed falls continuously onto the shelf and remains there. The hog can itself, by choice, then either eat from the shelf the dry material which has fallen there or can brush the feed from the shelf into the trough for mixing with water using a hog actuable nipple. This concept of the shelf which enables the feeder to be used as a wet feeder and a dry feeder so that the animal can choose its preferred condition of food was certainly not present in the original drawings submitted by Mr. Hofer nor in the subsequent drawings submitted for Mr. Hofer and therefore we had no indication that he had made any invention in this field.[50]

The argument of Ade and Co. was that subsequent to the Crystal Spring patent application, Daniel Hofer had come to it with a design very similar to that of Crystal Spring and "very different" from the original designs.[51]

Daniel Hofer maintained his position that, while the early drawings may not have included aspects of his ultimate invention, he had in fact invented a wet and dry hog feeder with an adjustable shelf, the idea for which was "stolen" by Crystal Spring. He stated:

> Our claim regarding this whole matter is that feeder patent # ... is our invention, evolved through large expenses over approximately two years of experiments. At the completed stage it was snatched by Crystal Spring who claimed patent under their name, to which we object. Our drawings at Ade will affirm this claim, the main part being the adjustable ledge under the feed compartment. I doubt if the feed compartment and feed trough below will be of any significance as all feeders always have had feed space and trough. Nevertheless, that's the way we designed it. Some of our early drawings are lacking some details. We were advised by Ade we have up to two years or more of making sure invention is satisfactory before applying for patent. This will however not cause a problem, as we can prove we sold some feeders of this type approximately a year before Crystal Spring ever made a feeder of this type.[52]

A matter that touches on Daniel Hofer's conduct was that throughout this period of disputing the patent, which had been going on for well over a year, Hofer did not inform the overseers of Lakeside of the situation. He did not show any of his correspondence with Ade and Co. or with the patent office or with C. and J. Jones to Michael Wollmann, Jacob Hofer, or Josh Hofer Jr., the managers of Lakeside.[53] While Daniel Hofer was the head of the stainless steel shop, with a degree of authority to act on his own, it would be a significant factor in assessing his credibility at trial that he had claimed the invention for Lakeside and disputed the patent of Crystal Spring and yet left the managers of Lakeside out of the picture. He had not informed the managers that he had been ordered to stop making the hog feeders.

While the details may not have been shared with the overseers, they certainly knew at least something about the dispute. At some point previously, when Daniel Hofer had told Jacob Hofer, one of the overseers, that Crystal Spring had stolen his invention, Jacob told Daniel to drive to Crystal Spring and tell the Kleinsasser brothers that they had stolen his invention. This was good advice, and Daniel drove to Crystal Spring Colony, only to find that both Kleinsasser brothers were away, but he did leave a message with Mike Kleinsasser.[54] Furthermore, much of the correspondence to Ade and Co. that Daniel Hofer initiated during the previous year was sent to Crystal Spring where, as president of that colony, the senior elder, Rev. Jacob Kleinsasser, received it.[55] The point was later made that while the overseers of Lakeside may not have known the details of the dispute, the senior elder in his capacity as head of the whole church knew about it yet did not investigate Daniel Hofer's claims on behalf of Lakeside, other than to rely on the opinion of Ade and Co.[56]

It was in August of 1986 that the overseers first learned that Lakeside might be infringing a patent that involved the manufacturing of hog feeders by Crystal Spring Colony. After receiving a phone call from Brian Miller of C. and J. Jones, the overseers came to Lakeside to meet with Daniel Hofer. When they arrived, Daniel Hofer apparently left the yard and "took off into the bush."[57] Later that evening, however, they had their meeting, and the overseers ordered Daniel not to manufacture feeders that might contravene the Crystal patent. At this stage the overseers were unaware of all the correspondence that had already transpired involving Daniel Hofer. Daniel objected to the order and told the overseers that the patent by Crystal was wrongful. Of significance to the subsequent claim that the overseers were in conspiracy with the senior elder was the fact that after this August meeting the overseers did nothing to investigate Daniel's claim. They simply ordered him not to manufacture feeders that contravened the patent.[58]

Daniel Hofer had a stubborn and independent streak. He continued on as before, manufacturing feeders and disputing the patent with Crystal. On 1 October 1986 he received a letter from Mr. J. Grariepy, commissioner for patents, which repeated the assertions of Ade and Co. that the Crystal Spring patent had features that were different from the original Hofer drawings and thus the patent agents, at least, had not acted improperly.[59] Daniel Hofer continued to write letters to the Patent Office in Ottawa during October and November of 1986, seeking cancellation of the patent to Crystal Spring Colony, but was ultimately advised that if his claim involved the fact that he had invented the device before it was patented by Crystal Spring, he would have to bring action in the Federal Court of Canada.[60]

The next step was for C. and J. Jones to take action against Lakeside. Brian Miller of C. and J. Jones went to Lakeside on 29 December 1986 and took pictures of feeders. He then contacted the overseers of Lakeside with the claim of patent infringement. On 10 January 1987 the overseers called a managers meeting at Lakeside which included the two overseers and the three inside leaders – Josh Jr., the secretary, and the two ministers, Joe and Paul. Daniel Hofer was called to this meeting, whereupon he strenuously disputed the claim of C. and J. Jones that Lakeside could not manufacture the feeders he had invented. However, by the end of the meeting, there appears to have been an agreement among the overseers to attempt to settle the matter with C. and J. Jones.[61]

The next day the overseers and the three inside leaders had a lengthy meeting in Winnipeg. Mr. Battison for Ade and Co. attended, as did Mr. Miller for C. and J. Jones. Daniel Hofer was not invited, allegedly because of his stormy behaviour at the Lakeside meeting the day before.[62] At this meeting the managers of Lakeside for the first time saw much of the correspondence between Daniel Hofer and the parties involved. But the overseers were apparently still not told that C. and J. Jones had a deal with Crystal to share patent infringement proceeds.[63] Again there would be an allegation on behalf of Daniel Hofer that the overseers did not sufficiently investigate his claim. Instead they agreed not to manufacture the feeders in the future and agreed to settle the current claim.

The overseers thought that since they had no personal knowledge that Daniel Hofer had been manufacturing a feeder that violated the patent, Lakeside could probably get out of the mess for nothing other than the promise to stop manufacturing any more of them.[64] Brian Miller of C. and J. Jones did not immediately agree to this, instead suggesting that he think about it over night and phone the overseers in the morning. The next day, 12 January 1987, Brian Miller negotiated a settlement with Lakeside for $10,000 for patent infringement on feeders that the Lakeside colony had been manufacturing. The agreement allowed Lakeside to manufacture up to fifty more of the feeders to fulfill an order from Souris Colony, but thereafter Lakeside could not manufacture the feeders again.[65]

The overseers would argue that the matter should have ended here. Surely a good Hutterite who subordinates his will to that of the group would let the matter rest at this stage even if he felt that the decision was unjust? But Daniel Hofer did not meekly bend. When he discovered that the overseers had settled the case with C. and J. Jones without putting the matter to a vote of the Lakeside members, and that he was not supposed to manufacture his feeders any longer, he was furious. Rather than accepting the decision of the overseers, he embarked on a path of rebellion. This rebellion was like a stone thrown into the pond. The impact was greatest on him and his family and on all of Lakeside Colony, but it also rippled out in wider circles to all the Schmiedeleut and to the whole Hutterian Brethren Church.

Excommunication

The rebellion against the overseers had started. On the bottom of a copy of the negotiated agreement to pay C. and J. Jones $10,000 for patent infringement, Daniel Hofer wrote: "All the above claims are false fabrications." Then he signed his name below this statement, as did other ordinary members of Lakeside, including Isaak Hofer, Joseph Hofer, Mike Hofer, Larry Hofer, and Daniel Hofer Jr. Beside these names, Daniel Hofer wrote that Ben Hofer had not been consulted about the agreement to pay $10,000, that Ministers Joe and Paul Hofer had disagreed with the idea of paying the claim, and that Josh Hofer was neutral. He added at the end, "Bank of Montreal is responsible from here on for any payments to C. and J. Jones.[66]

Daniel Hofer, armed with the signatures of more than a majority of the ordinary male voting members of Lakeside from both of the Hofer clans, went to the bank and put a stop-payment on the cheque to C. and J. Jones that had been signed by the outside overseeing officers of his colony. Hofer's position as stated in a letter written several days later was that "[n]o one in

the colony can spend $10,000 without consulting members, except for ne-
cessities like feed, fertilizers and repairs, etc. We owe Jones nothing. I wouldn't
settle this matter with him for a nickel if he made me the offer."[67]

At the subsequent trial, the overseers disputed Daniel's claim that they could
not make financial decisions without consultation of the members. The colony
was in "church receivership" and they claimed ample authority to run temporal affairs with or without the consent of the members, even if David
Waldner had historically chosen to consult in most circumstances.[68] In any
event, the original dispute was not between the two clans at Lakeside but
between the ordinary members of Lakeside and the outside overseers. Daniel
Hofer did not foresee that the dispute would bitterly divide his own colony.

The two key events, which numerous judges would later review, were the
meetings of the male voting members of Lakeside held on 21 January 1987
and ten days later on 31 January 1987. As a result of these two meetings,
some of the members who had signed Daniel Hofer's protest switched back
to obedience with the overseers, while Daniel Hofer and two of his sons
were allegedly excommunicated from the church and the colony.

Except for two members, the voting members of the colony (baptized
married males) met for what was supposed to be the annual meeting, on 21
January 1987. One of the missing members was David Hofer, a son of Daniel
Hofer Sr. David was the head mechanic at the colony machine shop. That it
was billed as an annual meeting rather than as a special meeting to deal
with the hog feeder matter meant that Daniel Hofer had no formal notice
that his actions would be on the agenda. The meeting turned out to be not
an annual meeting at all but a meeting solely about the hog feeder issue.

After a stormy exchange between the overseers and Daniel Hofer about
his dissent from the settlement with C. and J. Jones, his claim that he had
invented the feeder, and his refusal to stop manufacturing the feeders, Daniel
Hofer was ordered to leave the meeting. Minutes of the meeting, as prepared by the overseers, vary somewhat on the details. One set of minutes
notes that Daniel Hofer asked to leave the meeting and left with words to
the effect of, "It's time to get out of here."[69] Another account states that
Daniel Hofer was asked to leave the meeting.[70] At some point thereafter,
one of Daniel Hofer's sons, Daniel Hofer Jr., asked to leave the meeting,
saying something to the effect of, "I can't stand this any longer."[71] Daniel
Hofer Jr. was the head of the hog operation on the colony, a powerful position within most colonies. The other members of Lakeside granted Daniel
Jr. permission to leave.

The reason that Daniel Hofer Sr. was allegedly told to leave the meeting
was recounted at trial by the overseer, Rev. Mike Wollmann, who was the
chairman of the meeting: Daniel Hofer Sr. was objecting to the settlement
and Mike Wollmann was attempting to read from documents that had been
provided by C. and J. Jones and Ade and Co.:

A. And we – I told the audience and the brothers: "I'm going to read and prove you what documents we have, what position we're in and then we'll rule."

Q. And then we'll what?

A. Then we'll rule accordingly.

Q. Yes?

A. Well, it didn't come to that point. Daniel, in his vanity, he couldn't be controlled. I warned him, "Daniel let me read to the members what it is." He interfered and interfered, that we don't know what we're doing, that we don't understand. "It's all garbage what you got." I told him, "Man, we got the same papers you got from the same company, which we are a great surprise what we saw yesterday, what you did on your own." We're just so shocked that we barely looked at each other for minutes. And what avenue is Daniel taking? We carried on and tried to stop him and said, "Daniel hear me out. I am the president, the chairman. I like order in a meeting, not shouting and yelling and being in a defiant attitude." I didn't like that so I said, "Daniel, your last chance. If you don't let me read and finish whatever I have to say I'll have to take measures." He didn't care. He just said, "Okay, that's fine. You don't know what you're doing anyways. You did nothing more than make damage here." "All right, brothers, he is guilty. He may leave the room." So we all agreed he is guilty, he had to leave the room.[72]

By "agreement," Mike Wollmann did not mean that a vote was taken but that agreement is assumed unless someone registers dissent. The other overseer, Rev. Jake Hofer, recounted some of the events leading up to Daniel Hofer leaving the room:

A. We talked nicely to Danny and said, "Danny, this just does not work. You are going against the government and its regulations and against Ottawa, because there was letters presented to us which came from the Commissioner of Patent in Ottawa, as we told him, "We are not about to go and counsel about things like that and we advise you to accept this. There is no need to argue over a feeder invention. There's 101 other things to make. We don't want this in Lakeside."

Q. What did Danny Hofer say?

A. He repeated it again. He says, "That patent doesn't belong to Crystal Spring. That patent is Lakeside's. That's my patent. I invented it, and they stole it from us."[73]

Daniel Hofer's perception of the meeting was different. He was trying to get the overseers to listen to his arguments and they refused to hear his side of the story. They then expelled him from the meeting. Hofer stated:

Nobody expected that the patent issue would surface at that meeting, but then it did come up and Jake and Mike noticed that nobody was on their side. Didn't even see one member that agreed with them that they did the right thing to pay C. and J. Jones or to authorize the Crystal Spring Colony that they could have the patent regardless what Lakeside says. That was what they were trying to do, the direction they were heading, but nobody at that meeting agreed to that ... I explained at that meeting to the members what all those letters were about, the same way we're doing here now and then when Mike noticed what was going on ... the members got doubtful with Jake and Mike's opinion of the patent issue. So they didn't agree with them and after they saw how I explained it to the members, they excommunicated me from the meeting so that I couldn't further explain to the members what the whole issue was about.[74]

The minutes of the meeting do not give many details of the discussion after Daniel Hofer "left" the meeting. What is clear is that the overseers imposed some kind of punishment on Daniel Hofer for his behaviour. According to the following statements, prepared by the overseers after the event,

[i]t was then unanimously decided that Danny Hofer Senior *and all involved with him* shall not be classed as a brother or member any longer, and Daniel Sr. was asked to appear before the whole council, and told what the decision was. He cannot be a brother of Lakeside Colony with such a ... rebelling attitude for carrying on to build this same wet and dry feeder.[75]

After Daniel Hofer Sr. was called back in the meeting to see if he will accept church punishment for the above misconduct, he right away said he wants a higher court and that he has to go to make feeders.[76]

That the formal minutes are confusing as to what punishment was initially agreed to is indicated by the testimony of the overseers themselves. Rev. Jacob Hofer put it this way:

It was then discussed with the rest of the brothers that if Danny wants to proceed like this, he has caused some damage to Lakeside already. He's very stubborn in giving in, doesn't want to listen to counsel, he can't be a brother anymore. And for this conduct, he will have to eat in the bakehouse and sit in the hallway for church services. And all the members agreed. We called Danny back ...[77]

Q. Then what happened?
A. We called Danny back and asked, him, "Danny, with the conduct, the damage you have caused Lakeside, the conduct you have showed in this

meeting and expressed yourself and looked at us as if we were just children sitting in front and it's just scrap paper we're having and we should discard it, we can now sense your rebellious attitude towards us. And for this rebellion, we would like you to repent and come down from where you are. Until you do this, this is what is going to be imposed on you: Eat in the bakehouse and sit in the hallway.

Q. What did Dan Hofer say to that?

A. "I am not accepting it."

Q. Then what happened?

A. "Well, if you're not accepting it, where do you want to go?" "I'll find my right," he says ...

Q. Describe to us what transpired for the balance of the meeting?

A. So we said, "If that's the direction you want to go, Danny, you may leave." And as he left, he says, "I want 40 ministers, and you, Mike and Jake, you go home, we don't need you here."[78]

This reconstruction of the event indicates that Daniel Hofer was offered a form of church discipline, a milder form of shunning, which he did not accept. After Daniel left the meeting for the second time, that is, after he had not accepted the verdict that he should be shunned and had asked for a higher court within the church, an event allegedly took place, though this is highly contestable. The overseers would later claim that Daniel Hofer had been expelled from the colony and the church at this meeting.[79] Yet the minutes of the meeting mention no motion of excommunication or expulsion after Daniel refused the first punishment offered.[80]

The claim of the overseers that Daniel was now completely expelled from membership in the colony was confusing. The claim involved alternative grounds. One ground was that after Daniel left, even if it was not in the minutes, there was an actual pronouncement of excommunication with which the rest of the members agreed. Rev. Jake Hofer put it this way:

After he had left, we turned to the members again. We said, "Now what? He doesn't accept what we imposed on him. He's chasing us out, which he can't do in no shape or form. It's the church that's suppose to do it. If Danny wants to proceed like this, he is no more a brother." And the first punishment which we imposed on him is void. *He is no more a member and out of the church.*

Q. What was the reaction of the brotherhood to that statement?

A. The brotherhood accepted it unanimously.

Q. Who said that word; who pronounced that dictum or that saying?

A. ... Mike Wollmann.[81]

The other ground that the overseers stood on was the concept that once Daniel refused the lesser punishment and asked for a higher court, he was automatically excommunicated by his own choice in not accepting punishment. The matter was put this way by the senior elder, Jacob Kleinsasser, after being asked whether the excommunication took place on 21 January 1987:

Yes, with together the other information that was brought when first of all they had wanted him to be excluded from brotherhood, not to be in communion any more with the brothers in the dining hall nor in the worship. And after he rejected that, then out he goes even though it could have stayed if he would be decent only and accepted it as released from the brotherhood and be obedient to go and take his meal in separation of the rest of the faithful brothers. He could have stayed, but since he didn't then it ultimately was an expulsion and a total expulsion, not only a part expulsion, and it is him that made the choice, not the brothers. He was asked to make a choice.[82]

There is a hint in this testimony of at least three levels of church discipline within Hutterite colonies. One level involves some degree of the kind of shunning that Daniel rejected, where a person is still a member of the community but is not at peace and cannot partake in full communion until reconciled. Discipline occurs at another level when a person's membership is lifted and the person is shunned but not expelled from the colony. The last level of discipline occurs when the person's membership is taken away and he or she is also told to leave the colony.

On the other side of the coin, the interpretation Daniel Hofer gave to these events was that, when he called for the higher court, all discipline at the colony level was suspended until the matter was adjudicated by the higher court in the church. In other words, Hofer claimed he was not under any punishment at all as a result of the meeting of 21 January. But from the overseers' perspective, not accepting the punishment imposed by the group violates the very core of Hutterian inside law in terms of the individual submission required for community living. There was little doubt that according to inside law Daniel Hofer was in some state of church punishment, but that at this stage Daniel Hofer did not know he had been excommunicated at the third level, that is, expelled from the colony and the church. Indeed, that the colony continued to function "normally" for the next ten days would add support to his contention.[83] The testimony given at trial by Daniel Hofer included the following exchange:

Q. And what did you do then?
A. Nothing. I just appealed to a higher court, and then he [Mike Wollmann] told me exactly what – he used exactly the same words that Festus used in

Acts 25, "thou has appealed to the emperor, to the emperor thou will appear," exactly those words he used, meaning, I will get what I ask for, the higher court.[84]

After Daniel Hofer Sr. went off to make feeders, Daniel Hofer Jr. must have come back into the meeting of 21 January, as indicated by the minutes:

Daniel Jr. repeated saying he cannot stand for this because of the statements made against his father as there were difficult and many words exchanged back and forth. For this it was decided that Daniel Hofer Jr. should be reconciled with making an apology at the church service ... [85]

 Rev. Paul Hofer asked Mike Wollman[n] and Jacob Hofer, the overseers for Lakeside Colony, if they had permission to make an out of court settlement with C. and J. Jones ... After 20 minutes, Rev. Paul Hofer also asked to leave the meeting claiming he had a headache and didn't want to sit in discussion about hog feeder ... Paul said that this was a sad deal regarding the patent fight between Crystal Spring Colony and Lakeside Colony and that it was brother against brother.[86]

That the ordinary members agreed to have Daniel kicked off the colony at this meeting is highly doubtful. It is important to note that at this meeting of 21 January 1987, the overseers still had not seen the document used by Daniel Hofer to get the stop-payment at the bank. The day before, on 20 January, they had been made aware of the stop-payment and took action to overrule it, but they had not seen the signatures of all the ordinary members who supported Daniel Hofer. After the meeting, Josh Hofer Jr. told the overseers about the bank document; they told him to retrieve it from the bank. When he came back with it, they saw that some members had signed with Danny. Over the course of the next days, these members were brought to the overseers' trailer for a "discussion" about where they stood on this matter.[87]

Rather than having the matter go to a higher court within the church, ten days later, on 31 January 1987, the overseers called all voting members of Lakeside to another meeting, held at noon. Daniel Hofer Sr. was called but refused to attend the meeting. Arguably if he was no longer a member as of the 21st, as the overseers would later argue, why was he even called to the meeting on the 31st? Again, the minutes do not record what was said, but clearly the issue boiled down to those who stood with the overseers and those who dissented. By the end of this noontime meeting, the overseers appeared to have support nine to three. The male baptized members who did not agree to go along with the signing officers were Daniel Hofer Sr., and his twin sons, Daniel Hofer Jr. and David Hofer.[88] Daniel's brother, Rev. Paul Hofer, was still formally in the camp of the overseers. What is apparent is that even though a majority of the male members had initially signed with Daniel Hofer protesting the settlement, either before the meetings or as a result of them, and under the "guidance" of the overseers and the clear threat of discipline for disobedience, most of the members toed the line. However, Joseph Hofer, a grandson of Rev. Joseph Hofer, was in a little doubt about where he stood, so he was put under church punishment. He then went over into the overseers' camp.[89]

Daniel Hofer assumed that it was up to the overseers to go to the senior elder and arrange for some kind of hearing by one or more neutral ministers. However, Mike Wollmann and Jake Hofer asserted that the next move was up to Daniel: he was the one who should go to the elder and ask for a hearing.[90] In the meantime, as far as they were concerned, he was out of the church. In any event, that same afternoon, on 31 January 1987, Mike Wollmann and Jacob Hofer, the outside overseers, went to visit the senior elder, Jacob Kleinsasser, at Crystal Spring. Investigating the facts of the patent dispute was no longer the issue. The fundamental issue now was obedience and submission to congregational and conference authority.[91] If the overseers' position was correct, namely that Daniel Hofer had been excommunicated ten days earlier, they could argue that, even though the onus was on Daniel to take action, they were taking up the matter of a higher court to the senior elder. They would later argue that in Hutterite tradition one does not have the right to a higher court. All one has is the right to ask the senior elder to grant one. The senior elder may in his discretion intervene or refuse to intervene with the decisions made at the colony level.[92]

That afternoon, the senior elder was not interested in forming any higher court for someone who had so clearly rebelled against the overseers and the will of the congregation. Instead, he wrote a letter and gave it to the overseers. The letter stated that Daniel and his followers "should be separated from Lakeside" and that the "rebellion should be cut off with all those who follow Daniel." In addition, the second minister, Paul Hofer, "should immediately stop conducting worship services because his conduct is questionable as to whether he agrees with Daniel."[93]

Upon their return to Lakeside, the overseers, armed with the letter from the senior elder, called another meeting of the voting members of the colony for that evening. This time Daniel and his two sons Daniel Jr. and David refused to attend. The overseers read the letter from Jacob Kleinsasser and, as the minutes record, "[i]t was then agreed with the rest of the members that the above three were no more members and out of the church."[94] What happened on the evening of 31 January seems clear. The overseers got a majority vote to impose Ausschluss on the three men. That is, a decision was made to excommunicate them from the church and expel them from the colony. At this stage, Daniel Hofer and his two sons were supposed to leave the colony – and leave with but the shirt on their backs – to start a new life on the outside. They were supposed to leave their wives and children behind on the colony, unless the spouses and children chose to leave with them. In the alternative, they could seek repentance and bow to the majority will, and ask to be readmitted to the colony.

Daniel Hofer Sr., however, still had a differing view of what appealing to a higher church court meant. It was his view that once the appeal was made, the overseers were disentitled to act as overseers, not just in regard to any discipline of him but generally in regard to the colony, until the higher court established peace at the colony.[95] By "higher court" Daniel Hofer meant that the senior elder of the church would send a neutral minister or a number of ministers to Lakeside to investigate the matter and make a determination.[96]

Mutiny

Daniel Hofer now took further steps in clear defiance of the overseers. On 3 February 1987 the dissenting group held its own special meeting and decided to mutiny. In addition to the twin sons, Daniel Jr. and David, there was also son Larry Hofer, who was a baptized member of Lakeside but not married yet and thus not entitled to vote at membership meetings (he would not be allowed to vote until he was twenty-five years old and still unmarried). The dissenting group decided that Daniel Sr. should be appointed the "emergency president" of Lakeside, even though Daniel was not a minister of the church. Daniel Jr. was appointed secretary of the colony. It was then decided that all the ordinary members would be invited to join in the mutiny against the overseers and those who did not side with the dissenters would be placed under church punishment because they joined in with the "fraud and wrongdoing" of the overseers. So a degree of shunning was pronounced both ways: the dissenters, proclaiming themselves to be the true church, shunned the overseer group, and vice versa. The motive for the mutiny was no longer the patent dispute per se but, rather, the punishment issue. As Daniel Sr. stated:

> It wasn't really the fraud itself that inspired us to go that direction. If Jacob Hofer would have paid the ten thousand the way, the same way that he did with the combine and the shed, we probably would have just warned him again what you're doing is not agreeable with the church or with the law of the Hutterite, but what, what else happened there when they started punishing or intended to punish the members because they don't agree with their activities, that's where the break came. It really didn't come with the patent or with the payment of the patent, but after they decided to punish the members, like they did with me, to expel me from the meeting and punish me by sitting in the hall and [not] eating with the other members, it's just plain, sheer force. That's why we had to go to the extreme. It's not

only the mismanagement of the funds, but this is where really the thing came to a head.[97]

On 6 February 1987 Daniel Hofer sent a notice to the overseers that they had been removed until such time as the "breach of trust and fraud" was investigated by the Hutterian Brethren Church.[98] He went on working on hog feeders as the head of the manufacturing shop, and Daniel Jr. was still in charge of the hog barn, David was in charge of the garage, and Larry Hofer was in charge of the electrical shop. This meant that the dissenter group ran a substantial portion of the enterprises of the colony. As far as they were concerned, the overseers did not have authority to run the colony while the dispute was before a higher court. Daniel Hofer thought this situation would last a few weeks at most. He never contemplated that it would in fact last for years.[99]

Because the other members had voted to expel Daniel Hofer and his three sons, the "overseer" group had to shun the "renegade" group. When Daniel and his family entered the dining room to eat, the others would take their food and leave the room.[100] On 6 February 1987 Daniel Hofer Jr. locked the overseers out of the hog barn. The dissenting group also changed ignition and door-locking devices on a number of the colony vehicles so that they could use the vehicles without authorization of the overseer managers.[101] The next day, another Lakeside membership meeting was held. The overseers and the members who followed their orders approved the removal of Daniel Hofer and his sons from the positions they occupied in the economic affairs of the colony.[102] Of course, since the attitude of the dissenters was that the overseers and those that followed them had no authority to act until the higher court met, they continued to occupy the positions as before. Daniel Hofer Jr. would not allow Gary Hofer, the new overseer hog boss, into the hog barns. To bypass the overseers, the dissenting group opened a bank account for the "true" colony, as they called it, and tried to continue running key aspects of the commercial activities of the colony.

At a meeting of ministers at Milltown Colony with the senior elder on 10 February 1987, the issue of Daniel Hofer was brought to the attention of the assembly. As Jacob Kleinsasser, the senior elder, would later recount:

I brought all those letters to the attention of those brothers. "Here's a brother ... even though he may think he had been addressed a little wrongly maybe at the time of the meeting in Lakeside, but all the actions afterwards reveal a much worse and evil heart." And the brothers anticipated at that moment in time. And I said before that the whole room was shocked. We were sitting for minutes in quietness. "What are we going to do with such an evil brother? He can set himself up like Hamin in the Bible and many others of these that we can quote illustrations or – as illustrations in the Bible and here we are helpless. We can't do nothing. He doesn't move according to the decision." And all this was brought to our attention. But Jake and Mike, I remember well, and there were a few others that said, "Let's bring him anyhow to a meeting. See if – what he has to say anyhow."[103]

It was decided to allow Daniel to come to the meeting of ministers to be held the following month at Woodlands Colony. But rather than waiting for the church meeting at Woodlands where Daniel Hofer could make his case to a higher church court, Jacob Kleinsasser and the overseers took legal action.[104] The refusal to leave the colony after excommunication was probably not the trigger that caused the overseers to arguably set aside Hutterian norms to sue Daniel Hofer and his group. If Daniel Hofer and his sons had relinquished their positions of authority within the colony in the wake of their excommunications and simply "sat on their hands" while refusing to leave the colony, the lawsuit would likely not have been started, at least not at that point. It was the aggressive attempt to maintain control of key colony enterprises such as the hog operation and the manufacturing of hog feeders in clear defiance of the overseers that pushed them to take legal action so as to gain control of the management of the colony. However, as events unfolded over the next years, one might conclude in hindsight that the leaders of the church would have been far better off if they had moved the "faithful" members of Lakeside away from the Daniel Hofer group, rather than trying to force the "renegade" group off Lakeside at the point of a governmental gun. The lawsuit unleashed forces that would ultimately backfire on those who launched it, particularly on Jacob Kleinsasser, the senior elder.

6
Going to Court

Commencement of Litigation

On 16 February 1987 Michael Radcliffe, a lawyer in the Baker Radcliffe Murray and Kovnats law firm in Winnipeg, served a notice on Daniel Hofer and his twin sons. (Larry Hofer was not as yet included.) The thrust of the letter was that these three men had been excommunicated from the Hutterian Brethren Church and had to vacate Lakeside Colony within three days. If they would not do so, immediate legal action would be taken.[1] These threats to have the dissenters forcefully expelled from the colony took Daniel Hofer and his sons by surprise and escalated their anger against the overseers. Since when did the Hutterian church go to court to enforce church punishment by the force of the state sword? When the lawyer's letter arrived, both the wife of Daniel Jr. and the wife of David were in advanced stages of pregnancy. They began weeping over the contents of the letter. Daniel Jr. and his wife already had two children, while David and his wife had three. Daniel Sr. and his wife still had six younger children living in their household. Thus, in effect, seventeen people were at this stage being ordered off the colony. Those numbers increased in the future as sons of Rev. Paul Hofer were first added, and then finally Rev. Paul's whole family was affected. Of course, the dissenters would have to leave without any property, since all property on a colony is owned collectively and no expelled person is entitled to a share. However, the material difficulty of leaving with nothing is less important than the spiritual issue of eternal salvation and the enormous personal crisis of identity that results from expulsion from the church. The ideology of the Hutterites is that if a person should die while being in a state of church excommunication, they have no salvation, no expectation of getting to heaven. The argument could be made, of course, that only the three men at this stage were required to leave. The colony would continue to look after the women and children. Indeed, there were examples at Lakeside itself where men had been expelled from the colony, leaving their wives and children behind. However, while the bonds of family may be less important in a communitarian situation, it would be naïve to view them as irrelevant when applying a penalty of excommunication. The three families would stay or go together.

Daniel Hofer replied to Radcliffe of the Baker law firm. Among other things, he denied that he had been excommunicated by the Hutterian Brethren Church. "Our church does not operate the way you describe," he told Radcliffe.[2] Hofer also wrote a letter addressed to all members of the Hutterian church asserting that the expulsion order was a "horrendous crime ... We don't have to do any wrong to be excommunicated from our homes. We can as of now be excommunicated from our homes for opposing evil deeds, fraudulent deeds. Deeds we're about to prove are fraudulent, theft, breach of trust, etc."[3] Hofer said he was appealing this matter to the wider church, especially the Schmiedeleut ministers in the United States. The three-day deadline to leave passed and the three families refused to leave Lakeside colony.

On 25 February 1987, the Baker law firm filed a statement of claim against the dissenters on behalf of the overseers.[4] The lawsuit was brought in the name of Michael Wollmann, Jacob Hofer, and Joshua Hofer Jr. in their representative capacity for Lakeside Colony against Daniel Hofer and three of his sons, Daniel Jr., David, and Larry. Even though no notice of expulsion had been delivered to Larry, he was included in the lawsuit. The statement of claim sought declarations that these four men had been validly expelled from the colony, asked for court orders that they leave the colony and leave without any possessions of the colony, and that these orders be enforced by the police power of the state. Along with the statement of claim, the overseers sought an immediate court order that pending resolution of the case they be formally appointed by the court as receivers and managers of Lakeside colony.[5] On 6 March 1987 Mr. Justice Wright granted an order that the overseers could sue on behalf of Lakeside, but he did not formally appoint them as receivers and managers.[6]

The day the claim was issued, Daniel Hofer wrote to the "ex-officers" of Lakeside, as he called them: "Be advised that we Daniel Hofer Sr. (Pres.), Daniel Hofer Jr. (Sec.) have opened a partnership bank account to carry on business for Lakeside Co. Ltd ... Be advised also that we're requesting the sum of approx. four or five thousand dollars to carry on business for Lakeside Co. Ltd. including medical (human and animal), repair and hardware etc. which has been withheld by you (ex-signing officers). This is a temporary arrangement till church investigates matters ... Any properties held or used by us will become Lakeside Co. property immediately after church investigation."[7]

Daniel Hofer, again claiming to be the president of Lakeside, wrote to the Baker law firm and to the Manitoba Hog Commission asserting that the outside overseers and Josh Hofer Jr., the inside secretary, were temporarily "on hold" until the wider church had completed its investigation.[8] On 3 March 1987 the dissenter group started to ship hogs to market, but the overseers succeeded in getting the proceeds from the sale put into trust until the dispute was settled.[9] The dissenting group continued to order materials for the manufacture of feeders in the shop. The overseers sought an immediate court order to prohibit the dissenters from entering any hog barns or the metal shop on the colony.[10]

Before the pending motion could be heard in court, a meeting of the ministers of the Schmiedeleut branch of the church was called for 11 March 1987. Daniel Hofer was invited to attend should the ministers decide to hear him. However, in the wake of the statement of claim filed against him and the tremendous turbulence at Lakeside, Hofer wrote that he was not ready for a church meeting but that as soon as he was ready, he would so advise.[11] At the 11 March meeting of the Schmiedeleut ministers at Woodlands Colony the excommunication of Daniel Hofer was confirmed, following a discussion of the Lakeside situation. Rev. Jacob Kleinsasser described the meeting in his testimony:

Q. And what was the will or the resolution of the ministers of that meeting of March 11, 1987 touching on the issue of excommunication?
A. Increased shunning and avoidance was the decision, to increase it, that nobody should have anything to do with him 'cause we're a fear – we were afraid of him already.[12]

Nothing in the minutes of the 11 March meeting or in the testimony of Jacob Kleinsasser deals with the far more important point: excommunication from the church and increased shunning is one thing, going to court to invoke state violence to throw a person off the colony is quite another. There is no indication that the ministers collectively at the meeting of 11 March were either told about the lawsuit that had been initiated or that they gave their approval to it.

Court Orders

A few days after the Woodlands meeting, the lawyers for the overseers obtained a court order from Mr. Justice Monnin, of the Court of Queen's Bench. The dissenters still had no lawyer, so the order was granted on the basis of the affirmations submitted by the overseers. The order stated that "the Defendants be restrained and prohibited from entering into any hog barns or metal shop on Lakeside ... and be restrained and prohibited from interfering with any of the commercial activities of Lakeside."[13] Now that the overseers had a court order, they could call in the police to use governmental violence to remove the dissenters from areas of the colony. The court order included the usual enforcement language: "4. AND THIS COURT DOTH

FURTHER ORDER THAT all sheriffs, deputy sheriffs, constables and other peace officers within Manitoba shall do all such acts as may be necessary to enforce this order and for such purposes they and each of them, are hereby given full power and authority to enter upon any lands and premises whatsoever to enforce the terms of this order."[14]

Even though there had been no trial and judgment by the court as to whether the defendant men had been properly excommunicated, as a matter of a pretrial motion, the police power of the state was used to kick Daniel Hofer out of the steel shop that he had headed and to kick his son out of the hog barn. If they went into one of these buildings, the police could be called and the men would be charged with a breach of a court order. The police could violently remove them from the buildings, and repeated violations could result in their being thrown in jail.

If the overseers believed that they had regained control, they were quite mistaken. The order applied only to Daniel Hofer and his three baptized sons. They had to obey it, but a number of younger, unbaptized, and unmarried men were associated with the dissenter group, and they proceeded to engage in activities that disrupted the management of the overseer group. In addition to Jacob Hofer, the next oldest son of Daniel Hofer, there were four young men from families which were still in the overseer camp. Three sons of Rev. Paul Hofer and one son of Ben Hofer at this stage openly supported Daniel Hofer. The young men who sided with Daniel Hofer, but whose parents were still in the overseer camp, were told by the overseers not to live in their parents' housing units. Not having anywhere else to stay, the young men took over what had been the trailer of the overseers owned by James Valley Colony, changing the locks and effectively ousting the overseers from their business office.[15] The overseers claimed that on 19 March 1987 these five youths prevented the new hog boss, Gary Hofer, from unloading gilt pigs into the barn:

> [they] caused a front-end loader to be placed in the loading bay of the subject hog barn, placed the bucket of the front-end loader in such a position that the machine could not then be removed from the bay, removed the starter engine from the loader and threw the starter engine in the sewage lagoon appurtenant to the Colony. This action has totally prevented the said Gary Hofer, the designated hog manager, or any other member of the community for and on behalf of management at the present time to load or unload any livestock through the regular loading bay of the subject hog barn.[16]

The young men also attempted to remove the truck loaded with pigs from the yard. The overseers, in what would become a frequent occurrence, called in the RCMP detachment from Headingley. The overseers also sought a court order against the five young men so that they too would be prohibited from entering various places on the colony and interfering with the management of the colony.[17] More importantly, however, they sought to amend the statement of claim so that the three young men in this group who were over the age of majority, namely Paul Hofer Jr., Leonard Hofer, and John Gerald Hofer, would be added to the statement of claim in the lawsuit.[18] Thus, the overseers now were suing to expel seven men from the colony. Paul Jr. and John Gerald were sons of Rev. Paul Hofer; Leonard was the son of Ben Hofer. As time passed in the long struggle at Lakeside, the number of youths associated with Daniel Hofer grew. Three more sons of Rev. Paul Hofer became old enough to join the dissenting faction, as did another youth, Paul Wayne Hofer, son of Paul K. of the Joseph Hofer clan. Another youth who joined the Daniel Hofer crowd was actually a runaway from another Hutterite colony. At one point the following year, Rev. Paul Hofer having already moved over to his brother's camp, the dissenting group constituted pretty well half of the colony in terms of people living at Lakeside.[19]

While the overseers could argue that the baptized men had been excommunicated from the church and colony by a vote of members, none of the other young men had ever been baptized into membership. They could not be excommunicated from the church since they were never members of it. They had simply grown up at the colony and had spent most of their lives there. Thus, the theory of the overseers was that they "have been instructed by their parents to leave the Colony premises due to bad behavior and insubordination on their respective parts. The plaintiffs therefore state and the facts are that as these Defendants are not members of the Hutterian Brethren Church and have failed to comply with the instructions and directions of the clergy and management thereof, that they have no further right to remain on Lakeside Colony."[20] At least in the case of the sons of Rev. Paul Hofer, it was doubtful that the parents had ordered the children to leave. At the various court levels, the focus of the case was on the excommunication of Daniel Hofer Sr., and it is unfortunate that so little attention was paid to the status and rights and responsibilities of those who grow up on colonies but have not yet been baptized.

On 26 September 1987 the overseers called another meeting at Lakeside. They now included the baptized women who were not formally aligned with the three dissenting families. As the minutes record, "the purpose of the meeting was to ask all members if they want to go along with the church or side with Danny H. and his boys."[21] It was at this meeting that the second minister, Paul Hofer, a brother of Daniel Hofer Sr., declared that he was not sure which side to join. Paul had already been removed as second minister because of his possible support of Daniel, and two of his sons had been added as defendants to the lawsuit. The minutes state: "It was agreed that we will have no more communion or colony life with any brothers and sisters that side with Danny and his boys and young boys and girls included."[22]

At some stage Paul Hofer and his wife and one of their daughters walked out of the meeting, saying that "they want[ed] to have no part with a colony life like that."[23] Paul later apologized for his outbreak, but he remained in a tension between the two groups until he clearly joined in the activities of the dissenters the following year.

Defence and Countersuit

The dissenting men were by this time receiving an increasing volume of legal notices about court hearings involving motions made by the overseer camp. At some stage Daniel Hofer had received advice on the patent issue from commercial lawyer Donald Douglas of the Thompson Dorfman law firm. He now turned to Douglas for help in the face of the escalating legal attacks by the overseers. The first move was to file a countermotion for the upcoming hearings dealing with the young men. Daniel Hofer wanted the court order that ousted the dissenters from performing their colony duties lifted. Hofer's affirmation, reflecting his lawyer's advice, stated:

> My sons and I have devoted all of our efforts throughout our entire lives to the betterment of the Colony and we have no independent property or desire to have independent property or to leave the Colony or the Church ... the normal methods for resolving disputes within the Church have broken down because of the role of Kleinsasser as Senior Elder Minister is in conflict with his role as a member of Crystal Spring Colony and I would not now be prepared to submit to a higher court meeting of Ministers of the Church because I believe that the issue of the Patent must be finally resolved before the Ministers will be able to effectively deal with the remaining outstanding issues involving Lakeside Colony ... I submit that a Receiver and Manager of Lakeside Colony ought to be appointed by this Court with a direction that he act in the best interests of Lakeside Colony independently of the interests of the parties hereto and undue influences of Kleinsasser.[24]

When the motions and countermotions were argued at the hearings, the dissenters move to appoint independent management at Lakeside was not accepted by the court, and a new order was issued that added three of the youths (those over the age of majority) to the injunction not to go into the hog barns or metal shops or interfere with any of the commercial activities of the colony. The three youths over the age of majority were also added as defendants to the lawsuit.[25] While the court order now had more names attached to it, it would soon become apparent to the overseers that while they had regained control over hogs and hog feeder manufacturing at Lakeside, they had certainly not regained control of the colony.

On behalf of the dissenters, Douglas filed a statement of defence and counterclaim on 21 May 1987.[26] Arguments were included as to why the purported excommunications were not valid, including the allegations that the defendants had never been given proper notice that their expulsions would be considered at a meeting, nor were they given an opportunity to be heard. Furthermore, the young unbaptized men denied that they had been expelled by their parents or that they had breached Hutterian norms. But Daniel Hofer Sr. did not just defend against the overseer claim that he should be expelled from the colony. The effect of the counterclaim was to sue the overseers and especially the senior elder. That Daniel Hofer understood the meaning of a counterclaim is doubtful. In an assortment of subsequent letters, he always pointed out the wrongfulness of the overseer group going to the worldly court. However, a counterclaim is essentially a lawsuit brought against those who have sued you. Such a move goes beyond a simple defence of resisting or denying the claim brought against you. I doubt that Daniel Hofer at this stage separated the counterclaim in his mind from the filing of the defence to the overseers' attempt to force the dissenters off the colony. Lawyer Donald Douglas at this early stage of dealing with Hutterites would also not have the kind of background knowledge on Hutterian traditions that would have alerted him to the potential incompatibility between bringing counterclaims and Hutterian norms against going to law. In any event, a counterclaim may be an important tactical move in getting information so as to properly defend against a claim, and also for getting certain remedies that might be helpful to the defendants. It would not be until years later, in a second round of litigation, that the meaning of a counterclaim within the context of Hutterite law would have to be confronted.

Whatever the understanding of Daniel Hofer Sr., the reality was that the overseers had sued the dissenters and now the dissenters were suing the overseers: if the leaders had chosen to go to the outside court to deal with the dispute, the dissenters would make their case there. The counterclaim was brought not only against the overseers but also against the senior elder, Jacob Kleinsasser, two of his brothers from Crystal Spring, the Hutterian Brethren Church, and C. and J. Jones Co. The counterclaim asserted that the purported expulsion of Daniel Hofer was as a result of an unlawful and fraudulent conspiracy involving the senior elder, who was engaged in certain financial activities in violation of the federal statute that incorporated the Hutterian Brethren Church.[27] The counterclaim also asserted that the valuable patent was appropriated by Crystal Spring because of the need for that colony to maximize income to recover losses due to past financial dealings of the senior elder, and, further, that the appropriation of the patent was made possible by the "improper" control the senior elder exercised over the church. In addition, Rev. Wollmann, the outside president of Lakeside, was also the head of Spring Hill Colony, which had initiated a hog-killing plant in Neepawa, which was in deep financial trouble and was being sustained by the actions of the senior elder in enforcing a hog levy on all the colonies in Manitoba. Thus, the allegation was that Wollmann was not making decisions at Lakeside in any independent fashion but was strongly in need of Kleinsasser's support for his actions at Spring Hill.

As well as requesting a declaration and order that the defendants were still members in good standing of the colony, the counterclaim requested an order that the business and affairs of the wider Hutterian church be conducted in accordance with the requirements of the incorporating statute, and that the patent for the hog feeder be held in trust for Daniel Hofer on behalf of Lakeside and that an accounting be made of all profits derived from the patent thus far at Crystal.[28] While the issue as to the beneficial ownership of the patent was ultimately dropped from the counterclaim on jurisdictional grounds, since that was an issue exclusively within the domain of the Federal Court of Canada rather than the Queen's Bench of Manitoba, the central effect of the counterclaim was that the dissenting group at Lakeside was still suing the church overseers and the senior elder, alleging that the actions of these church leaders were illegal. This meant the lawsuit was no longer narrowly confined to what happened at Lakeside but had broadened to review the actions of the Schmiedeleut leadership. One can only imagine that upon receiving the counterclaim, the leaders might have had second thoughts about what they had done in starting the lawsuit. On 29 May 1987 a statement of defence to the counterclaim was filed alleging that the expulsion of Daniel Hofer and associates had nothing to do with any conspiracy involving financial matters with the senior elder from Crystal Spring or Michael Wollmann from Spring Hill.[29]

Discovery Wars

In October of 1987, Daniel Hofer spent several days in the offices of the Baker law firm, where he was examined for discovery by Michael Radcliffe. Daniel Hofer brought all his correspondence surrounding the hog feeder, his alleged expulsion from the colony, and his "mutiny," and provided them to the plaintiffs in the lawsuit against him. At one stage he even brought in a hog feeder. Several months later, when Donald Douglas was cross-examining Michael Wollmann, Jacob Hofer, Joshua Hofer Jr., and Jacob Kleinsasser on their affirmations filed in support of motions against the dissenting men, Douglas asked for the financial statements of Lakeside. The Hutterite leaders refused. Douglas also asked Wollmann about the financial statements for the hog-killing plant owned by Spring Hill and he asked Kleinsasser for financial records involving Crystal Spring Colony, various Schmiedeleut conference enterprises, and the agreement with C. and J. Jones Co. The overseer group refused to provide any financial records to the dissenters or answer any questions on these points. They would vigorously fight the attempt to widen the lawsuit to a review of their dealings outside Lakeside.

After repeated attempts over the winter to get the overseers to provide information, Donald Douglas filed a notice of motion in early May of 1988, asking the court to compel the Hutterite leaders to answer certain questions and provide records.[30] Before the hearing on this motion and other motions that were piling up from both sides of the case, Daniel Hofer and his three sons received a notice from the senior elder on 14 May 1988. It read: "Upon your request, that you asked to be heard at a Hutterian Ministers meeting, concerning your complaints and charges you make. We herewith invite you to a ministers meeting, which will be at Milltown Colony at 2 p.m. May 17, 1988. We ask you to be available at that time. If the ministers meeting will decide to hear you and call on you."[31] A separate note was sent to Rev. Paul Hofer inviting him to the meeting, even though he was not as yet a named defendant in the lawsuit. As noted below, May 1988 was a particularly difficult period for the dissenters, as several of their group were in jail at the time. Daniel Hofer replied to the invitation: "I will consult my lawyer for an answer ... As you are aware Kleinsasser and associates went to Law against the practices and rules of the Hutterian Church. So this issue is in front of the courts."[32]

Donald Douglas first approached Michael Radcliffe to ask whether he could accompany Daniel Hofer to the meeting. Radcliffe got back to Douglas with the message that the Hutterite leaders had refused. Douglas then asked whether they would provide financial records so that he could review them with Daniel before the meeting. The Hutterite leaders also refused this request.[33] The next day, after having consulted with Douglas, Hofer repeated the wrongfulness of having initiated the lawsuit and wrote that "the only satisfactory solution to this issue is the disclosure of financial funds (outside of the courts) ... Church monies handled by Crystal Spring Colony and Jacob Kleinsasser entrusted to him by the Hutterian Church. No meeting can be had before those financial figures are made public to us and to the Church."[34]

The idea of holding a hearing in front of the ministers was not refused by Daniel Hofer or his lawyer. Indeed, Douglas had asked for such a hearing, but it was conditional on having the financial records. A motion for disclosure had been adjourned precisely with the understanding that the case might be settled internally if the records were revealed.[35] But rather than disclosing the records and then calling a meeting, the senior elder refused to disclose the records and yet put the Lakeside matter on the agenda of a meeting anyway.

When the meeting took place at Milltown, with 106 ministers present from the colonies in Manitoba, South Dakota, Minnesota, and North

Dakota, the senior elder, Jacob Kleinsasser, was still firmly in charge of the Schmiedeleut. The minutes state:

> At the meeting it was presented to the assembly about the conduct and behaviour of the persons, which were excommunicated by the members of the Lakeside Colony and asked to leave the Colony. Points of discussion were, concerning the patent disputes, disobedience and the many slander-ous defamatory and arrogant letters with false accusations against the Elder Jacob Kleinsasser, and against all those that stand in support of the Elders. Also concerning the charge Daniel Hofer made about disclosure of financial statements about oil money, insurance, abattoir ... and of different colonies ... to this the ministers agreed this is not Daniel Hofer's business and should not be his concern, and [he] is not entitled to any of these financial state-ments. It was also brought to the ministers attention, about Daniel Hofer setting himself up as President of Lakeside Colony with his son Daniel Hofer Jr. as Secretary, setting up his own bank account etc. And it was unani-mously resolved, that Daniel Hofer and those in company with him, can in no way be members of the Hutterian Brethren Church. And that we all stand with one opinion that they should vacate the Colony premises and leave us. And that all support and encourage our Elder and want to stand with him ... It was also discussed about Paul Hofer from Lakeside, who like-wise was invited to the meeting at Milltown but refused to come. It was resolved to delegate another meeting to be held at Lakeside by a number of ministers concerning the problems with Paul Hofer and also other ques-tions at issue, which will be arranged at a later date.[36]

Again, the minutes do not disclose any vote on the part of the ministers to approve the taking of legal action against Daniel, although by now many of them would surely have known from Daniel's letters and other sources that this was taking place.

Since Daniel Hofer had asked for a higher church court all along – since 21 January 1987 – his decision not to appear at either of the meetings of the conference ministers of 11 March 1987 and 17 May 1988 did not bolster his case. It is true, of course, that both these meetings were held subsequent to the overseers already taking the matter against him to the worldly court. Daniel Hofer's lawyer was trying to get financial information from Kleinsasser and the overseers to defend the case, and thus the claim that Hofer should not appear until he had such information was not unreasonable. Further-more, there would be questions about whether the ministers' meetings in that form was the kind of higher court Hofer had in mind.

While examining Daniel Hofer at the trial that took place several years later, Donald Douglas suggested how the matter might have been handled:

Q. So, if we took all the Schmieden-Leut ministers, except Crystal and Lakeside, put all the names in a drum, shook it up, somebody picked out five names, said to those five people, you go away, and you interview Lakeside people, Crystal people, anybody you want to, who knows anything about who invented the feeder. And those people did that, and they came back after they concluded the reference. Now, the question is, ... what would your reaction be if the decision of that group of five ministers was that Crystal invented the invention?

A. I would be perfectly satisfied. The matter would be looked into, and that's the end of it.[37]

The motion to compel disclosure was finally heard before Justice Simonsen at the end of June 1988. The overseers made the point that, according to Hutterian custom, even members in good standing have no right within Hutterite law to see the books of the colony or conference, so why should the right be given to men who have been expelled from membership? Mr. Justice Simonsen, however, ordered the overseers to disclose the financial records of Lakeside and also the agreement involving C. and J. Jones Co. and Crystal Spring Colony. But he did not compel the overseers to reveal the financial affairs of Crystal Spring Colony, Spring Hill Colony, or the wider Hutterian Brethren Church.[38] Donald Douglas, on behalf of the defendants, appealed this order successfully to the Manitoba Court of Appeal. On 7 December 1988 Mr. Justice O'Sullivan, as he then was, stated for the court:

On the pleadings there is an attempt made by a federally-incorporated church to oust some of the adherents of the church from property belonging in equity to members of the church. In defence, the defendants allege there has been a serious conspiracy by the defendants by counterclaim to misuse the power of expulsion contained in the federal incorporation for private ends ... I would vary the order appealed from and require the defendants to attend for discovery and to answer all questions within their knowledge as to any colony or corporation which is alleged to be within the scope of the conspiracy pleaded.[39]

Now the plaintiff overseers and Jacob Kleinsasser were in trouble. The launching of the supposedly simple lawsuit to remove the defendants from Lakeside Colony turned itself around into a much wider examination of the financial dealings at the overseers' own colonies, and within the wider conference.

During the discovery stage of the litigation, Daniel Hofer wrote numerous letters addressed to all the Hutterite colonies in North America. Many of these letters, often quite intemperate, alleged that the senior elder, Jacob

Kleinsasser, was involved in corrupt practices and that Kleinsasser was refusing to disclose the accounts of various enterprises. A common theme was that Daniel had God on his side while the elder and his "cronnies," as he called them, were violating Hutterian tradition. The basic theme was that Daniel Hofer Jr. was a prophetic voice against the corruption in the church and that corruption would be exposed to the outside world because Kleinsasser and those associated with him had chosen to go that route (worldly court) to try to expel and silence him. It was Daniel who dared to speak against the leadership. It was Daniel who represented the true Hutterian faith and not Kleinsasser or the ministers who uncritically supported the elder. It was God who would vindicate Daniel. The victory at the Court of Appeal to compel wider disclosure was a step, but if vindication did come to Daniel Hofer in the end, the journey to that point involved years of struggle at Lakeside, including violence and never-ending trips by both sides to criminal and civil courts. In the process, both the reputation of Hutterites and their religious norm of non-violence took a beating.

Enterprising Dissenters

When the dissenters had been removed from their positions within the colony by court order, they decided to establish enterprises instead of sitting on their hands and doing nothing. Even though the majority of members had voted them off the colony, the colony continued to provide shelter and food to them until they could be forced off through the process of law enforcement. However, the overseer group refused to pay for clothing, medicine, dental work, gas, and other expenses of the group, not least of which were the mounting legal bills. To support the dissenting group and to keep the men busy, the true colony, as they thought of themselves, established their own enterprises. The plaintiff overseers would often use the enterprising skill of the group against them by claiming that the defendants had violated the norm of community of property by accumulating their own assets. But, in the context of the schism, Daniel Hofer and his associates claimed to be the "true colony," and they lived in a communal way like other Hutterites: the assets belonged to the church, not to any individual personally. Once the dispute was settled by a proper forum in the church, the dissenters' assets would go to Lakeside.[40] The overseer group, however, obviously did not want the dissenters to run enterprises from Lakeside but wanted the group to leave.[41]

The dissenting men worked on reclamation projects in one form or another. One enterprise involved the fixing of vehicles, particularly farm equipment and large trucks that had been involved in accidents. Such work required shop space, tools, and functional vehicles for hauling or towing. Another enterprise involved the manufacture of large containers out of scrap metal. These steel containers would stand outside buildings to hold garbage or scrap. Manufacturing such containers required welding equipment and hoists. The group became proficient at demolishing old buildings and factories and reclaiming materials for sale. This work required heavy equipment and vehicles, and also resulted in unsightly mounds of scrap materials on Lakeside land.

As mentioned above, at the beginning of the mutiny, the overseer group changed the locks on buildings and vehicles to prevent the dissenters from entering, even though there was as yet no such court order against the defendants. The dissenters had initially used only one half-tonne truck of the many vehicles available on the colony. But the overseer managers claimed that even the use of this truck was a theft.[42] Most of the equipment and vehicles the dissenters used was purchased with the funds generated by their own enterprises. Indeed, after just a year of operating these enterprises, the dissenter group had acquired an impressive list of vehicles and equipment, including two semi-trailer tractors, a five-ton flat-deck truck, seven five-ton trucks, two half-ton trucks, a forklift, a cargo van, and a new passenger van.

Given that the hog barns and stainless steel shop were off limits by court order and that Larry Hofer was still the colony's head electrician, the dissenters took over the electrical shop to run their enterprises, and they later also claimed one stall in the seven-stall colony garage. They needed the garage stall because it had the space for a hoist, which the electrical shop did not.

The original court order that applied to the seven adult men stated they could not go into the hog barns or metal shop or interfere with the commercial activities of the colony. For the dissenters, this would be analogous to you living in the same house you grew up in even though your parents were trying to get rid of you but thus far had only an enforceable order keeping you out of the den and furnace room. But the overseer camp soon went back to court to try to stop the dissenters from engaging in any of their new enterprises. Among other demands, the overseers sought a court order prohibiting the defendants from entering any nonresidential buildings whatsoever and bringing any vehicles or other property onto the colony.[43] If granted, such an order would have confined the men to their bedrooms, so to speak. Again in a countermotion, Daniel Hofer asked that the court order restricting the dissenters from the hog barn and metal shop be lifted and that the overseer managers allow the dissenters to participate in normal commercial activities at the colony until the larger issue could be resolved.[44] In the end, neither side got what they asked for. The current court order remained in place and the tense situation at Lakeside continued through the summer of 1987 and on through the winter, with complaints of harassment and vandalism on both sides. In the spring of 1988, a much more detailed court order was obtained which drew the lines as to which buildings the two groups could occupy.[45] But these new orders did not serve to keep the peace at Lakeside.

Before turning to the stories of violence and the larger turf battles at Lakeside, it should be noted that the most immediate commercial activity of the dissenters that provoked no end of battles was the reclaiming of copper by burning off insulation from wiring or from burning electric motors, and so forth. The dissenters alleged that before the dispute started, the colony had allowed scrap companies to come onto Lakeside land and burn insulation or other items to recover copper and then pay Lakeside for the services by providing a barter exchange of goods or services. But as soon as the dissenter group decided to burn for copper and make money in this way, the overseers called in the RCMP and municipal and provincial environmental agents. The alerted authorities established that the air pollution from this burning was excessive at times and that the ground at the burn site was contaminated with PCBs because of the burning of transformers. The provincial Environmental Management Department required the colony to clean up the burn site, and Larry Hofer and Paul Hofer Jr. were charged under the *Dangerous Goods Handling and Transportation Act*.[46] Although the burning of transformers ceased, the dissenting group continued to burn off insulation from wires and other electrical instruments in order to recover copper.

The Municipality of Cartier determined that the burning for copper violated zoning bylaws and ordered the dissenting group to stop. When the dissenters did not stop, it took legal action against the colony.[47] Despite the threat from the municipality, the dissenting group attempted to get authority from the provincial Clean Environment Commission for its reclamation program. A hearing of the commission was held on 10 March 1988 and an order issued on 30 March. The order imposed severe limitations on the reclamation program in terms of what could be burned and how it could be burned, but subject to meeting the requirements, the reclamation program was not prohibited by the commission.[48] Given the threat of litigation by the municipality, the dissenters proposed an alternative to their reclamation activities: if the overseers would allow them to run the chicken barn and use the profits to support themselves, they would stop entirely the scrap program.[49] But the overseers were not about to let the dissenters operate one of the normal activities of the colony and, at the beginning of May 1988, the overseers were successful in getting a court order against the seven defendants that prohibited them from operating the scrap metal reclamation enterprise on the land owned by Lakeside.[50]

Once again, the reach of a court order was frustrated. The seven defendants were prohibited, but not other persons associated with the dissenting group. This is when Rev. Paul Hofer clearly stopped walking a middle path between the two groups and came to his brother's aid. Paul Hofer had remained in a precarious position between the two groups for some time. Another membership meeting of the overseer group was held on 9 April 1988, and though Paul was called to come to the meeting, he did not show up, claiming he was ill.[51] As noted previously, the senior elder had already removed Paul from exercising his job as second minister of the colony. At this meeting, Paul Hofer was removed from the position of being the German schoolteacher at Lakeside. The next day, Daniel Hofer notified the supporters of Jacob Kleinsasser and the overseers that their meeting and their move to oust Paul was illegal and violated the articles of association of the colony.[52] Having been removed from his positions of authority at the colony, and in the face of the court orders against the defendants prohibiting their scrap reclamation activities, Rev. Paul Hofer took over the activity, aided by several of the young boys who also were not subject to the existing court order.

A Second Lakeside Lawsuit

Rather than attempting to excommunicate Paul and add him to the list of defendants subject to expulsion, the overseers launched a second lawsuit, this time against one of their own ministers, who had arguably not even been formally excommunicated from the church or the colony. They also sued children of the colony by adding six teenagers to the lawsuit. The statement of claim was against Rev. Paul Hofer; Nathan and George, sons of Paul Hofer; Jacob and Conrad, sons of Daniel Hofer; and Zach Gross, a runaway from Riverside; and Paul Wayne Hofer.[53] All these boys were under the age of majority. The lawsuit did not seek to expel Rev. Paul Hofer or the boys from the colony but sought only an order prohibiting them from doing any scrap metal reclamation work at Lakeside. With the second lawsuit added to the first, the overseers on behalf of the colony were directly suing fourteen of their own residents.

In what would become a continuing difficulty over the years, the dissenting group resisted the service of court documents. When the process server knocked on Rev. Paul Hofer's door to deliver papers, Paul would open the door, look at the man without saying a word, and then promptly close the door in his face and lock it.[54] When a lawyer from the Baker firm personally attempted to serve the dissenters with court documents, Paul on several occasions would jump into his truck and drive away, or run away into a field.[55]

At a hearing before Mr. Justice Schwartz on 3 August 1988, Rev. Paul Hofer arrived without legal representation; the motion was adjourned so that he could get a lawyer. However, in open court, Paul Hofer promised in the meantime that neither he nor any of the boys named in the suit would operate the scrap metal reclamation project.[56] The overseers were soon back in court with a motion for contempt because the dissenters were continuing to burn scrap and using even younger members of the group to light the match, alleging that so long as they did not actually light the match, they were not in violation of the court order, even though they had hauled the scrap onto the land and prepared everything for the copper recovery process.[57] Now being represented by Donald Douglas, Paul Hofer Sr. alleged that "during the month of August the copper recovery business has been continued and I admit that my nephew Roland (approximately 13 years of age) and my sons Steve and Gerald (being 14 and 13 years of age respectively) contrary to my specific instructions did engage in certain burning activity and, upon such activity becoming known to me, I firmly instructed them that no resumption of same was to take place whatsoever."[58] Fortunately for Paul, the motion for contempt was dismissed by Mr. Justice Schwartz on 6 September 1988, though he issued an order prohibiting the defendants from operating a scrap metal reclamation enterprise on Lakeside land, or even permitting such an operation.[59]

Within a year, the overseers brought another series of motions to have the defendants in both lawsuits found in contempt of court for violating these orders.[60] According to the overseer group, the scrap reclamation business never stopped despite the court orders against the fourteen individuals in the two lawsuits. The dissenters discontinued burning the scrap metal in large piles but instead burned scrap in old oil drums.[61] The defendants brought a countermotion asking the court to lift the restrictions on the scrap reclamation program, given the need to financially support the group, or in the alternative, order the overseer group to allow the dissenters to run the chicken operation or have the overseer group pay a proper sum of support to the dissenting families if they wanted them to sit on their hands and do nothing pending the resolution of the case.[62] By this stage, as I note below, the judges of the Queen's Bench had heard a steady stream of pre-trial motions in the *Lakeside* litigation for over two years. Mr. Justice Scollin in May 1989 ordered that the trial of the main case finally get going, rather than dealing with more motions for contempt of court orders. He set a trial date for June 1989 and ordered that discoveries be completed.[63] The second lawsuit was consolidated into the first lawsuit so that the issues could be tried together.

Violence Among the Pacifists
The struggle to shut down the enterprises of the defendants was the larger context for a much more damaging particularized turf war at Lakeside which often involved intimidation and harassment, and even violence. When the overseer group had lost the motion to confine the dissenters to their bedrooms, they conceded the electrical shop to the dissenters, but no more. When the dissenting group gained access to some of the stalls in the main garage in November 1987, the turf war turned violent. The garage had seven stalls and the dissenters wanted to use a couple of these stalls. The overseer

group shut the power off in the garage to force the renegades out. One of the dissenters in retaliation shut off the power for the whole colony. The overseer, Jacob Hofer, called in the RCMP to get the power restored, and the police suggested that the dissenters use just one of the stalls in the garage.[64] The overseers in a motion to court claimed that the dissenters had engaged in other acts of vandalism and harassment, which constituted contempt of the court order because they were interfering with the commercial operations of the colony.[65] However, at this stage, there was no court order excluding the dissenters from buildings other than the hog barns and metal shop. Nevertheless, apparently on the advice of their lawyers, the overseer group locked the dissenters out of the garage.[66]

The dissenters chose Remembrance Day to storm the garage, four days after being locked out of the garage. On 11 November 1987 Daniel Hofer asked William Hofer to open the garage just so that he, Daniel, could remove his forklift. When William opened the door, ten or so of the dissenters swarmed into the building. When William and Ike, of the overseer group, tried to prevent the dissenters from turning the power on, physical altercations ensued. The RCMP arrived and Larry Hofer, son of Daniel Hofer, was charged with assault causing bodily harm and assault with a weapon, for allegedly hitting William on the nose with a wrench.[67] Later that day, further violence broke out when Tommy Hofer, of the overseer camp, was driving a BobCat toward the garage and allegedly attempted to run down Paul Hofer Jr.[68] Tommy claimed that Paul Hofer Jr. jumped onto the BobCat and kicked his hands and head in an attempt to stop him from driving the vehicle to the garage.[69] Again the police were called in, and Paul Hofer Jr. was charged with assault causing bodily harm.

Another ugly confrontation occurred on 29 March 1988 when Joshua Hofer Sr. attempted to stop a vehicle carrying scrap from coming onto the colony. His story was that

> Daniel Hofer Sr. returned accompanying this vehicle and in spite of my instructions to the driver not to dump this load, Daniel Hofer Sr. instructed the driver to dump the load of armitures contained on the truck onto the Colony property. Daniel Hofer Sr. and Paul Wayne Hofer, followed me to the home of my son, Josh Hofer Jr., forced their way into his home and ripped the telephone off the wall and threw it outside as I was attempting to phone the Mounted Police for assistance.[70]

Daniel Hofer Sr. claimed that he was the one who was going to phone the police:

> After Joshua Hofer Sr. improperly attempted to interfere with a regular delivery of certain goods to the Colony for use in the scrap reclamation

business being operated by the Defendants, I attempted to use a telephone on the Colony to call the R.C.M.P. The said telephone is located in a building that serves not only as the residence of Joshua Hofer Jr. but also as an office for the business of the Colony and is normally used by such members without interference. I believe that Josh Hofer Sr. instructed Isaac Hofer to interfere with my use of the telephone. Isaac Hofer attempted so to do and Paul Wayne Hofer came to my defence with the result that Isaac Hofer engaged in a physical conflict with Paul Wayne Hofer during which conflict the telephone was inadvertently removed from the wall.[71]

The garage continued to be a flashpoint for violence. As the dispute escalated, more criminal charges were laid by the RCMP against members of both groups. By April of 1988, there were seven criminal charges against members of the overseer group and five charges involving the dissenting group.[72] The dissenting group did not want to share the garage any more than did the overseer group, and there were constant charges that one group or another was taking items belonging to the other group. It was impossible for the dissenters to do their welding and hoisting in the electrical shop, but they could easily modify the fire station at the colony to meet their needs.[73] If the fire truck were moved to the garage, the dissenters would give up the one bay of the garage that they were using and move to the fire station. But the overseer group never agreed to this solution to separate the parties and, in any event, the fire station was the working space for Joshua Hofer Sr.

So instead of rearranging the turf lines to accommodate the dissenters and keep the peace, at least until the trial was held, the overseers reversed their concession of the electrical shop and again attempted to get a court order to kick the dissenters out of all areas of the colony, including the dining rooms, kitchen, church, and school, and confine them to their living quarters.[74] Even more aggressively, the overseers also attempted to throw some of the men off the colony immediately and completely. The three young men targeted for immediate expulsion in March 1988 were Paul Hofer Jr., John Gerald Hofer, and Leonard Hofer.[75] Paul and John were sons of Rev. Paul Hofer, and Leonard was the son of Ben Hofer. These three men were adults but had never been baptized as members of the colony. The overseers also brought a private prosecution of petty trespass against Zach Gross, the runaway from Riverside Colony.[76] Given that Zach had permission from the dissenter group to be at Lakeside Colony, the charge was dismissed.

After several contentious hearings, the attempt to throw out the three men was dismissed, but another court order was issued on 4 May 1988 that attempted to draw a clearer line between the two camps. The order prohibited the named defendants from entering a long list of buildings at the colony and, most importantly, prohibited them from carrying on their scrap metal reclamation work on the colony property. However, it also granted to the dissenting group the right to use the electrical shop, the trailer, their homes, and the south stall of the garage to work on their own vehicles, and the overseer group was restrained from interfering in these areas controlled by the dissenters. So, while the overseer group had managed to reduce the territory of the dissenters even before any trial of the case took place, there was now a court order against the overseers to respect the little territory that the dissenters had.[77] But, as might have been predicted from the rejection of the fire hall alternative, the garage continued to be the flashpoint for further violence.

On 5 May 1988 Isaac (Ike) Hofer, one of the overseer members of Lakeside, and Rev. Paul Hofer, who was moving over to the dissenter side, had an altercation over a tractor in the overseer part of the garage. Previously, Paul had fixed up the old abandoned tractor and used it in the garden. The tractor was usually parked beside Paul's house. Ike Hofer took the tractor "without permission from Paul" and moved it into the garage to work on it, intending to use it to rototill around his own house. The taking of the tractor without permission made Paul angry and when he saw Ike working on it, he jumped on it to take it back to *his* house. Ike resisted this by pulling out the spark plug wires and smashing the starter to render the tractor inoperable. A physical altercation between the young Ike and the older Paul Hofer ensued. According to Paul,

> I indicated to the said Isaac Hofer that it was my intention to have the tractor removed from the garage. I went to the rear of the tractor to disconnect the roto-tiller and was jumped upon by Isaac. I fell on the roto-tiller with Isaac on top of me. He had a steel pipe in his hand and raised it over my head and said, "Nothing is going to happen to me, but you are going to shit" ... Just as Isaac was about to strike me, my son Paul Hofer Jr. arrived and pulled Isaac from me. Isaac fell on the floor and got up and proceeded to chase after my son but Isaac fell over the roto-tiller and appeared to sustain some injury to his ribs.[78]

Paul Hofer Jr.'s actions in coming to the aid of his father resulted in his being charged with assault and breach of the court order that prohibited him from leaving the south stall when in the garage. Not surprisingly, the story of Isaac Hofer differed in material respects from that of Paul. Isaac said that the tractor had been left abandoned in a slough for a week or so by youths and that he had no notice that Paul considered the tractor to be under his authority. Isaac said:

> I deny making any comments to Paul Hofer to the nature and extent as set out by him in his Affirmation, although I do admit that I had picked up a

steel pipe which was the extension bar for hooking up the roto-tiller to the tractor. Paul Hofer had previously removed this bar from the roto-tiller and placed it on the seat of the tractor. My intention was to take this bar and lock it up in the office of the garage together with the power takeoff in order that Paul was unable to abscond with the said tractor. I most emphatically deny that I ever threatened Paul Hofer in any fashion whatsoever with this steel bar nor in any other manner at this time ... That subsequent to these events, Paul Hofer advised his son, Stephen, to go get a wrench because it was his intention to start disassembling the mulcher or roto-tiller attached to the tractor. I positioned myself between Paul Hofer and the piece of machinery in order to prevent him from disassembling this equipment and it was at this point that Paul Hofer Sr. then called for assistance from his son who was working in the next stall in the garage ... Paul Hofer Jr. dashed into the stall ... threw me to the ground and started kneeing me in the chest so vigorously that it caused one of the ribs in my chest to be cracked and resulted in my having to seek medical attention at the emergency department of the Grace Hospital.[79]

Isaac also stated that after he left the garage to phone the police, he returned to the garage, whereupon Larry Hofer started pushing him around and an altercation broke out between the two groups. Paul Hofer Sr. had hotwired a second tractor and was moving it into position to drag the tractor in dispute out of the garage. Another tractor operated by a youth in the overseer camp was employed in a countermeasure of some kind. Paul Hofer Jr. then operated a forklift to disable the overseer tractor by lifting it off the ground in a way that was potentially dangerous to the driver. Joshua Hofer Sr. also claimed that he was assaulted while the tractor war was unfolding. Finally the police arrived on the colony, ending the skirmish before anyone was seriously hurt. Both Paul Hofer Jr. and John Gerald Hofer, sons of Rev. Paul Hofer, were arrested and taken into custody for assault and breach of the court order to stay in the one stall in the garage. The two young men were incarcerated for more than a week before bail was granted.[80]

The tractor war was just one of many incidents during the first two years of the conflict. The RCMP detachment in Headingley would be involved in an almost constant process of trying to maintain order at Lakeside Colony, by enforcing the court orders as to which territory the two groups were confined to. As well as laying criminal charges for assault, the RCMP laid charges against members of both sides for violating the court orders. By April of 1989 there were more than twenty criminal charges against the dissenting group alone that were scheduled for trial.[81] At this point, the provincial Crown prosecutions branch decided to stay the criminal charges dealing with breaches of court orders and inform the lawyers for the overseers that any future breaches would have to be handled by them through civil contempt proceedings.[82] The overseers claimed that the effect of this change of policy was that the dissenting group started to enter a number of buildings again, such as the kitchen and the metal shop.[83]

Another ugly confrontation between the two groups occurred when the dissenters removed a metal brake and metal shear from the stainless steel shop that they were prohibited from entering. Joshua Hofer Sr. stated that when he began to take pictures of the dissenters violating court orders, he was assaulted by John Gerald Hofer, and the RCMP were called in again. By the time the trial began, the animosity between the two groups at Lakeside was already at a level where any reconciliation seemed improbable. Both sides were entrenched in a very unhappy environment. Even the women associated with the dissenter group claimed that they were subjected to harassment and intimidation. According to Daniel Hofer Sr., "[m]uch tension has been created among the factions by the installation of listening devices by or on behalf of the Plaintiffs in the kitchen area so that they might overhear conversations among our wives and daughters who prepare food for us in the kitchen. Our wives and daughters were and are extremely offended at this practice and have, from time to time, ripped out wiring in the kitchen area that they believe to be connected to such listening devices."[84]

The Plaintiffs' Case
The trial finally commenced in the Manitoba Queen's Bench before Mr. Justice Ferg on Monday, 19 June 1989. The trial lasted three weeks, with testimony amounting to a transcript of over eighteen thousand pages; a selected group of exhibits alone added another four hundred pages.[85] There was not enough space in the courtroom for all the Hutterites who showed up to view the proceedings.[86]

In his opening remarks for the plaintiff overseers, Michael Radcliffe argued strenuously that the case should be confined to what happened at Lakeside in regard to the expulsion of Daniel Hofer, and that the court should not review the conduct of the senior elder and the affairs of the wider church. William Murray, who was conducting the case with Radcliffe, said that the plaintiffs were not seeking judicial review of the excommunication. Rather, the plaintiffs were asking the court to accept the excommunication as a fact and simply enforce it.[87] The plaintiffs were asking for the sword of the state to enforce an order of the church. For the defendants, Donald Douglas argued that the evidence should persuade the court to decline to enforce the purported expulsion.[88] Daniel Hofer and the other six defendants were not seeking a financial share of communal property so they could leave; all they were seeking was the right to remain on the colony.

The plaintiffs first called as an expert witness Dr. Victor Peters, a historian who had studied the Hutterites of Manitoba in the 1950s and written a highly favourable account of their way of life.[89] The thrust of Dr. Peters'

evidence was that the Hutterites were like a monastic order with democratic decision making, in which individualism needed to be wholly submerged into community identity and the individual must be unquestionably
obedient to the decisions of the majority once made.[90] The irony of having
a religion founded on principled rebellion from majority opinion turning
in time into a religion of majoritarian conformity was never explored.

As well as briefly highlighting Hutterian history and the structure of leadership at a colony, Dr. Peters asserted that the move to incorporate the church
at the federal level and the related adoption of a formal constitution for the
church were both completed as a response to concerns about governmental
action, but these were not documents that outlined the norms for how the
church operated internally.[91] The formal documents were written in outside law style in relation to demands of outside law but did not necessarily
reflect the inside law of the Hutterites.

On cross-examination, Dr. Peters asserted that the excommunication of a
male member from a colony meant that the wife and children of the man
had to choose between their religion and their husband or father.[92] If they
chose to follow the man out of the colony, they would have to leave the
colony with no property at all, however long they may have lived on the
colony. This was not unlike a person in a monastery who decides to leave.
Dr. Peters noted two levels of punishment available within the community
and gave them the German names: "Absonderung" – shunning – and
"Ausschluss" – excommunication.[93]

The plaintiffs then called another expert witness, Rev. Johann Christoph
Arnold, who was the senior elder of the Bruderhof. That the plaintiffs would
call on Rev. Arnold as a star witness on Hutterite beliefs and practice indicates the close alliance at this time between the leadership of the Schmiedeleut and the Bruderhof. That Arnold would be willing to give evidence on
behalf of a church seeking the power of the state sword to force so-called
ex-members off the colony would serve to increase the suspicion held by
many Hutterites that the Bruderhof influence on the Hutterite church was
dangerous.

Rather than looking at the formal outside law documents, it was through
Rev. Arnold that the ten baptismal points of Hutterites were introduced
into evidence as being the foundational inside law that should be examined by the court.[94] The allegations of the plaintiffs were that the baptismal
points constituted the contract, the inside law norms, and the expulsion of
the defendants was justified because they had breached the contract, particularly point number six, which stated: "Each must submit to and follow
brotherly warning, admonition, and discipline, and must practice the same
toward others in the House of God, so that no one may become co-guilty in
the sins of others."[95] But this term of the inside law contract was hardly free
of ambiguity. While the plaintiffs could point to Daniel Hofer's refusal to

accept discipline, Daniel Hofer would equally make the point that he had a duty to discipline as much as to accept discipline, and he had what he thought was evidence pointing to wrongdoing by the senior elder and the overseers of his colony. His refusal to step down from his allegations had to do with his refusal to be complicit in these so-called wrongful acts.

Rev. Arnold also gave evidence about the details of the baptismal, marriage, and Lord's Supper ceremonies, and provided a fairly lengthy exposition on Matthew 18:15-17 dealing with disputes between brothers. He outlined the three-step process of taking a matter up directly with a brother first, and then, if disagreement persisted, taking the matter up with a small group of two or three others, and, failing resolution in that forum, taking the matter in front of the church. At that final stage, a variety of disciplinary devices were available to lead the wrongdoer to repentance, but in some cases the penalty could be as high as excommunication. But even with excommunication, the goal was not penal but restorative: you wanted the wrongdoer to come back into the fold and you wanted thereafter to forgive him.[96]

In mentioning the range of disciplinary devices, Rev. Arnold noted the low-level punishment called Unfrieden. On cross-examination by Donald Douglas, this was explained as being excluded from a few church meetings, in contrast to Absonderung and Ausschluss. However, Rev. Arnold was quite vague about the distinctions between Absonderung and Ausschluss other than to suggest that the latter was a greater exclusion from the community than was the former.[97] As to whether there was a distinction between being in Ausschluss and being expelled from the colony, Rev. Arnold suggested that part of the baptismal vow was the promise to leave the community if ordered to.[98]

As to the idea of going to court to get the police power to throw people off a colony if they did not leave, Rev. Arnold testified:

Q. And what do you do? How do you get rid of him?

A. That's why we're here today.

Q. You go to the civil courts?

A. No, we don't.

Q. Not for anything?

A. I mean that is – that is not my – it depends. I mean if – we are citizens of a country, like of Canada or the United States and as citizens we also have certain rights, for example, freedom of religion, then we might ask for the protection of the court.

...

Q. In your experience have you ever heard of a situation where, in order to achieve the expulsion of a member off a colony, that the Hutterian community has resorted to the civil courts to get an order of the civil courts to achieve that?

A. I have never experienced it. I can speak only from my experience.[99]

Arnold was clearly on the defensive. His attempted escape hatch was to slide the case into the governmental arena, as if some fundamental issue of "freedom of religion" was at stake that the court needed to "protect." This sounded better than the reality that the church was unable to use physical violence to support its own internal norms and was going to the state to do so for it. "Freedom of religion" was being used not as a shield of the state to protect the group from attacks from without but as a sword of the state to deal with alleged attacks from within. Daniel Hofer had railed against the actions of the leaders of the church, and the church would supposedly collapse if the state did not intervene and protect it by forcing the so-called renegades out of the ark of salvation at the point of the state's gun. This was the plaintiffs' argument.

The issue of going to court to expel the defendants was also put into evidence on direct examination of the senior elder, Jacob Kleinsasser, who was the next witness:

Q. Reverend Kleinsasser, we've heard that the Hutterian communities are loath to come to the courts to seek aggressive acts. My understanding is that one of the vows of the Hutterian faith is that you are pacifists. Could you tell us, sir, what role you see for the civil court in the Hutterian lifestyle and in the Hutterian communities?

A. We go by Corinthians 7. I think it's Corinthians 7, where Paul, in his time and churches, rebuked the brothers that they were going to court one against the other, which is also not allowable to us today, real fundamental. If you're referring to the case at present why we're here in this court?

Q. Correct.

A. We were not asking to go to any court. We're going according the custom of ancient times. We believe according to the testament the government is ordained by God to protect the good and punish the evil. They are a protection to us by God, nothing unknown through the whole history of Hutterians that they were petitioning to the government and appealing to the government for various reasons. But it's also happened that they were dragged into court. In this case we have only been seeking the protection of the court to protect us from a rebellious, destructive situation that we were in. Not a brother, he was no brother to anyone anymore ...

Q. Have you faced divisiveness on previous occasions in the Province of Manitoba and had to resort to the courts for relief?

A. Yes. It also happened in the Hofer-Hofer case for their own benefit and for their own purposes or whatever it may be ... We resorted again to the government, as it is the custom, had always been ...

My lord, if you want to find where we have written it clear, you can find it in Peter Riedemann, "Authority of Government" I think, where it states as a – clearly how we stand with resorting to government and appealing.[100]

On cross-examination, Kleinsasser admitted that the legal action was commenced without first being approved by any meeting of the Schmiedeleut conference.[101] As to instituting a lawsuit, the cross-examination went as follows:

Q. In your experience as a senior elder of the Schmieden-Leut Conference, had you ever had cause to issue instructions to a lawyer to threaten, to institute legal action to effect the expulsion of a member of the Hutterian community from his colony?
A. Yes
Q. When?
A. Not I myself. But that sure happened by Interlake Colony ...
Q. Now, sir, it is my understanding that it is part of the Hutterian belief that you will not resort to the civil courts in order to effect a resolution of disputes among brothers; is that right?
A. This is not a dispute between brothers, and this is how it always had been understood.
Q. So that you are entitled, in your opinion, to resort to the courts as long as it's not dealing with the Brethren.
A. Right.
Q. And that is notwithstanding the provisions of First Corinthians 6.
A. No. It says brother and brother there.
Q. So in your view then, as long as Daniel Hofer, Sr. is excommunicated from the church, you were perfectly within Hutterian philosophy to seek the aid of the civil courts.[102]

Toward the end of the cross-examination, Donald Douglas returned to the issue of instituting a lawsuit:

Q. Now there was a question during the course of your examination concerning the case of *Hofer v. Hofer,* that is the 1966 case where you came to this court, and I put it to you that in *Hofer v. Hofer* what happened was exactly the opposite, that in *Hofer v. Hofer* there was a group of people and in that situation, which is entirely different from this situation, those people changed their faith. They changed their faith, and they sought a declaration of this court that the colony should be sold and the assets divided, and they sued and they dragged you into the world court in order to try to get relief. And upon their doing that, you responded in perhaps the only way you could have which was, you defended the claim and you sought the assistance of the court in removing them. I put it to you that this situation is entirely different. In this situation, you came to the court, you sought the assistance of the court, and Daniel Hofer Sr. and those with him simply responded months later. Now why did you come to the court?

A. We wanted them to vacate, I imagine.

Q. And on that basis alone you were prepared to put the affairs of the Hutterian Brethren Church before the world court?

A. Nothing to do with putting before the world court. The disobedience had to be removed.[103]

It is likely that the two senior elders, Arnold and Kleinsasser, had discussed the issue of initiating this lawsuit. They used the same argument of seeking the "protection of the court." They attempted to make the case look as if it was a matter of criminal law rather than civil litigation. Furthermore, Kleinsasser's use of the earlier *Hofer* case[104] as a precedent was effectively dealt with in cross-examination but, from an Anabaptist point of view, the most problematic admission by Kleinsasser was that he saw nothing wrong in aggressively suing a non-member. Kleinsasser took the one passage of Scripture dealing with disputes between Christians and then made the argument that because the defendants were not "Christians" in his view, properly so called, he could sue them.

The use of terms such as "protection of the court" served to feed the mistake made by the media. Report after report presented the trial as having been initiated by Daniel Hofer, when in fact it was the church that sued, while Hofer brought a counterclaim attached to the defence. But readers would not think this was the case as they read the following news reports:

Hofer has rejected more than 400 years of Hutterite tradition by taking the matter to civil court.[105]

Hofer and his supporters have filed suit to challenge the right of the colony to expel them and the colony had turned to the state to enforce the expulsion order.[106]

By dragging the matter into court, he said, Hofer has threatened this order to satisfy himself.[107]

Even when the plaintiffs and defendants finally got sorted out by the media, the situation was still misleadingly presented as if Daniel Hofer was the aggressive litigant, rather than the other way round:

> Renegade Hutterite Daniel Hofer sued the tradition-bound church after it asked the court to carry out an order to expel him from Lakeside colony near Winnipeg.[108]

Notice how the church is presented as "asking the court," but it is Daniel Hofer who "sued."

The Defendants' Case

It was the plaintiffs' position that the trial should be confined to the examination of how the defendants had breached Hutterite norms by not obeying the leadership and by not accepting the verdict of the majority and therefore the justifiability of expelling them from the colony. The position of the defendants was that the trial should expose the so-called wrongful actions of the leadership of the colony and particularly Senior Elder Kleinsasser. Donald Douglas at several points during the trial referred to a story in the *Great Chronicle* that highlighted the idea that a senior elder was not infallible and above correction.[109] The story involved a senior elder named Schutzinger who was the leader before Jacob Hutter. After a concern about the possibility that members of the community might be holding property for themselves rather than turning it over to the community, a search was made of members' rooms. Upon searching Schutzinger's room, a small amount of money was discovered. After being confronted with this, Schutzinger reached into the ceiling and pulled out a larger amount of money. Schutzinger was brought before the church and, even though he was the leader, he was judged as false and excommunicated.[110]

The complaints of Daniel Hofer against the senior elder brought out through cross-examination included more than the alleged violation of Hutterian doctrine in bringing a lawsuit against him, and bringing or threatening lawsuits through the front of C. and J. Jones Co. against certain colonies. In addition to the allegation that Crystal Spring Colony, which was headed by the senior elder, had "stolen" his invention and patented it, a host of other allegations were raised in the testimony. In the next section I will deal in more detail with the schism that developed within the Schmiedeleut conference over Kleinsasser's leadership as further information unfolded after the trial.

Donald Douglas opened the cross-examination of Jacob Kleinsasser by putting into evidence the fact that a corporation called H.B. Enterprises, of which the senior elder was one of two shareholders, had commenced a lawsuit against Don and Les Edel and Valley Agro Services Ltd. The statements of claim and defence were put into evidence.[111] It was then established that this lawsuit had its roots in a series of transactions going back to 1982. It was alleged that the senior elder had signed a broad power of attorney in favour of two men from New York who claimed they could get lower interest loans for the Hutterites. Mike Waldner, the leader of the Rosedale and Millbrook colonies in South Dakota, also dealt with the two New Yorkers. Later it was discovered that the men were con artists who defrauded Crystal, and particularly Rosedale and Millbrook, of millions of dollars.

To clean up the mess left by the con men, Senior Elder Kleinsasser, Mike Waldner, and Don Edel (who had unwittingly introduced the Hutterites to the con men) became involved in the formation of an Atlanta company called WELK Resources, which managed investments in oil workover rigs and other industries that the con men had acquired using Hutterite resources. Another corporation called RIDON was established as a limited partnership with WELK. Through H.B. Enterprises, Kleinsasser and Waldner were now suing Don Edel for allegedly failing to pay money owed to WELK Resources. While not much detail on these transactions was brought out at the trial (and I will deal with these matters in far more detail in the next section of this book), the evidence was raised in an attempt to establish two points. First, that the senior elder was involved in enterprises that went far beyond the traditional colony-based agricultural enterprises. Donald Douglas on behalf of the defendants suggested that this violated the narrower purposes allegedly permitted by the federal incorporating statute, or the constitution of the church. Second, while there was no evidence beyond the bad luck of dealing with the con men, the fact that Crystal Spring had lost money provided a good motive for that colony to acquire the profit-making patent of a hog feeder and suppress the claim of Daniel Hofer for Lakeside. Thus, the expulsion of the defendants was alleged to be a consequence of a conspiracy to "steal" the invention and then to get rid of the defendants when they did not go along with it.

In addition to the financial mess caused by the con men, another major allegation brought against the senior elder was his support and involvement with a Hutterite-owned hog-killing plant in Neepawa. When meat-packing plants closed in Winnipeg, this hog plant had been started by Spring Hill Colony and headed by Michael Wollmann, who was also the overseer president of Lakeside. As the hog plant proceeded to lose millions of dollars, the wider Schmiedeleut conference, headed by Jacob Kleinsasser as senior elder, agreed to buy into it and assess a hog levy for the plant on every Hutterite hog sent to the marketing board. The economic stability of the plant was a continuing problem, however, and the hog levy turned out to be controversial within the conference. According to the defendants, the hog levy was enforced by threatening to withdraw the privilege of having the Lord's Supper at Easter for colonies that were resisting it. The defendants alleged that, despite the levy, the Hutterite hog-killing plant continued to lose millions of dollars.

Again without going into the detail at this stage, the point of this evidence for the defendants was the attempt to show that Michael Wollmann was in a deeper relationship with Jacob Kleinsasser than would be most other ministers. As overseer head of Lakeside, he allegedly needed the support of the senior elder for the wider financial involvement of all Manitoba Schmiedeleut colonies in an effort to save his own colony's hog-killing plant just when the patent dispute came up, and thus Wollmann too had every incentive not to support Daniel Hofer's claim against Crystal Spring Colony. As with the allegation dealing with WELK, another argument was that the hog plant was a commercial activity that violated the traditional bounds of what Hutterites considered religiously acceptable for a colony. The hog plant, while owned by Hutterites, was managed by non-Hutterites, was not on a colony, and had union workers.

The plaintiffs, of course, asserted that all this evidence of various financial transactions involving the senior elder and Wollmann and Waldner had nothing whatsoever to do with the excommunication of Daniel Hofer at Lakeside. For example, a sharp exchange occurred in the cross-examination of Michael Wollmann:

Q. Sir, why wouldn't you investigate the allegation [of Daniel Hofer re the hog feeder]?
A. I didn't have to. I didn't know anything about it. As management, it was just short and sweet. And he insisted it's his, "It's mine." He didn't adhere to the management at all. And it's serious. That offence is serious in a colony in taking every member – in a colony, it's taken very sharply that if he just doesn't adhere to management, he's got a problem.
Q. So you were more concerned about keeping Danny Hofer in line than you were about the well-being of Lakeside?
A. No. Prove it. If you say it, you prove it. I can open my book for Lakeside, and you open yours.
Q. What did you do to prove it? You went to the Crystal patent agent to prove it; is that –
A. No, I take it over all the ten year now. You say Lakeside and I go back from '79.
Q. Sir, I put it to you that the reason you didn't take up Daniel Hofer's complaint or cause or concern for the benefit of Lakeside Colony is that you were concerned about offending Jacob Kleinsasser.
A. Douglas, Douglas [shaking head], you pity me.[112]

The courtroom was packed with Hutterites from many colonies as the evidence of various transactions involving the senior elder and the loss of millions of dollars was brought out. According to the press coverage, the financial revelations were a shock to the audience.[113] If the early press coverage portrayed Daniel Hofer and his group as "renegades" and "dissidents," the tide turned to some degree as the leadership of the church came under increased scrutiny. After the trial, an account in *Christian Week* stated:

> But Daniel Hofer's lawyer, Donald Douglas, demonstrated that all was far from well among Hutterite leadership ... But the case in the Manitoba Court, described as the first in 464 years of Hutterite history to see Hutterites turning to civil authorities to oust someone from their midst, also showed up church leadership which was unwilling to let colony members into their actions, was quite prepared to tell an untruth, and engaged in a variety of dubious business enterprises far away from normal colony life ... Hutterites have had their confidence in their leaders shaken by the revelations of financial wheeling and dealing that few knew about. The widely-watched case has left the colonies troubled. Too much power was held by too few people who felt little need to answer for their actions.[114]

In a similar vein, the *Mennonite Reporter* stated: "But the case has also turned into an examination of church leadership, and the picture has not been very pretty. It has revealed financial dealings, use of power and an attitude toward the truth which seem at odds with the way of Christ."[115]

After extensive cross-examination of the three managers of Lakeside – Jacob Hofer, Michael Wollmann, and Joshua Hofer Jr. – the defence called only two witnesses, Daniel Hofer and his brother Rev. Paul Hofer, who was not actually a defendant in the main suit. It will be recalled however that two of his sons were defendants, and after being removed from his position as minister and then from his position as German schoolteacher, he was clearly in the dissenters' camp. Certainly his appearance as a witness for Daniel Hofer was the last straw, if there was any doubt left, that he too would be expelled from Lakeside.

After extensive examination and cross-examination of each of the defence witnesses, the judge, Mr. Justice Ferg, engaged in his own further examination of the defence witnesses. The tenor of his questions pretty well signalled what the result would be. Paul Hofer had been particularly out of control on the witness stand, raving about Kleinsasser and the overseers. At one point during the cross-examination, Mr. Justice Ferg commented, "You're a bit more righteous than the Lord himself at the moment."[116] In his subsequent judgment, Ferg J. commented that Paul Hofer "was at times almost hysterical and shouting on the witness-stand."[117] This theme was picked up in the press: "At times during his testimony, an argumentative Paul Hofer railed church lawyer Bill Murray. 'You've got no respect for this church,' he said. At other times, almost in tears, Hofer spoke bitterly of the need for a public court battle to solve an internal matter. 'This is a sad, sad deal,' Hofer said repeatedly."[118]

Judgment

In closing arguments on 13 July 1989, Michael Radcliffe portrayed Daniel Hofer again as the individualist rebel who railed against the leaders instead of being obedient, like any good Hutterite would be. As noted in the press, "Radcliffe portrayed Hofer, 54, as a stubborn and spiteful man who has ripped apart the religious sect because of a personal vendetta against Manitoba's Hutterite leaders, especially senior elder Rev. Jacob Kleinsasser. 'These are not the actions of a man who is in harmony, who has brotherly love,' Radcliffe said of Hofer's attempts to persuade others in the province's 78 colonies that Kleinsasser was leading the church astray. 'The impertinence of this man knows no bounds.'"[119] Donald Douglas, on the other hand, had made the point in final argument that the boundaries of church and state were at stake. If the state court was going to enforce ecclesiastical judgments, such judgments had to conform in process with minimal standards of fairness as judged by the outside law. He reviewed how the process used in this case involved breaches of the notice requirement, the right to be heard requirement, and the right to an unbiased tribunal.

The judgment in *Lakeside Colony v. Hofer* was delivered by Mr. Justice Ferg on 31 October 1989.[120] The decision strongly supported the position of the overseer group and went against Daniel Hofer and his supporters on virtually every key point. Mr. Justice Ferg rejected the contention that the senior elder and the overseers had engaged in a conspiracy to steal the invention and then expel Daniel Hofer when he objected. Even though Jonathan and Daniel Kleinsasser, who took out the patent for Crystal Spring, were never called at trial, and the actual issue of the invention and patent was a matter of Federal Court jurisdiction, Mr. Justice Ferg came as close to a ruling as was possible and suggested that the hog feeder was invented at Crystal Spring even if Daniel Hofer honestly believed he had invented it.[121] While completely rejecting the conspiracy theory, the only line of Mr. Justice Ferg's judgment that gave something to Daniel Hofer's complaint was: "I would only question the propriety of one Hutterite colony accepting money extracted from a brother colony on a patent infringement. Although perfectly legal, that would seem to me to be contrary to the spirit and tenants of the church, but I make no further comment."[122]

Aside from this concern, the idea that Daniel Hofer Sr. had grounds to complain about the overseers and the senior elder was rejected by Mr. Justice Ferg. He described the good work the overseers had done and then noted how Hofer characterized the leaders in his letters: "damning in the most vitriolic and malicious terms Reverend Kleinsasser and the overseers, accusing them of fraud, deceit, conspiracy and theft, and made other equally serious accusations. It will be remembered all the overseers had done was devote hours and hours of their time, energies and wisdom to put Lakeside back on its feet, both spiritually and temporally."[123]

Little did anyone know at the time of this judgment that in a few years time, all the charges that Daniel Hofer made against the senior elder would be brought out in the church, and rightly or wrongly, a majority of Schmiedeleut ministers would reject the leadership of the senior elder. The senior elder may have won the court case and been vindicated by Mr. Justice Ferg, who rejected Daniel Hofer's "obstinate and dissident conduct and words,"[124] but in the end, as we will see, partly because of the information brought out in the case, the court victory turned into defeat as the church was split into two.

In terms of the disciplinary process, Mr. Justice Ferg took the position that colonies were independent congregations and there was no such thing as a higher court to which Daniel Hofer had a right to appeal.[125] Mr. Justice Ferg held that according to the articles of association of the colony[126] and the constitution of the church,[127] a member of a colony could be expelled by majority vote of the members. It was not necessary to decide whether the excommunication took place at the 21 January 1987 meeting or at the 31 January 1987 meeting. That it did take place was undoubtedly true. Ferg J. asserted that "[e]xcommunication means you remove yourself from the church, you are no longer welcome there, you remove yourself from association with other members entirely, and it necessarily follows you must leave the colony."[128]

The nub of the case in terms of legal issues was the position taken by Mr. Justice Ferg on judicial review of the excommunication. Daniel Hofer, whether he had any cause to complain about the hog feeder or not, had refused to abide by the decisions of the majority of the group and in refusing to accept punishment had expelled himself from membership. The only judicial review of the expulsion that Ferg J. entertained was that the court could ensure that the colony had properly followed its internal norms in expelling the defendants. On this point Mr. Justice Ferg turned to freedom of religion and asserted:

One could find the disciplines of the church and consequences which flow from them, to be harsh, but again it is not for the court to criticize. This country has always allowed for complete freedom of religion, and our laws now, found in the Canadian Constitution, guarantee that no government, no court, no man or woman, shall interfere with that freedom. The Hutterite colonies, as they have been described, have survived and lived for centuries by adherence to their baptismal vows. Without that adherence by members who voluntarily choose, as adults, to accept those vows, the colonies would not survive. The colonies have an absolute right to survival on their own terms.[129]

Thus, Mr. Justice Ferg did not judicially review the merits of the decision to expel Daniel Hofer and associates, nor the harsh consequences of the decision, although he did note anyway that the colony had good cause to expel and that the harsh consequences of expulsion were accepted by Hutterites in their baptismal vows. Nor did Mr. Justice Ferg impose what I call the "outside law" concept of natural justice to the process of discipline inside the Hutterite colony, even though he again judged the procedure to be fair in any case. That Daniel Hofer would call for natural justice and then refuse to attend meetings of the colony and the conference did not sit well with the judge.[130] Freedom of religion meant that the court in its judicial review simply had to determine whether the religious group had followed its own norms before enforcing the expulsion. Mr. Justice Ferg held that Lakeside had properly followed the Hutterian norms on how a member was excommunicated. That the plaintiffs may have violated the norm against litigation was not acknowledged.

The final result was that Mr. Justice Ferg ordered that

Daniel Hofer Sr. must leave the colony, and harsh as it may seem, [be] stripped of all worldly goods as his vow provides. The other defendants, who after being forewarned, chose to stand with Daniel Hofer Sr. shall also remove themselves or be expelled from the Colony in the same manner. All defendants shall have sixty (60) days from the date of the filing of this order, to remove themselves from Lakeside Colony. The only way the defendants can have a stay from this order would be in the event they were properly repentant, sought forgiveness of the church and submit themselves humbly in whatever repentance may be ordered by the ministers and members of the congregation, even if that means relocation to another colony, if any will have them. I am certain that in the spirit of the graciousness and forgiveness of their church, members in turn may in their hearts accept the defendants' repentance, if offered.[131]

The effect of losing the case went beyond the order of the court that the defendants leave the colony. The Canadian tradition in litigation, which differs from the American tradition, is that the loser pays a portion of the winning party's cost of litigation. This means that the dissenters not only would have to pay for all the expenses of defending the lawsuit brought against them, but they would have to pay a substantial portion of the legal bills of the overseer group that had sued them. The Baker law firm eventually submitted a bill of costs to the defendants for around $50,000.[132] Of course, the dissenter group would also have a much higher bill from its own lawyer. If Hutterites are expelled from the colony without a penny of assets, how can they possibly pay legal bills that are incurred fighting their expulsion? The overseer group could of course claim that the effective date of expulsion was January of 1987 and therefore the property the dissenters had accumulated in running their own enterprises over the last three years could be used to pay the legal bills. However, it would not be long, once the dissenters embarked on an appeal, before the overseers would claim that all the dissenters' property belonged to Lakeside, even if acquired after January 1987.

Despite the rough going during the trial, the plaintiffs were very pleased with the judgment. Maybe going to court was a good idea after all? As reported in the *Winnipeg Free Press*, "[l]awyer Bill Murray said the decision is a complete victory for the Hutterite Church, adding the ruling enforces the concept that individual religious organizations can govern themselves. 'We won everything,' Murray, who represented the Hutterite colony, said. 'The ruling is absolutely one-sided in our favor.' Murray said that if Hofer and his followers don't comply with the court's order voluntarily, the RCMP or the sheriff's office will forcibly evict them."[133]

Senior Elder Jacob Kleinsasser was jetting between Bruderhof communities when the word of the decision came out. As noted in the press: "He learned of the decision upon arrival at a branch of the church in Farmington, Pennsylvania where the 350-member community joined Elder Jacob Kleinsasser in thanksgiving to God for the decision."[134]

Daniel Hofer, on the other hand, was resolute in his defiance:

"If they want me out, they must come and get me," Daniel Hofer said, following a Manitoba Court of Queen's Bench ruling upholding the right of church elders to expel him. "If we have to end up in prison it will have to be," he said in a telephone interview last night. "We can't leave the colony because we'd be breaking our baptismal vows," he said in an interview at his lawyer's office ... For his part, Hofer insists Kleinsasser and his financial wheelings and dealings are undermining the entire Hutterite Church. "We're doing this for the church," Hofer said Wednesday. "We've done nothing wrong."[133]

At the end of the trial Justice Ferg had complemented the spectators: "'You are all a credit to the ways of your faith.' he said. 'I am acutely aware you're all going through an agonizing experience. Just remember that you gain spiritually through suffering. Some good can come out of this and I hope you find peace in your hearts.'"[136] But, as we will see, the effect of bringing this case to court and the revelations arising from it involved years of subsequent torment and conflict that rippled through the whole Hutterite church, and particularly the Schmiedeleut and the Bruderhof. "Peace in your hearts" would be a very long way off, if it ever came at all.

7
Lakeside under Appeal

More Court Orders and Conflicts

Daniel Hofer Sr. and his associates would not leave Lakeside after the judgment of Mr. Justice Ferg. Instead, the case was appealed to the Manitoba Court of Appeal. It had taken about three years before the dispute had been adjudicated at the trial level, and it would be somewhat more than another year before the Manitoba Court of Appeal would issue a judgment. During this year of appeal, throughout 1990, the two groups at Lakeside would remain as before, not only shunning each other but continuing their war of litigation, intimidation, and even occasional violence.

A notice of appeal of the trial court decision was filed on behalf of the defendants on 12 December 1989.[1] The appeal was set for oral argument in the Manitoba Court of Appeal for 23 and 24 May 1990. Given that the case was under appeal, the dissenting group asked the overseer group to consent to a stay of the order of Mr. Justice Ferg that the seven main defendants remove themselves from the colony. Of course, the overseer group, as was the pattern in the litigation from the beginning, would grant nothing to the renegades, and so the dissenters were forced to apply for a stay by way of a motion in court, which the overseer group would contest. The overseer group wanted the defendants expelled immediately, even if the case was under appeal.

To support its case for expulsion, the overseer group brought a number of recent transgressions on the part of the renegades to the court's attention. Larry Hofer had turned the power on and off during a particularly cold day (minus thirty degrees centigrade), thereby "terrorizing" the ordinary residents of Lakeside. He had also allegedly destroyed or interfered with the electrical security system of the colony. Furthermore, Daniel Hofer and his associates had other disaffected Hutterites visiting him at the colony too often, eating and drinking at colony expense. The overseer group had blocked a road at the colony, supposedly to stop hunters from entering, and the dissenters had then unblocked the road. Some of the dissenters' associates, not subject to any court order, had acted in objectionable ways in the common dining room, so that ordinary members picked up their food and returned to their homes to eat rather than remaining in the dining room.[2] All these arguments were met with counter-arguments by the defendants. For example, Larry Hofer claimed he was only doing regular maintenance of the standby generator when he shut the power off briefly. The frequency of visitors to the colony was no different from previously. That individuals who had the right to enter the dining hall were being disruptive was denied.[3]

However, the strong point for the overseer group was the continuation and even increase in the objectionable enterprises of the defendants, despite the numerous court orders against them. The burning for copper, the increasing amount of junk that was brought to the colony as a result of the demolition work, and the increased number of wrecked vehicles bought to rebuild at the colony had turned Lakeside into a junkyard.[4] To get a stay of execution of the expulsion order, Daniel Hofer had to promise that the defendants would obey the existing court orders as to where and what they could do at Lakeside Colony. Indeed, Mr. Justice Ferg, although he granted the stay of execution, included a strongly worded threat that if the defendants violated the court orders, the stay would be set aside and "the responsible Defendants will be ordered to forthwith vacate Lakeside Colony."[5]

It did not take long for the overseer group to attempt to implement Justice Ferg's threat of removal. On Valentine's Day of 1990, Daniel Hofer Sr. entered the new pumphouse at Lakeside in order to speak to Joshua Hofer Sr. about a dispute over a band saw. Joshua was not there, but his son Ken confronted Daniel Hofer Sr. and ordered him to leave. A physical struggle between the two men ensued; afterward each claimed he was motivated by self-defence.[6] This incident prompted the overseers to bring a court motion to have Daniel Hofer removed from the colony.[7] However, because the new pumphouse was not within the territory prohibited to the defendants, Mr. Justice DeGraves did not expel Daniel Hofer from the colony[8] but amended the court order to include the new pumphouse and the new chicken barn.[9]

Shortly thereafter, the overseers again felt compelled to go to court: when the power to the colony failed, they discovered that the standby generator in the room attached to the electrical shop was not functioning properly. Although the power was restored without reliance on the generator, in the process of fixing the generator over the next few days, the defendants allegedly blocked access to the room and in other ways harassed the overseers.[10]

Appeal Hearing

The hearing of the appeal took place in May 1990. The grounds for appeal as disclosed in the factum of the defendants[11] included the assertion that the trial court had not made a proper finding as to the inside law of Hutterites on conflict resolution. There was evidence at trial that if one colony had a conflict with another colony, the matter would be brought to the higher level of the conference. There was also debate over the precise meaning of "higher court" for internal disputes at a colony, but at minimum it was established at trial that such a process did exist if leave to appeal was granted by the senior elder, who in this case, according to the defendants, had a conflict of interest. Furthermore, as to the formal norms found in the constitutions, articles of association, and incorporation documents, the court should hold the church accountable to follow its own formalized norms. The argument that Hofer had in effect expelled himself was inconsistent with the formal requirement of a vote by the members to expel a member.

Donald Douglas also made a distinction between excommunication and expulsion. He took the position that the court did not have jurisdiction to review the excommunication of the defendants; this was a matter that should be left to the ecclesiastical authorities. However, given that the right to remain on the property was in question, Douglas asserted that the court did have jurisdiction to review the decision to expel. Excommunication could arguably happen without the person being required to leave the colony: the person would simply be excluded and shunned in an attempt to bring him or her back into the fold. Expulsion from the colony, on the other hand, involved temporal issues that the courts had jurisdiction over. The expulsion involved civil rights of entitlement or use of property. The effect of Mr. Justice Ferg's order was that the court was dispossessing the dissenter group of all the property it was holding collectively and also forcing the dissenters off the communal land and colony that they had spent a lifetime contributing to.[12]

At minimum, before the court enforced any decision to expel, the decision should conform to the outside law notions of natural justice and (or) procedural fairness. The argument continued that procedural defects in the purported expulsion violated the three basic rights of notice, fair opportunity to reply, and the right to an unbiased tribunal. To take just one example, all the decisions made by the senior elder as to whether to investigate, grant a hearing in the conference, and so forth, were made when the elder had an undisclosed conflict of interest. As to the expulsion of Daniel Hofer, it could be argued that he had no specific notice that this issue was on the agenda of the meetings of 21 January and 31 January 1987; nor any specific notice that he had been expelled from the property until he received notice of the impending lawsuit to throw him off. As to the other defendants, Douglas stated that, according to the evidence,

> [t]he Senior Elder clearly testified that anyone who affiliates himself with Daniel Hofer Sr. in the dispute is automatically excommunicated without the need of a hearing, or counselling, or accusations, or approaches or discussions. He concluded by indicating that Paul Hofer Sr. as well as the wife of Daniel Hofer Sr., even though they are not parties to these proceedings,

are no longer members of the Hutterian Brethren Church even though there have been no hearings or any kind of process or a vote to excommunicate or expel them. Reverend Hofer confirms that no hearings were held for Daniel Hofer Jr., Larry Hofer or David Hofer and that they were expelled simply for having affiliated with their father.[13]

It should be noted that the defendants did not appeal the dismissal at trial of the counterclaim. The argument on appeal was simply that, for a variety of reasons, the expulsion was void and should not be enforced.

While the appellants' (defendants') factum was around one hundred pages in length, the respondents' (plaintiffs') factum was only twenty-four pages and simply reiterated that the defendants had broken their vows by being disobedient to the collective will:

> Several of the essential points of this faith are that the individual will sub-merge his own will and opinion in that of the congregation or group and will obey unquestionably the orders of their superiors ... He agrees to accept such Church punishments as may be imposed upon him. Custom dictates that he shall conduct himself in a modest and humble manner and not disrupt the regular and orderly proceedings of his Church members nor be disrespectful of the person or office of his Elders. He shall not associate with those individuals who are shunned or under the ban.[14]

The oral arguments in May 1990 before the Court of Appeal attracted a packed courtroom of Hutterite spectators and, like the trial, considerable press coverage. While Donald Douglas outlined the natural justice arguments and the need for the dispute to be handled by a proper appeal mechanism within the church itself, Michael Radcliffe, for the colony, spoke to the court about the human cost of the dispute, laying the blame for the suffering at Lakeside squarely on the shoulders of Daniel Hofer:

> "They have suffered and suffered and suffered," Radcliffe said ... "They have suffered to such an extent it has gone to the very root of their own exist-ence." For instance, he said, in keeping with beliefs of the religion, colony members cannot eat with others they feel are "unclean." Since Hofer and his followers have been allowed to remain in the community, although shunted from the group's activities, the other residents have been forced to retreat to their homes for meals rather than eat in the communal dining hall. "They are fragmented into family units," he said. "This in itself shows how two disharmonious groups cannot live on the same property."[15]

After the hearing, the decision of the Court of Appeal was reserved, and the two camps at Lakeside continued to live in tension with each other.

Escalation of Conflict While Waiting for the Appeal Decision

Daniel Hofer and some of those associated with him came close to being expelled from Lakeside in the summer of 1990 when the defendants were hired to tear down and salvage what they could of the old Ogilvie Flour Mill on Higgins Avenue in Winnipeg. Again, the grounds of Lakeside were being littered with pieces of scrap.[16] In June Mr. Justice Morse issued a specific order that the defendants "be enjoined and prohibited from accumulating, storing, saving or in any way placing upon the property of Lakeside Holding Co. Ltd. any scrap metal, salvage, lumber, grain, equipment, machinery or material which has been salvaged from the Ogilvie Flour Mill or any other site until further order of the Court."[17] An application was made within a month of the order to have all seven of the defendants in the main litigation immediately expelled from Lakeside because of the breach of this order.[18]

Joshua Hofer Sr. was in charge of taking pictures and documenting the items the defendants had brought onto Lakeside land.[19] At one point, while taking pictures of George Hofer (son of Rev. Paul) allegedly dumping garbage on Lakeside land, Joshua Hofer Sr. stated "[t]hat during the period that I was taking the aforementioned photographs, George Hofer turned the loader around and pursued me attempting to run me down. This loader is a 30,000 lb. vehicle and would have easily crushed me to death or injured me. I was on foot and had to jump behind the loader. I had to run for my life. I am a 56 year old man, a grandfather, and luckily still quite fit because otherwise I would have been injured or killed. I was in real fear of losing my life."[20] On the other hand, Daniel Hofer alleged, "I am advised by John Gerald Hofer and do verily believe that he observed the incident in question and says that it was provoked by Joshua Hofer attempting to mount the loader in question while expressing verbal threats to the said George Hofer. Apparently, George Hofer moved the loader while Joshua Hofer was in its immediate vicinity, or on it, but at no time attempted to injure the said Joshua Hofer."[21]

As to the material brought to Lakeside, in reply to almost every allegation, Daniel Hofer claimed that the material in question was not material from salvaging the mill or other sites but was used by the men in their trade. When the matter was brought before Mr. Justice DeGraves, he agreed that most of the material was indeed not within the prohibitions of the court order but that there were salvage items that had been brought to Lakeside, even if temporarily, and therefore the injunction had been violated.[22] If Mr. Justice Ferg's pronouncement had been followed to the letter, those who had brought the material to Lakeside would be expelled. However, Mr. Justice DeGraves was more generous. Given that the parties were waiting for the decision of the Manitoba Court of Appeal and that the items that could be classified as falling within the prohibition were not substantial, Daniel Hofer was fined $750 for the contempt of the court order, while Daniel Hofer Jr., David Hofer, and John Gerald Hofer were each fined $100.

In addition, the defendants were to pay the plaintiffs $525 in costs.[23] While the defendants had been saved from expulsion by the skin of their teeth, they nevertheless requested that the finding of contempt and the order that they pay fines be appealed to the Court of Appeal.[24]

In the fall of 1990, the overseer group intensified its efforts to get rid of the defendants from the colony. There was a rapid stream of notices of motion for contempt and requests for immediate expulsion. One, for example, was based on the clash that occurred in the garage on the evening of 10 October 1990. The defendants had purchased used fuel tanks and cleaned them up so as to install them at Lakeside for their own use. The overseers claimed wrongly that these tanks were salvage material and thus fell within the injunction that the defendants not bring such materials to Lakeside. But more controversially, when Daniel Hofer Jr. and George Hofer (a teenage son of Paul) moved one of the tanks into their stall in the garage to spray-paint it, another violent incident occurred.

Ike Hofer, the main garage mechanic for the overseer group, had moved a tandem truck into the stall next to the defendants' stall in order to change the oil. In the evening, Daniel Hofer Jr. asked Ike to move the truck; Ike refused but did not tell Daniel that there was no oil in the engine, meaning that the truck could not be moved immediately.[25] Daniel and George moved their fuel tank as far away from the truck and near the open door of the garage as the length of the air compressor hoses would allow and proceeded to spray-paint the tank. Because paint was drifting onto the truck, Ike Hofer took a garden hose and began spraying the truck with hot water to wash off the drifting paint. However, according to Daniel Hofer Jr., Ike deliberately sprayed the fuel tank and George and Daniel as well. This resulted in a confrontation. According to Isaac Hofer,

> Daniel Hofer Jr. attempted to rip the nozzle out of my hand and words were exchanged between himself and me ... I proceeded to persist in spraying the Louisville Truck with the water. Daniel Hofer Jr. then charged me that if I did not quit spraying with the hose that he would spray the entire Tandem Truck with paint. The situation quickly deteriorated whereby George and Daniel Hofer were wrestling with me to try and take the nozzle away from me. [After George shut off the water, h]e picked up the paint sprayer and Daniel Hofer instructed George Hofer to spray my person and he did and he covered my clothing and my hair with the same paint that had been used on the large steel tank ... I succeeded in turning the water supply back on in my hose and I proceeded to hose down George Hofer with water. George Hofer took the nozzle off the end of the paint sprayer and smeared paint over the entire Louisville Truck and in addition, my clothes as well ... After George Hofer smeared my person with paint from the paint sprayer I chased him from the garage and proceeded to clean off the truck.[26]

Whereas Isaac admitted that in the heat of the struggle he had sprayed George with water, Daniel Jr. denied that he or George had sprayed Isaac with paint:

I stepped between Isaac and the tank and he deliberately sprayed me with hot water from the hose. I grabbed the hose in an attempt to direct the water away from the tank. George Hofer disconnected the paint spraying equipment and turned off the water but in the ensuing struggle with Isaac Hofer, a can of paint attached to the sprayer came away from the sprayer and spilled over the three of us. In addition, Isaac Hofer kicked over a five gallon pail of the primer paint we were using which spread over everything in its immediate vicinity. At no time, to my observation, did George Hofer spray Isaac Hofer and I never stated that we would spray either the truck or Isaac Hofer with paint. In fact, neither George Hofer nor I did spray or smear paint on the truck and any paint that splashed the truck could easily be removed as it was a latex paint and readily soluble in water.[27]

The fight continued as Larry Hofer joined Daniel and George in confronting Isaac and his brother Tom, who was also cleaning the truck. It wasn't until the RCMP arrived that the nozzle wars, like the previous tractor wars, came to an end, at least for that day. The next day, as the fuel tank was again being spray-painted, the confrontation repeated itself, but this time with William Hofer, another brother of Isaac, who was washing down the truck. According to Daniel Jr.,

[t]he hot water in question is too hot to bear but, notwithstanding this fact, William Hofer sprayed water directly into my face. William Hofer soaked George Hofer with hot water and, in response, George picked up a handful of gravel and indicated to William that, if he sprayed him any further, he would throw the gravel. William Hofer then deliberately sprayed George once again and George responded by throwing gravel. The RCMP once again attended and, after the matter had been reviewed with them, offered to lay charges against William Hofer but I indicated to them that this would not be my wishes. We then proceeded to finish painting the tank in an orderly way.[28]

According to William Hofer, the stones in question ranged as large as half an inch to an inch.[29] The overseer group asserted that Daniel Hofer Jr. and Larry Hofer should be found in contempt of the order that they remain in the one stall of the garage, because both of them had entered the overseer area in their struggle with Isaac. George was not a defendant to the main litigation and thus there was no court order against him as to territory (though there was an order against him as to participation in junk reclamation activity since he was a defendant in the secondary lawsuit). Therefore the overseers asked for the immediate expulsion of only Daniel Jr. and Larry.[30] The overseers also claimed that the installation of the fuel tanks at Lakeside violated an earlier court order against the defendants regarding the erection or modification of buildings or structures at Lakeside.[31]

On 17 October 1990 Mr. Justice Kennedy allowed the defendants to use the fuel tank they had installed, and on 18 October 1990, Mr. Justice Morse rejected the argument that the fuel tanks were salvage within the meaning of any existing order. However, he adjourned the matters of the contempt motions dealing with the installation of the tanks, and violation of territory in the garage and the assault on Isaac Hofer, for the chief justice of the court to look into.[32] The chief justice then assigned these matters to Mr. Justice Ferg. On 6 December 1990 Mr. Justice Ferg found that Paul Hofer Jr. and Daniel Hofer Jr. had violated an order by erecting a structure to hold the new fuel tanks, and he fined each $500 plus costs of about $1,000.[33]

As the motions for contempt and expulsions continued to accumulate, Donald Douglas told the defendants that although he was representing them on the appeal, he could not run to the courthouse every day to deal with another Lakeside motion. On 21 November 1990 a notice was filed that the seven defendants would be acting on their own, without a lawyer.[34] The overseer group immediately seized the opportunity and filed yet more motions, this time concentrating on the enterprise of fixing wrecked vehicles and farm machinery. The overseers argued that this was also a "salvage activity" that fell within a previous court order and that David Hofer, Daniel Hofer Jr., Paul Hofer Jr., and Larry Hofer, the prime four engaged in this business, should be found in contempt and immediately expelled.[35]

While the contempt hearings related to bringing wrecked vehicles onto Lakeside land were adjourned for hearings in January 1991, the overseers were successful in getting a new order from Mr. Justice Ferg that prohibited the defendants from bringing wrecked vehicles to Lakeside in order to engage in the auto body business.[36] The order was potentially crippling to the enterprise of the defendants, as it stated: "This court orders that the defendants named herein and their associates be enjoined and prohibited from transporting or driving onto the property owned by Lakeside Holding Co. Ltd. any wrecked, damaged or disabled motor vehicles, tractors, farm implements, equipment and machinery of any kind whatsoever until further Order of the Court ... This court orders that Daniel Hofer Jr., David Hofer, Paul Hofer Jr. and Larry Hofer forthwith remove all wrecked or damaged motor vehicles, tractors, farm implements, equipment and machinery which they or their associates have brought onto the property owned by Lakeside Holding Co. Ltd."[37] Acting without a lawyer, Daniel Hofer Sr. immediately launched an appeal to the Manitoba Court of Appeal of the prohibition on fixing vehicles at Lakeside.[38] Just after Christmas, Mr. Charles Huband of the Manitoba Court of Appeal allowed the Daniel Hofer group to keep on an interim basis one highway tractor and one field tractor at Lakeside, but he did not stay the rest of the order that prohibited the dissenters from bringing damaged vehicles or equipment to Lakeside.[39] Thus, on the eve of the Court of Appeal judgment being rendered, the defendants' ability to generate funds to sustain the dissenting group at Lakeside was under intense attack. When the decision of the Court of Appeal went against the dissenters, one might have concluded that this would be the end of the road for them. But that would be to underestimate Daniel Hofer Sr.'s stubbornness and that of his lawyer, Donald Douglas.

Manitoba Court of Appeal Decision

The judgment of the Manitoba Court of Appeal was delivered on 23 January 1991.[40] By a margin of two to one, the judgment of the trial court was affirmed. However, it is important to note that, aside from affirming the result, the reasoning of the Court of Appeal differed significantly from the trial decision. The majority decision of Mr. Justice Huband (Mr. Justice Lyon concurring) and the dissenting judgment of Mr. Justice O'Sullivan had some points of agreement. Both decisions asserted that the court could judicially review the excommunication of the defendants by applying the rules of natural justice to the process used at Lakeside. Both judgments also went beyond this, asserting that even if the process was fair, the court could review the merits of the decision, at least to the extent of being satisfied that there was reasonable cause for the expulsion. This potential review of the merits of decisions made by ecclesiastical bodies (as opposed to procedure only) might potentially be dangerous to the integrity of religious organizations as courts get entangled with issues of doctrine that they are ill-suited to deal with.

The fundamental disagreement in the decision was that Huband J.A. for the majority held that the process used at Lakeside to expel the defendants did not violate the rules of natural justice, and that there was also reasonable cause for the decision to expel the defendants, whereas O'Sullivan J.A. in dissent asserted that the Lakeside process had violated the rules of natural justice, and there had not been a good reason to expel the defendants. As to the rules of natural justice, Mr. Justice O'Sullivan was of the view that the purported excommunication or expulsion did not occur at the meeting of 21 January 1987 but at the 31 January 1987 meeting.[41] Daniel Hofer did not excommunicate himself by refusing to accept the shunning verdict at the 21 January meeting but, rather, after the consultation with the senior elder on 31 January, a meeting at Lakeside was held where those in attendance at the meeting voted to excommunicate Daniel Hofer. Even though Daniel Hofer and two of his sons were invited to the meeting, O'Sullivan concluded that they were not given explicit notice that their excommuni-

cation and expulsion was the topic of the meeting and they were not therefore provided with an opportunity to be heard on whether they should or
should not be expelled.[42] As to the subsequent meetings of conference ministers that Daniel Hofer declined to participate in, O'Sullivan J.A. said:

> There is no doubt that he was invited to a number of meetings at which he
> was told he would have the opportunity to prove his allegations against the
> elders of the church. But this notice was far from satisfying the requirement
> of natural justice, in my opinion. What was needed was the articulation of
> an offence which would have justified excommunication. In fact, he was
> excommunicated because he was a "railer," because he criticized the elders
> of the church in what appeared to them as an unseemly way. He was never
> charged with this offence or given the opportunity to defend himself against
> it. On the contrary, he was excommunicated on the spot when he criti-
> cized. When he appealed to a higher court within the church, he was de-
> nied a hearing at which the question of his excommunication would be
> reviewed. He was given an opportunity to prove his allegations, but that is
> quite a different thing from being given the opportunity to defend himself
> from the allegations of disobedience and criticism, and from the allega-
> tions that such disobedience and criticism were sufficiently grave to war-
> rant excommunication and expulsion.[43]

As to the merits, Mr. Justice O'Sullivan painted a very different picture of
Daniel Hofer compared with that given in the trial judgment. The idea that
the defendants could be expelled from the church for disobedience of the
orders of the overseers clearly touched a raw nerve in O'Sullivan J.A. His
language became extravagant and provocative:

> [T]he effect of the decision of the majority in this case is, in my opinion, to
> place Hutterites in a state of bondage ... the effect of the majority decision
> must be compared to the famous Dred Scott decision which did so much
> not only to discredit American justice, but also to bolster the institution of
> slavery in North America. In my opinion, the unintended effect of the deci-
> sion of the majority in this case is to impose bondage on thousands of our
> fellow Hutterite citizens ... It would indeed be surprising if the tradition of
> anabaptism espoused by Hutterites should end in a regime where the tyr-
> anny of a Kleinsasser and other elders should outrival the worst pretensions
> of Popes and prelates of times past ... In my opinion, it is not part of the
> Hutterite covenant to provide blind obedience to elders or to men of any
> kind ... But the effect of the majority judgment, in my opinion, turns
> Hutterites into zombies who can be expelled from the church for daring to
> question the conduct and orders of the elders, at least if such questioning is
> vigorous and determined. If Hutterites are so bereft of freedom that they

cannot challenge the establishment without fear of being thrown out without even the shirt on their backs then theirs is a condition of slavery ... Yet Hutterites who are formed since childhood to accept the way of life of the Hutterites are condemned to a form of slavery worse than the slavery of the blacks in the United States. Their only recourse against the unjust conduct of the elders is to speak out at the risk of losing their livelihood ... Much has been said in this case about freedom of religion as if the Canadian *Charter of Rights and Freedoms* protected religious bodies in their freedom to oppress their members. What the *Charter,* as distinguished from the American First Amendment, protects is not freedom of a religious group to conduct itself in whatever manner it pleases, but rather the freedom of the individual to liberty of conscience and religion. I see nothing in the Hutterian belief or practices which militate against liberty of conscience ... I would not be prepared to disturb the finding of the learned trial judge as to the conduct of Mr. Kleinsasser and the other elders, but I think the evidence is overwhelming that Mr. Daniel Hofer Sr. had good cause to question what the elders were doing.[44]

Mr. Justice Lyon, who concurred with the majority judgment of Huband J.A., had this to say about some of O'Sullivan's comments: "With respect, these comments are completely unwarranted. They bear no relevance whatsoever to the facts and circumstances or to the trial and majority judgments of the case at bar. They represent, at best, an overdrawn and mischievous flight of fancy in a dissenting opinion which otherwise deserves to be read and considered seriously."[45]

Whatever the extravagance of the language, the dissent of O'Sullivan was probably crucial to the ability of the dissenters to prolong their time at Lakeside. There is no right to appeal a case involving civil litigation to the Supreme Court of Canada in Ottawa; rather, that court must grant leave to appeal based on the importance of the case. It is far easier to argue before the Supreme Court that the legal issues in question should be reviewed when there is a vigorous dissent at the provincial Court of Appeal level as to what the law ought to be, as compared with a situation where the Court of Appeal decision is unanimously against a party seeking leave to appeal. Thus the dissent of O'Sullivan provided the dissenters with a leg to stand on in the subsequent leave to appeal process.

Huband J.A., for the majority, rejected the argument that excommunication was different from expulsion. He took the view that at the meeting of 21 January 1987, Daniel Hofer Sr. was offered Absonderung, a mild form of punishment. In refusing to accept the punishment, Daniel Hofer Sr. expelled himself from the church. Huband J.A. stated:

It does not appear that any formal vote was taken to confirm the excommunication of Daniel Hofer Sr. from the congregation. There was simply a common understanding that if one did not submit to absonderung the only alternative was excommunication. It might seem incredible that the degrees of punishment should be escalated so dramatically, but there is logic to it. The shunning is intended as a temporary condition, lasting until the individual is ready to accept the will of the community, and resume his place within it. But if it becomes clear that there is no willingness to accept the shunning, and therefore no hope of reconciliation, then the only alternative becomes excommunication, and expulsion from the colony.[46]

Huband asserted that the excommunication was confirmed by the members of Lakeside at the meeting of 31 January 1987.

Huband J.A. put the rules of natural justice into the context of the Hutterian traditions. Regarding formalities such as having proper notices of meetings and the like, he asserted that Daniel Hofer could hardly claim to be surprised that his conduct would be the subject of the meetings of 21 and 31 January.[47] As to the meetings held after 21 January, Huband J.A. stated: "Daniel Hofer Sr. and his followers were afforded the opportunity to attend and explain, and perhaps begin a process which would lead to reconciliation. They elected not to do so. Under these circumstances, a complaint of procedural unfairness seems out of place."[48]

In regard to the sufficiency of the cause for expulsion, Huband J.A. focused on obedience: "Obedience is crucial. The colonies themselves make many of their own decisions, particularly those related to business operations. A majority vote decides matters, but it is simply a majority of the adult male members of the community. Once a decision is made, strict adherence is demanded from all the colony. The promise of obedience in the baptismal vow is the practical requirement of maintaining the system. Dissent, non-co-operation, or rejection of majority decisions makes the successful operation of a colony next to impossible."[49]

Even though he upheld the trial court decision, Mr. Justice Huband's portrait of Daniel Hofer Sr. was more positive than the one given in the trial decision of Mr. Justice Ferg. Huband J.A. said: "Although I dismiss the appeal, I have considerable sympathy for Daniel Hofer Sr. and his followers. Concerning Daniel Hofer Sr. himself, I find his stubborn and relentless pursuit of his idea of justice to be admirable. Unfortunately, what is commendable in a larger society becomes destructive in the context of a Hutterite Colony."[50]

Furthermore, as has happened in courts in the past, Mr. Justice Huband was not entirely happy with the consequences of his decision. The effect of the enforcement of the church punishment was that these people would be sent out into the world without any share of the church property. Mr. Justice Huband stated: "As to Daniel Hofer Sr. and the others, it seems manifestly inequitable that these individuals should be forced out of the colony without a share in the value of the property that they have helped to acquire and develop. Further, it is cruel to require wives and children of expelled members to either separate and stay or be cast adrift with husbands and fathers without any material resources."[51]

Michael Radcliffe had made the argument in his closing remarks that while the dissident group should leave the colony without any of the property belonging to the colony as of the January 1987 expulsion, the group had since that time earned money from their own enterprises, so it was hardly accurate to say that they would leave the colony with no resources. Yet, as became apparent during the second round of litigation, it would be only a matter of time before the overseers changed their minds and tried to kick the defendants off the colony, while at the same time claiming all the assets that the group had acquired since 1987. Despite judicial regrets about the effect of its decision, the majority of the court nevertheless ordered the seven defendants to vacate Lakeside.

Reaction and Final Appeal

Daniel Hofer's reaction to the Court of Appeal decision was reported in the press:

> "No court can force me to break my vows I made with God. That's between me and God," Hofer said ... "In the end, it's going to be the Hutterite Church that resolves this matter. This is a religious problem. There's no way an outside court can resolve this," Hofer said ... "He (Kleinsasser) says we broke our vows. That's the only reason we're staying, that we won't break our vows" ... Kleinsasser, "sold his birthright to the judge and lawyers in Winnipeg. Like Saul, he went to the witches when he was in trouble. He turned away from the Lord," said Rev. Paul Hofer, Danny's brother.[52]

Now that the Court of Appeal had confirmed the decision of Mr. Justice Ferg, the overseer group immediately sought to evict the seven defendants from Lakeside. A notice of motion to evict was filed on 29 January 1991, as well as a demand that the defendants remove all their equipment from Lakeside and pay the $40,000 in costs for the trial level to the Baker law firm.[53] While the dissenters were now acting without a lawyer in the face of the motions that were constantly brought against them, Donald Douglas did file a motion in the Court of Appeal for a stay of the order of expulsion pending a decision to seek leave to appeal to the Supreme Court of Canada.[54]

On 31 January 1991 Mr. Justice Kerr Twaddle of the Manitoba Court of Appeal ruled, despite the strenuous arguments of Radcliffe on behalf of the overseer group, that it would be unreasonable for the Hofer group to be expelled, at least until the leave to appeal decision had been made by the Supreme Court.[55] However, the stay was subject to all the previous court orders that restricted the dissenters' movements and activities at Lakeside. Indeed, Mr. Justice Twaddle added another clause of his own, that "the parties hereto and those affiliated with them are not to act in a manner reasonably likely to result in a breach of the peace at Lakeside Colony."[56] If the leave to appeal was granted by the Supreme Court, Twaddle J.A. would decide at that point whether a further stay of the order would be granted. Obviously, if the Supreme Court refused leave to appeal, that would be the end of the matter, and the defendants would be forced off Lakeside.[57]

As it turned out, leave to appeal was granted by La Forest, Cory, and Stevenson J.J. on 4 July 1991. No reasons are ever given as to why Canada's highest court decides to hear a particular case. One can only surmise that the state enforcement of ecclesiastical judgments to remove people from colonies, leaving them penniless, was sufficiently important that the court decided to examine it.

When the dissenters moved in the Manitoba Court of Appeal to extend the stay of eviction now that the Supreme Court had agreed to hear the case, the motion was again fought by the overseer group, which wanted the dissenters removed. But the claims of new sins that it presented were weak. The group argued that the renegades had dumped plasterboard and gravel from a wrecking site onto the Lakeside yard, once burned copper in a trash barrel, fixed a truck in the garage stall, and held a wedding party for Paul Jr. which was too loud, and that the trailer that had been formerly used by the overseers was now full of unwanted renegade household items.[58] Furthermore, the renegades had fed lunches to workers outside the colony and had left the garage door open on cold days, and the wives and children of the renegades were sometimes abusive in the kitchen to those members who had good standing in the colony.[59]

The "renegades" argued that the gravel and plasterboard were in fact used to construct a volleyball court for children, the burning barrel contained sweepings from the electrical shop, the truck that was in the garage briefly for repair was taken there on the plea of a friend who asked for help when it broke down close to the colony, the wedding party was no different from any others that had been held at Lakeside, and on it went.[60] Not surprisingly, the Court of Appeal extended the stay of expulsion pending the hearing and decision by the Supreme Court of Canada.

Notice of appeal on behalf of the defendants to the Supreme Court of Canada was filed on 23 September 1991. Oral argument before a panel of seven Supreme Court justices did not take place until 5 May 1992. The judgment of the court was delivered on 29 October 1992. Thus, the effect of appealing the decision to the Supreme Court was that the defendants were allowed to stay at Lakeside for several more years, even though there had been a trial court decision and majority decision of the Court of Appeal that the overseer group could evict them using the power of the state sword.

Eviction While Waiting for the Supremes?

While the eviction of the defendants had been postponed by taking a further appeal to the Supreme Court of Canada, the court orders restricting the defendants' activity at Lakeside continued. As well as the orders relating to territorial boundaries between the two groups and prohibiting the bringing of salvage materials to Lakeside, the most recent order of Mr. Justice Ferg, that the dissenters should not bring any motor vehicles or farm implements to Lakeside for purposes of fixing, was particularly crushing to the dissenter group.[61] It was now pretty much impossible for the dissenters to work at Lakeside. Given the predicament they were in, an old friend of Daniel Hofer offered to rent his small farm (240 acres) to the dissenters with an option to eventually purchase it. The farm was in the municipality of Rosser, north of Winnipeg, and the owner of the land was Abraham Block, who lived in Winnipeg. The dissenters rented the Block land, intending to live on it if they were evicted from Lakeside. They moved fire-damaged trailers onto the land to be fixed up in at least a minimal way, to provide housing should they be evicted from Lakeside. In the meantime, the dissenting group started operating its salvage business from this land.

The new work location turned out to be no more inviting than Lakeside, although this time, rather than the overseer group, the adversary was the municipal authorities, who soon were alerted to the piles of equipment and to the salvage operations that were being conducted on land zoned as agricultural. However, before the conflict on the Block land came to a head, the animosity of the overseer group toward Daniel Hofer and his supporters reached a high point, in the first few months of 1991. Instead of being content with the new reality that the dissenters were away most of the time working at the Block farm, the overseer group decided to display in a decisive way that they controlled Lakeside territory.

If the overseer group could not evict the dissenters, despite the numerous court orders and charges of contempt of court and the appeal judgment that confirmed the legality of the church eviction order, the overseer group would try to at least get rid of all the property at Lakeside that the dissenters were using in their enterprises, even though much of the dissenters' equipment had already been moved to the Block farm. The overseers noted that the dissenters were still using a loader at Lakeside that they had restored, and that they had brought a truck cab, a mixing machine for flour, a loader frame from a burnt tractor, and a golf cart to Lakeside.[62] Mr. Justice Ferg ordered that the sheriff could remove the equipment and charge the costs of removal to the dissenters.[63] As reported in the newspaper, "Hofer came home Friday to find that a front-end loader and golf cart had been towed away by order of the colony's elders. Winnipeg lawyer Michael Radcliffe said ... 'The elder's attitude is: if you want to do these kinds of things, do it on your own property, not on our property ... It's a breach of authority. It turns on who is going to control the property.' ... Radcliffe said Hofer is free to remove the loader and cart from a Winnipeg compound."[64]

Again acting without a lawyer, Daniel Hofer filed a notice of appeal of this decision to the Manitoba Court of Appeal.[65] In response, the overseer group stated that the renegades had never given a dime of money from their own enterprises to help pay for the food and lodging that had been provided to them and now that they had their own property (the Block land), they could move their stuff there.[66] Daniel Hofer asserted that fixing damaged vehicles was the main source of income for the dissenter group to pay for all those items that the overseer group refused to provide.[67] However, the appeal was dismissed by Mr. Justice Twaddle after a hearing on 28 February 1991.[68]

The overseer group then made a list of thirty-one pieces of equipment, materials, and vehicles they wanted removed from Lakeside property.[69] The sheriff's office was not willing to seize these items unless Lakeside Colony signed an indemnity agreement for the costs of moving and storage and future litigation costs involving these items, if the dissenters would not or could not pay these costs.[70] Armed with the indemnity agreement, the sheriff's office made a contract with Hi-Way Towing to remove the items. On the morning of 13 March 1991, accompanied by a fleet of heavily armed RCMP and sheriff's officers, a convoy of three flat-deck trucks, two one-tonnes, two tractor-trailers, one semi-tow truck, and one front-end loader rolled into Lakeside Colony to remove the equipment and so-called junk of the Donald Hofer group. As reported in the press, "[o]ne sheriff's officer – who asked that his name not be used – said RCMP and sheriff's officers wore bulletproof vests, fearful of the possibility the Hutterites might retaliate. 'It was going to be hairy,' the officer said. 'Everyone was wearing vests here. We were informed there would be arms here, but it went all right.'"[71] That police officers believed, rightly or wrongly, that they needed bulletproof vests when coming onto a Hutterite colony is a sad commentary indeed.

Daniel Hofer was particularly upset that the raid on the equipment came at a time when the dissenters were attempting to move stuff to the Block farm, and that the very equipment that was being used for moving was itself seized. In particular, Daniel Hofer said that a Caterpillar front-end loader and a John Deere tractor were parked on the highway allowance when the armed enforcers for the state loaded them and took them to a compound in Winnipeg.[72] The overseer group denied that the vehicles were on the highway rather than on colony land when seized.[73] According to Daniel Hofer, the point of the raid at a time when the dissenters were moving their stuff to the Block farm was not so much a genuine desire to clean up Lakeside land as it was another step in trying to intimidate the dissenters and finally drive them away.[74] The dissenting group had to pay $15,000 for the hauling and storage fees to get its equipment back.[75]

That Daniel Hofer was not a purist when it came to launching his own lawsuits is indicated by the fact that he went to small claims court against Hi-Way Towing, alleging that it had removed fifty sheets of wood that went beyond the terms of the court order.[76] Paul Hofer also sued in small claims court, alleging that those items belonging to the women of the dissenter group that were beyond the terms of the court order were also seized.[77] Both these claims were dismissed by a small claims adjudicator. Daniel Hofer brought motions related to the seizure of property, including one that alleged Mr. Justice Ferg was biased against the dissenter group and should not be the judge hearing further motions involving the case.[78] Alleging that a judge is biased against you is hardly a promising tactic to embrace in the course of litigation. On hearing the motion, Mr. Justice Hanssen told Daniel that the proper procedure was to ask the judge hearing the motion to disqualify himself or herself, and if he or she denies the argument of bias and does not do so, the next step would be to appeal the issue to the Court of Appeal.[79]

Difficulties on the Block Land

Lakeside Colony now looked nicer, even if it was a more bitterly divided territory than ever before. However, for the dissenters, the Block land did not turn out to be a haven, even though the dissenter group successfully obtained several demolition contracts, outbidding Winnipeg demolition firms who then claimed that government regulations were needed because the Hutterites could outbid them, since the communal group did not have to pay worker's compensation or minimum wages and the like.[80] In May of 1991, the South Interlake Planning District Board launched a lawsuit against Abraham Block as owner of the land and Daniel Hofer as the user of the land.[81] The Block land was zoned agricultural, but the property was being used for burning of scrap, burying refuse and stockpiling junk.[82] The Planning Board sought an interim injunction to prohibit Hofer from using the land contrary to the zoning law and also an injunction to restore the land to its former state. At the end of May 1991, Daniel Hofer appeared without a lawyer at a hearing before Mr. Justice Kroft who then issued a court order prohibiting the Lakeside dissenters from "operating a metal salvage business on the land in question and from continuing to stockpile or burn scrap metal or related materials."[83] Daniel Hofer made a motion to have the injunction lifted, but after a hearing before Mr. Justice Hanssen, this motion was dismissed.[84]

Neither Daniel Hofer nor Abraham Block filed a statement of defence to the claim, and the dissenter group carried on with their activities on the Block land, despite the court order against them. The accumulation of junk on a portion of Hutterite property would probably not be very noticeable to immediate neighbours given the size and relative isolation of most colonies. However the neighbours around the Block farm were hardly happy with the constant burning, the accumulation of unsightly scrap, and the heavy truck traffic to and fro. The neighbours made a series of complaints to municipal officials.[85] Brian Savage, investigator for the Board, stated that "in the past thirty years I have had considerable contact with farmers and I have never seen a farmsite or farm operation in shoddy conditions similar to those which I observed on the subject property. I observed equipment and machinery strewn on the site which were not functional and/or had no connection with a farm operation of any sort."[86] While one can understand the frustration of the dissenters at not being able to work at Lakeside, and also having to live under the constant threat of expulsion, the behaviour of the group toward the municipal officials was hardly an example of fostering a positive image of Hutterites in the host society. Municipal officials were allegedly met with foul language and their attempts to serve court documents were met with hostility and even intimidation.[87]

When the case was tried before Mr. Justice Mykle in March of 1992, he concluded that Daniel Hofer was violating the permitted agricultural uses for the land under the zoning law, and that a permanent injunction should be issued. Furthermore he concluded that a mandatory injunction should be issued requiring Daniel Hofer to clean up the land so as to restore it to its previous condition. Mr. Justice Mykle stated:

> To what degree has the property changed since April 1, 1991? It has been established that the property was clear of debris and buildings until Hofer took possession of it. Since then, it has become a blight on the landscape with an incredible collection of old motors, trailer vans, scrap lumber and metal, concrete rubble, partially demolished camper trailers, damaged trucks and truck bodies, and an aggregation of other items related to Hofer's salvage operation, and with no connection to any agricultural purpose.
>
> Hofer has been warned repeatedly and constantly by the plaintiff about the non-conforming uses to which he has put the property. He has ignored the interim injunction, and has knowingly failed to comply with the requirements of law. The plaintiff has proceeded with vigilance, in attempting firstly to reason with Hofer before resorting, in a timely fashion, to the Courts. Hofer has proceeded deliberately on a course of conduct which he knew was not permitted.[88]

Mr. Justice Mykle gave Hofer until 30 June 1992 to remove all the items from the Block farm.

Over the next months, municipal officials determined that the Hofer group appeared to be complying with the injunction not to bring further materials to the Block farm, but they were not in compliance with the order to move all the previous materials and vehicles off the property.[89] Although the Hofer group had sold a lot of the materials through an auction and "received one cent on the dollar" for it,[90] a motion to find Hofer in contempt of court was filed on 12 August 1992.[91] This motion was heard by Justice Kroft on 3 September 1992, but given that Daniel Hofer was not present in court, the motion for contempt was adjourned. However, Mr. Justice Kroft issued a new order that the municipal officials could remove all the offending materials from the Block farm, hold the materials for thirty days, and then sell them at an auction.[92]

Toward a "Renegade Free" Colony

The living situation at Lakeside continued to be challenging. While clashes were not always recorded in the court documents available to me, Ken Hofer, who was by this time the colony plumber and electrician, did recount an event at the pumphouse the evening of 2 March 1992. He stated:

> I had occasion to be in the pump house at Lakeside Colony with some of my friends who were visiting me from another Colony. The door was unlocked and Conrad Hofer [son of Daniel] and John Gerald Hofer [son of Paul] burst into the pump house. I asked them to leave and they refused. I met them at the door to prevent their further entry into the building ... I keep this building secured at all times and "renegade free" in order to suffer no loss of any materials and to prevent water contamination. The only people who enter or work in this building are my helper and me.[93]

Ken Hofer went on to recount John Gerald's attack on him, despite that as a baptized member of the church, he (Ken) could not fight back. Ultimately, however, in desperation and frustration, he had hit John Gerald, for which he was placed under church penalty.[94]

After more than five years of conflict, the ordinary members of Lakeside were indeed waiting for a "renegade free" colony. Although the number of court motions had dropped dramatically once the dissenters moved their main activities to the Block farm, the overseers tried one more time to evict the defendants before the Supreme Court decision was delivered in the fall of 1992. The best complaint the overseers could come up with was that Leonard Hofer, son of Ben Hofer, appeared to be fixing the trailer that the dissenters had taken over from the overseers. For some time, the trailer had been used by the dissenters for storage rather than as a place of residence for displaced youth, as it was meant to be when it had been taken over by the dissenters.[95] While the trailer was ordered to be returned to the plaintiff overseers, the motion for contempt and eviction of the defendants was dismissed by Justice Wright on 22 July 1992.[96] Everybody was waiting for the Supreme Court to speak.

The Supreme Court of Canada

On 29 October 1992, in what must have been a sweet albeit short-lived victory for Daniel Hofer and his associates, the Supreme Court of Canada by a six-to-one margin reversed the decisions of the trial judge and the Manitoba Court of Appeal.[97] The court ruled that the colony had not followed the procedural requirements of natural justice in making the decision to excommunicate Daniel Hofer and the other defendants, and so for the moment at least, the defendants were, in the eyes of the law, still members of the colony and the police power of the state could not be invoked by the overseers to throw them off the colony.

Jurisdiction

Mr. Justice Gonthier wrote a lengthy decision with which five other justices concurred. On the first issue of the jurisdiction of the civil courts to adjudicate the dispute – that is, either to enforce the expulsion from the colony or declare the expulsion void – it appears that the defendants did not raise this issue as a possible ground for appeal and thus Gonthier J.A. did not expand on it. Obviously, the plaintiffs did not object to the jurisdiction of the courts, since the whole point of their action was to get the court to exercise jurisdiction and get the police force of the state into action to enforce the decision of the church. Huband J.A. in the Manitoba Court of Appeal had stated:

> Should the court become involved at all in resolving internal disputes in voluntary associations, including religious bodies? The general rule is that unless civil rights or property rights are implicated, the courts should not adjudicate issues of faith or doctrine: *Ukrainian Greek Orthodox Church et al. v. Trustees of Ukrainian Greek Orthodox Cathedral of St. Mary (no. 2)* (1939), 47 Man. R. 64 (C.A.), affirmed [1940] S.C.R. 586. Where an issue, such as the validity of excommunication from a religious body, impacts solely on the individual's status within a voluntary association, the court will not become involved in adjudicating the matter. It makes no difference whether the procedures for excommunication comply with the requirements of natural justice or not. It is otherwise, however, where the excommunication is linked with a property issue.[98]

Huband J.A. then pointed out that the property link here was that the colony wanted to expel the defendants from the colony property, whereas the defendants claimed that they were still members and had the right to remain on the property and participate in colony life. Gonthier J.A. at the Supreme Court of Canada took a similar position on the jurisdictional issue: "The courts are slow to exercise jurisdiction over the question of membership in a voluntary association, especially a religious one. However, the courts have exercised jurisdiction where a property or civil right turns on the question of membership."[99]

In this case Gonthier J.A. asserted that the right to remain on the colony was more a matter of contract rights arising out of the articles of association of the colony than it was a matter of property rights. In any event, what is interesting is that Gonthier did not close the jurisdictional issue after finding a contract right to adjudicate but added further requirements that might have an impact in future cases involving judicial review of disputes generated from within churches. Gonthier J. stated: "If the defendants have a right to stay, the question is not so much whether this is a property right or a contractual right, but whether it is of sufficient importance to deserve the intervention of the court and whether the remedy sought is susceptible of enforcement by the court."[100]

Standard of Review

Now that it had established that it had jurisdiction to review the expulsion from the colony, the next issue for the Supreme Court was what standard of review it should use. In other words, if we expect that the courts are going to invoke the violence of the state to coerce people to obey the expulsion decision of a church, what procedural standards are we going to require of the church before such a drastic step is taken?

Mr. Justice Gonthier applied two basic sets of norms to determine whether the expulsion was valid. First he looked at the applicable rules of the colony and the church to see if the expulsion had been properly dealt with according to the church's own rules. Second, he applied the principles of natural justice and duty to act in good faith to the process. Gonthier J. asserted: "It is not incumbent on the court to review the merits of the decision to expel. It is, however, called upon to determine whether the purported expulsion was carried out according to the applicable rules, with regard to the principles of natural justice, and without mala fides."[101]

The Inside Law: Hutterian Rules

After establishing jurisdiction, and what the standard of review should be, the next task of the Supreme Court of Canada was to determine what the rules of the Hutterian Brethren Church were in regard to expelling people from the colony, so as to see if the inside law of the church had been followed. One of the arguments that had been made by Donald Douglas for the defendants right from the start of the litigation was that the expulsions of the defendants violated the process laid down in the 1951 federal statute *Act to Incorporate the Hutterite Brethren Church*.[102] Section 5 of the act stated: "The Church dogma and church discipline and all the temporal affairs of the Corporation shall be administered, managed, exercised, transacted, conducted and controlled by a board of nine managers." Did this mean that church discipline by way of expulsion from a colony was actually a matter for the board of managers of the nationally incorporated church, as opposed to being a matter for each individual colony, or a matter involving at a higher level the three individual conferences of the church? Certainly there was no evidence that the Hutterian Brethren Board of Managers had ever dealt with discipline at the colony level.

Before dealing with Gonthier's determination of this issue, I should briefly outline the formal legal documents involved. A year before the federal legislation of 1951, the colonies from all three conferences of the church (Schmiedeleut, Dariusleut, and Lehrerleut) had agreed to the *Constitution of the Hutterian Brethren Church and Rules as to Community of Property*.[103] This constitution was a foundational document in the church. Individual colonies from the three subgroups would sign it. The constitution served as articles of association for a higher Hutterian Brethren Church composed of colonies from all three conferences. This constitution formalized certain powers and processes for three levels of the church. Regarding the highest level, the constitution stated:

> 6. The church dogma and church discipline and the affairs, powers, privileges and all matters affecting and pertaining to Hutterian Brethren generally shall be administered, managed, exercised, transacted, conducted and controlled by a Board of nine managers, three of whom shall be appointed by each of the said Conferences, provided, however, that except as to matters of a purely administrative nature, no resolution or decision of the said Board shall be binding or effective until approved, ratified and confirmed by each of the said Conferences.[104]

As to matters dealt with at the level of the three separate conferences of the church, the constitution stated:

> 20. The affairs, powers and privileges of each of the said Conferences shall be administered, managed, exercised, transacted, conducted and controlled by a Board consisting of two delegates from each of the congregations or communities comprising the Conferences.
>
> ...
>
> 23. The Conference Board shall exercise control over the Church dogma and Church discipline within their respective Conference, and shall have

charge of all matters pertaining to Hutterian Brethren generally within their respective Conferences, and shall have power to take such action as they deem meet in respect to matters affecting or pertaining to the Hutterian Brethren within their respective Conferences.[105]

And as to matters at the colony level, the constitution stated:

46. Any member of a congregation or community may be expelled or dismissed therefrom at any annual or general meeting of that congregation or community upon a majority vote of all the members thereof, or upon the request of such member.[106]

When a church is composed of three levels, it may be difficult to determine the exact jurisdictional powers of each. On the basis of the constitution it would appear that the highest level of the church, namely the Board of Managers from all the conferences, had the least power, in that decisions had to be accepted and approved by each of the conferences. Arguably, however, church discipline might take place at any of the three levels. Perhaps it could be the entity subject to discipline that varied from level to level. For example, an individual may be disciplined at the colony level, at the conference level a colony could be disciplined, and at the highest level a conference could be disciplined. But this line of argument might not work if a decision at the highest level to discipline had to be approved by all three conferences: hardly likely if one of them was the subject of the discipline.

An argument could be made, on the basis of the considerable power of each of the conference boards as stated in article 23, that the Schmiedeleut Conference Board would have at least concurrent jurisdiction to deal with the defendants. But how does that conference jurisdiction relate to the clear jurisdiction given by the constitution itself in section 46 to individual colonies to expel members from the congregation? The constitution contains no explicit provisions allowing appeals of decisions made at the colony level to the senior elder of the Leut or to the conference board of the Leut.

The term "church discipline" as used at the conference level is ambiguous. The power to deal with "church discipline" might refer to the power to set the rules about what a Hutterite is allowed to wear, or what grade a Hutterite must stop school at, or what consumer goods are disallowed, and so forth. This is a different use of the term "church discipline," and thus one might argue that the conference board does not have concurrent or appeal jurisdiction to adjudicate whether any particular person has violated a norm of the church – that is a matter for enforcement at the colony level.

However, in addition to the 1951 statutory provisions and the 1950 *Constitution of the Hutterian Brethren Church*, most, if not all, colonies have their own articles of association. Just as each colony is associated as a member of the wider church by signing the constitution of the church, so each individual member of a colony after baptism would become associated with fellow members of that colony by signing the articles of association of his or her colony. The colony is usually an unincorporated association based on these articles. The farming enterprise of the colony is then incorporated, and the land and assets usually held by another corporation and leased to the farming corporation. These corporations are in turn operated and held in trust for the members of the colony.

For purposes of discipline the *Articles of Association of Lakeside Colony of Hutterian Brethren* stated:

> 39. Any member of the Colony may be expelled or dismissed from the Colony at any general or special meeting of the Colony upon a majority vote of the voting members thereof for his or her having left or abandoned the Colony or having refused to obey the rules and regulations.[107]

Note as well:

> 12. No member shall be entitled to vote at any meeting unless:
>
> ...
>
> (d) He is not under any Church penalty, which Church penalty may be imposed either by the members of the Colony *or by the elders of the Schmieden-Leut Group of Hutterian Brethren.*[108]

So now we see from the articles of association of the colony themselves an explicit recognition that there is authority to discipline individuals at the conference level concurrent to or beyond the discipline exercised within a particular colony. Concurrent jurisdiction is not the same thing as appellate jurisdiction, but the colony articles and the church constitution do not foreclose arguments that the inside law of the Hutterites as expressed in outside law contract terms might include appeals of disciplinary matters to the senior elder or the conference board.

In addition to these formal written documents of the church, the traditions and customs of the church are also in question. Here the courts encounter difficulty. Can a custom within the church *contradict* a formally written rule, and if so, can the customary rule be recognized by the court rather than the formally written one? Or can the customary rules simply *supplement* the formally written ones? How do courts determine what the customary rules of the church are without getting into a morass of doctrinal and theological issues that the courts are ill-equipped to understand? For example, in *Lakeside* much of the evidence related to customary patterns of discipline and to the powers of the senior elder. This evidence was also contested as to just what the customary practice was.

Now that I have outlined some of the inside law provisions, what important contribution did Mr. Justice Gonthier's decision make to these matters? Even though it was strictly unnecessary for Gonthier to put so much effort into sorting out the formal legal structures of the Hutterian church, he did so, and his effort was useful in terms of providing guidance for future litigation involving Hutterites, and also useful for providing an authoritative interpretation as a baseline for future changes to the formal rules within the church.

First, on the issue of customary norms, Gonthier was not actually faced with a conflict requiring a choice between a customary practice and a formally written rule. However, on the issue of the relationship between the alleged customary power of the senior elder to appoint conference ministers to investigate and adjudicate cases and the formalized norms of the powers of the conference and colony, Gonthier J. allowed the customary norm to form a kind of gloss or supplement or interpretative provision to add to the formal norms. What is crucial is that he affirmed that the court could use the customary norms of the group in the process of asking whether the group followed its own rules. He stated: "[T]o rely exclusively on the written documents without reference to the tradition and customs of Hutterites would seem unwise. From a point of view inside the Hutterite society, it seems probable that tradition and custom are in fact the highest source of authority, and the written documents are merely imperfect attempts to capture these sources."[109] After pointing out the problems for a court in finding out what the traditions are, he stated further: "Once the court assumes jurisdiction, there is no alternative but to come to the best understanding possible of the applicable tradition and custom. Even in other contexts it has been held that a sufficiently well-established tradition or custom may be considered an implied term in the contract making up the articles of association of a voluntary association."[110]

That courts tend to focus on the formalized norms, however, was born out in Gonthier's own decision as he embarked on an exhaustive examination of the relationships between the various levels of the Hutterian Brethren Church and an examination of the formal rules to see if the expulsions had been carried out in accordance with them.

The church constitution and the colony articles were treated by Gonthier J. as the fundamental documents in question. He also held that colony articles must conform to the church constitution and that in cases of inconsistency, the constitution would prevail. Before applying the colony articles and the church constitution to see whether the Lakeside expulsions were valid according to the inside law, Gonthier had to deal with the federal statute that incorporated the Hutterian Brethren Church.[111] How do the rules and provisions contained in this legislation relate to the rules and practices contained in the church constitution and colony articles?

As suggested earlier by Huband J.A. in the Manitoba Court of Appeal, Gonthier J. concluded on this issue that the "constituted church" was a separate entity from the "incorporated church." The purpose of the incorporated church was to deal with issues of concern common to all three conferences, such as discriminatory practices of government. The rules in the constitution, which were drafted before the legislation, were not bylaws of the subsequent Canadian corporation. The corporation as an entity set up by Canadian statute had some authority to deal with common concerns of all three Hutterite tribes in Canada, but the constitution of the church in theory could serve to associate all the colonies from anywhere in the world that were willing to be governed by it and accepted into membership by the church as constituted. Thus Gonthier stated: "In analysing the relationship between the Act and the constitution, it is readily apparent that the Act casts only the top layer of the structure established by the constitution into legislative form. This is consistent with the view that the purpose of the corporation was to deal with external threats that affected each Hutterite conference equally ... The church corporation and the church should therefore be seen as technically distinct entities which in practice have the same members, and are governed by the same managers at the same meetings."[112] This conclusion would take care of any argument that the excommunication of the Hofer group at Lakeside was improper because the statute incorporating the church required that the "discipline" had to take place at the level of the nine managers of the incorporated church. The function of the church as incorporated was separate from the whole church as constituted.

Turning then to the rules found in the church constitution and colony articles, Gonthier J. concluded that a person could be expelled from a colony by majority vote at the colony level. On the issue of voting, Gonthier recognized Hutterite customary practice: "Whether a vote has been taken is essentially a question of fact and need not be formal. Given the Hutterite preference for operating by consensus rather than by formal votes if possible, it will be a question of fact in any given situation whether a consensus has been reached that is sufficiently unambiguous to qualify as a vote."[113]

Gonthier also concluded that a member of a colony could be expelled from the church at the conference level, and this would lead to automatic expulsion from the colony without any need for a vote at the colony level. This rule, however, was not in issue in the *Lakeside* case.

Applying the rule that the colony could expel the defendants by majority vote, Gonthier J. recognized that the disciplinary practices of the church made it difficult to sort out whether a person had been repelled from the colony or just expelled from membership, or whether the person was still a member and was just receiving an extreme form of shunning. Even after a vote to expel from membership, a person might be given time to repent before being asked to leave the colony. Gonthier J. concluded that a vote to expel Daniel Hofer in the ultimate form of ordering him to leave the colony did indeed take place at the 21 January 1987 meeting. After Daniel Hofer refused to accept a mild punishment for his behaviour, the majority expelled him from membership in the colony. A vote to expel two of his sons took place at the 31 January meeting, and a vote to expel Larry Hofer took place at a meeting on 21 July 1988.

At least in regard to the expulsion of the defendants who had been members (as opposed to the young defendants who never were members), Mr. Justice Gonthier found that the inside law had been fulfilled. A majority vote at the colony level was sufficient and there was no inside law that gave the dissenters a right to an appeal tribunal within the church. However, Madam Justice McLachlin in dissent disagreed fundamentally with the majority view of what the inside law was, while agreeing that no breach of Hutterian norms occurred. Gonthier's interpretation was that a member had to be expelled by majority vote, aside from the issue of being expelled from the church at the conference level. Even if the Hutterites customarily spoke of members expelling themselves by their behaviour, the rules required a majority vote to formalize the decision. McLachlin, on the other hand, asserted that no vote was necessary. McLachlin focused on Hutterian custom as she understood it from the evidence. A mild form of punishment was offered to Daniel Hofer Sr., who did not accept it. In not accepting it, Daniel Hofer excommunicated himself. The members did not make the decision by any majority vote, because it was not their decision to make.[114]

The Outside Law of Natural Justice

Having examined the formal rules of the church itself, Gonthier J. turned to the application of the principles of natural justice. Here is where we see the potential danger of litigating church matters. It is not enough to see if the inside law of the church has been fulfilled. The courts will also apply what I call "outside law" to the situation. If the outside law is just a procedural gloss that adds requirements to the inside law but does not fundamentally contradict the particular religious norms of the group, the difficulty may not be apparent. But there may well be cases in the future where the outside law arguably conflicts with the inside norms of the religious group, which then would raise questions as to whether the judicial review and enforcement of ecclesiastical judgments constituted an interference with freedom of religion.

As to the outside law of natural justice, Gonthier stated: "The content of the principles of natural justice is flexible and depends on the circumstances in which the question arises. However, the most basic requirements are that of notice, opportunity to make representations, and an unbiased tribunal."[115] It was on the first arm of this trinity that Gonthier J. hung the decision that the Lakeside expulsions be declared void: "A member must be given notice of the cause for which he is to be expelled. It is insufficient merely to give notice that the conduct of a member is to be considered at a meeting."[116]

Gonthier J. concluded that the defendants did not have sufficient notice that their expulsions from the colony would be considered by the colony's voting members. Daniel Hofer Sr. of course had notice that an annual meeting of the colony would be held on 21 January 1987, and he probably suspected that his conduct would come under review, but at this stage no one intended to expel him. Only after the events at the meeting and his refusal to accept punishment was the next step of expulsion taken. Gonthier J. asserted that

> [w]hen Daniel Hofer Sr.'s conduct during the meeting, and his refusal to accept the mild penalty imposed, brought his expulsion into issue, he was specifically warned, as found by the trial judge, that he was "expelling himself" if he did not repent. Despite this warning, Daniel Hofer Sr. did not accept the mild penalty and was expelled.
>
> There is a sense in which Daniel Hofer Sr. had notice of the charge against him and an opportunity to make representations on whether or not he ought to be expelled. However, there were really only a few moments of notice that expulsion was being considered before the issue was decided. One wonders whether such short notice is really adequate when a decision of this magnitude is to be made.[117]

After noting further that two voting members were absent from the meeting when the decision was made to expel and that these two members did not have notice that such a decision would be made, Gonthier J. concluded: "A proper procedure would have been to defer consideration of the issue of expulsion to a subsequent meeting called for that reason with adequate notice to all voting members of the colony."[118]

As to the obvious argument that such later meetings of both the colony and the conference were held confirming the decision to expel, and that Daniel Hofer and at least some of the defendants had notice of these meetings, Gonthier J. concluded that if Hofer had been expelled from membership on 21 January, the meeting of 31 January was called for purposes of seeing whether Daniel Hofer Sr. would repent and seek readmission into membership. The meeting was therefore not a reconsideration of the original decision to expel and so could not cure the procedural defect of the original decision. He stated further: "This conclusion applies to all further meetings which were held, especially since they were all held after the statement of claim had been issued."[119]

As for the sons of Daniel Hofer, they had no specific notice that their expulsion from the colony would be considered at the relevant meetings where they were purportedly voted out. While they may have known full well what was going to happen, Gonthier J. concluded: "[I]t must be remembered that natural justice requires procedural fairness no matter how obvious the decision to be made may be. It does not matter whether it was utterly obvious that Daniel Hofer Jr., David Hofer and Larry Hofer would be expelled. Natural justice requires that they be given notice of a meeting to consider the matter, and opportunity to make representations concerning it. This may not change anything, but it is what the law requires."[120]

One matter that Mr. Justice Gonthier left open was the issue of the expulsion of non-members from the colony. Gonthier J. concluded that the defendants who were unbaptized adults had no adequate notice of any decision to expel them, and thus their expulsion was void as well, since it violated the principles of natural justice. However, the whole issue of the church's process for expelling non-members was not addressed in the judgment.

Madam Justice McLachlin in dissent took strong exception to the majority interpretation of the notice requirements. On one hand, given her interpretation that no majority vote of the members was necessary and that the defendants excommunicated themselves, no notice would be required, since the decision was their own to make by choosing to be disobedient and thus expelled, or obedient and thus still a member, even if under discipline. However, even assuming that a vote was taken and was required, McLachlin J. thought that there was adequate notice in this context. She stated:

> Turning to the specific requirement of notice, the authorities show that advance notice of a decision is not required where the purpose of the notice requirement is fulfilled ...
>
> if one were to find that some sort of decision to expel was made by the colony, one would be bound to conclude that the appellants were fully aware in advance of what was to be decided and had full opportunity to present their defences ...
>
> it is clear that Mr. Hofer was fully aware of the fact that continued defiance made continued membership in the colony impossible and that the colony would have no alternative given its theological beliefs but to view him as expelled ... In short, he had full knowledge of what would happen; making formal notice was unnecessary.[121]

But the other justices of the Supreme Court agreed with Gonthier J. that a decision to expel had to be made by the members by majority vote and that formal notice had to be given.

Having disposed of the case on the basis of the notice requirement, Gonthier J. did not have to deal with the other two parts of the natural justice test, though he did acknowledge the difficulty of applying the third test involving bias to cases of this kind. His remarks are important because it would be on the bias issue that much of the second round of litigation would be fought. He stated:

> There is no doubt that an unbiased tribunal is one of the central require-
> ments of natural justice. However, given the close relationship amongst
> members of voluntary associations, it seems rather likely that members of
> the relevant tribunal will have had some previous contact with the issue
> in question and, given the structure of a voluntary association, it is al-
> most inevitable that the decision-makers will have at least an indirect in-
> terest in the question. Furthermore, the procedures set out in the rules of
> the association may often require that certain persons make certain kinds
> of decisions without allowing for an alternative procedure in the case of
> bias.
>
> While the defendants did raise the question of bias, I would be reluctant
> to address the issue in any definitive manner because the appropriate stan-
> dard in the context of voluntary associations was not argued by the parties
> before us.[122]

The result of the Supreme Court decision was that Daniel Hofer and his sons were still in law members of Lakeside Colony because the expulsion of them was void, having breached the requirements of natural justice in that proper notice of the expulsion hearings were not provided to them. That the colony could simply turn around and expel them properly was not lost on the court. The decision did not purport to look at the merits of the decision to expel but, rather, insisted that proper procedures must be fol-lowed before a court will enforce the decisions of a voluntary association. The court awarded costs to the defendants, not just for the Supreme Court level but for all the previous levels as well.

Reaction

What had the leaders of the church accomplished by launching the lawsuit in an attempt to use the power of the state to expel the defendants from Lakeside? Aside from the issue of arguably breaching the norms of the church in launching the lawsuit in the first place, the lawsuit opened up a potential loss of autonomy for the church to live by its own norms. The highest court clearly imposed on the church (and as a matter of precedent on all other churches and voluntary associations) a standard of procedural fairness which might well be applauded as a minimum protection of members' rights but which also might be decried as a potential loss of autonomy for religious groups to live by their own norms in ecclesiastical matters, rather than be regulated by outside law.

Furthermore, the course of the litigation illustrated all too well problems with formal court adjudication. One such problem is the delay associated with litigation: it was almost six years since the decision had been made to expel the defendants before the final word on the legality of that decision was rendered. Another is cost: Donald Douglas submitted a bill of costs for fees and disbursements to Lakeside for over $300,000.[123] Lakeside would be liable to pay its own lawyers at the Baker firm a great deal of money as well. It is safe to assume that the litigation easily cost over a half a million dollars, with the end result being the declaration that the defendants had not been properly excommunicated from the colony.

Most importantly, the litigation had not resolved anything. This is often the case with litigation, as disputes are abstracted into legal issues, having little to do with the substance of the matter. The actual dispute between the parties had nothing to do with whether notice was properly given. The dispute had to do with whether an invention was stolen, whether the leaders were acting according to Hutterian norms, whether the elders of the Leut should hear the case, whether Daniel Hofer had violated Hutterian norms to the point that expulsion from the colony was justified, and so forth. The effect of the litigation was simply to return everyone back to square one.

The decision of the Supreme Court of Canada on 19 October 1992 received considerable press coverage. The Canadian Press quoted Daniel Hofer as saying, "At least sometimes things come out right, the way God planned it from the start ... I admit it would be fairly difficult to adjust to living with these people, the way they've been harassing us and taking us to court. It will take a little bit of time to forget all that."[124] In a *Winnipeg Free Press* front-page story complete with colour photograph of Daniel Hofer and his wife, Daniel is quoted as saying, "It was God's battle too and he's the one who gives the victory."[125]

But victory was still a long way off. If Daniel Hofer and his supporters thought that the Supreme Court judgment would translate into reconciliation with the colony, their hopes were soon to be dashed. Meanwhile, the overseers, and particularly the senior elder, were swept up in a whirlwind of controversy. Instead of reconciliation, there was a great confrontation and division.

Part Four
The Schism in the Schmiedeleut and
Lakeside Litigation: Round Two

8
Lakeside and the Schism within the Schmiedeleut

On 29 October 1992 the Supreme Court of Canada declared that in the eyes of the law, Daniel Hofer and his three baptized sons were still members of Lakeside Colony. Furthermore, the court held that the three other adult defendants who were not baptized could not be expelled from the colony without a proper hearing. But the two groups in reality were unreconciled, and the geographical boundaries and relationships between the two did not disappear with the pronouncement that the dissenters were still members. Showing great restraint, the dissenters did not grab their licence of membership and attempt to aggressively push back the boundaries of the arrangements that had developed. For this they certainly got no credit, however, as the logic of the Supreme Court's decision kicked in. If the overseer group had not followed the outside law of natural justice the first time around, they would simply have to do so in a second round of expulsions.

Donald Douglas, lawyer for the dissenter group, wrote a letter to Michael Radcliffe, lawyer for the overseer group, on 2 November 1992. Douglas suggested that the Supreme Court had set a high standard for the notice requirement, and by implication the standard for the "opportunity to be heard" and "the need for an unbiased tribunal" should also be set at a high level. Douglas concluded:

It may be that either the Senior Elder or the officers and certain members of Lakeside Colony are considering further expulsion proceedings respecting the Daniel Hofer Sr. group. I sincerely hope that this is not the case. Clearly, given the many unfortunate occurrences during the last 5-½ years, neither the officers nor any of the members of Lakeside Colony could sit as unbiased members of a tribunal. The role of the Senior Elder in selecting a body of ministers would likewise be suspect. The only possible unbiased tribunal would be the Conference Board of the Schmied-Leut, consisting of two delegates of each of the congregations, excluding Lakeside and Crystal Spring. The nature of the hearing, the right to counsel, the right to examine and cross-examine witnesses and other such matters are all complex issues which I believe the Hutterian Brethren Church ought to avoid unless it wishes its procedures to be further controlled by Court made rules.

Before any firm decisions are made, I request an opportunity for a meeting among our respective clients and their counsel. From a practical perspective, it may be that the members of Lakeside Colony should no longer reside together. Perhaps the financial assistance of the Church and other colonies might be required if Lakeside Colony does not possess sufficient wealth to allow for a split in the normal way. Both colonies could then continue as members of the Schmied-Leut Conference.[1]

The overseer group at Lakeside was willing to reconcile with the renegades if they repented and asked for forgiveness, but this was presumably the position that they had always taken. Losing in the Supreme Court did not lead to a willingness to set aside a "they are wrong and need to repent" position with some new attitude such as "maybe we are both wrong and need to reconcile." Douglas's suggestion was that the Daniel Hofer group, at least in law, were still members of the church, so they could leave Lakeside without breaking their baptismal vows. Why not end this dispute by a pro rata division of the colony assets? But as far as the overseer group was concerned, the rebels were not members of the church, irrespective of what the Supreme Court said, and rather than *giving* them assets to go, the overseer group decided that they would *take* assets from them: the defeat at the Supreme Court could be turned into a victory.

Unreconciled Grab for Assets

On 14 November 1992, barely two weeks after the Supreme Court judgment, the overseer president of Lakeside, Michael Wollmann, signed a letter that was likely drafted in the Baker law offices. This letter, formally delivered to Daniel Hofer on 16 November, stated: "On behalf of Lakeside Colony, we would ask that you please provide financial statements including full disclosure of all assets and liabilities accumulated by you, Daniel Hofer Jr., David Hofer, Paul Hofer Sr. and all your associates since 1987 and your families, including a list of all vehicles, equipment, machinery, chattels, bank accounts, real property or lease hold interests and all debts accumulated by this group ... Would you please arrange to have this information furnished to us in writing within the next ten days."[2]

What was going on? The Supreme Court had said that in the eyes of the law the Hofer group were still members of the colony and had been since 1987. But in the eyes of the overseers, in both a temporal and spiritual sense, the renegades were not members of the colony. There was no acceptance that since Daniel Sr. was still a member he could go back into the machine shed. There was no acceptance that since Daniel Jr. was still a member he could run the hog operation again. Nothing changed at the colony after the Supreme Court decision, except that for the moment the police power of the state could not be invoked to use force to throw the defendants off the colony.

Yet the overseers found a way to use the decision of the Supreme Court as a weapon, as it were, in their favour. Without offering the Hofer group any of the real benefits of legal membership, the majority group claimed that all the property of the minority group at the colony that they had accumulated since 1987 after being expelled from colony enterprises belonged to the colony, since the minority group were still members in law with the majority. This was logical. If the dissenters claimed they were still members and had always been so, then all the property accumulated by them belonged to the colony. But as perceived by Daniel Hofer, this move was made with no intention of ever accepting the minority back into membership in fact, although the overseer group later argued that a request for an accounting should be perceived as a first step in reconciliation. If the request for an accounting of property had been made as a real step in bringing the dispute to a church body for adjudication or resolution, Daniel Hofer would have likely readily accepted it.

The Daniel Hofer group had formed a colony within a colony when it was expelled from the economic activities of Lakeside. The dissenters formed their own enterprises, always stating that once reconciliation came about, all the assets of the minority colony would go into the Lakeside pot. Like other Hutterites, the dissenters did not own personal property but rather their assets belonged to the church, and as far as they were concerned, after 1987 they were the more faithful church at Lakeside than the majority.

Whether the attempt by the overseer group to seize the dissenter group's assets was made in good faith as a step to reconciliation as claimed by one side, or as a cynical tactic as claimed by the other, the move certainly had advantages for the overseer group. First, it provided a great bargaining chip in getting rid of the renegades. Since the group would not leave if it were voted out, seizing the assets would allow the overseers the opportunity to offer the assets back to the group as a gift of sorts if they would leave. Second, given that the overseer group was responsible for a substantial portion of the dissenter group's legal costs for the first round of litigation, it could grab the dissenter group's property to pay that bill. Finally, the request for the assets provided a potential ground for the next round of expulsions. Knowing that the Hofer group would not hand over its subcolony to the overseers without reconciliation, the overseer group could claim that the Hofer group was violating Hutterian tradition by holding "private property" separate from the communal pot. Daniel Hofer probably did not anticipate this last point, and he would have been much better off to at least give the overseer group a complete list of the assets, even if he thought the overseers' motivation for the request was questionable. Because he did not do so, the overseer group had the ammunition with which to make the argument that the dissenter group was violating Hutterian norms by holding personal assets.

The issue of what to do about assets in the hands of the minority, since these people were still in law members of the colony, had not been ignored by Mr. Justice Gonthier, who stated at the end of his judgment:

> The status of the property which the defendants have been accumulating raises an ancillary issue. The colony had asked for an order that the defendants return all colony property to the colony. Given the provisions of the Articles of Association relating to the ownership of property, it seems possible that the colony would be entitled to such an order even though the defendants have not been validly expelled. However, the order for the return of property was not sought on the basis that the defendants were still members, but rather on the basis that they had been expelled. Therefore, the action should be simply dismissed, preserving the right of the colony to take other proceedings to protect its property if that should be required.[3]

There is a recognition here of tension between the formal rules and the reality at Lakeside. The formal rules mandated that those who are expelled have no right to take common property with them. Thus, if the expulsions had been valid, the order to return common property would extend only to whatever equipment or assets had belonged to Lakeside as at the date of the expulsion. In the first round of litigation, the overseer group took the position that the defendants were no longer members of the colony as of 21 December 1987 or thereabouts. If these ex-members subsequently started enterprises of their own, the colony would have no claim to those. After all, the assets of the Hofer group were accumulated by ex-members on their own. What might be claimed in the first round, had the overseer group been successful in the litigation, was reimbursement for the use by the so-called ex-members of colony food and housing and machinery shed space and the like to run their enterprises. But now that the highest court in the country had declared that the Hofer group had not been validly expelled, the formal rules would indeed state that members must not hold any property separate from the collective pot. So despite losing the case, the majority would win the property of the dissenter group. But the problem was that the reality did not fit the rule, because the minority did not and would not receive a reciprocal benefit from the use of common property. Lakeside remained in a state of schism, with two unreconciled groups maintaining separate enterprises on the same colony. To put all the post-schism assets in the common pot controlled by the majority group, while at the same time kicking out the minority group, would leave the minority group with nothing.

That Daniel Hofer was furious when he received the letter asking for an accounting of the property is an understatement. The victory at the Supreme Court level meant nothing. The wheels were grinding him down again. Daniel Hofer's letter to Michael Wollmann on 17 November 1992 was intemperate. After calling Wollmann "evil and heartless and pitiless" and reviewing complaints by the Hofer group about the behaviour of the overseer group at Lakeside over the last years, Hofer stated:

> Now you have the gall as a spiritual leader to ask us to provide you and the likes of you with a list of our properties. Why didn't you poor lost souls come with an offer to get united in Christ and the Church in peace where and when we could have embraced each other in love and forgiveness and become one in Christ Jesus and the Church ...
>
> Our request from the beginning was to be heard by a higher court in the Hutterian Church. (We were granted that request but it never materialized). To date this is still our request ...
>
> Naturally upon a satisfactory settlement of all issues temporal and spiritual all properties will be or become church property. We agree that all people will abide by the rules and judgements and decisions reached by said ministers.[4]

Daniel Hofer suggested that the higher court be composed of John Wipf, the senior elder of the Hutterian Brethren Church, with ten to twenty ministers of his choosing; joined with Joseph Wipf, assistant senior elder of the Schmiedeleut, with ten to twenty ministers of his choosing from the American side; and by ten to twenty ministers from Manitoba, half selected by Wollmann, and half selected by Hofer. Such a huge assembly of judges from such distances would no doubt have constituted a much grander assembly than the circumstances demanded but, in any event, the overseer group was not apparently interested in any higher court decision in the church. It was up to the renegades to come back, repent, and obey.

Giving Proper Notice

The next step was for the overseers to follow the notice requirements of the Supreme Court judgment. On 2 December 1992 Michael Wollmann signed notices that stated:

> TAKE NOTICE that you are hereby requested to attend a special meeting of Lakeside Colony members on 11th day of Dec., 1992 at 2 o'clock in the afternoon at the Lakeside Colony Church to discuss the following issues regarding your behaviour within the Lakeside Colony congregation, namely:
>
> 1. In failing to advise Reverend Michael Wollmann or Reverend Jacob Hofer or Reverend Josh Hofer of your financial affairs as requested in Reverend

Wollmann's letter to you including a list of all vehicles, equipment, machinery, bank accounts, real property or leasehold interests and all debts.

2. In participating in preparing a letter of November 17, 1992 from Daniel Hofer to Michael Wollmann or alternatively your agreement with the contents of this letter.

TAKE NOTICE THAT YOUR EXPULSION FROM LAKESIDE COLONY WILL BE CONSIDERED AT THIS MEETING.

If you fail to attend a decision will be made in your absence as the members of the community will deem proper.[5]

It is interesting that this notice was sent only to Daniel Hofer Sr., Daniel Hofer Jr., David Hofer, and Paul Hofer Sr.; it was not sent to Larry Hofer, who had been a defendant in the first round of litigation and was a baptized member of Lakeside. It also was not sent to any of the unbaptized young men who supported Daniel Hofer. Thus, of the original group of seven defendants in the first litigation, the notices were sent to only three of them. Of importance is that Rev. Paul Hofer was finally added to the group to be formally expelled. The overseer group probably knew that if the four named individuals were forced off the colony, the rest of the renegades would follow, despite that spouses and children of expelled members are entitled to stay on the colony. Thus, nothing really was to be gained by having more defendants.

The four men returned the notices unopened, but they obviously knew what was going on. Daniel Hofer made it abundantly clear that his group would not be showing up for the meeting. His letter to Wollmann on 3 December 1992 stated that the matter should be dealt with at the higher church level, but of course this was being delayed because of the refusal of Kleinsasser to "confess or at least admit some of his dealings."[6] Hofer then put the overseers on a kind of counter-notice that the matter would be dealt with at the higher level. As further evidence that there was again an escalation of tension at Lakeside, Hofer complained about

your recent actions whereby you cut the electrical wiring serving the house trailer one of our families has been struggling to move into after refurbishing during the summer. This has caused these families great grief as at present they're living in intolerable crowded conditions. While the ones that support you and Jake Hofer are living comfortably in new homes that we helped build and in house trailers supplied to them for their support of you and Jake Kleinsasser. Also your shameful and despicable actions of throwing our children's toys into the lagoon is continuing, just recently I again pulled a new children's bike out of the lagoon – last and final words written or oral to you and supporters of Jacob Kleinsasser – direct all your correspondence or requests or suggestions etc. to the church leaders mentioned in our previous letters ...

P.S. I advised our very upset members effected by your despicable acts to do like Isaac did (Genesis 26:21) and try to be patient until the church investigates said matters, and hold onto and live according to the teachings of Christ Jesus.[7]

Voted Out Again

Round two of the Lakeside expulsions became official, as it were, at the meeting of overseer Lakeside members on 11 December 1992, almost a full six years after the original alleged expulsions in January 1987. Since that earlier date, a number of males had been baptized and then married, bringing the number of voting members on the overseer side to fourteen. Josh Hofer Jr., the inside secretary, had become the second minister of the colony, after the movement of Rev. Paul Hofer to the renegade group. At the meeting on 11 December, thirteen of the fourteen voting male members of the majority group were present. Ben Hofer was absent because he was under church punishment.

The minutes of the 11 December meeting indicate that the notices sent to the dissenter group and the replies by Daniel Hofer were read at the meeting. Then the three inside leaders, the first minister, elderly Rev. Joseph Hofer; the second minister, Rev. Josh Hofer Jr.; and the new farm boss, Garry Hofer, expressed the opinion that the four members should be expelled. The other ten male voting members signed their names in agreement, and the meeting was over. It had taken barely an hour.[8] On 16 December 1992, all four of the defendants in the second round of litigation received notice of their expulsion and the demand that they leave Lakeside.[9]

As predicted, the dissenter group did not leave, and thus the overseer group would once again invoke the power of the state sword by going to court to get rid of the "renegades." Of great significance to the subsequent litigation was the fact that the meeting at Lakeside on 11 December 1992 took place *one day after* Jacob Kleinsasser lost a vote of confidence in his leadership of the Schmiedeleut. He refused to step down, which then led to a schism in the Schmiedeleut. For our purposes, the members and colonies loyal to the senior elder will be called Group One, whereas those who disassociated themselves with the leadership of the senior elder will be called Group Two. What is crucial here is that eventually it was Group Two that was accepted by the Dariusleut and Lehrerleut as the legitimate representatives of the Schmiedeleut branch in the wider Hutterian Brethren Church as reconstituted, while Jacob Kleinsasser and Group One were treated as having fallen away from the church. For its part, Group One claimed to be the true church, and asserted that it was Group Two that had fallen away.

Thus, aside from whatever issues of procedural due process there might be in the second round of expulsions, bias being the most important one, there was now a new argument to raise, namely that the overseer group at Lakeside colony, that is, the Group One majority, did not have the authority to expel the minority group, which wanted to be associated with Group Two. Even if the traditional rule was that persons could be expelled from the colony by majority vote of the members, this was subject to the more fundamental rule that the colony was held in trust for members of the Hutterian Brethren Church. Thus, if a court held that the minority group was voted out by a majority group consisting of those who were themselves *no longer members,* because they had lost their status as being in the Hutterian Brethren Church, the expulsions of the minority would be invalid. The authority of the majority Group One to expel would not depend on the reciprocal question of the status of the minority group. Even if the minority was not as yet formally accepted into the Group Two church, the point would be that a court would have to determine if the Group One majority were still properly members of the Hutterian Brethren Church, with the authority to expel anyone by majority vote.

In addition to the question of authority, there might also be the question of ultimate ownership of the colony's common property. If Group One had lost membership in the church, an argument could be made that it was really the minority group that retained membership, and thus the whole Lakeside colony belonged to the minority group, because the property was held in trust for the true members of the church. At this level of the argument, the status of the minority in relation to Group Two might well come into play. In any event, the litigation certainly took on a new flavour the second time round, with two competing claims between Group One and Group Two that they were the only true and exclusive Hutterite church. From now on the schism at Lakeside would need to be viewed in terms of the larger, developing schism within the whole conference. Thus we turn to how that schism happened, before returning to the developments at Lakeside.

The Gibb Indictment

In June 1992, before the Supreme Court decision in *Lakeside* had been delivered, Hutterite colonies in Manitoba and the United States received a lengthy manuscript written by I. Donald Gibb, a banker living in Cos Cob, Connecticut.[10] Gibb's manuscript contained over a hundred pages of his own narrative, plus an exhibit book of several hundred pages containing 120 exhibits. Many of these exhibits came from the first trial in the *Lakeside* case and from depositions taken during various lawsuits in Canada and in the United States.[11] Gibb was well known by many of the Schmiedeleut ministers. His covering letter to the manuscript indicates that he grew up in Manitoba near colonies, and he later went on to deal with the banking needs of Hutterites, both as head of agricultural services departments at several Canadian banks and then in a variety of positions with American banks. Gibb stated that in 1991, a loan made by Rabobank Netherlands to Hutterite colonies had been "compromised." Gibb had been involved in securing the loan for these colonies, and in the end the bank was left with a shortfall of about $652,000 plus unpaid legal fees. Furthermore, certain Hutterite colonies had been left with losses that Gibb calculated to be at least $8 million. This motivated Gibb to write his detailed account.

The circulation of the Gibb manuscript was of utmost importance to the eventual schism of the Schmiedeleut conference. At the Lakeside trial back in 1989, Donald Douglas had raised a number of issues dealing with losses to Crystal Spring Colony, headed by the senior elder, in an attempt to show that Crystal Spring conspired to get the patent and manufacture the profitable hog feeders because it needed to recoup the considerable debts it had acquired. However, the information at the Lakeside trial as to the financial transactions involving the fraud artists was sketchy, and the trial judge had emphatically disagreed with any sort of conspiracy theory.

The details of these transactions were now being provided by Gibb, who introduced his manuscript with this indictment:

> Attached is a lengthy analysis and factual background narrative on the various misadventures incurred over approximately the past decade by, generally, the Rosedale, Millbrook and Crystal Spring Colonies and involving especially Mike Waldner and Bishop Jacob Kleinsasser, amongst others ...
>
> What follows is a sad story of incompetence, inexperience, and ineptitude, all compounded by lying, deceit, misrepresentation and outright theft of Hutterite Brethren Colony resources ...
>
> This sad litany is a sober indictment of Bishop Kleinsasser and his badly flawed judgement, and an even worse indictment of Mike Waldner, his lieutenant ... Surely this is no way for a Bishop to treat his Brothers.[12]

While the Gibb manuscript includes a great amount of detail on many transactions, I shall only attempt a brief overview, including additional materials from the court files subsequent to Gibb's analysis. I should point out that I am dealing with the allegations Gibb made because these allegations are crucial to understanding why the schism took place; I am not here suggesting that the allegations are necessarily always fair. From the point of view of Jacob Kleinsasser's supporters, even though the Gibb manuscript included a host of documentary exhibits, it was in some respects based on, in the words of Michael Radcliffe, "suspicions, gossip in the Hutterite community which was totally unsubstantiated by fact, prejudice."[13] But from the point of view of those who ultimately rejected the leadership of the senior elder, the Gibb manuscript at minimum raised issues that were not answered satisfactorily when the senior elder had to defend himself in light of it.

Powers of Attorney to Fraud Artists

According to Gibb, the story began in 1982 when the interest rates in Canada were very high. Rev. Jacob Kleinsasser, on behalf of his own colony at Crystal Spring and on behalf of the whole Schmiedeleut conference, had been involved in attempts to get lower interest money to finance the colonies. Don and Les Edel of Valley Agro Services in Morris, Manitoba, were also interested in getting low-interest financing for their company, which, among other items, manufactured grain bins and grain-handling equipment. In 1982 Valley Agro had a debt to a bank in excess of $600,000.[14] The majority of Valley Agro's clients were Hutterite colonies, and it was this relationship between the Edels and the Hutterites that started the ball rolling.

According to Gibb, the Edels came across an advertisement for low-interest loans in a farm magazine. They phoned the number listed and talked to a Mr. Al Deleo, who offered to assist them in finding low-interest financing through Dell-Cornell Group Inc., a company formed by Deleo and his partner, Harold Cornell. Deleo and Cornell were in fact retired schoolteachers from Long Island, New York, and, according to Gibb, fraud artists with no particular business experience. Several days later, Don Edel mentioned Dell-Cornell to Joe Kleinsasser of Crystal Spring, a brother of Jacob Kleinsasser, and Joe also phoned Al Deleo. As a result of the tantalizing prospects held out by Dell-Cornell, Jacob Kleinsasser and Don Edel flew to Montreal in December 1982 to meet with Deleo and Cornell. Joseph Kleinsasser, the secretary of Crystal Spring, and David Decker, from a colony in South Dakota, also joined the group on the trip.

Deleo and Cornell apparently were effective in their persuasion, because Jacob and Joe Kleinsasser provided $5,000 to the smooth talkers and signed an irrevocable noncircumvention agreement with Deleo and Cornell dated 10 December 1982 that purported to last for five years and be renewed automatically on a yearly basis. The effect of the agreement was to bind Crystal Spring Colony to deal only with Dell-Cornell to arrange financing with any institutions that Dell-Cornell had introduced to them.[15] One of these ventures later involved negotiations in West Palm Beach, Florida, to provide Hutterite financing for a new bank to be established in the Bahamas. This proved unsuccessful.[16]

On 24 March 1983 Jacob and Joe Kleinsasser signed a power of attorney, the wording of which was undoubtedly composed by Deleo and Cornell. The twelve-month power of attorney that was granted to Deleo and Cornell was far broader than the power to negotiate for low-interest loans. It stated: "This includes any and all: general business transactions, chattels and/or goods transactions, bond and/or shares, and/or commodities transactions, banking transactions, insurance transactions, claims and/or litigations trans-actions, records and/or reports and/or statements transactions, and all other matters."[17]

Gibb asserted that another problem with the power of attorney and an accompanying certificate of authority[18] was that Jacob Kleinsasser did not just sign as the president of Crystal Spring Colony but he was also described in the documents as the bishop of the whole Hutterian Brethren Church. Even if he was not in his own mind signing the document so as to bind the wider church to anything, his using the title "bishop," arguably, according to Gibb, allowed the fraud artists to accomplish greater amounts of mis-chief by having a power of attorney from the head of the whole church and not just from one colony. In the end, no money from any colonies other than those that dealt with Deleo and Cornell was ever put at risk.

Eventually, according to Gibb, Jacob and Joe Kleinsasser made a formal request to Deleo and Cornell to get a loan of US$2 million for Crystal Spring. To secure these loans if needed, Crystal Spring requested and received two offers of "letters of credit" for US$2 million. One offer was from the Bank of Montreal and the other from the Royal Bank.[19] In addition, Crystal Spring opened a bank account with First National in Great Falls, Montana, and on the basis of a letter of credit from the Bank of Montreal, received a loan from First National for US$500,000. It would appear that because US inter-est rates were lower than in Canada, the loan from First National was fil-tered through Millbrook Colony in South Dakota, which was headed by Rev. Mike Waldner. According to Gibb, this $500,000 from Crystal Spring channelled through Millbrook was eventually entrusted to Deleo and Cornell through a transfer of the money to Marine Midland Bank in Gens Falls, New York.[20] A substantial portion of this money was later transferred by Deleo and Cornell to Key Bank, New York.[21]

By July of 1983 Deleo and Cornell had decided to approach Rev. Mike Waldner, the head of Millbrook Colony in South Dakota. Millbrook had just split off in June 1983 from Rosedale Colony, where Mike Waldner had been minister. A power of attorney similar to the one signed by Crystal Spring was signed by Mike Waldner on 28 July 1983. The problem, accord-ing to Gibb, was that Mike Waldner signed as president of Rosedale Colony and Millbrook Colony, even though he was at that time only president of the new daughter colony, Millbrook. Thereafter, Mike Waldner continued to sign a series of documents for Deleo and Cornell on behalf of Rosedale Colony, as well as Millbrook. Mike Waldner's signing for Rosedale Colony, when he had no authority for that colony, was a "fraudulent" act according to Gibb.[22] The contrary view is that Mike Waldner at the time of the colony division still had authority over both colonies.[23]

The events of the summer and fall of 1983 are just one example of the mess Rosedale Colony later found itself in. By the end of August 1983, Deleo and Cornell were given the power by Mike Waldner to act for Rosedale Colony as "chief financial investment officers" and authorized to negotiate, procure, and execute "lease and/or security agreements with First Savings Leasing Corporation."[24] Gibb alleges that Deleo also decided to use the powers of attorney of Rosedale to buy oil workover rigs valued at US$1,200,000. However, according to Gibb, Deleo obtained financing of US$1,720,000 for the equipment by way of a fake document he gave to the bank as to the value of the rigs so that he could use the difference to fund his own interests and personal debts. The deal for the rigs was arranged through First Florida Leasing and financed through a loan from Consumers Bank in Massachusetts. In September 1983, First Florida executed an assignment whereby Rosedale and Crystal Spring were indebted directly to Consumers Bank for repayment of the oil rig leases.[25] When Consumers Bank discovered the true value of the oil rigs, a plan was negotiated whereby the rigs would indeed be refurbished at a cost of US$370,000, and the loan from Consumers was increased to almost US$2 million, with the lease payments to be made over five years amounting to $2,740,500.

On 14 November 1983 Mike Waldner signed an "unbelievable" letter of commitment that purported to make Rosedale and Millbrook Colonies a financial guarantor of all investments made by Dell-Cornell, waive all potential lawsuits against Deleo and Cornell, give Deleo and Cornell power to transfer funds at will, and most importantly, grant 100 percent ownership to Deleo and Cornell of all investments made on behalf of Rosedale Colony, the Hutterian Brethren Church, and other colonies.[26] Clearly Waldner, who claimed he was authorizing only the obtaining of low-interest loans, was being fooled by the fraud artists.[27] After the horses had long since escaped from the barn, Waldner started to have his doubts about Deleo and Cornell, and he flew to New York to investigate why the low-interest funds were not being secured. Shortly thereafter he sent a letter trying to reverse the authorizations he had given to Dell-Cornell.

Of crucial importance is the question of whether the senior elder, Jacob Kleinsasser, was aware of all the transactions involving Mike Waldner, or whether he was aware only of his own limited transaction involving Crystal Spring seeking a loan. On this point, Gibb concluded: "This agreement and power of attorney [Mike Waldner's] is wrong, irrational and utterly illegal. It could not have been done without Jacob Kleinsasser's knowledge and approval. Clearly, this is the ultimate 'smoking gun' and an instrument of fraud on the entire church!"[28] That Kleinsasser knew about Waldner's transactions would later be flatly denied. According to Radcliffe, it would only be months later when the fraud became evident that Kleinsasser discovered what Deleo and Cornell had done through their relationship with Waldner.[29]

According to Gibb, with the broad power of attorney from Crystal Spring, Rosedale, and Millbrook Colonies, and the US$4 million offers of letters of credit from the Bank of Montreal and the Royal Bank, and armed with the US$500,000 "loan" from Crystal Spring through Millbrook, Deleo and Cornell attempted to get low-interest financing for the colonies, including attempting to borrow money in Switzerland.[30] But in reality what they were doing was quite the reverse. They went on a fraudulent buying spree that would ultimately, according to Gibb, result in the loss of more than US$8 million to Rosedale, Millbrook, and Crystal Spring.

Deleo and Cornell entered into a host of leasing transactions with First Savings Leasing Corporation of Milwaukee involving trucks, trailers, and all-terrain vehicles. As noted, they also purchased and refurbished oil workover rigs using fraudulent documentation. They purchased interests in oil wells in Texas through Western States Energy. They bought a luxury property on Long Lake, New York, in the name of Rosedale Colony. They invested in Cleveland Plastics. They invested in a clock factory just before it went bankrupt. There were other transactions, such as an investment in a trucking company in Texas.[31] And, of course, the fraud artists, according to Gibb, were living the high life of corporate tycoons at Hutterite expense. As is common with fraudulent transactions, Deleo and Cornell started to make payments to Mike Waldner at Millbrook Colony to give the appearance that the investments were paying off. Of course, Deleo and Cornell were actually paying Millbrook with Crystal Spring and Millbrook's own $500,000 pot. Eventually, cheques would bounce and the whole mess would come to light.[32]

Chasing after Bad Money

In early 1984 Kleinsasser and Waldner realized that Deleo and Cornell could not be trusted. With the help of Don Edel, the powers of attorney were revoked and Deleo and Cornell were convicted of fraud.[33] Waldner testified at one of the criminal trials against Deleo.[34] In addition to reporting the fraud artists to the police, the Hutterites brought lawsuits against them.[35] The willingness of the colonies to start lawsuits was reciprocated by a host of lawsuits that would eventually be brought against the colonies by others who demanded their due from the borrowing and investments of the fraud artists.

When the dust settled, Crystal Spring, Rosedale, and Millbrook Colonies were owners of a host of money-losing enterprises that Deleo and Cornell had got them into with the powers of attorneys they had granted. According to Gibb, Mike Waldner and Jacob Kleinsasser appointed Don Edel as their principal agent to help them clean up the mess. Of all the investments, Edel felt that certain oil rights the con men had purchased on behalf of the colonies through Western States Energy might be worthwhile. Thus, instead of divesting themselves of all the investments and cutting their losses, Kleinsasser and Waldner arguably dug themselves in even deeper.

At a meeting in Winnipeg involving all the players, including Edel, it was decided that a corporation should be formed in Atlanta, Georgia, to be called WELK Resources. The purpose of the corporation would be to investigate the transactions that the fraud artists had entered into on behalf of Crystal Spring, Rosedale, and Millbrook, and to divest or manage these investments. Gibb also asserts that the purpose of WELK included further attempts to get low-interest financing for the colonies through a centralized loan from Rabobank.[36] The name WELK stood for Waldner, Edel, Lay, and Kleinsasser. Richard Lay was a lawyer in Atlanta who had earlier been promoting investments to Deleo and Cornell, including a gold mine enterprise that he was personally involved in.

Another corporation, RIDON (*Ri*chard Lay and *Don* Edel), was formed for the purposes of managing WELK. Gibb states that Edel soon fired Richard Lay after he persisted in trying to invest WELK money in his own personal business interests. According to Gibb, Lay later committed suicide when his gold mining venture collapsed.[37] RIDON, the corporation that was managing WELK, was restructured so that it was 60 percent owned by Don Edel and 40 percent by Waldner.[38] To replace the lawyer Richard Lay, another Atlanta lawyer by the name of James Youngblood was hired to work on WELK interests, and Myles Bender was hired to manage the oil interests. When Edel resigned or was fired by Kleinsasser in early 1985, RIDON was owned solely by Waldner.[39]

Through an unsecured loan from Rabobank, Michael Waldner, on behalf of Millbrook and Rosedale Colonies, borrowed US$1.5 million to provide working capital for WELK Resources. Gibb, who was working for Rabobank, states that he had no idea at the time that the funds were going to be used to fund Deleo's and Cornell's past mistakes.[40] According to Gibb, WELK was involved in oil-well interests, gold mining equipment, a plastics factory, trucking firms, and other companies.[41] Given that Don Edel was now spending almost all his time running WELK and that he also needed low-interest financing for his company back home, several advances from WELK to Edel and Valley Agro were made in 1984 totalling US$170,000, although a portion of these were for expenses directly related to Edel's work for WELK. Michael Waldner later asserted that he was not aware of, nor did he authorize, some of these initial cash advances of WELK money to Edel.[42] When he discovered them, he made sure that Edel signed backdated promissory notes for the advances so that they would be treated as loans from WELK to Edel and Valley Agro.[43]

What is clear is that rather than divesting, WELK was involved in a host of further investing activities, particularly in Texas oil interests. For a brief period it appeared that perhaps WELK would make a profit, but this hope soon disappeared in a flood of red ink and litigation. According to Gibb, belief that WELK Resources would rescue Kleinsasser and Waldner and provide a rich source of income for their colonies turned out to be utterly false. I recall that when I was at law school many years ago, one professor described an oil well as a hole in the ground surrounded by lawsuits. This certainly proved to be the case for the Hutterian leaders. WELK Resources operated for two years, between May 1984 and May 1986.[44] It appears from the Gibb account that it was basically lawsuits over debts, rather than any flow of income from investments, that characterized the activities of the company.

The Consumers Bank Litigation

Consumers Bank demanded payment under the terms of the fraudulent loan Deleo and Cornell had obtained to purchase oil rigs and other equipment. A meeting was held in Worcester, Massachusetts, on 15 February 1984 and attended by Joe Kleinsasser (brother of Jake) and Mike Waldner. At that time they agreed to continue payments on the leases on a reduced rate to the Consumers Bank on behalf of Rosedale/Millbrook and Crystal Spring.[45] An assignment of a term deposit at the Bank of Montreal in Winnipeg for US$300,000 was also provided by Crystal Spring as further collateral for the loan payments. However, by September 1984 both Rosedale/Millbrook and Crystal Spring stopped payment to Consumers Bank and a lawsuit was commenced by the bank against the colonies. When Consumers Bank tried to collect the $300,000 term deposit in Winnipeg as part of the amount owing, Jacob Kleinsasser on behalf of Crystal Spring Colony sued in Manitoba.[46] Crystal Spring sought a court order prohibiting the Bank of Montreal from sending the $300,000 to Consumers Bank, because Consumers was allegedly involved in the fraud with First Florida Leasing, and the assignment should therefore be declared void for fraud.[47] It was more than a little suspicious that First Florida was now a wholly owned subsidiary of Consumers Bank. Pending the trial, Crystal Spring was successful in getting an interim injunction to stop the term deposit money from going to Consumers. But at the same time, the amount actually owing by the colonies was much greater than the $300,000 being fought over, and the lawsuit continued in Massachusetts.

In January 1985 at a meeting in Chicago, this lawsuit was settled by the payment by Rosedale and Crystal Spring Colonies of over $2 million plus legal fees. Crystal paid $750,000 through two cheques drawn on the Bank of Montreal, while Rosedale paid $750,000 through a secured loan negotiated with Rabobank.[48] Some of the rest of the money came from the sale of the oil workover equipment.

The most sensitive aspects of the Gibb manuscript deal with allegations of how the senior elder dealt with the protests of Rosedale at being stuck with losses alongside Crystal Spring and Millbrook.[49] I will not deal with these matters here, other than to note that the charges were ultimately vigorously debated on both sides of the developing divide.

Hutterian Leaders Sue Their Former Business Partners

After two years WELK was dissolved in a blizzard of further lawsuits and losses.[50] One of the lawsuits was brought by Kleinsasser and Waldner against Edel.[51] As noted in the *Lakeside* trial, the corporation H.B. Enterprises, with Jacob Kleinsasser as one of its principal shareholders, was formed in Manitoba for the sole purpose of suing Don and Les Edel and their company, Valley Agro. The lawsuit against the Edels was launched on 8 November 1985. WELK Resources assigned to H.B. Enterprises the promissory notes for US$150,000 that Edel had signed for advances to himself or Valley Agro from WELK, and then H.B. Enterprises sued in Manitoba.[52] In defence, Edel asserted that he had spent huge amounts of time on WELK business at the request of Jacob Kleinsasser and that there was an informal agreement that he would be paid $80,000 a year for his work. Never having been paid, he now asserted that the loans should be set off against salary owing and he counterclaimed against WELK and H.B. Enterprises for payment for services rendered.[53] Kleinsasser and Waldner denied that there was any service contract with Edel, asserting that Edel had been motivated to help the colonies put out the fires because in a way it was he who had got them into the mess by introducing them to the fraud artists, and that he too was motivated by the desire to get low-interest financing through WELK. If there was any reimbursement for management fees, it was confined to Edel's interest in RIDON, which was contingent on a cash flow in WELK that did not materialize.

This bitter litigation, with discovery wars, motions of various kinds, and delays, extended over a decade, well past the writing of the Gibb manuscript, the split in the Schmiedeleut, and even the second round of the Lakeside dispute.[54] H.B. Enterprises particularly fought any attempt to have Jacob Kleinsasser examined for discovery. After five years of conflict, a settlement agreement was made in 1991, where the Edels would pay Cdn$60,000, instead of the US$150,000 alleged as debt owing from the WELK advances. Furthermore, the settlement was structured so that the payments by the Edels could be made at $12,000 a year over five years. However, to ensure the payments would be made, the Edels granted a series of consents to judgment to Kleinsasser's lawyers so that if a payment was not made, the amount that would be due and collectible would be twice the aggregate amount left owing under the agreement.[55] As part of the settlement, Kleinsasser and Waldner also demanded that all documents dealing with Crystal Spring, Rosedale, Millbrook, and WELK in the possession of the Edels be given to Kleinsasser, and that the Edels would not discuss the details of the litigation with anybody. I presume it was the lawyers for Kleinsasser who were successful in getting many of the documents in the court file declared confidential and thus placed in a lockup unavailable to me or other researchers.[56]

Given that the Edels did a lot of their business with Hutterite colonies, they in turn stipulated that

6. H.B. Enterprises Ltd., Baker, Zivot and Co., and Michael Waldner, on behalf of Millbrook Colony of Hutterian Brethren, shall each provide a letter to the Defendants confirming that the settlement has been reached on a basis acceptable to all parties, each in the form attached hereto. The Defendants shall be at liberty to use such letters as they see fit.

7. Reverend Jacob Kleinsasser will, on enquiry or request from any Hutterite Colony, advise that an amiable and satisfactory resolution of this litigation has been reached by the parties.[57]

These provisions were important to the Edels because they needed to rebuild the goodwill they had lost with many Hutterite colonies. Leslie Edel stated:

During the course of the within action I was repeatedly asked by Ministers and farm bosses of virtually every Colony from whom I sought business why, "I had sued their Bishop" ... Further, during the course of the within action virtually all of the colonies with whom I had previously carried on business advised me, through their respective Ministers or farm bosses, that Jacob Kleinsasser had directed that they should not under any circumstances carry on business with me or Valley Agro ... and that if they were to purchase products from me or to be seen to be even meeting with me that they would likely face retribution from Jacob Kleinsasser in one form or another.[58]

The Edels made their first payment in 1992 but thereafter refused to pay because they claimed that Kleinsasser failed to live up to the settlement agreement and had continued to denounce them and direct colonies under his leadership not to deal with them or Valley Agro. A fresh lawsuit against H.B. Enterprises and Jacob Kleinsasser was instituted.[59] The claim was for a counter-judgment of $12,000 and unspecified damages for lost profits, as well as for an interim injunction against H.B. Enterprises to prevent it from filing the consent judgments, and against Jacob Kleinsasser, ordering him to stop talking about any matters dealing with the lawsuit to other people.[60]

Jacob Kleinsasser denied that he had ever ordered colonies not to deal with the Edels or Valley Agro.[61] In defence, Kleinsasser filed twenty-five affirmations from ministers and secretaries of colonies within his leadership group. These people denied that Kleinsasser had made negative comments about the Edels or ordered the colonies not to deal with Valley Agro. A few were still dealing with Valley Agro, while others claimed that other suppliers offered a better price or product and that is why they did not contract with Valley Agro, rather than because of any directive of their bishop.

After a stalemate that lasted for several years, the Edels in June 1995 renewed the application for a court injunction to prevent H.B. Enterprises from using the consents for judgments and to prohibit Jacob Kleinsasser from making negative comments.[62] Leslie Edel stated: "The breaches of the settlement agreement ... remain unremedied and despite various attempts which I have made to meet personally with the defendant, Jacob Kleinsasser for the purposes of resolving our differences, Kleinsasser continues to refuse to meet."[63]

In the end, after a number of adjournments of the motions and counter-motions, the Edels submitted a certified cheque for the amount owing under the original settlement agreement and agreed to pay costs, but H.B. Enterprises sent the cheque back, insisting that it would proceed to file the consents for judgment, which would have doubled the amount the Edels would have to pay. Finally Justice Duval, in a hearing in August 1995, in essence affirmed the original settlement agreement, dismissing both the application of H.B. Enterprises to immediately use the consent judgments and the application of the Edels to have injunctive relief against Kleinsasser.[64]

Thus, after a prolonged battle of more than a decade, the Edels paid $60,000 plus costs as a debt for advances made by WELK, rather than the US$150,000 claimed. However, the legal costs and the costs to their business in terms of being sued by, and in turn suing, Jacob Kleinsasser were probably far greater than the original claim. Whether or not Kleinsasser said anything to ministers of other colonies, decisions to deal with a supplier could hardly not be affected by the widely known fact that the head of the church, Jacob Kleinsasser, was involved in a bitter dispute with that supplier. And as for Kleinsasser, the bringing of the lawsuit against the Edels might be characterized as a disaster. A great deal of the information that would ultimately split the church became public, both at the *Lakeside* trial and more particularly in the Gibb manuscript, because of the materials that were placed on public record through the litigation process, despite the sealing of other documents in the file.

Other Financial Issues

In his manuscript, Gibb also took aim at the performance of H.B. Credit, a company formed in Canada in 1984 to act as a kind of Hutterite savings and loan company. Gibb reviewed the financial transactions undertaken by H.B. Credit up to 1991, noting the numerous loans made to Crystal Spring Colony and the loans made to prop up the hog-killing plant in Neepawa started by Spring Hill Colony, and the levies imposed on Manitoba colonies to fund H.B. Credit. Gibb estimated that "there has been over $15 million dollars spent on the killing plant to date to primarily finance its losses."[65]

Gibb also reviewed the patent transactions involving Crystal Spring and C. and J. Jones Company in Canada and Gro Master in the United States. Gibb expressed his dismay at the way Crystal Spring Colony, headed by the leader of the church, was suing other Hutterite colonies, using the outside corporations as "strawmen."[66]

To conclude, the Gibb manuscript was read by many a Hutterian minister over the summer and fall of 1992. It would not be long before Gibb would be a household name in Hutterite circles. To some Hutterites, he would be the hero who blew the whistle on Kleinsasser, the leader of the church jetting to exotic locales, involved in high finance, oil wells, and lawsuits. No doubt for others, the Gibb manuscript was treachery, to be burned in the communal furnace: Kleinsasser had been a victim of fraud and had intended only to modernize and advance the financial security of the colonies. If the transactions would have paid off, he would have been a big hero. It was because they failed that he was in big trouble, not because of doing something wrong. Indeed, when the schism started, the informal language used to refer to the two groups in the Schmiedeleut was the "Gibbs (Group Two) v. the Oilers (Group One)."[67]

The Bruderhof Connection
The involvement of the senior elder, Jacob Kleinsasser, in various financial transactions and enterprises and the litigation arising therefrom was an important aspect leading to the schism in the church, but it was only half of the story. Probably of even greater importance were the conflicts generated at particular colonies and within the Hutterite community generally due to Kleinsasser's close association with the Bruderhof and the kind of spiritual and cultural changes that were seen as stemming from that association. The changes were a curious combination of liberalization on one hand – less restrictive clothing norms, the movement to accept high school and even secondary education, the willingness to participate in missions, the affirmation of a more individualistic spirituality, the movement to industry and manufacturing, a greater involvement in the wider society – and yet alleged authoritarianism on the other hand – a greater stress on obedience to leaders, and harsher church punishments. Changes in church doctrine and practice are bound to lead to disagreements, and the test of leadership is not the absence of conflict but how those conflicts are managed. To many of those who found themselves in disagreement over the direction Kleinsasser was steering the church, the management of conflict appeared to them to be the sheer authoritarian imposition of the will of the leader to crush opposition.

Thus, the schism was also caused because many people came to believe that the kind of strong-arm use of church punishments and shunning utilized by the senior elder to maintain power and control and impose his will was inappropriate.[68] Aside from the *Lakeside* case, litigation involving the Oak Bluff Colony also arose, and there were other colony hot spots as well. Before dealing with these developments, it should be noted that the first split in the church over the association of Kleinsasser with the Bruderhof occurred at the highest constitutional level, where Kleinsasser was removed as senior elder of the wider church, and in effect, while he remained senior elder of the Schmiedeleut, that branch was in a schism with the Darius and Lehrer branches of the church.

Every two years a meeting of the nine managers of the Hutterian Brethren Church takes place. As noted previously, this Board of Managers has jurisdiction over two separate entities, one involving the church as constituted and one involving the church as incorporated. There are three representatives from each of the three conferences. The nine managers when they meet elect from among themselves a senior elder and a second senior elder. Rev. Jacob Kleinsasser, the Schmiedeleut senior elder, was elected the senior elder of the whole Hutterian Brethren Church in 1980.[69]

A review of the minutes of meetings of this Board of Managers, at least for the corporate side of its function, since the first meeting was held in 1951, indicates that aside from admitting newly established colonies, the nine managers discuss legal and political issues that affect all the colonies. Since 1951 the church has retained one law firm to represent its interests – the Baker law firm in Winnipeg. The firm received an annual fee from each Hutterite colony in Canada as a retainer to represent the Hutterites collectively on various issues.

In 1978 the topic for discussion was discriminatory land use planning.[70] When Kleinsasser was elected senior elder in 1980, the major issue was the Hutterian response to the Canadian Pension Plan. At the next meeting in 1982, issues included the National Produce Marketing Board and the revision of the federal legislation dealing with nonprofit corporations.[71] In 1984 the meeting dealt with commodity quotas, the House of Commons Committee on Visible Minorities, eligibility for federal grant programs, income tax issues upon the split of a colony, and so forth.[72]

In 1986 a significant event happened. The meeting of the managers, which was to take place in Alberta in July, did not happen; Kleinsasser cancelled the meeting. A meeting was finally held in October 1987 at Bernard Colony in Manitoba. The minutes of the 1987 meeting have an altogether different flavour to them. The focus, instead of being on external relations, was on internal relations. The minutes include the following:

A discussion was held with regard to the postponement of the bi-annual meeting ... Jacob Kleinsasser advised that he would inform the members of the meeting of the reason for the postponement of the said meeting after the lawyers had withdrawn from the conference room ... On a motion made, seconded and duly passed, it was resolved that the Chairman alone, would not be allowed to postpone any meeting, but such postponement would only be done in consultation with the managers of the corporation ... A further discussion was held with regard to several points which were in contention between the different conferences and Jacob Kleinsasser stated that he was willing to clarify these issues subsequently in the meeting.[73]

The next meeting in 1989 at Lakeside Colony, Alberta, was unprecedented. The senior elder and chairperson of the meeting, Jacob Kleinsasser, did not show up.[74] Rev. John Wipf, from Parkland Colony in Alberta (Dariusleut), was elected senior elder. Behind all these tensions was Jacob Kleinsasser's relationship with the Bruderhof.

In 1990 the leaders of the Lehrerleut and Dariusleut sent a letter to the "Society of Brothers who call themselves Hutterian Brethren."[75] The letter contains ten points of disagreement with the practices of the Bruderhof. Some of these points of disagreement illustrate what would be seen by most of us as a narrow and inflexible legalistic view of Christian worship and ethics but, nevertheless, for the Hutterites, certain customs and prohibitions have taken on a sacred quality. The two Hutterite Leuts objected to the Bruderhof use of musical instruments and drama in worship, preaching new sermons instead of reading the old ones, lighting candles at worship services (too close to idolatry), presenting babies in church for dedication (too close to infant baptism), using emersion baptism instead of sprinkling, and so forth. Another objection was stated to be the Bruderhof support for the doctrine of the millennium.

For our purposes, however, the most interesting objections related more to the stance of the Bruderhof to the outside world. They allowed their older children to leave the colony for a time and attend colleges and universities. The Darius and Lehrer leaders also objected to the Bruderhof political involvement such as taking part in demonstrations against the death penalty. In regard to Rev. Arnold's giving testimony at the *Lakeside* case, it is interesting that the Hutterite leaders of the other two conferences had this to say: "The condoning or abetting of one Colony or Colony Member suing another in a secular court of law, in which you have been a willing and aggressive partner in complete contrast to the advice of Paul ... is also against the stand Hutterites have taken for 4 1/2 centuries."[76]

The letter ends with the Lehrerleut and Dariusleut revoking the 1974 unification or alliance with the Bruderhof. This disfellowship of the Bruderhof could be interpreted as a fundamental break with the Schmiedeleut as well, because Jacob Kleinsasser was actively involved in leading the union between the Eastern Bruderhof and the Western Hutterites. As noted previously, there were many intermarriages between the Schmiedeleut and the Bruderhof, and visitors flowing East and West, and there were also joint projects.

At the next meeting of the managers of the Hutterian Brethren Church in 1991 in Alberta, the schism was even more apparent. Not only did Jacob

Kleinsasser not show up but neither did the other two managers from the Schmiedeleut. Thus, the meeting included only the managers from the Lehrerleut and the Dariusleut. Roy Baker and Michael Radcliffe, the lawyers from Winnipeg who were closely associated with Kleinsasser, were in attendance at this meeting. The minutes state:

> A discussion was held on a number of different issues of concern to the Church, namely the general effect of membership by the American colonies and that the proper name of the corporation is Hutterian Brethren Church and not Hutterian Brethren Church of Canada ... An inquiry was made as to whether the Daniel Hofer matter was in order and the meeting was advised as to the status of this litigation. An inquiry was made as to the status of the Woodcrest Colony of Hutterian Brethren [Bruderhof] and the meeting was advised that no steps had been taken to bring Woodcrest Colonies into the Hutterian Brethren Church ... A discussion was held regarding the complaint by the Schmieden-Leut that they had been criticized at the meeting held August 16, 1989.[77]

As it turned out, by the time the next Board of Managers meeting took place, Jacob Kleinsasser, who had already lost his leadership position at the highest level of the church, would also lose his position as leader of the majority of the Schmiedeleut colonies, again in no small part because of his insistence that the Bruderhof be associated with the Hutterites. That the Dariusleut and Lehrerleut had already removed Kleinsasser as senior elder for the whole church made it much easier for the dissenters within the Schmiedeleut to later challenge the senior elder of their Leut. Even within the context of the considerable autonomy of the Leuts, dissenters could point out that they had the support of two-thirds of the church.

Jacob's Ladder

While on a plane trip years ago, I picked up the April 1992 edition of *Saturday Night* magazine. Nothing on the cover whet my appetite. The cover picture and lead story dealt with a man and his elephant. The cover also advertised two other stories, one on Lucien Bouchard, then leader of the Bloc Québécois, and one on some Canadians in a Brazilian jail. I nevertheless flipped through the magazine and was astonished to find a ten-page article entitled "Jacob's Ladder" by Brian Preston, written before the Supreme Court judgment in *Lakeside* was handed down.[78] There is a black-and-white photograph of Jacob Kleinsasser hunched over his kitchen table, a similar picture of Daniel Hofer, a colour photograph of Christoph Arnold and his wife, and a colour photograph of the family of Kleinsasser's daughter, Dora, who had married into the Bruderhof group. Despite the misleading caption attached to Daniel Hofer's picture – "Hutterites are taught to suffer wrong passively. Danny Hofer (below), excommunicated by the bishop, hit back with a lawsuit" – the article is overall an insightful overview of Schmiedeleut colony hot spots, and the role of the senior elder. Preston outlines some of the Manitoba hot spots where the "authoritarian" leadership of Kleinsasser was in question.

The first sketch dealt with Pine Creek Colony, where overseers had been appointed about the same time that Lakeside had experienced that fate. Unlike Lakeside, however, the Pine Creek people did not accept the overseers. According to Preston, this led to a feud with Kleinsasser, who excommunicated all the members of the colony from the Hutterian Brethren Church and then tried to get them to leave the colony so that the conference could take it over. Preston quotes the minister of Pine Creek as saying: "He wanted us out of here! There were twenty semis out on the road, sheriffs and police and whatnot ever, standing to take all the assets. He was just leaving us between heaven and earth, with nowhere to go, no sympathy, no Christianity, nothing. Off the colony! If you're disobedient to his orders, just go!"[79] The Pine Creek people managed to stay on the land by exploiting a clause in their mortgage that allowed them to stay on the home quarter, even as the feed company to which they were indebted took over the colony.[80] Lawyer Michael Radcliffe later pointed out that "[t]he excommunication of members at Pine Creek Colony was done by the Schmiedenleut Conference, all assembled ministers. Joe Kleinsasser from Sunnyside was the senior elder at the time who chaired this meeting, not Jake Kleinsasser. Therefore to blame Jake Kleinsasser for this action is inappropriate."[81] Another hot spot Preston mentions is Rainbow Colony, where again Kleinsasser had allegedly appointed an overseer minister after disapproving of the colony's choice of minister.[82] Rainbow Colony members refused the overseer, and Preston notes that the colony at that time was facing the threat of legal action by Kleinsasser to bring it into line.[83]

As for Lakeside Colony, Preston interviews Daniel Hofer, who thought that Kleinsasser's style of leadership came from the Bruderhof connection. Daniel Hofer is quoted as saying of the Woodcresters: "They're a hundred percent dictators down there. And he brought it over here, that system. The way Kleinsasser is trying to run the colonies here now is exactly like they've been running the colonies there for years."[84]

After reviewing the Bruderhof connection, Preston concludes his article with ambivalence: Kleinsasser was certainly a controversial leader, but perhaps he was a visionary who was working for the spiritual and economic renewal of the Hutterites, a renewal that was necessary for the survival of Hutterianism in the twenty-first century.

Another sketch in the Preston article deals with the Oak Bluff Colony, where four families, objecting to the Bruderhof influence, were under threat of excommunication and eviction.[85] Not being able to interview these people,

Preston does not elaborate on this hot spot. He notes, however, that the majority of the colony would not allow the children of the dissenters to attend the colony school. As a result of this decision, the minority group instituted litigation. Because the Oak Bluff conflict, like Lakeside, was a fundamental factor in the schism to follow, I will outline it briefly, based on information in the court files.

Oak Bluff Litigation

The conflict at Oak Bluff goes back to 1989, when the minister of the colony, Jacob T. Maendel, a strong supporter of the Bruderhof, went on a mission, and in turn a Bruderhof minister and other Bruderhof members came to Oak Bluff for several weeks. As a result of objections and actions taken to what they perceived as wrongful influences of the Bruderhof, Paul Maendel and Jake H. Maendel, two brothers, were excommunicated, and Paul was also removed from his position as vice-president of Oak Bluff. The two men later repented and were taken back into fellowship, although Paul was not returned to his former high position at the colony. Within a year, however, new conflicts broke out, triggered by disciplinary inquiries the minister had made of Jake Maendel's eleven-year-old daughter. Heated confrontations between Jake H. and Jacob T. occurred, and a series of church punishments and repentance phases took place, but eventually, because of various actions of Jake and Paul, including writing an intemperate letter to Kleinsasser, the two men were excommunicated at a congregational meeting at Oak Bluff on 15 July 1990.[86]

Unlike with the Lakeside situation, a higher court hearing of sorts was held within the church on the Oak Bluff conflict. On 23 July 1990, eighteen ministers gathered at Crystal Spring Colony to deal with the matter, and ten of those ministers were chosen to go to Oak Bluff and talk to the dissenting brothers. Apparently, after the ministers confirmed the excommunications and sought repentance, the dissenting men were still defiant – until the ministers had a meeting with the wife of one of the men. Thereafter there was again a repentance phase during which the men ate in the bakehouse and sat in the hall during worship services. This phase fell apart when Jake disobeyed an order to kill over $100,000 worth of bees he was looking after. According to Jake, there was no reason for this order to be given other than to test his obedience.[87]

The minority group did not leave the colony, which now was split into two groups just as at Lakeside. The dissenting group consisted of ten adults and twenty-one children.[88] Just as at Lakeside, the dissenters tried to establish enterprises to support themselves. According to one Hutterite leader, the dissenters at Oak Bluff were treated far worse than those at Lakeside in that they were not even given food.[89] Jacob Kleinsasser allegedly directed that no one from other colonies aid the dissenters, and if they did, they would be subject to church punishments. This harsh treatment of withholding bread from even the children led Samuel Kleinsasser, the minister of Concord Colony and one of Jacob Kleinsasser's brothers, to violate the order and come to the aid of the Oak Bluff dissenters.[90] His action was discovered and he barely avoided being placed in exclusion and having his ministerial position suspended. The Oak Bluff conflict arose directly out of objections to the relationship of the Hutterites with the Bruderhof, and given the strong views on this matter by the senior elder, the "renegades" at Oak Bluff were probably considered more dangerous than the "renegades" at Lakeside, where the dispute could be more directly pegged on hog feeders and disobedience rather than on religious ideology.

Also unlike the Lakeside situation, it was the dissenters at Oak Bluff who took the matter to court. The immediate reason for the litigation was that in an attempt to put pressure on the dissenters to leave, the majority group planned to privatize the colony school and hire its own teacher from the Bruderhof and then exclude from the school the sixteen school-aged children from the four dissenting families. The four families, following their religious faith, could not send their children to a public school off the colony. At the court hearing, lawyer Blair Filyk, acting for the dissenters, stated that the Red River School Division had offered to send a teacher to instruct the outcast children, but the colony would not allow the teacher on its property.[91] It might be recalled that in the Lakeside conflict, the children of Daniel and Paul were either married with preschool children, or they were living at home as young teenagers who were finishing or had already finished school. Thus, the fight at Lakeside did not involve conflicts over the education of the children as it did at Oak Bluff.

While the dissenters sued to get a court injunction allowing their children to attend school, the statement of claim was far broader than that. The dissenters claimed that their expulsions were void and that they were members in good standing of the church and colony, that the Schmiedeleut leaders under the direction of Kleinsasser were breaching the terms of the trust under which the Hutterite church was established, and that the dissenter group was the legitimate and rightful group to hold all the property of the colony, rather than the Kleinsasser group. Furthermore, the dissenters sought a court order restraining the Schmiedeleut from allowing the Bruderhof (Arnoldleut) to be members of the Hutterian Brethren Church, and a declaration that Jacob Kleinsasser had breached the terms of the church trust and should be restrained from acting as senior elder until approved by a vote of all the members of the conference. To similar effect was the assertion that the minister of Oak Bluff had breached the terms of the church trust and therefore should not act as minister until a proper vote was taken.[92]

None of these claims was ever adjudicated, as the immediate application for an injunction dealing with schooling became the focus, given that the school year was to start within days.[93]

The majority group at Oak Bluff claimed that it wanted a private school for its own children because the two streams of children from the two sides of the dispute had been involved in clashes and abusive conduct toward each other over the course of the last two years. Furthermore, it claimed that the dissenters had made allegations of child abuse against the minister and German schoolteacher, and so the majority group leaders felt incapacitated from exercising any discipline in the circumstances.[94] The colony proposed to rent an old rundown farmhouse adjacent to the colony and allow the dissenters to establish a school there.

For their part, the dissenters stated that they were never told of problems with the conduct of their children in school, and they denied that they had ever threatened the minister or teacher with claims of child abuse. The dissenters filed report cards and other materials that indicated the good behaviour of their children in school. The dissenters stated that, irrespective of the shunning of the parents, the children should be educated together, but if the two streams of children had to be separated, the dissenters at least wanted to use part of the schoolhouse or the kindergarten space rather than the uninhabitable house off the colony.[95]

When the matter came before Mr. Justice Vern Simonsen, he pleaded with the two groups of Oak Bluff to settle their differences without resorting to litigation. He is quoted as saying: "It (going to court) just isn't the way that people who live under a spiritual network should involve themselves."[96]

Given the number of times Jacob Kleinsasser and other Schmiedeleut leaders had launched aggressive lawsuits, it was almost comical when Michael Radcliffe cross-examined Jake Maendel. After presenting the ten baptismal points, as he had done at the Lakeside trial, Radcliffe asked Maendel,

Q. And by bringing this court action through these gentlemen here (referring to the lawyers for the dissenters) you feel that you are still in sympathy with these principles expressed in this book?
A. I would say yes.
Q. That seems, at first glance, to be a contradiction to me. Could you explain, sir, how [bringing this action] in a world court proceeding – that that is in conformity to the discipline and precepts of the Hutterian Brethren Church?
A. I would say with all the documents that we can show here today, that we tried hard with the Hutterian Brethren Church as a whole and to the best of our knowledge, there was no alternative available than making that move that we did.

Q. In some circles, sir, it would be considered an adversarial or an aggressive step to call somebody to the world court and I am asking you, sir, whether you, in fact, adopt that position, that you are being aggressive and adversarial? "Adversary" means opposite or opposed or aggressive to the Hutterian Brethren Church and the people that you have named as defendants.[97]

This same tone of righteous indignation at the violation of Hutterian norms would soon be used against Daniel Hofer at the second Lakeside trial even though, as we have seen, the lawyers for Kleinsasser and other Group One leaders appeared to have no qualms about launching aggressive lawsuits on behalf of their Hutterite clients.

As the weeks of the school term passed without a settlement, and under the pressure of Mr. Justice Simonsen, the colony finally suggested that it move a trailer onto the colony and allow the public schoolteacher to come onto colony land and teach the dissenters' children in the trailer.[98] The dissenters finally accepted this proposal, and so there was no need for a court order.

However, according to the dissenters, the misuse of shunning by placing innocent children into the circle of contamination continued. The portable classroom was used for one year, after which the lease was up and the owner of the trailer removed it. Radcliffe argued that the colony had no obligation to facilitate any education of the dissenters' children because the dissenters had been excommunicated from the church.[99] This argument that a colony has no fiduciary duty for the welfare of children who have been born into and are living on a colony, just because their parents are allegedly not in good standing, seems fundamentally contradictory to the notion that colony life involves significant colony responsibility for the welfare and socialization of children that transcends "normal" parental control.

Now the dissenters had to bring a new series of motions to get a court order so that their children could go to school.[100] The Kleinsasser group argued that if the dissenter group would not bus the children to St. Agathe (a nearby town), it should pay all the costs of reassembling the trailer and all past and future costs of heating it, as well as pay rent to the colony for the use of it. In the end Mr. Justice DeGraves ordered the colony to move the school trailer back to the colony at colony expense, but he also ordered the dissenter group to pay half the lease and utility costs.[101] Justice DeGraves is reported to have said: "My prayerful hope is these things are much better settled in your chapel or living room than in this forum."[102] As we will see, however, that hope was unrealized. The litigation at Lakeside and Oak Bluff was only the beginning of many more lawsuits between colony factions. I will return to Oak Bluff when examining the aftermath of the schism that was about to engulf the church.

Debating the Leadership of the Senior Elder

It was the assistant senior elder, Rev. Joseph Wipf of Plainview Colony, South Dakota, who led the movement to challenge the leadership of the senior elder, Rev. Jacob Kleinsasser. Wipf had been in the assistant position since 1971. After reading the Gibb manuscript, Wipf organized a meeting of Schmiedeleut ministers in South Dakota in August of 1992. The meeting came to the attention of the senior elder, who sent several letters ordering the ministers not to meet without his permission.[103] However, despite the orders of the senior elder, forty-four South Dakota ministers met, and from that discussion, Joseph Wipf formulated a twelve-point letter of concern about Kleinsasser's leadership, which was circulated throughout the colonies on 29 August 1992.[104]

Included in the twelve points were questions about how Rosedale Colony had been treated, why the powers of attorney and letters of credit were given without consultation with the conference or with the colonies concerned, and why Crystal Spring was suing other colonies over the patent issue. There were also questions about whether the American colonies were being shortchanged by the Hutterian insurance scheme, about a lack of accounting for the levies paid to the conference by each colony, about how litigation at Lakeside and Oak Bluff was being handled, about why the Schmiedeleut was cut off from the other two conferences, and, of course, the issue of the Bruderhof. In this regard, Wipf wrote, "It is our plea and request that we do not want to have anything to do with them further."[105]

Faced with a twelve-point indictment, the senior elder had to defend himself. Over the next months, meetings of ministers were called to deal with the concerns. A smaller meeting of Manitoba ministers was held at Crystal Spring on 7 September 1992. However, it was decided that a meeting of all the Manitoba ministers should be held on 15 September.[106] At this meeting, chaired by Mike Wollmann, Kleinsasser went through the twelve points and dismissed them all, but some of the ministers thought certain points had validity and wanted to hear from Joseph Wipf. Nothing was resolved. Another small meeting of Manitoba ministers took place on 19 October 1992, and it was decided that a meeting of all the ministers – on both sides of the border – would have to be called to deal with the growing controversy. The meeting was called for 5 November 1992 at Starlite Colony in Manitoba.

The meeting at Starlite, involving around 150 ministers, lasted three days, as Wipf's twelve points were debated with intensity. Joseph Wipf did not back down from his allegations, nor did Jacob Kleinsasser back down from affirming his innocence. The final result was that Jacob Kleinsasser said that "[h]e did not accept any of the 12. They were all lies and false. He told everyone to go home and think about it."[107] At the meeting Jacob Kleinsasser had also told those who persisted in affirming the twelve points against him that "they had no Senior Elder."[108]

Given the unwillingness of Kleinsasser to admit to any of the charges, Joseph Wipf circulated a letter on 19 November 1992 on behalf of forty-nine ministers who questioned the leadership of Kleinsasser. Wipf concluded his letter by calling for a meeting of all the ministers to be held at New Elmspring Colony, South Dakota, on 1 December 1992. By this time it was clear to all that the leadership issue had to be resolved, and rather than let the opposition control the location and agenda, Jacob Kleinsasser responded with a letter on 23 November calling for a meeting of all the ministers for 9 December, back at Starlite in Manitoba.

Before the Starlite meeting took place, the leaders of the other two conferences, the Dariusleut and the Lehrerleut, circulated a lengthy letter to the Schmiedeleut ministers dated 1 December 1992.[109] The leaders of the other conferences repeated many of the ten points that had led them to disassociate with the Bruderhof back in 1990. They also elaborated further on their disagreement with the Bruderhof, including the undemocratic hereditary leadership style of the Bruderhof, which had devolved within a particular family, from Arnold to his son and then to his grandson. Most importantly they noted the autocratic disciplinary approach of the Bruderhof leadership. The thrust of the letter was that Jacob Kleinsasser was solidly aligned with the Bruderhof, and they wanted it to end.

Based on the Gibb manuscript and other sources, the leaders of the Lehrerleut and Dariusleut added further points as to why Kleinsasser should be removed. The language was strong:

> One after another he [Kleinsasser] has abandoned the time-tried ordinances, traditions and practices that have held the Hutterian Brethren Church together for hundreds of years ...
>
> Like no other Hutterian Elder before him, Kleinsasser uses the well known Arnoldian practice of using the Elder powers to force change; to intimidate his fellow Servants of the Word and silence any opposition among those that do not agree with his policies in the Schmiedleut conference, to attain his goal of bringing the Arnoldleut fully into the Hutterian Church, with all their destructive, anti-Hutterian practices, which will certainly destroy the Hutterian Church if left unchecked. This has been his goal even before he became the Schmiedleut Elder ...
>
> We have weighed all the evidence that has come to light in the fear of the Lord, and can only conclude that he [Kleinsasser] has abandoned the true Hutterian path that our forefathers walked in their sojourn on this earth, and has been led astray through lofty minded pride and the Arnold influence ...

The cause of this present crisis that is dividing the Darius and Lehrerleut from the Schmiedleut can be laid squarely at the door of Jacob Kleinsasser, the apostate Elder of the Schmiedleut and those that stand by him ...

We have discussed this issue at great length in the fear of the Lord and declare openly that we do not recognize Jacob Kleinsasser as an Elder nor as a Servant of the Word anymore, but support Joseph Wipf Vetter, Plainview Colony, S. Dak. and all those that are struggling with him in their fight to preserve the integrity and honour of the Hutterian Brethren Church.[110]

That the leaders of the other two conferences were willing to call Jacob Kleinsasser "an apostate" was as strong a signal of support for Joseph Wipf as there could possibly be. On the other side of the debate, in support of Kleinsasser, some Bruderhof members faxed communications to the colonies. They asserted that the forty-nine ministers who stood with Wipf were no longer recognized by the Bruderhof as ministers in the Hutterian Brethren Church. They stated: "We are deeply pained that our beloved Jake Kleinsasser Vetter of Crystal Spring, who has served the Church so faithfully for so many years, and has been our Elder for so many years, is now so viciously attacked. We would like to remind Joseph Vetter and the Servants and brothers and sisters holding to the same spirit of defiance, that you will not be able to remove the brothers and sisters in the East so simply. You will not be able to remove Jake Kleinsasser Vetter from the Eldership so simply."[111]

At the pivotal meeting of Schmiedeleut ministers on 9 and 10 December 1992 at Starlite Colony, Rev. Joseph Wipf was asked if he still affirmed his twelve points. He stated that he did. Jacob Kleinsasser was asked whether he would admit to some of the concerns and questionable behaviour and promise to correct the problem. Kleinsasser refused to budge.[112]

The two sides that emerged each put their own, very different, spin on the events of the meeting. Kleinsasser supporters wrote their own minutes, to the effect that Kleinsasser was never removed from his position but, rather, that the Schmiedeleut split on 9 December, with one side agreeing to remain at Starlite and the other side going off to Westroc Colony. Part of Kleinsasser's minutes read:

After a lengthy discussion, Jacob Wipf, Spring Creek Colony, South Dakota, very impolite, rude and insensible, read a letter of false accusations and untruths to Bishop-Elder, Jacob Kleinsasser that he was no longer Elder. This letter was a predetermined decision, which he had in his pocket before coming to the Meeting.

Jacob Kleinsasser, Bishop-Elder told everyone, this letter is not and will not be accepted, because it is full of untruths and false accusations.

Joseph Wipf, Plainview Colony, South Dakota, without further counsel got up and said to the group, whoever stands for the truth shall be in Westroc Colony tomorrow at 1:30 pm, we will have our own meeting.

Jacob Kleinsasser, Bishop-Elder and Chairman told the group: whoever is with this letter of untruths and accusations, can go to Westroc Colony, you are on your own, you are separated (abgesondert) from the Church. Further-more, you cannot preach the gospel or Word of God with this revolt, rebel-lion and exaltation. All of you who stand with the Church and Elder shall be here tomorrow at 1:00 pm at Starlite Colony.

This was unanimously accepted by everyone present and therefore was the official split of the Schmiedenleut Hutterian Brethren.[113]

However, a different interpretation of the meeting of 9 and 10 December was that the ministers who supported Joe Wipf did not want to break up the church: they wanted a resolution to the matter, not a split. They did not want to go to Westroc for a separate meeting and persuaded Wipf to stay and join in the meeting the next day. This change of plans was read to all at the Starlite supper table on 9 December.[114]

The Senior Elder Loses a Vote of Confidence
The hope for a resolution was dashed on 10 December 1992. After more discussion on the twelve points, some ministers again asked Kleinsasser to step down as senior elder. Instead of doing so, he called for what was in effect a vote of confidence in his leadership. Many of those who supported Wipf did not want a vote. They did not want to remove the senior elder: they wanted him either to step down on his own accord or to admit to the problems and correct them. After much discussion on whether to call a vote, Jacob Kleinsasser left the meeting for a half hour. When he came back, the process started all over again. Despite some ministers not wanting to have a vote, it was clear that Kleinsasser was intent on drawing a line and dividing the conference.[115] On a motion seconded by Mike Wollmann, Kleinsasser asked those that supported him to stand. The evidence is clear that more remained seated than stood up in support.

There was some confusion about counting bodies. The minutes of the meeting prepared by Joseph Wipf state that 78 ministers stood up in favour of Kleinsasser and 95 remained seated.[116] This would mean that 173 minis-ters had voted. However, the count as recalled by Leonard Kleinsasser, min-ister of Delta Colony, who was also not a supporter of the senior elder, was that 78 stood up and 90 remained seated, but this was in the context of his recollection that there were 168 ministers at the meeting, not 173.[117] This 90 to 78 figure also conforms to press reports.[118] However, Michael Wollmann, a supporter of the senior elder, said at the second Lakeside trial that the vote was 78 to 95.[119] The minutes of Jacob Kleinsasser, on the other hand, stated that 80 had stood up at the meeting. The number 80 was subsequently confirmed by Rev. Jacob Hofer of Starlite when he gave testimony at the second Lakeside trial.[120] Even by his own count, Kleinsasser lost the vote.

The Joseph Wipf minutes of the meetings state that after the vote was counted, the meeting ended in the following way: "On motion duly made from the floor by Rev. John Hofer, and seconded by Mike Tschetter, a majority vote was declared that Rev. Jacob Kleinsasser no longer be an elder of the Hutterian Brethren Church, and Schmiedleut Congregation, and therefore, must step down from that position. The meeting then adjourned on motion by Reverend Jacob Kleinsasser and seconded by Rev. Joseph Wipf."[121]

Jacob Kleinsasser, however, did not accept the vote or the motion that he step down. According to the Kleinsasser minutes,[122]

> Jacob Kleinsasser, Bishop Elder said: this affair does not go by majority. You separated yourself from us (the Church) yesterday.
>
> To end the Meeting, Jacob Kleinsasser, Bishop-Elder said, "All that are with the Church shall stay and sign their Name so we know where you are from. The rest go home and think over what they have done."
>
> Present at the Meeting were 168
> Signed for the Church 90
> Dissidents 78

Notice how in the Kleinsasser minutes the results of the vote are reversed, as if a majority had supported his leadership. To explain the reversal of vote counts, supporters noted that nine ministers changed their minds and phoned back after a few days indicating their support for Kleinsasser.[123] The Bruderhof, of course, jumped in and added to the confusion. It claimed that 110 ministers stood up to support Kleinsasser, while 95 remained seated. This was accomplished by arguing that Jacob Maendel of the Pleasant View Bruderhof community in Ulster Park, New York, was at the meeting, and he actually represented all "29 ministers from the 'Eastern' Hutterites."[124]

Determining the correct number of members who stood in support of the elder or who sat in opposition to the elder was not the only controversy. Equally problematic was the meaning to be given to the vote in the first place. As noted above, those who remained seated found themselves to be in the majority and therefore concluded that the senior elder would have to step down. The senior elder had lost a vote of confidence that he himself had called and had therefore removed himself from the position. But another argument was that the senior elder could not be removed by any vote of ministers. The senior elder was elected to the position by all the male members of the Schmiedeleut and had the position for life, no matter what he did: the vote was not a vote to remove the elder but a vote to identify those who did not support the elder, and these ministers were out of the church he led, even if they constituted a majority. But the majority of the ministers who did not support the senior elder did not think they were leaving their church to start a new one; they thought the senior elder and his supporters were being disobedient to the church by not stepping down in obedience to the majority will.

As noted previously, in this narrative I will use the simple division of Group One (Kleinsasser supporters) and Group Two (Wipf supporters). Group Two claimed that it was the true Schmiedeleut and that Jacob Kleinsasser was removed from his position on 10 December 1992. Group One claimed that Group Two had left the true Schmiedeleut and formed its own association, and that Group One constituted the true Schmiedeleut.

Group One and Group Two Divide

If Rev. Jacob Kleinsasser had stepped down as senior elder of the Schmiedeleut after the pivotal vote of 10 December 1992, the Schmiedeleut would still be together, although the formal connection with the Bruderhof and the Schmiedeleut would have come to an abrupt end. After the vote of December 1992, the Schmiedeleut colonies were not immediately split into two camps. It would take some time and a lot of pain before separation was achieved. That the lines would be drawn fairly quickly, however, became apparent when Jacob Kleinsasser concluded that those who had voted against him should conform again or be expelled from the church. If the managers of a particular colony – the first and second minister and the secretary, for example – were all in one camp or the other, and the ordinary members of the colony were also in agreement with the position taken by the leaders, the effect of the schism would be less painful: the colony would clearly be a Group One or a Group Two colony. However, as with the Lakeside and Oak Bluff situations, many colonies were internally divided, and so the schism was painful indeed, largely because of the approach of Group One, which demanded that Group Two be shunned. Families and colonies were torn apart as people were excluded and expelled from the church for not supporting the senior elder. As noted in the press, "[o]bservers say that the movement between colonies is similar to a small civil war with refugees fleeing from one colony to another."[125] The rift between families affected even those at the top. One of Jacob Kleinsasser's brothers became one of the leading spokesmen for the anti-Kleinsasser forces.[126] Jake Hofer, overseer minister at Lakeside and minister of Starlite, was a prominent Group One leader, whereas his brother, John Hofer, minister of James Valley, was a prominent Group Two leader. Throughout the Leut, families were torn apart.

The use of expulsion and shunning is illustrated in a letter (said to be typical) sent to a troubled colony. Jacob Kleinsasser states:

Be it known by all members of the Hutterian Brethren Church that there
are persons who have stated openly that they no longer wish to recognize
Jacob Kleinsasser as the Elder of the Schmiedleuts Hutterian Brethren. They
have chosen a course of action which violates the rules, tenets, teachings,
and practices of the Hutterian Brethren and have stated openly that they
are no longer part of the church.

Because of their statements and actions, the Hutterian Brethren Church
accepts their withdrawal from the Church and recognizes that they are no
longer members of the Hutterian Church by their withdrawal. These persons include the following:

[names deleted]

All members of the Hutterian Brethren Church are to recognize and remember that the above persons are no longer members of the Church and
they have given up all rights and privileges of such membership, including,
but not limited to, the right to vote on any questions to be decided by the
members of the Colony made up of members of the Hutterian Brethren
Chruch.[127]

The power that the senior elder was exercising was quite breathtaking.
Without any need to go through the procedural due process steps laid down
by the Supreme Court of Canada, a vast number of Hutterites were allegedly expelled from the church, simply on the word of the senior elder. If
taken literally, these people would be tossed out of their colonies simply
because they did not recognize a leader who had been voted out of office.
For their part, Group Two leaders claimed they did not reciprocate with
similar tactics. While it is true that Group Two claimed it was the true church
and that Jacob Kleinsasser had no authority to speak for the church any
longer, Group Two nevertheless agreed that it would not use shunning
against Group One minorities at Group Two colonies.[128]

Group Two had to scramble to get organized in the face of the aggressive
moves to discipline Group Two members and ministers. The intention of
Group Two to recognize Joseph Wipf rather than Jacob Kleinsasser as the
true senior elder was soon moot because Wipf died. Rather than choosing
another senior elder, Group Two settled on a conference structure (at least
for the time being), which included a nine-person executive committee (eight
elders plus a chairperson) for the Manitoba colonies, and a similar committee for the American colonies. The two committees would consult and the
regular annual and special conference board meetings as outlined in the
church constitution would continue.[129]

One of the first problems faced by Group Two ministers was that Jacob
Kleinsasser, without any notice to them, had managed to get their licences
to marry people revoked. The senior elder was the designated ecclesiastical
authority for the Hutterian Brethren Church to register those ministers of

the denomination who would be granted licences to perform marriages. Jacob Kleinsasser went to the provincial Department of Vital Statistics and argued that the licences of all the ministers who opposed him should not be renewed, as the ministers were no longer members of the Hutterian Brethren Church.[130] If these ministers wanted a licence, they would have to register under a different name than that of "Hutterian Brethren."

The Group Two ministers met on 8 and 9 February 1993 at the Delta Colony in Manitoba to consult with lawyers and chart a course of action.[131] What was perceived as the vindictive move to revoke the licences of ministers to perform marriages backfired on Group One and its legal counsel. Several Schmiedeleut ministers visited the leaders of the Dariusleut and Lehrerleut. After hearing how the senior elder claimed that his group was the only true Hutterian Brethren, and that the Baker law firm was supporting him in this contention, the leaders of the other two branches of the Hutterian Brethren Church promptly travelled to Winnipeg, arriving at the offices of the law firm and demanding that the official books of the Hutterian Brethren Church be handed over to them. Radcliffe complied, and this brought to an end the longstanding relationship between that law firm and the church as constituted and incorporated.[132] Mr. P.K. Matkin of the law firm Macleod Dixon in Calgary was retained as solicitor for the wider church, and Group Two ministers and colonies in Manitoba also retained Sidney Wolchock as their legal counsel to deal with the legal questions arising from the schism. Jeffrey Sveen, an attorney in South Dakota, represented Group Two in the United States.

Aside from dealing with the disputes over management and property that would arise between it and Group One at particular colonies, how would Group Two colonies disengage themselves from, or make claims for, the assets of the various enterprises the Schmiedeleut conference itself owned and which were firmly under the control of Kleinsasser supporters? Lawyer Sidney Wolchock first prepared a lengthy report on "Hutterite Business Ventures and Dealings" in February 1993.[133] But of more immediate importance, Wolchock suggested a reaffirmation process, whereby the Group Two colonies would formally demonstrate that they, rather than Group One, were the proper Schmiedeleut branch of the Hutterian Brethren Church.[134]

Reaffirmation Process

When Jacob Kleinsasser did not show up for the 1989 meeting of managers of the Hutterian Brethren Church, Rev. John Wipf from Parkland Colony in Alberta was chosen as senior elder of the church. In April of 1993, John Wipf issued a statement to all Schmiedeleut congregations that asserted that Jacob Kleinsasser had been voted out of the position of elder on 10 December 1992. Wipf then said: "Therefore, everyone should know that Reverend Jacob Kleinsasser is no longer an Elder of the Church, and has no right or authority to speak for the Hutterian Brethren Church. I wish to make it clear in this letter that no one is to take any instructions from Reverend Jacob Kleinsasser because he has no authority to speak for or on behalf of the Hutterian Brethren Church and the Schmied-Leut Congregation."[135]

That Group Two was going to be the recognized and accepted member of the Hutterian Brethren Church required more formality than the declaration by the senior elder of the church. A meeting of the managers of the Hutterian Brethren Church was called for 9 June 1993 in the offices of Macleod Dixon. Lawyers Matkin, Wolchock, and Sveen were in attendance. The six Lehrerleut and Dariusleut managers were at the meeting, but no managers from the Schmiedeleut were officially in attendance. In attendance, but not voting, were some Group Two Schmiedeleut ministers. At this meeting, a motion was approved that "Jacob Kleinsasser, Crystal [Spring] Colony, Manitoba, through his actions over the past year and the vote which took place at Starlite Colony on December 10, 1992, was removed as Elder, Minister, Manager or Representative in any way of the Schmied-Leut Conference of the Hutterian Brethren Church and that the Board of Managers accept that vote."[136]

Given the split in the Schmiedeleut conference, it was agreed that a document should be drafted, entitled "Reaffirmation of Membership in the Hutterian Brethren Church." This document would be circulated to every colony in all three conferences and signed by two managers on behalf of each colony. The document was drafted and approved at the Calgary meeting of 9 June.[137] It was also agreed that Matkin, Wolchock, and Sveen would draft a new constitution to be approved at a later date.

With the circulation of the reaffirmation document it would become more apparent as to which colonies stood with the wider church and which stood with Kleinsasser. Of course, Kleinsasser and his supporters would claim that this reaffirmation process was illegal for a number of reasons, one being that the three managers of the Schmiedeleut, as appointed by Group One, were not given notice of, nor were they in attendance at, the Calgary meeting. Michael Radcliffe, from the Baker law firm, sent a letter to the Schmiedeleut colonies telling them not to sign the reaffirmation document. He claimed that "[t]his documentation may have the legal effect of changing the inherent nature of the Hutterian Brethren Church from one of a collection of independent colonies to that of a vertically structured association or corporation, all having direct responsibility to the Elder and Board of nine Managers. This is not the current status of the organization and I would suggest that it is extremely dangerous to change the nature of the Hutterian Brethren Church into an organization as I have described."[138]

This argument no doubt caused a few chuckles within Group Two circles, given that it was Radcliffe's client, Jacob Kleinsasser, who was perceived by them as the one who had exercised a dominating, centralizing authority as a senior elder that ran contrary to the traditions of having "a collection of independent colonies."

As expected, all the Darius and Lehrer colonies from both sides of the border signed the reaffirmation document, as did the Group Two colonies of the Schmiedeleut. However, the reaffirmation documents were thrown in the garbage at colonies controlled by Group One managers. Just as there was a contest as to the numbers of the votes at the 10 December meeting, there was now a contest as to the numbers of colonies affiliated with Group One and Group Two. It was reported that at the time of reaffirmation, there were 150 Schmiedeleut colonies, and that 87 had reaffirmed, whereas 63 had not.[139] But while the majority of Schmied colonies had reaffirmed, there was a big difference between the numbers on either side of the border. The vast majority of the Schmied colonies in the United States (53 out of 65) reaffirmed, but in Manitoba, the Group One colonies had a clear majority. If there were around 85 colonies in Manitoba in 1993, only 34 of them reaffirmed at that time, while 51 did not.

Because Jacob Kleinsasser still had a majority in Manitoba, and because the Hutterian Brethren Church as incorporated existed as a Canadian entity by virtue of a Canadian statute and therefore did not include the American colonies, and because, according to Radcliffe, the American colonies were not signatories to the 1950 constitution of the church,[140] Group One continued to argue that the purported change to the constitution by adding American colonies was illegal, and that Group One was the true Hutterian Brethren Church in terms of law. Of course, the numbers of colonies supporting either Group One or Group Two changed over the course of the years. At the time of this writing there are about 105 colonies in Manitoba; 54 of them are Group Two colonies, which means that Group One no longer is in the majority. Instead, there is an almost even split between the two groups.[141]

New Constitution

Another meeting of the Board of Managers of the Hutterian Brethren Church took place on 7 July 1993, where by resolution of the board, a new constitution was approved.[142] The original 1950 *Constitution of the Hutterian Brethren Church and Rules as to Community of Property* was replaced with a new document having the same title.[143] It was resolved at this Board of Managers meeting that colonies would sign up and agree to the new constitution, and then the first biannual meeting of the Board of Managers under the new constitution would take place on 21 July 1993 at Starland Colony, Drumheller. The new members of the Board of Managers were to be nominated using the new constitution. In this way, the Schmiedeleut would have new managers elected from Group Two, which consisted of the colonies that had reaffirmed.

Under the new constitution, there was to be a fifteen-person Board of Managers for the church as constituted, five to be elected from each conference. Group Two Schmiedeleut leaders met on 13 July 1993. The leaders of the fifty-three American colonies met at Glendale Colony, while the leaders representing thirty-four Manitoba colonies met at Sommerfeld Colony. At these meetings the new constitution was read, discussed, approved, and signed by representatives of each colony. The list of nominees for the five managers from the Schmiedeleut who were to be appointed to sit on the Board of Managers under the new constitution was also approved. Even though the number of reaffirmed colonies was greater in the United States than in Canada, three of the five managers were from Manitoba.[144] This was necessary in any case, because out of the Board of Managers of the transnational church as constituted, there would have to be three people to serve on the board of the Canadian church as incorporated.

Group One responded to these developments by presenting a rival slate of candidates for the meeting of the Board of Managers that was called for 21 July 1993. Michael Radcliffe, claiming to still be the solicitor of the Schmiedeleut conference, properly so called, wrote a letter to John Wipf, the senior elder, with the names of the three Schmiedeleut minister managers who should attend the meeting of the Board of Managers of the church as incorporated at Drumheller.[145] Now that they were no longer members of the church as newly constituted, Matkin in effect told the Kleinsasser managers to stay away. The managers who were part of the church as incorporated were to be appointed by the provisions of the church as constituted. Radcliffe's clients were attempting to attend a meeting of a church to which they no longer belonged.

The first biannual meeting of the fifteen-member Board of Managers took place on 21 July 1993 at Starland, near Drumheller, Alberta. In addition to the fifteen managers, well over 150 Hutterite ministers from across North America were in attendance.[146] John Wipf, a Lehrerleut from Parkland, Alberta, was again elected president of the church, and Michael Stahl, a Dariusleut from Alberta, was elected vice-president, while John Stahl, another Dariusleut from Alberta, was elected secretary-treasurer. The fifteen-member Board of Managers then elected the nine members to sit as the Board of Directors for the corporate church in Canada. The officers of the church as incorporated were the same three who were elected president, vice-president, and secretary-treasurer for the church as constituted. At the meeting, the reaffirmation process and new constitution were reviewed and approved. It was also noted that "those colonies which, to date, had not reaffirmed their membership in the Church could in the future again be accepted in membership in the Church on terms as may be established by the Board of Managers."[147]

Having been accepted as *the* Schmiedeleut branch of the Hutterian Brethren Church, Group Two was able to convince the government officials in Manitoba that they were worthy of using the name Hutterian Brethren to obtain licences to marry people. But this did not happen without a prolonged fight by Group One to discredit the legality of the new constitution.[148] In the end, the government decided that both groups could use the name Hutterian Brethren, at least for marriage licence purposes. It seems to me that this should have been the obvious solution from the start of the dispute.

Subsequently, having been spurned by the wider church, Group One incorporated its own conference in Manitoba.[149] Eventually Group One also incorporated federally using the name "Schmied-Leut Conference of the Hutterian Brethren Church Inc."[150] Given the confusion as to the name of this federal corporation with the corporation set up in 1950, the federal minister of Industry, after a prolonged dispute between Group One and Group Two, issued Supplementary Letters Patent changing the name of Group One's federal incorporation to a numbered company.[151] The Group One church as federally incorporated is currently called "3272656 Canada Inc."[152]

Old Constitution versus New Constitution

The disputes between Group One and Group Two would soon proliferate and include a great deal of litigation. Before detailing this, however, it may be helpful to first give a brief overview of how the 1993 constitution differs from the 1950 constitution.

Following the exposition of Mr. Justice Gonthier of the Supreme Court of Canada in the *Lakeside* case, the new constitution clearly separates two distinct entities: the constitutional church and the incorporated church. The church as constituted is composed of all the reaffirmed colonies, the three conferences (Lehrer, Darius, and Schmied), and the central Board of Managers. From the Board of Managers, representatives are then chosen to sit as the Board of Managers for a separate entity called the incorporated church that exists only in Canada.[153] As for the church as constituted, does the new constitution change any of the former rules or practices at the three levels of the church: the central Board of Managers level, the conference board level, and finally, the local colony level?

As to the power of the new fifteen-person central Board of Managers of the constitutional church, the new constitution states:

7. The Church dogma and Church discipline and the affairs, powers, privileges and all matters affecting and pertaining to Hutterian Brethren generally and subject to the rights of each Conference as set forth in Article 22

hereof, shall be administered, managed, exercised, transacted, conducted and controlled by a Board of fifteen (15) managers, five (5) of whom shall be chosen as set forth in Article 30 hereof by each of the said Conferences.[154]

Whether the new constitution gives significant ecclesiastical and administrative powers to the new Board of Managers depends on the relationship between article 7 and article 22, which states:

22. Each Conference Board shall exercise control over the Church dogma and Church discipline within its respective Conference, and shall have charge of all matters pertaining to the Church and the Hutterian Brethren within its Conference, and shall have power to take such action as it deems appropriate in respect to matters affecting or pertaining to the Church and the Hutterian Brethren of that Conference. The senior elder is recognized as the spiritual and ecclesiastical leader for a Conference. To the extent that the decisions of the Conference might affect the Church generally then such decisions shall be subject to review by the Board of Managers who have the right, in accordance with the provisions of Article 7 hereof, to overrule any such decision pertaining only to matters which are of concern to the whole of the Church or which may affect the working, administration or operation of the Church generally.[155]

It may be recalled that under the old constitution, each conference had the right to veto any ecclesiastical ruling made by the central Board of Managers.[156] The effect of the new constitution is very different: it is now the central Board of Managers that can veto a conference decision if it involves a matter "of concern to the whole of the Church." While it is obviously unclear and open to dispute as to when matters are, or are not, of concern to the whole of the church, there is no doubt that the new constitution gives the central Board of Managers potentially far more power than previously.

It is interesting to note that a senior elder of a conference can, and will probably, be elected as a member of the central board, but under the new constitution, a senior elder of a conference cannot be the senior elder of the church:

8. The Managers shall elect from among their numbers
(a) a President;
(b) a Vice-President; and
(c) a Secretary-Treasurer.
The Senior Elder of a Conference shall not be eligible to serve as President and if the President is elected as the Senior Elder of a Conference, he shall, from that time cease to serve as the President.[157]

Regarding the conference level, where each colony elects two members to sit on the conference board, the new constitution states:

> 21. Each Conference Board, following the ways of the Hutterian Brethren, shall select from their number a Senior Elder and an Assistant Senior Elder, who shall hold office for life subject to ill health, misfeasance or malfeasance at the pleasure of the Conference Board, and by a majority vote of the Conference Board a Senior Elder or Assistant Senior Elder may be directed to stand down, and the Conference Board may elect another in his place and stead.[158]

So under the new constitution there is specific authority as to how to remove a senior elder. Under the old constitution there was no such guidance, though one could argue that as a member of the conference board, the senior elder could be removed, like any other member of the board, by majority vote.[159]

As for the provisions of the new constitution relating to the rules of community of property of a colony, and the rules regarding rights and duties of members, the articles often are word for word the same as in the old constitution. The whole scheme of community of property, and the absolute bar on ever having any private claim to a share, is repeated several times over. While the article dealing with exclusion of members is cleaned up, the basic principle remains that a majority of the members of a colony can exclude someone from the colony. Article 46 reads:

> 46. Any member of a Colony may be excluded from membership in that Colony or otherwise disciplined at any meeting of that Colony upon a majority vote of all the voting members thereof in accordance with the doctrine of the Church as set forth in the aforementioned work of Peter Riedemann and as set forth in the New Testament. Each colony may make its own rules and procedures with respect to the expulsion of the member and the conduct of such meetings provided such rules and procedures are in keeping with the doctrine of the Church.[160]

It seems to me that there is a potential here for a court to attempt a review on the merits of an expulsion, because the article incorporates reference to Riedemann and the New Testament. That is, even if a person was removed based on a majority vote, perhaps he or she could argue in court that he or she was faithful to Riedemann or the New Testament, and it was the majority that violated these fundamental documents.

In any case, in the light of *Lakeside* and the many other cases of litigation that we will look at here, it is unfortunate that the new constitution did not include provisions for dealing with disputes between colonies, or between members of a colony. The drafting of a new constitution provided a golden opportunity to put into place mechanisms that might prevent disputes and deal with disputes in the church without resorting to litigation. For example, why not have a conference board of inquiry defined in the constitution and established to deal with appeals from aggrieved members of a colony?

9
Litigating Again at Lakeside

Daniel and Paul Hofer and the twin sons of Daniel Hofer, it may be recalled, were voted out of Lakeside by a majority of the members at a meeting on 11 December 1992, a day *after* the crucial vote on the leadership of the senior elder. Mike Wollmann and Jake Hofer, the outside overseers, and Joshua Hofer Jr., the inside leader of Lakeside, were key supporters of Kleinsasser and Group One, while the Daniel Hofer group would have felt a clear sense of affinity for Group Two, which had after all agreed with much of Daniel's criticism of the Kleinsasser style of leadership.

Given the chaos surrounding the schism of the Schmiedeleut, the Baker law firm was preoccupied with much greater difficulties than the dissenters at Lakeside, and thus it took somewhat longer this time round for legal proceedings to start.

Upon receiving the notice that they had been voted out again, and after hearing about the 10 December meeting where Jacob Kleinsasser had been allegedly voted out but had refused to step down, Daniel Hofer Sr. wrote to Wollmann on 28 December 1992, again asking for the Lakeside matter to go to an impartial court in the church:

> May I ask, "Where are you headed?" Can we offer you any more than we already have? Is our offer to be heard by the church and to abide by the decisions of the church not satisfactory to you and Jake Kleinsasser? And if so does the Supreme Court decision mean nothing to you and J.K.? ... surely if you are in the right they (church court) will never side with us, could you involve the church in this matter on that basis and call Minister Joe Wipf and the President of the Hutt. Church and have this matter resolved?[1]

After receiving a demand from Radcliffe regarding a disputed colony tractor, Daniel Hofer wrote to Radcliffe on 28 January 1993, noting that it was Radcliffe's clients who were in mutiny from the Hutterian Brethren Church, and all Hofer wanted in due course was a proper hearing from the true church.[2] After a face-to-face meeting with the two outside overseers on the morning of 3 February 1993, Hofer wrote to them, expressly raising the issue of church authority. Since the Schmiedeleut was splitting into two camps, Hofer wanted to affiliate himself and get his claim heard by the side that did not support Jacob Kleinsasser as senior elder. Hofer wrote:

> Again as we are aware and have discussed at our meeting, the church at this time is experiencing a split over the behaviour and dealings of Jacob Kleinsasser (the Hutt. Bishop) who admits nothing (reported to me) about the contents of the documents gathered by Don Gibb and presented to the Hutt. ministers and the church and all other disputed matters ...
>
> Our only request is for a fair and unbiased hearing in the church as outlined in our previous letter regarding all past happenings which have led to the present problems ...
>
> We wish to inform you at this time in the event of a split in the church we will side with the party opposing wrong doings ... It is our understanding that you are a supporter of Jacob Kleinsasser and of wrongdoings so any decision made by you ... regarding any matters would be of no consequence whatsoever.[3]

Kleinsasser and the overseers now went right back to invoking the jurisdiction of the worldly court and the violent police power of the state to throw the dissenting group off Lakeside.

Three Lawsuits

The statement of claim on behalf of Lakeside Colony was issued on 29 April 1993.[4] Once again the overseer group sought a declaration that the defendants, in this case Daniel Hofer Sr., Paul Hofer Sr., Daniel Hofer Jr., and David Hofer, had no legal right to remain at Lakeside Colony, and an order of the court to force them off the colony. The claim also demanded an accounting of all the property of the defendant group, and an order to dispossess the defendants of all property belonging to Lakeside. The ground asserted for the expulsion was the failure of the defendants to account for the property that belonged to the collective pot managed by the outside overseers and the inside secretary, Joshua Hofer Jr.

On the same day, the overseers launched a second lawsuit.[5] This action was taken against Leonard Hofer (one of the original defendants in the first case), Paul Wayne Hofer (one of the teenage defendants in the secondary scrap metal reclamation case), and Paul K. Hofer, the father of Paul Wayne. Paul K. Hofer had left the colony sometime in 1983-84, after being expelled from the church for "drunkenness and 'stealing' a vehicle."[6] As noted previously, his older brother, Joe Hofer (K.O.), had also been expelled at some stage and had left the colony. Now both men had come back to the colony and to their families, but Joe joined the overseer group, while Paul K. joined with the dissenters. That Joe had difficulties is indicated by the court records, which reveal that he had several impaired-driving convictions while out selling colony produce and was even at one point arrested and jailed for refusing a Breathalyzer.[7]

In any event, Paul K. Hofer and his son Paul Wayne and nephew Leonard had ripped off an old vestibule, approximately 10 by 8 feet, attached to the front door of the Paul K. Hofer residence and were in the process of building a slightly larger (20 by 12 feet) structure in its place. The defendants bought supplies for the building project from the dissenter pot and proceeded with the work without authorization from the Lakeside managers. Thus, they were first served formally with a written order to stop construction, and when they did not, a lawsuit was launched. The overseers wanted to put an immediate stop to this rebellion against their authority, and they wanted the defendants to tear down the new structure and return the old, rotting vestibule to its rightful place.

At about the same time as the second expulsion lawsuit and the construction lawsuit were commenced by the managers of Lakeside, a third lawsuit was launched, this time against the Hutterian Brethren Church and Lakeside Colony by the law firm of Thompson Dorfman, seeking about $300,000 in legal fees and disbursements from defending the dissenters in the first round of litigation.[8] Both of the new lawsuits against the defendants claimed costs to be paid to the plaintiff colony, assuming that the colony would win the case. The issue of costs was of course something that Donald Douglas was particularly interested in. Douglas, who had represented the dissenters for more than five years, had not yet received any fees for the huge amount of time he had spent drafting and arguing motions, defending the case at trial, appealing the case to the Court of Appeal and the Supreme Court, and so forth. The plaintiffs were responsible according to the Supreme Court for some of the costs of the defendants throughout the course of the past litigation. But, however substantial, court-awarded costs against the loser of the lawsuit are still only a portion of the actual legal fees that are charged to the client. If the defendants were in fact members of the colony during this time, as the Supreme Court had held, and if the assets of the dissenter group belonged to the colony, as the overseers were now claiming, then surely the colony should be responsible for the entire legal bill owing to Donald Douglas and the Thompson Dorfman firm. Donald Douglas was also finding a way to turn the Supreme Court ruling into a victory. How could the colony argue that no person could earn and hold private property, and then turn around and sue its own member, expecting that somehow that member would be responsible for his own legal fees?

The first legal battle to hit the courts was the construction lawsuit. Without giving the men notice, the overseers sought an immediate court order through an *ex parte* motion to have the new structure ripped down.[9] The issue was purely the authority of the management to control Lakeside. The new structure was obviously an improvement, and none of the other residents of the quadruplex building in question disagreed with or complained about it.[10] On the morning of 30 April, Mr. Justice Smith refused to allow the plaintiffs to proceed without notice and adjourned the hearing to the afternoon of that day, so that the defendants could appear. Donald Douglas appeared in the afternoon and, pending the trial of the case, Mr. Justice Smith ordered the defendants to stop further construction (they were allowed to install the door and window so that the structure would be enclosed).[11]

The statement of defence in the construction case was issued on 10 May, the defendants asserting that they had the right to reside at Lakeside and that according to the church constitution and colony articles, the managers of the colony had a duty to equitably allocate the common property of the colony, including the equitable provision of accommodation in that there should be "no significant distinction between the quality of the residential facilities provided by Lakeside Colony to all persons residing thereat."[12] The defence claimed that the managers of Lakeside had been in flagrant breach of their duty not to discriminate as to the provisions of basic goods such as housing for the members and residents of Lakeside. Interestingly, by launching the second lawsuit, the overseers were faced with the other side of the coin in terms of the implications of the Supreme Court declaration of membership in law. If they grabbed the assets that the dissenters had accumulated since 1987 because the court had pronounced that the dissenters were members, it would bolster the dissenters' claim that the colony had a duty to provide basic services to them, rather than treating them as lepers.

On behalf of the defendants, Donald Douglas filed a motion to join Katie Hofer, wife of Paul K., to the lawsuit as a defendant, and he sought an order that Lakeside colony pay the legal costs for Katie Hofer to defend the case.[13] Bringing in Katie Hofer might force the issue of the responsibility of the colony for legal bills. The overseer managers quickly responded that the renegades ran their own enterprises and never contributed any of the profits to Lakeside; that Katie Hofer could not make a contract for legal services without the consent and direction of the managers; and that they had no intention whatsoever of paying the legal bills of ex-members or residents who disobeyed their directions.[14]

As for the issue of equitable housing, it will be recalled that Paul K. and his son and nephew were part of the Rev. Joseph Wipf clan. They lived in an old quadruplex housing unit at Lakeside. Typically at Hutterite colonies, families live in side-by-side two-storey housing units of various sizes. In this case, the four units of the quadruplex were occupied by the old patriarch, Rev. Joseph Hofer, and the three families of his sons, Ben, Joe, and Paul K. Unless the colony is brand new, housing accommodations at a colony are often a source of friction over time. After the dissenter group had formed in 1987, the overseers had, understandably, made no attempt to improve or maintain the housing of the dissenters. They wanted them to leave, rather than making their life more comfortable. Thus, both Daniel Hofer Jr. and his wife, Josie, with their four children, and David Hofer, and wife, Kathleen, with their four children, had lived in a mobile home on the colony for the nine years since they were married. Paul Hofer Jr., with his wife and three children, lived in an old trailer without running water.[15] If the schism at Lakeside had not occurred, these families would long since have been provided with normal colony residential facilities. But applied to the Paul K. family, the argument of equity would probably not be accepted.

After a contested hearing before Mr. Justice Oliphant on 3 September 1993, the motion of the plaintiffs to force an immediate destruction of the new structure was denied.[16] Instead, the earlier order of Mr. Justice Smith that the structure stand at least until the case was tried was confirmed. At the same time, while Katie Hofer was added as a defendant, the motion that the plaintiffs should pay her legal costs was denied. Since the new structure was already up, though incomplete, the construction lawsuit faded away as the second round of litigation in the expulsion case proceeded. However, that the issue of authority would be a central feature of the case was already indicated when Donald Douglas cross-examined Joshua Hofer Jr. on his affirmation in the construction case. Joshua Hofer Jr. admitted that if the defendants were unhappy with the decision of the managers that they not build the new vestibule, they could appeal to the senior elder. Donald Douglas asked who the senior elder was. Rev. Joshua Hofer Jr. asserted that it was Jacob Kleinsasser. When Joshua Jr. admitted that he had been at the conference meeting dealing with the leadership issue, and Donald Douglas started asking questions about what went on there, the atmosphere became tense, with Radcliffe instructing his client to stop answering any more questions.[17]

The situation at the colony became hotter as well. Just a few days after the statement of claim for expulsion of the dissenters had been served on the defendants, violence broke out again. Joshua Hofer Sr. noticed a group of renegades removing raspberry roots from the colony garden on the evening of 3 May 1993. He grabbed his camera and jumped on a garden tractor so that he could take photos to use in a court motion. In the heat of having another round of litigation commenced against them, the dissenters gave Joshua Hofer Sr. more than he bargained for. According to Joshua, the hotheaded Paul Hofer Sr., waving an upraised shovel, "jumped up on the tractor and attempted to choke me around the neck. Paul Hofer summoned his associates to come and help him. Gerald Hofer [youngest son of Paul] jumped up on the tractor on my left side and also started choking me. Roland Hofer [youngest son of Daniel] circled behind me and also got up on the tractor and tried to remove my camera from my pocket where I had placed it."[18]

During the confrontation, the tractor was out of control and could have injured the infant children of the dissenters, who were also there. Joshua Hofer Sr. continued:

> I was successful in shrugging off Paul Hofer and his associates. I abandoned the tractor. The defendants vandalized the tractor by ripping out the wires to the ignition. I ran for my home on the Colony as fast as I could, calling for help from my family ... My son Ken Hofer and Tommy Hofer, a nephew, were driving to assist me in a half-ton truck and drove on a causeway between two large lagoons to the said raspberry patch. Daniel Hofer Sr. was in the vicinity. He observed Ken and Tommy Hofer coming to my assistance and deliberately drove his half-ton truck down the causeway ahead of them to block their progress so they were unable to reach me ... I was walking to my home on the Colony to summon the Police when I was accosted by Paul Wayne Hofer [who] tried to impede my progress by pulling at my shirt front but I was able to ward him off with a defensive gesture ... I succeeded in reaching my home and called the RCMP who attended the Colony.[19]

The overseers made a motion to have Paul and his son Gerald removed from the colony.[20]

Claiming the Dissenter Assets

In the wake of the most recent encounter between the two groups, Donald Douglas on behalf of the dissenter group again sought to negotiate a colony split. In the first lawsuit, the counterclaim by the defendants dealt with the patent issue and the conformance of the leaders of the church to legal norms, but the defendants never made a claim for colony property. They simply wanted to stay at Lakeside and have their claim heard by an independent tribunal in the church. But within the context of a split in the wider church, it was possible for the dissenters to contemplate a colony split between the two groups at Lakeside, because even if they had been excommunicated by the majority, the dissenters might be accepted and affiliated with the true church, as they viewed it. In a letter dated 25 May 1993, Douglas asserted that it was no longer realistic to expect the two groups at Lakeside to live together and, therefore, with a complete disclosure of assets by both groups and a proportionate division of assets, a new colony should be established. Which group would go and which would stay should be determined by the usual custom in the establishment of new colonies. Douglas also made it clear that if the proposal to split the colony was not accepted, the defendants would once again vigorously defend themselves in the expulsion lawsuit.[21]

The overseer leaders and the majority members of Lakeside were not about to divide the assets of Lakeside and give the dissenters a fair share. Instead, they took precisely the opposite approach: they made a motion to seize the assets of the dissenters in order to add them to the overseer-controlled pot, while at the same time proceeding with the lawsuit to kick the dissenters off the colony, leaving them without any assets whatsoever. Claiming that all the assets and undertakings of the dissenters belonged to Lakeside, the overseers sought to have an independent receiver appointed to take over all the assets of the dissenters pending the resolution of the expulsion case.[22]

After a contentious hearing before Mr. Justice DeGraves, the plaintiffs were successful.[23] The order appointed an interlocutory receiver, L.C. Taylor and Co., Trustees in Bankruptcy, to determine the assets controlled by the four named defendants, and then take possession of these assets. While the order stated that the receiver "shall allow the Defendants' possession of assets of personal use and shall set a budget for the Defendants and their dependents for their personal needs to be paid from any bank accounts which the Receiver may take into possession,"[24] the dissenters would be running their enterprises under the control and direction of L.C. Taylor, and with all the expenses of the receivership deducted. Furthermore, should the expulsion case go against them, it would appear as a foregone conclusion that the effect of Mr. Justice DeGraves decision was that the assets would go to Lakeside. The dissenters were now in a far worse position, financially, than they would have been if they had lost at the Supreme Court, in which case they would at least have been able to go to the Block land, and have modest assets accumulated since 1987 with which to start a new colony.

By far, however, the most damaging effect of the appointment of the receiver was the decision justifying the motion. Mr. Justice DeGraves stated: "The defendants have, notwithstanding the plaintiffs' demands, refused delivery of possession of certain property to the plaintiffs *asserting their personal ownership*."[25] Justice DeGraves characterized the property holding by the dissenter group as evidence of having private property in violation of Hutterian community property norms, rather than characterizing the dispute as involving a schism in a colony between two groups who both affirm community property norms. This initial characterization, I will argue, in the end doomed the case for the defendants. An appeal of the receivership order was filed, but given that the main litigation quickly proceeded to trial, no further action on the appeal was taken.[26]

Last-Ditch Negotiations

The overseers and the majority at Lakeside were aligned with the Group One branch of the Schmiedeleut. Daniel Hofer and his group were very much interested in being recognized by the Group Two branch, which was now the recognized church under the new constitution of the Hutterian Brethren Church. Douglas argued that since Kleinsasser was arguably no longer the senior elder at the time the 11 December vote was taken, and since by tradition the members of a colony had the right to ask the elder for a hearing, Daniel Hofer Sr. should be allowed to go to the Committee of Elders of the Group Two conference and ask for a hearing.[27] That this would be unacceptable to the overseer group at Lakeside was probably obvious to Douglas, but it might form an interesting issue of procedural justice in the litigation to follow.

For Daniel Hofer, the issue of an appeal to the church was crucial. The idea of leaving Lakeside with nothing, or of setting up a new colony with the assets the group had accumulated over the last five years, was not the issue. Indeed, even the request to have Lakeside divided into proportional shares would not have satisfied Daniel Hofer, unless that new colony would be part of the church. The issue was fundamentally about church membership, rather than property. It was about eternal salvation, rather than temporal survival. What was fundamental was that any new colony established by the Hofer group had to be recognized as a part of the church, and the church that Daniel Hofer Sr. recognized was the reaffirmed church – Group Two. So Daniel Hofer appealed to the Group Two leaders, placing his case in their hands.

As I will explain in the next part, many colonies were riddled by disputes in the wake of the schism, and the most pressing concern of the reaffirmed leadership was not the Lakeside situation. Just because Daniel Hofer also disagreed with the actions of Jacob Kleinsasser, and indeed that Daniel Hofer to a degree had been instrumental in helping bring all these matters to a head, did not mean that the dissenter group would accept him without question. Daniel Hofer and his group would have to explain much in terms of their behaviour before they would be accepted into the church.[28] But Daniel Hofer was willing to put his case in their hands and accept their verdict. The problem, of course, was that the decision of the Group Two leaders would not be recognized by the Group One leaders of Lakeside.

Leonard Kleinsasser, minister of Delta Colony, was one of the Group Two ministers who later gave evidence about Daniel Hofer's attempt at affiliation with Group Two. According to Leonard Kleinsasser, after several meetings with Daniel Hofer, the Group Two ministers told Daniel to admit that he had done wrong, repent of it, and then a possible reconciliation would be possible. The Daniel Hofer group could then establish a colony aligned with Group Two.[29] But Daniel Hofer refused to admit to any wrongdoing in standing up against the senior elder and his overseers. Thus, while Group Two ministers were willing to mediate or negotiate a settlement at Lakeside, they felt that they could not embrace Daniel Hofer Sr. and his group back into the church. Daniel Hofer Sr. was in the horrible position of having been tossed out of the Group One conference, without being accepted into the Group Two conference.

Still, some Group Two leaders wanted to help Daniel Hofer Sr. They approached the overseers to see if a settlement could be mediated. However, according to Leonard Kleinsasser, Mike Wollmann told them to stay out of the affairs at Lakeside.[30] Eventually, though, the reaffirmed ministers told Daniel Hofer Sr. that perhaps if he could not be reconciled with Lakeside colony, he could start his own colony anyway and, after a period of proving that community life was being properly upheld, the colony might gain acceptance.[31] Daniel Hofer Sr. replied that leaving Lakeside without reconciliation first would be breaking his baptismal vows.

But the idea of leaving Lakeside with at least the potential of being accepted as a Group Two colony after a period of probation was not entirely rejected. The matter came close to resolution, largely through the efforts of John Hofer, the Group Two minister of James Valley Colony. On 12 July 1993, William Murray of the Baker law firm faxed a letter to John S. Hofer, which read:

> This will confirm that the following proposal would be given serious consideration:
> 1. Daniel Hofer and associates leave Lakeside immediately;
> 2. Daniel Hofer and associates be allowed to retain the property they have accumulated;
> 3. Daniel Hofer and associates release Lakeside of all claims including legal costs and legal fees.
> In terms of their departure they may also take the residential trailers they currently occupy.[32]

This hardly amounted to much on the part of Lakeside, but Rev. John Hofer of James Valley (Group Two) replied on 17 July 1993 seeking further clarification of what "immediately" meant, and seeking more particulars about what the costs and fees were. He also noted that the farm lot (the Block land) that the Hofer group had been using as a base was not adequate for establishing any sort of colony, given that it was not suitable for future expansion and livestock operations, nor did it have a suitable water supply. As well, the land was zoned for one dwelling per eighty acres. Furthermore, the trailers might serve as temporary dwellings but would not pass inspection for long-term use.[33] Still, the offer was not rejected out of hand, and Rev. John Hofer requested a mediation session with Taylor, the court-appointed receiver, acting as mediator. That negotiations looked promising was also evidenced by the fact that the Thompson Dorfman law firm filed a notice of discontinuance of its claim against the church and colony for fees.[34]

L.C. Taylor, the receiver, met with the overseers of Lakeside, "as well as several members of the [Kleinsasser] church hierarchy"[35] at the Baker law firm on 20 July 1993. The offer that the overseer group made was that if a number of conditions were met, the dissenter group could have all the property in the receiver's possession, as well as the four trailers in which the dissenters lived. Again a colony split in the usual way was rejected. The conditions for allowing the dissenters to have their assets returned included formulating a viable plan for leaving the colony by 1 September; that the equipment in the hands of the receiver would not be released until the dissenters had left; that the Daniel Hofer group would immediately stop using the colony gardens and the colony tractor; that they would not invite visitors to the colony without the consent of Joshua Hofer Jr.; and, finally, that they would discontinue all appeals of court orders.[36] Taylor noted that earlier, Daniel Hofer Sr. stated that any agreement he made about leaving Lakeside was subject to approval by a committee of reaffirmed ministers (Group Two).[37]

At a meeting in Taylor's office on 4 August 1993 with Daniel Hofer Sr., Paul Hofer Sr., and Rev. John Hofer of James Valley, the dissenters accepted the proposal, even though it gave virtually everything to the overseer group. The proposal was still subject to the acceptance by the Group Two ministers who were meeting on 8 August. In the agreement Taylor subsequently wrote, he stated that Daniel Hofer Sr. had agreed to three preliminary points and that there was no need for these three points to be approved by the Group Two ministers. These three points were:

> 1. That you and your family will vacate the main dining hall to allow it to be used by the rest of the colony. You indicated that you are prepared to use the "children's dining hall," which you indicated would allow the two groups sufficient separation and should be acceptable to the rest of the colony.
> 2. You agreed to stop using the colony's garden and agreed that the Receiver will chain and padlock the garden tractors so they cannot be used.
> 3. You agreed not to invite anyone on the colony without the permission of Josh Hofer Jr.[38]

This information was passed on to the overseers of Lakeside. But just as the parties were coming close to a settlement, everything came crashing down. What seems to have been the crucial event that made Daniel Hofer Sr. and his group dig in for the court battle was the destruction of a small garden on the colony that the Hofer group had been tending. In a letter to L.C. Taylor on 10 August, Daniel Hofer Sr. wrote:

> I just took a walk to the garden we tended and planted and weeded etc. for the last approx. 8 years. None of the [overseer group] have entered said garden we tended and planted and weeded etc. for about 8 years or more, except to on occasion pass through. Now after our proposed agreement,

Mike Wollmann, Jacob Hofer, Joshua Hofer Jr. etc. and who ever else is responsible, have entered said garden with heavy machinery and destroyed our road and dug trenches deliberately. With sad and heavy hearts we have to look on as our 3 to 4 acres we've tended is being destroyed. We [Lakeside] own 3000 acres or more. These people have to destroy these few acres where we tend our trees and plants. We have not agreed to this destruction [in the proposal]. The colony is the property of the Hutterite church and the property of all persons residing in the colony. None had more or less than the next. I doubt Mike Wollmann and Jacob Hofer, etc. will come up with a very good reason they so urgently had to destroy our garden road which was our favourite spot to take our children and grandchildren for walks and rides in our hand pushed carts during the summer. How is it possible to negotiate under such behaviour? We know this was done in the hope our side would retaliate and police would attend and Court actions started. We won't retaliate.[39]

The negotiations collapsed; it appears that taking over a few acres of dissenter turf a few months too soon was the reason. The lawsuit to expel commenced, and the law firm of Thompson Dorfman in turn reinstituted the legal fees lawsuit against Lakeside and the Group One branch of the Schmiedeleut.

Defence and Counterclaim

When the lawsuit over legal fees was reinstituted, the Baker law firm issued a statement of defence to the Thompson claim on 3 September 1993. Predictably, it asserted that the Hofer group had no authority from the management to retain legal counsel and that these expenses were personal and Lakeside Colony was not responsible for them.[40] In turn, Donald Douglas, on behalf of the defendants, filed a statement of defence and counterclaim to the second-round action initiated by the overseers.[41] This time, given the schism in the Schmiedeleut, there was a new argument as to why the court should not enforce the purported expulsion of the defendants. It had to do with the authority of the plaintiffs to bring the action on behalf of Lakeside colony in the first place. The managers of Lakeside had thrown the reaffirmation document in the garbage. However, according to the articles of association of the colony, one could not be a member of a colony unless he or she was a member of the church. Thus claimed Douglas: "The defendants say further that the aforesaid failure, refusal or neglect of the individual plaintiffs to execute and return the Reaffirmation of Membership on behalf of Lakeside resulted in Lakeside's ceasing to be a congregation of the Church with the result that the individual plaintiffs are no longer members of the Church and no longer have the right either to act as the managers of Lakeside or to pursue this action on its behalf."[42]

Furthermore, as to the purported expulsion of the defendants, the issue this time round was one of bias. Given the bitter acrimony of the last six years or so between the two camps, how was it possible that a fair and impartial hearing was given to the defendants in terms of the decision to expel them from membership again? As stated by Douglas:

> The defendants say that the members of Lakeside who attended the meeting on December 11, 1992 to consider the expulsion of the defendants have been closely involved, both physically and emotionally, in the aforesaid disputes and conflicts between the parties. The defendants say further that it is a requirement of the rules of natural justice that the circumstances in which a hearing is held must not create a reasonable likelihood of bias, or a reasonable apprehension or suspicion of bias by a decision maker. The defendants say that, in the circumstances of this matter, it was not possible for the voting membership of Lakeside to hold and they did not hold a hearing into the conduct of the defendants which met the requirements of the rules of natural justice and their purported expulsions are void.[43]

It was the counterclaim, however, that potentially had the most impact, not just on Lakeside but on the schisms that were taking place at numerous other colonies. By having a counterclaim, the defendants went beyond simply asking the court not to enforce the expulsion from the colony. If the courts struck down the expulsion as violating the natural justice requirement, or struck out the claim due to lack of authority of the plaintiffs to bring the suit or expel anyone, what would have been solved in the basic disputes between the parties? The two sides would continue to live in schism and likely the process of litigation would start all over again. So the counterclaim asked for two alternative solutions. The first involved a series of orders by the court that all the inside members of Lakeside individually vote for or against reaffirmation and then the whole colony and the assets of both groups be given to the members who voted for reaffirmation, while those who voted against would be out with nothing. The second alternative counterclaim was that the court place Lakeside in receivership and have a proportional partition and sale of the colony to force a colony split between the two groups.

It should be noted that the defendants did not claim that ex-members of a colony who leave the church or are expelled from it should be given a share of the assets. Their claim was that they were members of a colony and they were not being treated equitably by the other members in terms of being given access to and use of the common property of the whole group. Indeed, at bottom the claim was that the whole colony really belonged to them, as reaffirmed Group Two supporters, rather than to the overseer supporters, who were in rebellion from the true church. However, one of the prime difficulties with this claim was that the Daniel Hofer group could not point out any formal process by which they had in fact been readmitted into the church. The defendants were simply willing to sign the reaffirmation document, which was geared to colony acceptance, not individual acceptance. But this was not unlike the situation at other colonies, where disputes and litigation arose between a minority faction which was expelled by a majority faction. Would a court simply grant all the colony assets to the majority of any colony, and allow a minority to be kicked out empty-handed in the context of a schism, or would a court order a proportional share division, or actually make a determination as to who the true church was, and give the property to that group, even if it was a minority? As we will see, these interesting questions were ultimately avoided in the *Lakeside* case.

The trial started before Mr. Justice DeGraves on 22 November 1993. It was a lengthy affair again, taking up the better part of three weeks of court time. Much of the evidence related to the schism in the church, and I have already noted much of this in the proceeding narrative.

Trial

In his opening statement, Michael Radcliffe for the plaintiffs, after reviewing the authority structure of the various levels of the church, asserted that Daniel Hofer Sr. was "dismembered" because his individual defiance simply did not fit into the collectivist fabric of a Hutterite colony. In terms of the bias issue, Radcliffe returned to the notion that it was really the individual member who chose to be expelled, rather than it being a decision by the group. He implied that even though the Supreme Court of Canada required that a vote be taken, there was really no decision to be made by the majority group, so one could hardly argue that the decision was biased. It had always been an option for Daniel Hofer Sr. and his group to admit they were wrong, and they would have been brought back into the group. The decision was black and white, as it were, with no deliberation needed, and the decision was on Daniel Hofer's own shoulders.

Radcliffe also pointed out that the defendants had not agreed to an accounting of the property they had accumulated, and, of course, Hutterites believed in having no private property. From failure to provide an accounting, Radcliffe jumped to the assertion that the Hofer group held private property.

As to the issue of the schism within the conference and the question of authority that it raised, Radcliffe asserted that this was all irrelevant in terms of what happened at Lakeside. The colonies were in essence independent congregations and the structure of the church was not hierarchical or episcopal. As to the counterclaim, Radcliffe argued that any property issues should be left for a separate trial at a later date, if necessary. The court should at this point concentrate on whether or not to enforce the decision that Daniel Hofer and his group had made to expel themselves from Lakeside.

Donald Douglas for the defendants declined to make an opening statement, and the plaintiffs called to the stand Mike Wollmann, the outside overseer minister of Spring Hill Colony and president of Lakeside. The direct examination of Rev. Wollmann consisted of a short overview of the notices given to the defendants and the expulsion decision made at the meeting of 11 December 1992. The cross-examination, however, was extensive and took about two days.

After establishing the role of the wider conference in the appointment of ministers at a colony and in the decision to split a colony, Douglas asked Wollmann about his appointment as president of Lakeside back in 1979. Wollmann admitted that overseers appointed by the conference did not fall into the provisions of the colony articles, but that nevertheless this was part of the custom of the Hutterian Brethren Church.[44] The point to be made in this series of questions was that colonies in general, and particularly Lakeside, were not completely independent of conference authority. Wollmann also admitted that the statement by the senior elder Jacob Kleinsasser that anyone who sided with Daniel Hofer Sr. would be out of the church was still in operation. There was no deliberation to be made. Furthermore, Wollmann established that Jacob Kleinsasser had been consulted about the second-round of expulsions at Lakeside, and while he could not provide the minutes, he asserted that the Kleinsasser conference had approved the bringing of this lawsuit to enforce the expulsion.[45]

On the issue of asking for an accounting after the Supreme Court of Canada decision, Rev. Wollmann in a confusing series of interchanges finally asserted that in the eyes of the law, the defendants had been members since 1987, but in the eyes of the colony, they had not been. Thus, the property the defendants had accumulated through their own enterprises since 1987 was personal property that the colony was not seeking to get, unless the defendants were first fully reconciled to the colony. "We do not want that property. It didn't come in under the right door," said Wollmann.[46] However, Wollmann admitted that the accounting was asked for without any attempt to give the defendants membership rights in the colony enterprises from which they had been excluded.[47] So the Hofer group property was treated as colony property for which an accounting was sought, and at the same time it was treated by the overseers as "private" property for purposes of blaming the group for breaching Hutterian norms.

The questions shifted to the events at the conference and wider church. Regarding the vote to remove the senior elder, Wollmann admitted that a majority had remained seated when the vote was called. However, this had meant that a majority had left the church. When shown the new constitution of the Hutterian Brethren Church, Wollmann looked at the document with disdain and said, "I don't know anything about this one. I have not read it."[48] When he had received the reaffirmation documents for Lakeside, he had thrown them in the garbage and not presented them for a vote.[49] When Douglas presented the documents to Wollmann during cross-examination, Wollmann displayed hostility and said, "I don't want to read it. I am not interested in it."[50] He admitted that a majority of colonies in the former Schmiedeleut conference did not support Jacob Kleinsasser, but it was they who had fallen away from the church.

The next witness was Garry Hofer, the farm boss at Lakeside. His testimony focused on his service of the letters of notice to the defendants, as well as on the defendants' return of the unopened notices to him.

The second overseer of Lakeside, Rev. Jacob Hofer from Starlite Colony, was called to the stand. He asserted that it was common to ask for an accounting from someone who had left the colony and then returned to it, so that is why the overseers had asked Daniel Hofer's group for such an accounting. Daniel Hofer's reply had been: "[T]hat is the least and the last."[51] In direct examination, Jacob Hofer asserted that a senior elder was appointed for life and could not be removed, "anymore than a son or daughter can remove their father."[52] Jacob Hofer's position was that there never was a vote to remove the senior elder but only a count of who had fallen away from the church by their refusal to follow the God-ordained senior elder.

The cross-examination was lengthy and covered the events at Lakeside back to 1987 and the split of the Schmiedeleut conference. Jacob Hofer admitted that in the eyes of the colony, they had not been dealing with members of the church at the Lakeside meeting of 11 December 1992.[53] They had been, for a second time, expelling people who had actually been expelled in 1987. They were, however, still open to having the group repent. Rev. Hofer repeated his position that although the senior elder was elected, he could not be removed, even if he had done wrong; one could counsel the elder and the elder could resign, but he could never be voted out. While the conference could remove a minister from a colony, the senior elder could not be removed from his position.

The fourth and final witness for the plaintiffs was Rev. Joshua Hofer Jr., who was the inside secretary and minister of Lakeside Colony. All four witnesses were asked in direct examination whether the members who voted to expel the defendants at the meeting at Lakeside on 11 December 1992 had done so eagerly, given the events of the last six years. Joshua gave the same answer as the others and claimed that they had been surprised that the defendants did not show up, and that they made the expulsion decision with sorrow and some with tears in their eyes.[54]

In cross-examination, Donald Douglas concentrated on the many conflicts that had occurred over the years between the groups, leading to many criminal charges, injuries, and court orders. Joshua Hofer admitted to all of this. Douglas was attempting to cast doubt on the contention that the members of Lakeside could be unbiased in any decision to expel those they called "renegades" from the colony. Joshua admitted that the renegades may have been members according to the Supreme Court of Canada, but they were at best "members in unfrieden" from the inside perspective.[55]

The defendants called Sidney Wolchock to the stand. Wolchock was the lawyer acting for the Group Two colonies and conference and also acting for the wider Hutterian Brethren Church for issues in Manitoba. He gave details of the events leading up to the passing of the new constitution and reaffirmation process.

The thrust of William Murray's questions on cross-examination related to the structure of the church. Now that Kleinsasser's group had been cut off from the wider church, Murray tried to carve the Hutterian church up into many different units. For example, where did the Bruderhof fit under the old constitution? If it was not part of the church as constituted, there must be some Hutterian Brethren Church of the world that was larger than the church as constituted. And within the Schmiedeleut, there was allegedly a division between the American colonies and the Manitoba colonies. The line of questioning was suggesting that Group One was still the majority in Manitoba and had full legitimacy, even though reaffirmation had been rejected. Wolchock avoided getting drawn into any debate on larger issues of how many Hutterian groups might exist. He concentrated on the reorganization of the traditional three groups of the Lehrerleut, Dariusleut, and Schmiedeleut that resulted in the reaffirmation process and the creation of a new constitution. Murray, of course, was arguing that the new constitution was itself unconstitutional, because Kleinsasser's group had not been represented in the decision to repeal the old constitution. Wolchock noted that he had no interest in this particular case one way or the other but was simply providing information on the newly constituted Hutterian Brethren Church. The fact of the matter was that all the Group One colonies had been invited to sign the new constitution and they had declined: they were no longer a part of the Hutterian Brethren Church as constituted.

The defendants' second witness was Brian Millar of C. and J. Jones Company, who had been subpoenaed to answer a few brief questions about the patent agreement that had been at the heart of the original dispute at Lakeside.

Then the defendants called Rev. Leonard Kleinsasser, the minister of Delta Colony near Austin, Manitoba, and one of the leaders of the reaffirmed Group Two colonies in Manitoba. Rev. Leonard Kleinsasser gave a detailed account of the events leading up to and including Kleinsasser's calling of a vote of confidence in his leadership. He also reviewed the negotiations between Group Two leaders and Daniel Hofer over leaving Lakeside and joining the Group Two wing of the church.

Daniel Hofer Sr. finally took the stand. His position was that he still was waiting for a higher court in the Schmiedeleut to resolve the patent issue. Because that court had not met, he did not attend the meeting of Lakeside at the colony level on 11 December 1992. The questioning then focused on how the group operated. Daniel Hofer Sr.'s group had formed an association called L.S. Colony and ran a number of enterprises. In terms of the money earned, the dissenting group handled assets like any other colony. The money went to the secretary and was not owned by anyone individually. The secretary would purchase temporal goods for the group such as clothing or fuel and machines for the group's enterprises as needed. Hofer claimed that the group held its own worship services and for the last several years ran its own German school for the children within the group.[56] A list of the names of the families of the defendants in the Hofer group was provided to the court.[57] Thirty-six people were listed. However, the group was actually bigger than this; some of the young men from other families were not on the list provided to the court.

Daniel Hofer Sr. then affirmed that he fully believed the baptismal points of the church and the authority of Scripture and the foundational overview of the Hutterian theology as found in Riedemann, and he outlined the process of Hutterian discipline as he understood it.[58] As to taking a person to court who was under either Unfrieden or Ausschluss to get the power of the state to expel him or her from the colony, Hofer asserted that it was strictly forbidden and he had never heard of it happening before this case.

After the Supreme Court decision, it was Hofer's opinion that the managers of Lakeside had not met with the Hofer group in an attempt to reconcile, even though the court had declared them still to be members. Instead, they had written a letter asking for an accounting. Hofer claimed that this was "un-Christian."[59] He claimed that the overseer group focused on getting temporal goods rather than on resolving the differences that separated the two groups. Hofer stated that he was now seeking to have the colony split only because the case could not be resolved at the colony level, and the conference level was not willing to resolve it either. Hofer also reviewed his attempts to pass the original dispute over the hog feeder and the subsequent discipline and seizure of the group's machinery and assets over to the reaffirmed Group Two ministers, and how that process had collapsed.

William Murray's cross-examination led to a dramatic moment in the trial. Murray suggested that a person in Ausschluss was just like a thief on a colony, and that if a thief came on a colony it would be proper to call the police. Therefore, this lawsuit was proper since it was analogous to using police power to expel a thief. Daniel Hofer Sr. stated he was not so sure that it would be proper to call in the police if it meant going to court. Murray then asked:

Q. Well you are here now.

A. Yes, but not by my will.

Q. Well you have a counterclaim.

A. ... If making a counterclaim is a form of "going to court" then it is wrong.

Q. So you are not asking this court to order that property at Lakeside should go to your group?

A. We are only making a suggestion as to how to resolve the dispute.[60]

As was done with the Oak Bluff dissenters and would be done in other litigation that I will examine in the next section, the lawyers who acted on behalf of Group One Hutterites, the group that initiated the lawsuit, nevertheless would argue that any claim brought against their clients violated the religious norms of the Hutterites. After further exchanges on this theme, a recess was called and Donald Douglas met with his clients, followed by a meeting between counsel for both sides and Mr. Justice DeGraves. The case was adjourned until the next day, to allow for a further meeting between Douglas and his clients.

As a result of these meetings, the counterclaim was discontinued by the defendants, who acknowledged that it was a violation of their beliefs to counterclaim for a property division or an order for the colony to be placed in Group Two hands. The next morning, Donald Douglas read to the court the passage from Riedemann about how Christians should not go to law or sit in judgment.[61]

The dropping of the counterclaim was no doubt a huge relief to the overseers, but in the overall context of the claims for assets being made between Group One and Group Two supporters at various colonies, it was probably also a relief to Group Two leaders. The *Lakeside* case was not a good baseline judicial precedent for these matters anyway. The difficulty was that the dispute at Lakeside predated the schism in the church, and at that stage the defendants were not really part of the Group Two side of the schism. This was not a particularly promising case for the judicial determination of asset ownership between Group One and Group Two.

The dropping of the counterclaim, as an example of the defendants' willingness to remain true to Hutterian beliefs, and arguably as an indication that the defendants were more true to those norms than the overseer group, probably did not impress the judge but may have made it easier for the Hofer group to ultimately be admitted into Group Two.

The cross-examination of Daniel Hofer continued. Murray's line of questioning focused on how successful the Hofer group was at fending for itself. It had started with zero assets in 1987 and now had equipment worth $600,000. The implication was that if the court enforced the expulsion, and the defendants were allowed by the colony to take "their" assets with them and even pay off their own legal fees, they would still be able to survive.

Again the plaintiffs played it both ways, claiming all the assets, while also suggesting that those assets could be used by the defendants to pay their bills and start a colony. As for the failed attempt to be reconciled with even the Group Two wing of the church, Daniel Hofer Sr. admitted that he was not reconciled, but he had wanted to know specifically what he had done wrong that needed to be repented of.

The other three defendants took their turn on the stand, but their testimony was much shorter, given that it was Friday, the last day scheduled for the trial. Rev. Paul Hofer, who had been so emotional on the stand in the first trial, was more controlled this time. He reviewed the events surrounding his removal as the second minister by Mike Wollmann and his joining with the L.S. Colony group. He confirmed the testimony of Daniel Hofer Sr. as to how the group lived and what they believed. The cross-examination was short. Paul Hofer's most damaging admission was that, after being removed as minister at Lakeside subsequent to the hog feeder dispute, he had not truly acted as minister for the L.S. group. Members took turns at reading the sermons, and none of them had taken part in the Lord's Supper since the events of 1987.

Daniel Hofer Jr. and David Hofer were asked a few questions about their removal by court order from the positions they had held at Lakeside and their subsequent work with L.S. Colony. They both affirmed their belief in community of property and the Hutterian Brethren faith. Again the cross-examination was short, and the case closed with oral argument scheduled for a subsequent Friday, 17 December 1993.

In his final argument, Radcliffe referred to the two lines of evidence in the case, one pertaining to whether the colony decision to expel was made according to the proper Hutterian process and the rules of natural justice, the other pertaining to the so-called removal of the senior elder and whether that resulted in lack of authority to act at Lakeside. Radcliffe repeated his opening-statement portrayal of Daniel Hofer as a man who was "a round peg in a square hole," an individualist unable to live in communal harmony by being obedient to the group consensus.[62] The ordinary members of Lakeside were always willing to take him back if he would repent. They were not a biased tribunal in the circumstances. Daniel Hofer would not surrender and this indicated his individualist refusal to blend in with the group.

Radcliffe suggested that the "removal" of the elder was irrelevant and should not be addressed by the court at all, though he went on to address it anyway. His argument was that no vote to impeach the elder had been held. Rather, Jacob Kleinsasser had in effect told the ministers that they were outside the circle of the church if, after all the discussion, they still believed in the twelve points against him. Those who remained seated during the vote indicated that they had left the church, and the real Schmiedeleut was not

the reaffirmed Group Two but the Kleinsasser group. The elder was not putting his position on the line within the Schmiedeleut but was calling for a
count of who was remaining loyal to the church and who was leaving it.[63]
Radcliffe asserted that the elder was appointed for life and could not be
removed by any vote, unlike Daniel Hofer Sr., who could be removed by a
vote of his colony.

In any event, argued Radcliffe, suppose that the senior elder *was* impeached
and the conference had split into two groups. This would make no difference to the Lakeside problem. Irrespective of which group a colony was
affiliated with, the decision to expel members was made by majority vote at
the colony level. Even Leonard Kleinsasser of the reaffirmed group had admitted that the problem of Lakeside would have to be solved at the colony
level. Mr. Justice DeGraves pushed Radcliffe to clarify the relationship between colony and conference: could a colony have no relationship with the
conference and yet be part of the Hutterian Brethren Church? Radcliffe,
although wanting to emphasize the congregational concept, was not willing to go this far.[64]

Donald Douglas in his argument asked whether the plaintiffs had the
authority to initiate the action on behalf of Lakeside Colony. He noted provisions in the colony articles of association that require a person to be a
member of the Hutterian Brethren Church in order to represent the colony.
For example, article 2 states that the purpose of the colony was to worship
God according to the religious belief of the Hutterian Brethren Church.
Article 13 states: "The property and business of the Colony shall be managed by a Board of Managers of not less than three, and not more than
seven, who shall at all times be members in good standing of the Hutterian
Brethren Church and under no form of church penalty."[65] Article 30 states
that all colony property belongs to the Hutterian Brethren Church. To be a
member of the Hutterian Brethren Church was a condition of membership
at a colony. It was Douglas's argument that the church referred to in the
articles of association was the church as formalized in the 1950 constitution. That constitution was repealed and replaced by a new one in 1993,
and the managers of Lakeside did not reaffirm and sign up with the church
as constituted. Thus, they had no authority to bring this lawsuit.

Douglas reviewed the tradition of how the conference appointed a minister for a colony. It involved the drawing of lots among candidates with an
initial number of votes – calling on God to appoint, as it were. Yet the
minister could be removed by the vote of the conference or as a result of a
hearing by a number of conference ministers. However, the court was being
told that the senior elder was not appointed by having a lot taken of the
leading candidates: the senior elder was appointed by a popularity contest
of an election. At the same time, his election was apparently so divine that
he could not be removed by vote, no matter how great the case against him.

In effect, the senior elder had made himself the centre of a circle and proclaimed that all those outside the circle were no longer in his church. It was
Jacob Kleinsasser who would not surrender to the group, not Daniel Hofer
Sr.[66] Douglas claimed that it was Jacob Kleinsasser who had fallen away from
the Schmiedeleut group as traditionally constituted, rather than the other
way around.

In terms of natural justice, Donald Douglas noted how, despite six years
or so of being counsel to the defendants, notice was never sent to him about
the calling of a meeting to expel the defendants. Furthermore, regarding
the return of the notices by the defendants, they had insisted long ago that
all communication was to be made through their counsel or named individuals. As to bias, Douglas suggested that by analogy to the notice requirements formulated by the Supreme Court, the bias standard was also a high
standard. The consequences of expulsion for the defendants were enormous.
They had spent their whole lives at the colony. They were required to leave
with nothing. It was not that the tribunal in this context could have no
prior relationship with the parties or that it could have no knowledge of the
details of the situation, but surely some degree of unbiased judgment was
required, and Douglas submitted that the evidence showed not only an
apprehension of bias but actual bias. Anyone siding with Daniel Hofer Sr.
was out of the church. That edict by the senior elder back in 1987 was still
in effect.

Judgment

Mr. Justice DeGraves delivered his judgment on 21 March 1994.[67] He granted
to the plaintiffs what they sought, namely an order enforceable by the state
to evict the defendants from the colony and take the assets the defendants had
accumulated as L.S. Colony since 1987 and up to 11 December 1992, which
was now the legally recognized date for the expulsion of the "renegades."

Justice DeGraves reviewed the earlier Supreme Court decision in *Lakeside*
and outlined the inside law of the Hutterites, both in terms of the formal
documents and the applicable customs. As to the issue of the authority of
the plaintiffs to bring the action or of the majority of the colony to expel
the minority, DeGraves J. carefully reviewed the events culminating in the
meetings of 9 and 10 December 1992, and the subsequent reaffirmation
process and the passing of the new constitution. DeGraves J. drew conclusions that might be interpreted as giving legitimacy to the claim of Group
Two leaders that they were the true Hutterian Brethren Church.

First, DeGraves J. noted the argument made by the plaintiffs claiming
that Hutterian tradition and custom included the notion that the senior
elder was appointed for life, unless the elder consented to his removal or
ceased acting as elder. He then stated: "I am accepting the historical assertion or interpretation advanced by the plaintiffs. But in doing so I must

find, in any event, that the Senior Elder, Jacob Kleinsasser, put himself out of office on December 10, 1992 by challenging the assembly by asking for a 'vote of confidence' and losing it, and in effect consenting to his removal or deposition."[68]

Second, as to the drafting of the new constitution of the church in 1993 and the reaffirmation process, DeGraves J. noted the formerly unified Schmiedeleut conference was now split into two groups, with some colonies reaffirming the new constitution and others not. While not getting into the merits of one position or the other, DeGraves concluded: "From a review of the proceedings leading to the adoption of the new constitution, I must conclude that the constitution was validly passed at the biannual meeting of July 21, 1993."[69]

Here we see again, I would suggest, how bringing this action backfired, even if the decision was squarely in favour of the plaintiffs. Just as the first round of litigation had a significant effect in opening up a can of worms surrounding the business deals of the senior elder, so the second round included rulings that might have an effect far beyond the particular situation at Lakeside. These findings by DeGraves J. that the elder had been removed and that the reaffirmed conference was the legitimate offspring of the original Schmiedeleut did not amount to a definitive ruling that the Group One Kleinsasser wing was no longer entitled in law to claim the name "Hutterian Brethren Church" or was in law not entitled to the assets of any colonies or the conference, which were held in trust for that church. However, the findings could point in that direction, and certainly at minimum contradict the claims made by Group One that it was the only group with the rightful claim to be in the Hutterian Brethren Church and hold church assets. The conclusions of Mr. Justice DeGraves could be valuable to the Group Two leaders in negotiations with Group One and in resisting the litigation brought against them by Group One, despite the statement by DeGraves J. that his findings were "only to apply to these proceedings."[70]

The central question on the authority issue, however, was whether any of this mattered in terms of the Lakeside expulsions. Even if Lakeside was in a schism with the church, and even if Lakeside's articles of association made it clear that the managers had to be members in good standing of the Hutterian Brethren Church, DeGraves J. concluded that this did not affect the authority of the plaintiffs to bring the case, or the authority of the majority to expel the defendants.

It will be recalled that at the time the defendants were expelled, 11 January 1992, and at the time the action was brought, 23 April 1993, the schism had begun, but that the reaffirmation process and the passing of the new constitution were events that happened subsequent to these dates. Mr. Justice DeGraves concluded that these subsequent events should not be given retrospective effect:

The net effect of what I am finding is that the events and happenings of and the decision at the meeting of December 10, 1992 at Starlite Colony in no way affected the continuing authority of Lakeside Colony to have its own internal meeting of December 11, 1992 and to institute and continue the action to enforce Lakeside Colony's decision. Subsequent events, which may have changed somewhat the structure and leadership of the Church, cannot have retrospective effect (unless expressly said to be so) on the authority of the Colony in respect to its internal administration. On a practical level, the autonomy of a colony to regulate its membership, unless expressly modified or taken away, remains vested and continues in the Colony.[71]

While the argument against retroactive application of the effects of the schism to the key events at Lakeside seems to me to be a good one, there was a second reason for the validity of the authority of the majority to vote out the minority that DeGraves J. suggested. Even if the senior elder had been removed from office, and even if his supporters were in a schism with the church as reconstituted, DeGraves J. concluded that the autonomy of colonies to expel people by majority vote continued. It appears that DeGraves J. accepted the argument that the ecclesiastical polity of the Hutterian Brethren was congregational. He stated: "Article 39 of the Articles of Association is clear and explicit that Lakeside Colony has the means of expulsion at a duly constituted meeting and this right has not been diminished or abridged by the three collateral events I have described [senior elder deposed, new Constitution validly passed, Lakeside colony in schism]. Accordingly, I find that Lakeside Colony had jurisdiction to convene and conduct the meeting of December 11, 1992 and to institute and maintain this action to enforce its decision."[72] DeGraves J. found support for this concept of colony autonomy in the fact that Rev. Leonard Kleinsasser, as a Group Two leader, had negotiated with the Group One managers of Lakeside and had also suggested to Daniel Hofer that he repent and be reconciled with his Group One colony, perhaps as a prelude to a subsequent decision to leave and form a Group Two colony. That is, even assuming that Lakeside was in schism with the Hutterite church, properly so called, DeGraves argued that Group Two leaders themselves were recognizing the continuing validity of the internal authority at Group One colonies to manage their own affairs.

With respect, it seems to me that recognizing the reality that a colony is run by Group One managers and majorities, and negotiating with them, does not mean that as a matter of law their authority is affirmed. By negotiating or trying to mediate, one is simply dealing with the reality of the situation, rather than making a representation of what the normative rules are in the situation. And this is particularly so in a context where the Daniel Hofer group had not been accepted even by the Group Two wing of the church. Furthermore, one might question the autonomy of colonies, at least in the context where a senior elder has such power that on his own proclamation he can expel people from a colony. It was a clear admission at the trial that the order of the senior elder that anyone siding with the Lakeside dissenters was out of the church was still in effect.

In any event, what was the implication of this decision for the cases that would soon be filling Manitoba courtrooms? Even though the counterclaim had been withdrawn, the implication of the decision as to authority was that the majority rules, whether it is a Group One majority or a Group Two majority. The decision does not, it seems to me, support the alternative positions that the whole colony should go to the judicially determined true church supporters, even if in a minority; nor does it support a pro rata division of colony assets between groups at a divided colony.

After concluding that the defendants had adequate notice, DeGraves J. turned to the crucial issue of whether the tribunal had the impartiality demanded by the outside law principles of natural justice. He concluded that the majority had not been biased in voting the defendants off the colony, stating at the outset the factual basis from which the decision flowed:

> Since 1987 the plaintiffs claim, and it is not disputed, that the defendants have accumulated and retain property in their own right and separate from other members of Lakeside Colony. The plaintiffs assert that in doing so the defendants have defied the legitimate authority of Lakeside Colony in refusing to deliver, transfer and account to Lakeside Colony for said property. The plaintiffs maintain that the defendants are in breach of a major tenet of the Hutterian Brethren Church, namely that personal ownership of property is prohibited and that all property is held communally for the Colony and its members. Accordingly, the defendants, the plaintiffs aver, being in breach of the church tenet of community of property and having refused to deliver or account for said property, after demand by Lakeside Colony, must be expelled from Lakeside Colony.[73]

That Mr. Justice DeGraves completely accepted this argument of the plaintiffs was evident when he turned to the bias arm of the natural justice requirements. His argument was similar to the one previously made by the plaintiffs' lawyer, Michael Radcliffe, that there was no decision to be made since the defendants expelled themselves. Mr. Justice DeGraves asserted that there was indeed a decision to be made, but the decision was absolutely obvious: one could not assert that the tribunal was biased if the decision flowed unambiguously out of the very ethos of the organization. He stated: "The members of Lakeside Colony, at the meeting of December 11, 1992, had no choice, if they were to act in accordance with their beliefs, but to find the defendants in flagrant breach of the Hutterian tenet of community of property."[74]

But was this really an "undisputed" fact, and an "obvious" choice? I do not think so. While it was in retrospect foolish for Daniel Hofer Sr. not to provide an accounting of the group's property, and while it was also not disputed that one group held property separate from the other *for the time being,* how these facts should be characterized was indeed disputable. The defendants were in a schism within the colony, and they held property, not as personal property but as a colony within a colony. It seems to me that the dispute could be characterized as a conflict between two groups over church membership and collective church property rather than as between individuals holding personal property in violation of group norms. Mr. Justice DeGraves did not comment on the fact that, before the new expulsions, the Lakeside overseers claimed the dissidents' property as part of the common pot but at the same time refused to grant to the dissident group as members access to the common pot, or access to the positions in the collective life of the community that would allow them to contribute to the common pot. To suggest that the dissenters were expelled because of their breach of the common property norm was a convenient ground on which to avoid the difficult question of what an unbiased tribunal in these circumstances might mean, but, with respect, it ignored the reality that it was the rebellion of the dissenters against the actions of the overseers and the senior elder, Jacob Kleinsasser, in dealing with the patent dispute that remained the true ground for the schism at Lakeside, not any pretext dealing with the failure to account for dissenter assets. Do we really believe that the renegades were expelled by the Lakeside overseer majority because they failed to provide an accounting of the assets held in the dissenters' pot?

Fight over Costs and Appeal

After the statement of claim was issued for the second round of the *Lakeside* litigation, the overseers had, as noted previously, gone to court and obtained an order placing the Hofer group's assets into receivership. Now that the judgment in the case had proclaimed that those assets belonged to the colony (at least those assets acquired until 11 December 1992), another hearing took place before Mr. Justice DeGraves on 13 May 1994, dealing with the issue of the payments of debts in relation to those assets. The majority group at Lakeside extended no mercy toward the plight of the minority. The overseer group claimed that even the Block land should go to Lakeside Colony, and that Lakeside should receive all the dissenters' assets without deduction for legal fees owing to the Thompson Dorfman law firm.[75] However, Mr. Justice DeGraves was more merciful. It was enough that the dissenters would leave with no assets; surely it would be overreaching to expect them to leave saddled with a massive debt. As it happened, the Block lands were not yet owned by the dissenters, and Mr. Justice DeGraves ordered that the debts of the Hofer group, particularly the legal fees owed as at 11 December 1992, be paid out of the value of the assets in receivership, before the receiver returned those assets to Lakeside.[76] Finally, it looked as though the law firm for the dissenters would be paid, at least for the first-round action. The minority group would still have legal fees and costs arising from the second round of the litigation.

Daniel Hofer Sr. had always said that he would not leave Lakeside simply because a court had ordered him to. As in the first round, the dissenters got a stay of the order of expulsion,[77] and filed a notice of appeal to the Manitoba Court of Appeal.[78] Both the authority of the colony to expel the defendants, given the failure of Lakeside to reaffirm, and the question of natural justice in terms of a biased tribunal were cited as grounds for the appeal. Not to be outdone, the overseer group filed a cross-appeal on the grounds that DeGraves J. should not have ordered that legal fees be paid out of the assets seized from the defendants before those assets were turned over to Lakeside Colony.[79]

The appeal by the majority against paying legal fees for the minority group out of the assets accumulated by that group led to its own litigation war. While the bill for legal services to the dissenter group for the first round amounted to about $300,000, there was no doubt that Lakeside Colony was responsible for a portion of those costs as a result of the costs award by the Supreme Court. This was assessed by a court officer as amounting to $77,364.68.[80] The colony owed this money quite apart from any further debts for legal fees that were to be deducted from the property of the defendants subject to the receivership. Donald Douglas brought a motion to have the colony placed in receivership because Lakeside refused to pay even this portion of the legal fees.[81] The overseer group continued to fight against any claim that the colony was responsible for the overall legal fees of the defendants, even as a set off against the property that they had accumulated since being excommunicated, and furthermore, as to the court-assessed costs for the first round, these should be set off against the costs the dissenters owed to the colony for the second-round litigation.[82] Given that the second round was under appeal, the overseer managers at least wanted questions regarding first-round costs postponed pending the second-round appeal.

While all these fee disputes may have aided the dissenters by putting pressure on Lakeside to negotiate a settlement, once the order had been made that legal fees could be deducted from assets of the dissenters taken into receivership on behalf of the colony, there was also a potential conflict of interest that Donald Douglas might have in any subsequent fight to challenge or appeal the colony claim to those assets. One might make the argument that if the assets went to the colony, Douglas and the Thompson

Dorfman firm would be more likely to be paid as a charge on those assets than if those assets went back to Douglas's clients for, perhaps, purposes of establishing a new colony. Thus Douglas had to be careful not to be drawn into a situation where the argument would be made that he did not wish to have his clients succeed.

Having lost the second-round case, the dissenters at Lakeside went through a difficult period. Clearly the only way that they could leave Lakeside as the law required them to do would be through the help and affirmation of the Group Two leaders of the church. While these negotiations were taking place, litigation had already broken out in other colonies besides Lakeside and Oak Bluff. We turn now to this story before returning to Lakeside.

Part Five
Litigating, Leaving, and Sometimes Dividing: Lakeside and Other Schmiedeleut Schisms

10

Litigating at Rock Lake, Huron, Cypress, Sprucewood, Poinsett, and Leaving Lakeside

While the *Lakeside* case was before the courts, litigation also broke out at the Oak Bluff colony. But these were not the only Hutterite cases that were flooding the court docket. As the lines were drawn between Group One and Group Two, several more colony disputes also ended up in litigation, and in each case the litigation arose because of an unwillingness by Group One supporters when they were in a clear minority position at a colony to give up management control to the majority Group Two supporters. Indeed, Group One supporters, even in a minority position, either claimed full rights to the common property or made a claim for shares of the assets.

These are useful cases to compare with *Lakeside* because in many respects the situation was now reversed. The Group One leaders who had treated the minority members at Lakeside as if they had no common property claims now found themselves leading a minority group of "renegades" within several other colonies. Would they be treated the way they had treated the minority at Lakeside? Would they be excommunicated and expelled, sued, and dumped on the section line without a penny of colony assets, as directed by the court and enforced by the power of the state sword?

The *Rock Lake* Case

The conflict at Rock Lake Colony involved the minister of the colony and a few of his supporters who were in Group One, that is, loyal to Jacob Kleinsasser. However, the clear majority of members was affiliated with Group Two, those who had reaffirmed their membership in the Hutterian Brethren Church. Two managers of Rock Lake, Tim Hofer, the vice-president, and Ben Hofer, the secretary, had been removed from their positions by an assembly of Schmiedeleut ministers in 1989. Subsequently, the management of the colony passed to Dave Hofer, who became the minister and president, while Ike Hofer became vice-president, and Sam Hofer was appointed secretary.

After the schism, Dave and Sam, who were aligned with Group One, and Ike, who was aligned with Group Two, had a disagreement. Knowing that the clear majority of members was aligned with Group Two, Dave and Sam, still having the signing authority as minister and secretary of the colony, proceeded to obtain permits to create a new colony on Rock Lake land, dividing the colony between the two groups. They did this allegedly behind the backs of the ordinary members of Rock Lake. When they revealed their plans to the ordinary members, the plan to subdivide was voted down, whereupon their "unauthorized" action was discovered. Despite the wishes of the majority, the management team of Dave and Sam declared that they would go ahead and divide the colony in any case. They declared that the Group Two members, who were in the clear majority, were apostate for not supporting the senior elder, and therefore their vote did not count any more.[1]

At a duly constituted emergency meeting on 24 June 1993, a resolution was passed removing Dave and Sam from their leadership positions. Ike was voted in as president, and Ben Hofer returned to the position of secretary. The vote by the male voting membership of the colony to align Rock Lake with Group Two and put in the new management team was recorded as thirteen to five.[2] Despite being voted out of management, Dave and Sam did not resign but continued to insist they were the rightful managers and had signing authority for the colony. It would have been one thing for them to continue to attempt to run Rock Lake as a colony, but much more damaging, while purporting to retain their signing authority, they apparently decided to take as much of Rock Lake as they could so as to establish a daughter colony for the benefit of the five Kleinsasser loyalists and their families. They formed a new corporation, Keystone Holding Ltd., and without authorization from the majority of the colony, transferred about three thousand acres of Rock Lake land to Keystone. This was more than half of the land owned by the colony. Purporting to have signing authority for Rock Lake, they also proceeded to contract with suppliers on behalf of Rock Lake to provide lumber and equipment to build Keystone Colony using Rock Lake money and credit. They also removed items from the current colony site to take to the new colony. Against the wishes of the majority of the members, Group One spent within a few months between $1 million and $1.5 million in colony assets to begin construction of Keystone.[3]

As we have seen, when Group One supporters were in the majority at a colony, such as Lakeside and Oak Bluff, they did not support the idea that the assets of the colony could be split to let the minority establish its own colony. Indeed, they accused the minority of theft if it took or even used common property. But when the tables were turned and Group One supporters were in the minority, and especially when the group included those who had previously been signing officers, they were quite willing to grab whatever assets they could, under the claim that they were the true church and therefore the majority vote did not count. The Group Two majority at Rock Lake was powerless to stop them, because Group Two was committed to nonresistance, rather than taking aggressive court action. On the other hand, the Group One branch of Hutterites had certainly shown a willingness to take court action when it suited its purpose, but it was quite content to continue to build Keystone free of legal challenge rather than go to court to establish its authority. The Group One claim to be the only true Schmiedeleut as a legal position was questionable, as would be apparent in a few months' time, when the decision in the *Lakeside* case would give legitimacy to the Group Two members' claim to be the true members of the Hutterian Brethren Church. Furthermore, even if this status did not necessarily translate into a right of Group Two to claim all the assets of every colony, the *Lakeside* decision at minimum supported the right of the majority Group Two at Rock Lake to control all the property of that colony, and to have the assets taken by the Group One minority returned to the control of Group Two. However, in the *Rock Lake* case, the majority group could not sue without violating its religious norms, while the minority group had every reason not to go to court in an attempt to legitimize its actions.

Thus Rock Lake was torn apart. Not only were two competing groups claiming the right to manage the colony but one of those groups was actively using the assets to establish a daughter colony for itself. The splitting of assets and the holding of separate accounts by the two groups eventually forced the Bank of Montreal to refuse to honour cheques drawn on the common Rock Lake Colony line of credit. In consequence, creditors could not get payment from the colony. The Rock Lake matter finally came to court in a curious way. Precision Feeds Ltd., the main supplier of feed for the colony, brought an application under section 234 of the *Corporations Act* of Manitoba.[4] Dana Nelko of the law firm Fillmore and Riley represented Precision Feeds. Section 234, among other things, allows a complainant to apply for a court order to remedy an "oppression" brought about by a corporation against the interests of a creditor. If the oppression is found to exist, the court is given considerable power to remedy the situation, including the power to change the bylaws or articles of a corporation, appoint a receiver to run the corporation, and even liquidate or dissolve a corporation.[5]

In this case the plaintiff company had a relationship with the colony going back about twenty years and was currently supplying it with feed worth about $60,000 per month. Indeed, to protect its own interest in the livestock of the colony, the feed company paid the colony's hydro bill when Manitoba Hydro threatened to cut off the power to the colony because of unpaid bills. While neither group at the colony was denying that the plaintiff should be paid, the two groups could not agree on how payments to creditors should be made.

Thus, instead of just suing the colony for money owing, Precision Feeds applied under section 234 for a court order that would clarify the management authority at Rock Lake so as to enable future payments of accounts, not just payments of past debts. If the court would not determine who the true managers were, Precision Feeds requested that the court at least appoint a neutral receiver/manager to run Rock Lake as a financial enterprise until the management dispute was resolved.[6] Thus, through this indirect route, precisely the issue that the parties to the dispute were unwilling to bring to the court was in fact brought before the court: which management team was legally in charge of Rock Lake? That question could hardly be answered without getting into the fundamental religious dispute between Groups One and Two and the effect of that dispute on the ownership of particular colonies.

Given that the colony as a corporation was now a respondent to an application brought by a creditor, both sides of the dispute made a series of applications in the context of the litigation. James Cox and Sidney Wolchock represented the majority Group Two members, while William Murray and Michael Radcliffe represented the Group One minority. Even for Group Two, there was an exceedingly thin line between refusing to sue in court and at the same time making applications and asking for court orders, albeit in the context of a case originally brought by a creditor. Once the motion under the *Corporations Act* was made by Precision Feeds, the majority members requested that the court appoint their management team as sole signing authority for Rock Lake, declare that Group One had wrongfully used colony assets, and order a return of those assets to Rock Lake.[7]

Of course, Dave Hofer and those associated with Group One claimed that they were the true Schmiedeleut, that the majority at Rock Lake was acting without legal authority, and that, indeed, all the Rock Lake property belonged to Group One.[8] They also claimed that the action by Precision Feeds was part of a conspiracy used by the majority group to get a lawsuit launched against the minority group while still claiming to uphold the religious position against launching lawsuits,[9] even though Precision Feeds had earlier denied that it was interested in which side had control or ownership. All it wanted was for the issue to be clarified one way or the other so that creditors would be paid and the colony would function smoothly.[10]

On 19 November 1993, just days before the second-round trial in *Lakeside*, Mr. Justice Schulman heard the first oral arguments in the case. As it turned out, there would be a continuous stream of court applications, hearings, judgments, and orders in the *Rock Lake* case that would occupy Mr. Justice Schulman's attention over the next two years. In his first judgment, Schulman J. established that while the court obviously wanted to avoid taking sides in a religious dispute, Precision Feeds could use section 234 to ask for a remedy. Schulman J. said: "The respondent [colony], after all did not have to incorporate. It chose to avail itself of the advantages of the Manitoba *Corporations Act,* and as such, has brought itself within the jurisdiction of this court, under Section 234 of the statute."[11]

Schulman J. concluded that the management dispute, the holding of separate bank accounts between the two groups, the freezing of the line of credit, the appropriation of assets by one of the groups, and so forth, was oppressive to the creditors. As to remedy, he first awarded the plaintiff a sum of about $200,000 for money owing for feed and ordered the Bank of Montreal to pay the amount from the colony line of credit. Second, he ordered an accounting from each group for assets of the colony that it had put into separate bank accounts, as opposed to the common bank account at the Bank of Montreal, and then he made an order that both sides henceforth deposit all funds to one bank account. Of particular importance, Schulman J. also took the next step of trying to deal with the situation at Rock Lake to prevent the same problem from arising again. He considered a number of options for dealing with the colony's leadership vacuum. One option Mr. Justice Schulman suggested was that one representative of each feuding group be chosen as an officer of the colony for the time being, and that all decisions would have to be made unanimously by both of them, and that both would have to sign any cheques. After consultation with their lawyers, the two groups agreed to attempt this arrangment.[12]

Not surprisingly, given the nature of the dispute, dual management did not work. The attempt to run the colony with Ben Hofer representing Group Two and Sam Hofer representing the Group One minority collapsed with the claim that the minority did not account for funds, continued to remove equipment to the Keystone site, and submitted cheques for signature that applied to costs for building the Keystone site, rather than for legitimate Rock Lake enterprises.[13] Mr. Justice Schulman issued an order restraining Group One from removing any more assets from the Rock Lake site.[14]

Despite the prohibition on bringing lawsuits, the majority Group Two, within the context of the litigation brought by the feed company, filed another notice of motion, asking to have the court remove Sam from the management duo; recognize the majority managers, or in the alternative have a majority vote on who the managers should be; and require the minority to return all colony property.[15] Predictably, Group One filed a motion to remove Ben from the management duo, recognize the Group One managers, restrain the majority group from interfering in the management of the colony, and so forth.

More telling, however, was that once again, as they had done in the *Lakeside* and *Oak Bluff* cases, the Group One forces played the litigation card against their opponents. William Murray of the Baker firm, knowing full well that the majority had religious scruples against bringing a lawsuit, asked for "an order requiring Ben Hofer and Ike Hofer to be joined in the matter as party plaintiffs and that they be required to issue a Statement of Claim."[16] While the litigation card was played in an attempt to gain advantage, there was still some truth behind it. Although it was Precision Feeds that had opened the door to the courthouse, the case was increasingly being fought independently between the two groups as if they were fully engaged in a lawsuit. In the meantime, other creditors that were owed or were holding money for the construction of Keystone were also coming forward to the court with claims for payment or for direction about the disposition of deposits made.[17]

In the face of these diametrically opposed motions between the two groups, Mr. Justice Schulman made some controversial moves in a judgment on 31 January 1994. Even though neither side had asked for the appointment of a receiver to run the colony, Schulman J. ordered that unless the two groups agreed on the process for payment of creditors by a certain date, Rock Lake Colony would be placed in court receiver-management.[18] The deadline soon passed, and Deloitte and Touche Ltd. was appointed the receiver/manager of Rock Lake on 8 February 1994.[19] Now all the assets of Rock Lake Colony, including the Keystone site, were in the hands and control of a neutral third party. Even if it had not asked for a receiver, the Group Two majority had the most to gain by having a receiver. For a long time, the Group Two supporters had watched as the Group One minority openly took assets away from the colony, while they, given their non-violent beliefs, could do nothing to stop what they considered to be outright theft. With a receiver in control, such action would at least stop.

In addition to appointing a receiver, Schulman J. ordered that a trial between the two groups be held to deal with issues such as who were the proper officers and directors of Rock Lake, whether the court had jurisdiction to determine which of the two competing church groups had the legal authority to control the colony, whether the assets removed from Rock Lake should be returned, whether a vote on these issues should be taken and who would have the right to vote, and so forth. The motion by Murray to make Group Two the plaintiffs against their wishes was reversed by Mr. Justice Schulman. He ordered that Group One be the plaintiffs and that Group Two be the defendants.[20] Playing the litigation card backfired on Group One, which was ordered by the court to take the initiative to justify its actions by proving that the minority group had the legal authority to run the colony or control the assets. Again Group Two had the most to gain, because it was the one which had arguably demonstrated far greater consistency of religious principle against bringing cases to court. Being cast in the role of defendant would be much less odious.

Mr. Justice Schulman had given Group One a deadline to file a statement of claim, but it refused to meet the deadline, which prompted Group Two to bring a motion for contempt of court against Group One.[21] In response, Group One brought a motion for a stay of proceedings of the court-ordered trial pending an appeal that Group One brought to the Court of Appeal. On appeal, Group One now claimed, with supreme irony, that it had religious objections to being ordered to be plaintiffs in a lawsuit.[22] Schulman J. dismissed the motion for a stay and ordered the minority group to file a statement of claim.[23] The judge did not accept the legitimacy of Group One's claim of religious objection, as he noted that Radcliffe and Murray had instituted the *Lakeside* case as plaintiffs for the same segment of the church that was now claiming religious conscience against lawsuits.[24]

The Court of Appeal on 15 April 1994 stated that the receivership order was proper but that Schulman J. had exceeded his jurisdiction in directing a trial of the dispute, at least in terms of some of the issues he had directed to be litigated, when in fact the original plaintiff, the feed company, was basically no longer involved. The court made no mention of any grounds of religious objection to being a plaintiff in a lawsuit.[25] Because the Court of Appeal struck down Schulman's remedy of forcing a litigation of the fundamental issues, the dispute at Rock Lake continued on as before, except that a receiver/manager was in place.

In his first report to the court, Arthur Holmes, the receiver, noted that one of the most difficult decisions for the receiver was what to do about the Keystone site. The position of the majority group was that the building of this second colony was illegal and the creditors owed money to this point should not be paid. However, while Holmes halted further work at the site for the time being, he authorized the payments to creditors.[26] But it was clear that the intention of Group One was to complete Keystone and move there; the minority group was taking the position that it had the right to control all of Rock Lake, but given the reality of its minority status, it had been authorized by the leaders of Group One to split the colony into pro rata shares. Just as at Lakeside, the minority at Rock Lake consisted of about one-third of the population. While arguing in one courtroom that the Lakeside minority should not get a penny of the assets, the same group argued in a different courtroom that as a minority it should get one-third of a colony estimated to be worth at least $12 million to $14 million.[27]

Having avoided direct litigation by its successful appeal to the Manitoba Court of Appeal, Group One brought a motion to have the receivership terminated so that it could continue to build Keystone, while a countermotion was brought by Group Two to have its own management appointed as the receiver. The costs of having an outside receiver run the colony were estimated to be $15,000 a month.[28] At the same time, the receiver, with Donald Douglas acting as counsel, sought an order against Sam Hofer of Group One, who refused to provide some of the vehicles and other equipment taken to the Keystone site to help harvest the 1994 crop at Rock Lake, even though the equipment would be returned thereafter to the Keystone site. On 4 August 1994 Schulman found Sam Hofer of Group One in contempt of court for refusing to turn over to the receiver certain equipment needed for the operation of the colony. He ordered that combines, swathers, trucks, tractors, and other equipment that had been taken to the Keystone site be delivered into the hands of the receiver. The full violence of the police power could be used to effect this transfer if necessary.[29]

On 30 August 1994 Schulman J. had to deal with the motions piling up from both groups.[30] Group One suggested that it leave the Rock Lake Colony to go to Keystone and then let Group Two sue it for the return of assets if they were wrongfully taken. The motivation for this move might be questioned, given that Group Two had a religious bar to initiating lawsuits and Group One knew it. Schulman J. noted that removing the receiver would merely start a new round of disputes, as Group One would take even more assets. As to appointing the managers of Group Two as the receiver, this would not be acceptable to the other group. Thus, Schulman rejected both the motions that had been brought and concluded that the receivership should remain in place. Schulman J. started his judgment by saying: "It is never an easy task for a judge to decide a case where neither party wants the court to get involved."[31]

Given that neither side was willing to negotiate a settlement or go to court, or have the case go to arbitration, the neutral third-party receiver offered that he make a proposal and have it put to a vote of all the Rock Lake members of both groups. For the proposal to be accepted and implemented by the court, each group, voting separately, would have to have its majority in favour of the settlement.

The proposal by the receiver formulated in writing on 12 October 1994 was that the two groups should indeed split up, and that the minority group should get some assets to start its own colony. However, in the opinion of the receiver, the Keystone site, despite being half built, was too close to the existing Rock Lake site and therefore another colony should be established, at least twenty-five miles away. The minority group would be provided with up to $600,000 to purchase a new site, plus it would be allowed to take all the buildings, vehicles, and equipment currently at the Keystone site and move them to the new site. In the meantime, while the new colony was being built, a modest sum would be used to complete houses and kitchen facilities at the Keystone site so that the minority members could move there. It was proposed that all of the minority group would move away from the Rock Lake home base by 30 November 1994 and would leave the Keystone land by 31 August 1995.

During the period of disengagement between the two groups, the receiver would continue to pay certain living expenses to the minority group. The receiver also noted that if the proposal was rejected, the receiver would make an application to the court which might then result in a court-ordered split of the assets, or might well result in a court order that one group be expelled with nothing, and that all the assets of the colony would belong to the remaining group, which was essentially the result in the *Lakeside* case. The receiver noted the expense and delay that a court determination would involve. He also noted that, should the proposal be rejected, something would have to be done while the matter was before the court. One option was to require all the minority members to move to the Keystone site while the case was heard, but without giving any further funds to build up any more structures or enterprises at the site. The other option was to try to give the minority members certain jobs to do within the main Rock Lake enterprises pending the decision of the court.[32] The proposal to divide Rock Lake between the two groups was likely heavily influenced by Donald Douglas, the lawyer for the receiver.

Both groups rejected the receiver's proposal. Perhaps the majority group felt that the minority group would get too much, or the minority group felt that it would not get enough. However, it may well be that for some voting members in both groups, the amounts in question were irrelevant. Rather, it was the principle: a colony simply does not give assets to departing or expelled members; all colony assets go to those who are properly within the Hutterian Brethren Church. I will return to this issue of dividing assets in due course.

As he had given notice he would do, Arthur Holmes, the receiver, made a motion before Mr. Justice Schulman to have the schism in the colony, and by necessity the schism in the conference, litigated, even though both sides did not want this.[33] Donald Douglas for the receiver proposed to present evidence to the court as to whether each group was or was not an adherent to the practices and beliefs of the Hutterian Brethren Church. After hearing the evidence, the court would determine that the colony should go to one group or the other or, alternatively, that the colony should be divided between the two groups. Or, the court might put management by majority vote in place, with the option that those who disagreed had to leave with no claim to the assets. That the receiver/manager had a preference, or perhaps more precisely that Donald Douglas had a preference, for the outcome was made clear in Holmes's affidavit.[34]

Would the court really want to judge which group was the true Hutterite group and give all assets to that group? As I outlined previously, while Group Two was in the majority in terms of total Schmiedeleut colonies (that is, within Manitoba, North Dakota, South Dakota, and Minnesota), the court would have jurisdiction over only the Manitoba colonies, and in Manitoba, the situation was different, with Group One having the majority of colonies, at least at this stage. At the time of reaffirmation there were 85 colonies in Manitoba; 34 were Group Two, while 51 were Group One. If the court said that Group Two was the only proper church, potentially all the Group One colonies could be handed over to Group Two. Alternatively, if the court found that the reaffirmation process and the new constitution were fatally flawed, all the assets of the Group Two colonies could be transferred into the hands of the Group One conference. As well, there were many colonies where allegiances were divided between the two groups, just as at Rock Lake. The idea of handing all the assets to one group or another did not seem appealing. The idea of letting the majority rule at a particular colony, irrespective of wider conference affiliation, would not necessarily solve the disputes in a context where the majority might not take legal action to enforce this principle. The implication was clear that the receiver thought that equitable divisions of colonies in the face of internal schism made sense.

But what would be the implications on Hutterian norms of having a court-ordered division of assets? Would this precedent threaten the fundamental norm that those who leave or are expelled from a colony have no share in the assets? The legal stability of community of property was at stake in this litigation, and neither group looked forward to the proceedings. However, it appeared that Group One was again the most afraid of what a court might say. Group One at Rock Lake pleaded with Mr. Justice Schulman to simply let it have the Keystone site and the equipment already at Keystone, rather than ordering litigation. Group One claimed that at a meeting of Group One leaders held at Baker Colony on 11 November 1994, the decision of the conference was that the majority members of Rock Lake were unfaithful, and that while David and Sam were the rightful managers of the whole colony, Rock Lake should nevertheless be divided on a fair and equitable per capita basis to complete Keystone Colony. With some irony, in an affirmation submitted by Michael Radcliffe, Sam Hofer claimed that the true church had spoken, and quoted at length from 1 Corinthians about the horrors of taking recourse to "heathen courts."[35] The claim that the church had spoken in favour of dividing assets between the groups might have had more credence if Group One had agreed that Group Two minorities at Lakeside or Oak Bluff were also entitled to a pro rata share of their colonies.

On 23 December 1994 Schulman J. again made a decision on the conflicting motions in front of him.[36] He ruled that a variation of enforced dispute resolution should proceed. The receiver was directed to initiate the litigation by way of an application; the two groups would be separate respondents. Arguably, in a kind of hair-splitting way, neither Hutterite group was bringing a lawsuit against the other. Both would be respondents to a suit brought by the receiver. Schulman J. also granted the motion by the receiver to spend about $50,000 on the Keystone site so at least the kitchen and residences were available for use and habitation. Group One, despite the clear indication that the receiver supported a pro rata split of Rock Lake, did not want a court determination of the issue, and so a second appeal was taken to the Manitoba Court of Appeal.[37] Murray argued for his clients that the receiver should be dismissed, that Sam and Dave should be recognized as the managers of Rock Lake on the undertaking that they would effect a pro rata split to establish Keystone. If the majority members did not like the division, they could sue.[38]

By now the expenses of having a receiver, and all the legal expenses of the endless motions, hearings, and appeals, had taken its toll. Unless the two sides came up with a solution, a court determination of the issue would soon take place. However, before returning to the story of what happened at Lakeside and Rock Lake, it is important to note that litigation had broken out at other colonies as well. This added to the pressure facing the two groups to negotiate a settlement rather than face the dangers of a court determination that one or other group was illegitimate.

The *Huron* Case

In many respects, the situation that arose at the Huron Colony mirrored what was going on at Rock Lake Colony. A management dispute between the two groups at Huron Colony led to the Bank of Montreal freezing the colony accounts. The Group Two majority arranged new banking with the Royal Bank, and then this bank, again with lawyer Dana Nelko acting for the creditor, made application to the court for the appointment of an interim receiver.[39] As in Rock Lake, the Group One minority claimed that the court application was a conspiracy by the Group Two majority to find an indirect way of launching a lawsuit.[40]

However, there were also differences between the Rock Lake and Huron situations. At Rock Lake, both the minister and the secretary of the colony had sided with Group One against the wishes of the majority. At Huron Colony, the minister, Dave Waldner, had signed the reaffirmation documents. It was the secretary, Levi Waldner, who sided with Group One against the wishes of the majority. Thus, at Huron Colony, the majority was not taking the more radical step of removing the minister as head of the colony. Having the minister on board probably made it somewhat easier for the Group Two majority to control the situation as compared with Rock Lake.

On 25 May 1993 Levi Waldner was removed by majority vote from the position of secretary and replaced by Willie Kleinsasser. According to one account, Waldner had "already siphoned off large sums of money, unsuspected."[41] As at Rock Lake, the Group One minority continued to argue that the secretary, despite purported removal by majority vote, was the rightful signing officer for Huron, and that the majority members were the real renegades who had left the true church by not supporting the senior elder. Because of certain actions that Waldner took in his rebellion, the majority voted to expel Levi Waldner and his brother, Joshua Waldner, from membership in Huron Colony. The vote of male members was eight to two for expulsion.[42] The procedure for the expulsion was governed by the Supreme Court ruling in *Lakeside*. The notices of the meeting to consider expulsion were obviously drafted by lawyers and included a list of offences that the two men had allegedly committed. There was also an invitation to the "accused" to attend and speak to the charges.[43] Emerging out of the bitter schism in the colony were forty-four people in the majority group (Group Two), while eighteen affiliated themselves with the minority (Group One).[44] When counting each family member affiliated with minority groups within a colony, we see that all these cases (Lakeside, Oak Bluff, Rock Lake, and now Huron) involved substantial minorities, usually at least one-third of the population and sometimes more.

Levi Waldner did not leave Huron but continued to act as if he was in charge of the financial management of the colony and had the proper signing authority for all financial matters. When Waldner refused to hand over the books and records in his possession, there was fear that the Group One minority would transfer colony land to itself, as had been done at Rock Lake, so Dave Waldner, the minister and head of his colony, went to the bank and had the safety deposit box drilled in order to recover the duplicate certificates of title belonging to the colony. However, allegedly sums of money were still being deposited by the Levi Waldner group into separate bank accounts, and colony grain was taken and stored at a neighbouring Group One colony. It was also alleged that Levi Waldner forged the signature of Dave Waldner on a letter of direction and then used that letter to unlawfully remove the minute books of the colony from the Wolchock law offices.[45]

The grabbing of colony assets was supposed to end when Mr. Justice Nathan Nurgitz, on a motion brought by the Royal Bank, appointed Arthur Holmes of Deloitte and Touche Inc. as the interim receiver/manager of Huron Colony on 15 April 1994.[46] Holmes was still managing Rock Lake Colony at the time. But the grabbing of assets apparently did not end. As it had done in *Rock Lake*, the Baker firm on behalf of Group One immediately appealed the receivership order to the Court of Appeal, but again there was no stay of the order pending this appeal.[47]

The receiver was given a frosty reception by the Levi Waldner group. Within a few days, the receiver got an *ex parte* court order to take control of certain areas of the colony and restrain anyone within the Levi Waldner group from interfering with the receiver's possession and control of the colony.[48] This time the receiver was represented by the law firm of Taylor McCaffrey. Further motions by the receiver were necessary to get at the bank accounts held by the Waldner group and to get the grain returned. The planting of the crops and the supervision of primary colony enterprises were all assigned to

Group Two, while the receiver/manager allowed the minority members to engage in manufacturing and repair work using colony equipment, so long as they properly deposited any proceeds into the common bank account. However, as time went by, the receiver noted that the Levi Waldner group was extremely uncooperative with accounting for purchases or for income from its enterprises.[49] They basically ran their own enterprises outside the control of the receiver/manager.[50] Given the extreme animosity between the two groups, the garage at Huron Colony was a constant flashpoint, not unlike in the Lakeside situation. The majority group had trouble using the garage for regular maintenance, so long as the minority group worked there.[51]

Eventually it came to Holmes's attention that Levi Waldner had a bank account in his own name with approximately $220,000 of colony funds in it, and he instituted an action for the recovery of these sums.[52] Levi Waldner's failure to account for his group's activity to the court-appointed receiver led to an order by Mr. Justice Nurgitz that the group provide a detailed accounting to the receiver for all purchases and income of the group. The judge made it clear that a failure to comply would lead to contempt charges.[53] Subsequently, the receiver discovered that Levi Waldner had another bank account in his own name, and another court order was obtained to seize it.[54] Despite the court order to account for all assets, the receiver over the course of several months discovered yet more bank accounts that had been opened in Levi Waldner's name, a vehicle that had been purchased by the group and registered in the name of the colony, and several business transactions for which Waldner did not account. The receiver noted to the court that "[i]t is apparent from the activities of Levi Waldner that he has no respect for the Order of this Court nor the administration of this Receivership and has taken continual steps to interfere with and to delay the Receivership or to remove assets or cash out of the Huron Colony enterprise in some fashion, directly or indirectly to his benefit, and to the detriment of Huron Colony and the Receiver's administration."[55]

Now facing a motion for contempt of court, Levi Waldner claimed that Group One was the only true Hutterian Brethren Church and therefore he represented the rightful owners and managers of the colony, and that while it was true that he had not complied at all times with the court orders, a combination of inadvertence and other circumstances were to blame. To avoid further trouble, he had temporarily moved to Crystal Spring Colony, the colony of the senior elder, until the court motions and orders were heard.[56] Moving off the colony saved Levi Waldner, at least for the time being, from being found in contempt of court. On 23 March 1995 Mr. Justice Nurgitz adjourned the contempt motion but ordered that in the meantime Levi Waldner be banished from the colony, that he hand over all colony vehicles and equipment, and that once again he provide a complete accounting for the activities of Group One.[57]

As in the Rock Lake situation, significant amounts of colony assets were being drained into the costs of outside management and legal bills, and the overall financial health of the colony was slipping, as the minority group could not, or would not, contribute to the functioning of the colony to anywhere near the extent that it had before the dispute arose. It was the opinion of the receiver that the colony could not financially sustain outside management for an extended period. Holmes, as with Rock Lake, was prepared to ask the court to adjudicate the underlying dispute as to which group should properly control the colony or, in the alternative, whether the colony should be split.[58] Here was another case in which the judicial determination of the underlying dispute between Group One and Group Two seemed imminent.

The *Cypress* and *Sprucewood* Cases

Both Cypress Colony, near Cypress River, Manitoba, and Sprucewood Colony, near Brookdale, Manitoba, became Group Two colonies. Each colony had a minority group of Jacob Kleinsasser loyalists, and again, as in the *Rock Lake* and *Huron* cases, this minority, especially when it included former managers, took action to obtain colony assets, so as to establish its own Group One colony. At both Cypress and Sprucewood, the minority group, with the help of William Murray of the Baker firm as legal counsel, formed new corporations, and then, purporting to still have signing authority for the colony corporation, managed to transfer colony land titles to the name of the new corporation. In both cases, the Group Two majority viewed these land transactions as "fraudulent," but given the prohibition on bringing lawsuits, what could the majority do? Sidney Wolchock and James Cox, acting for Group Two, placed caveats on the transferred titles. Group One, of course, claimed that it was acting properly because all assets are held in trust for members of the church, and the majority were renegades, not true members.

Ultimately, the ministers at both Cypress and Sprucewood did make an application to court on behalf of their colonies, asking that the lands be reconveyed to the colonies in question.[59] These applications were made despite the attitude of Group Two that initiating lawsuits was not permitted. The applications may well have been made as a bargaining tool to induce a final agreement within the context of a tentative agreement in principle that had already been reached between Group One and Group Two leaders.[60] Whatever the motivation, it appears that, at least in regard to protecting title to lands, some Group Two colonies did take court action against those who had been their brethren, which might have earlier been considered a violation of the fundamental religious norms of the community.

In defence, despite the implications of the *Lakeside* decision to the contrary, William Murray on behalf of Group One again argued that the minority group at the colony consisted of the members of the only true branch of the Schmiedeleut. However, in a concession surely motivated by Group One's weak legal position, Murray stated that the church had decided to make no claim for the assets of those colonies where an overwhelming majority had affiliated with the renegade Group Two, but in those colonies where a significant minority was affiliated with either Group One or Group Two, it was the position of the Group One church that those colonies be split on a pro rata basis.[61] As we will see, after much debate within the leadership of Group Two, this became the opinion of Group Two as well, at least in Manitoba.

The *Poinsett* Case

The dynamics of the schism were somewhat different on the other side of the border. At the time of the reaffirmation process, the overwhelming majority of American colonies joined Group Two. Predictably, the litigation in the United States arose from Group One minorities at Group Two colonies. The oddity is that in Manitoba, aside from Lakeside and Oak Bluff, the litigation also arose from Group One minorities at Group Two colonies, even though there were far more Group Two minorities at Group One colonies in Manitoba. This might well be evidence of the different attitudes of the two groups about bringing lawsuits.

Of the lawsuits that were brought in the United States,[62] one case involved the Poinsett Colony in South Dakota. This colony was apparently in the process of getting ready to establish a daughter colony called Claremont when the schism took place. Perhaps if it had played its cards in a more restrained way, the minority Group One at Poinsett could have moved to Claremont as a part of the normal process of establishing a daughter colony.[63] In the end, however, the Group One minority leaders decided to sue the Group Two majority in Federal Court.[64] Even though it had not been expelled by Group Two, Group One feared that it would be expelled.[65] Thus, it went to court seeking injunctive relief from such a possibility.

However, Chief Judge Jones threw the case out because, aside from the jurisdictional question of whether the matter was for the state or federal courts, unlike Canadian courts, American courts often refuse to adjudicate cases that are at bottom cases involving church disputes. After noting the religious schism between Group One and Group Two, the federal judge stated:

> The court is unable to envision any set of facts which would more entangle the Court in matters of religious doctrine and practice. The religious communal system present in this case involves more than a matter of religious faith, it involves a religious lifestyle. An individual Hutterian colony member's entire life – essentially from cradle to grave – is governed by the church. Any resolution of a property dispute between a colony and its members would require extensive inquiry into religious doctrine and beliefs. It

would be a gross violation of First Amendment and Supreme Court man-
dates for this Court to become involved in this dispute.[66]

Since the courts refused to take jurisdiction over the membership and
property disputes between the two groups, the issue was left for the Hutterites
to resolve for themselves, and de facto the majority at any colony would
have the stronger claim to rule. But this did not mean that the majority had
to toss the minority out with nothing. There is a difference between what
the law allows and what morality dictates. At one point in the *Poinsett* case,
Judge Jones himself suggested that perhaps the colonies could trade dissident members.[67] In the end, as far as we know, the Group One minority left
with nothing. Thus, Group Two was allowed to control both the new colony,
Claremont, and the old colony, Poinsett, which was arguably far more than
it needed. While it might be said that Group One reaped the reward of
going to law, many Group Two Manitoba leaders did not agree with this
approach.[68]

The *Delta* and *Hidden Valley* Cases
The litigation involving Delta and Hidden Valley was different. Here the
issue was not internal division between the two groups at the colony but
the schism at the higher conference level. Both Delta and Hidden Valley
were Group Two colonies that were sued by the Group One insurance company.[69] After the schism, Group Two colonies pulled out of the common
insurance scheme at the conference level. Now the Group One insurance
company was claiming that Delta and Hidden Valley still owed money for
coverage provided by the company for some periods in 1992 or 1993. Both
colonies claimed that they had not asked for coverage during these periods.
The litigation in both cases was eventually discontinued, but for our purposes it again illustrates the willingness of Group One to launch lawsuits to
deal with internal Hutterite disputes.

Leaving Lakeside Colony and Establishing Heartland Colony
As the litigation at other colonies began to heat up, the litigation at Lakeside
was finally winding down. While there were many parallels and connections between the *Lakeside* case and others, there was also a fundamental
difference. As noted previously, the Lakeside dispute occurred before the
schism in the church, making the dynamics of the dispute at Lakeside somewhat different from an internal conflict at a colony between Group One
and Group Two supporters arising after the schism. And in the second-round
litigation, the minority group at Lakeside was not clearly associated with
Group Two, not because it did not want to be but because it had not yet
been accepted into Group Two membership.

When Daniel Hofer Sr. came to realize that the victory at the Supreme Court of Canada meant nothing to the majority group at Lakeside in terms of its intention to get rid of the minority group unless that group capitulated into obedience, Hofer wrote at the end of one of his letters: "I advised our very upset members effected by your despicable acts to do like Isaac did (Genesis 26:21) and try to be patient until the church investigates said matters, and hold onto and live according to the teachings of Christ Jesus."[70] As it turned out, Daniel Hofer Sr. was prophetic when he cited Genesis 26:21, a story about disputed territory, peace being found only after two quarrels: "Isaac's servants dug in the valley and discovered a well of fresh water there. But the herdsmen of Gerar quarreled with Isaac's herdsmen and said, 'The water is ours!' So he named the well Esek [dispute], because they disputed with him. Then they dug another well, but they quarreled over that one also; so he named it Sitnah [opposition]. He moved on from there and dug another well, and no one quarreled over it. He named it Rehoboth [room], saying, 'Now the Lord has given us room and we will flourish in the land.'"[71]

Perhaps in some cases the best response to a prolonged conflict is to exit from it. People leave a contested space or relationship, even if they have legitimate claims to it or commitments, because they want to find a space or situation where they can do something or hold value without facing opposition at every turn. In church disputes, for example, people may leave the congregation and start up their own fellowship or join a different church when reconciliation with the opposition seems impossible. Thus, while it had appealed the decision of Mr. Justice DeGraves to the Manitoba Court of Appeal, the case came to an end, as the minority group left Lakeside in 1995 and established its own colony, Heartland. The colony is in Hazelridge, near Beausejour, Manitoba, and it appears to have plenty of room and is already flourishing, despite that the minority group left Lakeside with no assets.[72] How did it happen that the minority group finally agreed to leave Lakeside, as the court had ordered?

As I mentioned above, often the key to walking away from church disputes is to have another church to go to. The minority could leave Lakeside to establish a new colony only if it had a realistic hope that it would be accepted into membership as a Group Two colony. The key to allowing the minority to leave Lakeside was provided by Group Two's Committee of Elders, but the decision to provide it was controversial and involved a split within the committee.[73] However, under the pressure imposed by the deadline of the court order to leave Lakeside, the elders finally gave the Lakeside minority enough to allow them to start moving. The elders suggested that the individuals in the Daniel Hofer group be given an opportunity to be reconciled with the church through a process of first placing the "renegades" and their families in Group Two colonies for significant periods – six months or so. This would allow the Committee of Elders to see whether the individuals in question could live by the rules of the colony. If the elders and colony leaders were satisfied, there would be a readmittance into the church, the ceremony taking place at the colony where the person was temporarily living. After being readmitted into the church, the Lakeside people could move to their new colony, which would be a Group Two colony. Even as late as the second trial, Daniel Hofer had resisted the idea that he had done anything wrong in his rebellion against the management and majority of his colony. But the acceptance of this process by individuals in the Lakeside group was an admission that, despite sharing the Group Two opposition to the leadership of Kleinsasser, in the course of the dispute at Lakeside the dissenters had not always acted according to Hutterite norms and that they needed to repent for their behaviour.

Interestingly, Larry Hofer, who had so often been implicated in violent confrontations during the dispute, was apparently the first person to go through the repentance and reconciliation process and move to Heartland Colony.[74] Eventually Daniel Sr. and Paul Hofer Sr. and their wives went to live at Cypress Colony, while Daniel Jr. and David and their families went to Sommerfeld, Paul K. and his wife to Mayfair Colony, others to Concord Colony, and so forth. This process of reclaiming church membership was done over different periods for different individuals. After they were all re-admitted into the church, the families moved from Group One Lakeside to the new Group Two Heartland Colony they were building.

In addition to providing a process of church membership, which was foundational to leaving Lakeside, the Group Two leadership had to provide human and financial resources to help in the building of the new colony. After the minority group had its assets frozen by court order, as well as losing the second-round case at trial, Daniel and Paul had searched desperately for help from various colonies, trying to get funding to buy a farm on which to develop a colony and enable them to leave Lakeside. They made various trips to the United States and to Alberta seeking help.[75] Usually a new colony is established as a daughter colony of a well-established colony that has accumulated assets for many years precisely for that purpose. To establish a new colony from scratch involves millions of dollars.

Loans from some colonies allowed the group to purchase land for the new colony, and once the church membership process was in place, each Group Two colony provided a modest sum to help Heartland. As well, some provided more substantial gifts, and also contributed labour to help build the colony. But in the end, it was the proven entrepreneurial skill and effort of the Hofer group that built the colony, rather than the modest resources provided by the church. Today, the huge garage structures at Heartland make the old Lakeside stalls that were so bitterly fought over look like toy sheds. As it did at Lakeside, the group engages in the business of repairing large trucks and other equipment for resale. Heartland Colony also has a major manufacturing enterprise involving the production of venting systems for animal barns. Two massive and modern barns have been built where the colony operates a chicken breeding enterprise (the production of eggs for hatching). Although more housing units need to be built, the finished ones are attractive and spacious.

Somewhat more controversially, after the move to Heartland, Daniel Hofer Sr. continued working "off the colony" on demolition projects and also continued to be involved in controversy involving the Block land.[76] One of the most interesting "off the colony" ventures of Heartland was the purchase of an old brewery, which was then demolished, with much of the purchase price regained by way of sales of salvageable materials. At the time of this writing, the land is ready to be sold by the colony, and estimates are that the colony will make a substantial profit from this salvage transaction. An even more ambitious proposal was that Heartland would purchase and demolish an abandoned slaughterhouse in Winnipeg. The elders of the Group Two church, and others as well, counselled against this move because the land had likely been contaminated and development of it was very risky compared with development of the brewery land. In any case, Heartland Colony, after its first years of development, seems to be on the road to economic success. Of course, the issue that really ought to matter most at any colony is not the outward material growth but the inward spiritual health of the community. We are obviously in no position to judge such things.

The formal management of Heartland has fallen to the next generation. When it came time to appoint a minister, Daniel Jr., David, and Larry (now married with children) were nominated. In a traditional ceremony and casting of lots at James Valley Colony, the lot fell on Larry; he is now the president and minister of Heartland.[77] Daniel Jr. is the secretary and David is the farm boss. Several of Daniel Hofer Sr.'s younger sons married and established families at Heartland. Only Jacob, who suffered an injury during the violence at Lakeside, is living outside the colony. All of Paul Hofer's sons joined the church and live at Heartland, some of them heading enterprises. Five of the sons are married. Heartland is thus composed of the extended families of Daniel, Paul, and Paul K., who previously lived at Lakeside. But in addition, there are families at Heartland that left Group One colonies to join this Group Two colony. One family left Baker Colony and another left Spring Hill Colony to join Heartland. The family from Spring Hill is the family of Daniel and Paul's youngest sister, Lissy. At the time of my visit, eighty-one people lived at Heartland, eighteen of whom were male voting members.[78]

While the deadline to leave Lakeside would have been some time in 1995, it is clear that the agreement to leave and move to Heartland was negotiated and accepted by the end of 1994.[79] After various motions and countermotions, a settlement for the payment of legal fees was reached, in November 1994.[80] The appeal to the Court of Appeal was also discontinued,[81] as was the litigation brought by the law firm against the colony.[82] The litigation brought by the overseer group against dissenters over the building of Paul K. Hofer's vestibule was discontinued on 2 December 1994.[83]

There was nothing dramatic when the renegades finally left Lakeside. There was no goodbye party. The two sides had shunned and fought each other for many years. The dissenters drifted over to Heartland over an extended period; the whole group didn't leave Lakeside on a particular day. Eventually Lakeside was free of those who were referred to as the "renegades." The pattern of life continued. Lakeside was left to the three extended families of Rev. Joseph Hofer,[84] namely the families of Joseph (K.O.), Joshua, and Ben Hofer. New babies were born. Young men at Lakeside got married and established families, while some young women left the colony to get married and join their husbands' colonies. By around 2000, the number of people at Lakeside increased to ninety-three. The overseers apparently gradually left the colony to its own management, with Josh Hofer Jr. as minister and his brother, Sammy, as secretary.[85] One of the former renegades, Leonard, son of Ben, had left the colony while the dispute was unresolved. When he was ready to return to colony life, he did not go to Heartland but returned to Lakeside, the colony that had twice sued him. Nevertheless, he joined Lakeside, was baptized, and later got married at Lakeside.

Now that there has been a schism, people throughout the Schmiedeleut might well have parents and siblings at a colony that is a member of the rival branch of Hutterites. For example, the minister of Lakeside, Joshua Hofer Jr., is married to a woman from Hidden Valley, now a Group Two colony. His brother, Sammy, is in the same position, also married to a Hidden Valley woman. Just as the schism was underway, another brother, Kenny, married a woman from Blumengard, also now a Group Two colony. The iron curtain of shunning initially imposed by the senior elder appears to have been moderated in many places, but the unwritten rules regarding visits to relatives varies from colony to colony. Some Group One colonies have been known to exercise church discipline over their members for visiting too long or in the wrong place with Group Two relatives. A married woman in a Group One colony, for example, was prohibited for many years from seeing her parents on a Group Two colony.[86]

Despite the bitter dispute that took place at Lakeside, visiting between Lakeside and Heartland appears to be possible, at least for those with close relatives at the other colony. Paul and his wife at Heartland may visit their daughter Rachel, married to Mike at Lakeside. Josie, wife of Daniel Jr. at Heartland, may visit with her parents from Lakeside. That the schism is real, however, is illustrated by the fact that four of Ben's sons all married women from a Group One colony. On the other side of the divide, three of

Daniel Hofer's daughters got married once Heartland was established, and they all married men from Group Two colonies. Furthermore, three of Daniel Hofer's sons (Larry, Conrad, and Roland) all married women from Group Two colonies. It would appear that the marriage pool among the Manitoba Hutterites has been cut in half, unless there is some kind of federation or reunification between the two rival groups.

Financially, the majority group at Lakeside won the war of litigation. Aside from old residential trailers the renegades were told they could take with them, not one dollar of regular colony assets was given to the departing minority. Furthermore, all the legal fees and costs of the lawsuit were allegedly taken out of the minority-acquired asset pool, leaving little if anything for them.[87] The refusal of the majority at Lakeside to give substantial assets to the departing minority was moderated by the arguments that the colony had housed and fed the dissenters for eight or nine years during the dispute; that the colony had suffered from reduced productivity since the dispute had put so many people on the sidelines of colony enterprises; and, finally, that Lakeside was not itself a particularly financially prosperous colony, as it incurred significant debts in constructing a new hog barn, and so forth.[88] But the bottom line is that just as the Group One minority at Poinsett left its former colony without any claim to assets, so the Group Two minority at Lakeside left its former colony. Perhaps this is as it should be, but as we will see below, the resolution of other colony conflicts turned out to be quite different. While Group One at Lakeside had clearly won the war over control of Lakeside's common property, how would this group apply the lessons of Lakeside at all the colonies where the situation was reversed, that is, where Group One was in the minority position at Group Two colonies?

11
Agreeing to Divide Assets, Further Schism, and Yet More Litigation

Division as Compromise

During the period 1993-95, the Group Two Manitoba Committee of Elders held several meetings and eventually agreed that subdivisions of some colonies should be permitted as a means of ending the disputes that were before the courts. Some leaders also supported subdivision as a matter of fairness. Even though in certain cases individuals in the departing group had acted in ways that clearly violated Hutterian norms and in theory deserved to be expelled with no claim to property, each group also had women and children and other innocents who had been caught in the crossfire. As noted by Rev. Samuel Kleinsasser,

> [a] point of interest at this meeting was that all committee members who had agreed to subdivision gave their reason why permitting subdivision of warring communities was a must. They all to a man added, among other words, that this was still the better choice between two evils. They said this very sincerely and I am doubly sure they meant every word of it, that to permit subdivision was a lesser evil than losing one-time, well established hofs, which, partly because of theft, were sinking from day to day into unbearable depths and bankruptcy due to a breakdown of the communal system.[1]

The willingness to divide colonies was thus a compromise that went against the traditional rule that those who leave a colony, or are expelled by majority vote, have no claim to the assets. But this rule had to be read within the light of another rule, namely that the common property of Hutterite colonies is to be held in trust by members of the Hutterian Brethren Church. A court might be persuaded that a minority group, even if expelled by majority vote, was in fact the group that was properly the Hutterian Brethren Church, and the court could then award all the common property to the minority group, wiping out the validity of the expulsion by majority vote.

To agree to a subdivision of colonies where there was a significant conflict between the two groups might be seen as a violation of the trusteeship rule, because Group Two believed that it was the proper Hutterian Brethren Church, and to give property to Group One was to give property to those who were no longer members of the church, properly so called. Of course, Group One made the claim that it was the proper church, and to give assets to Group Two would violate the trusteeship rule. As a compromise of the trusteeship rule, an agreement to divide colonies would at least remove the risk to either group of a court determination that it was not the true Hutterian Brethren Church.

Clearly the decision by Group Two leaders to try to peacefully divide some colonies between the two groups, as the lesser of two evils, was an action that might threaten the traditional rules by setting a bad precedent or opening the floodgates to a division of assets at each and every colony with any dissent. But at the same time, the decision affirmed the traditional rules in that it fully recognized that in order to resolve the conflicts and litigation at some colonies, the rules would be compromised in these cases.

This is very different from the idea that the division of colonies between the two groups might actually be the right thing to do as a matter of morality in these circumstances. That is, each group might say that, irrespective of legal rights, we recognize that our unity as a church body has been broken, but rather than claiming all the assets, we will give a fair share of the assets to the other side. To agree to give common property to the other side is not a compromise of the trusteeship rule but an acknowledgment that, whatever differences there are, both groups are still similar enough in practice to claim that they are Hutterian Brethren. This is not a situation where one group is leaving the Hutterite church to join the Baptist church, for example, but one in which a socio-religious-ethnic community has split into two groups. Even though fundamental disagreements have obviously led to this split, common property is not being given to individuals who are leaving: the property remains common property, used by one group or the other to establish a new colony affiliated with one or the other branch of what used to be the one Schmiedeleut tree. The fundamental religious principle of holding property in common is not compromised by the voluntary division of assets between the two groups.

However, it appears to me that this idea of division as normative, as opposed to exceptional, was not the position adopted by most Group Two leaders. Indeed, even, at minimum, the idea that a division of assets was a one-time exceptional solution was hotly contested. The pros and cons of division were debated at a meeting of Group Two leaders, including the leaders from the United States.[2] The American leaders of Group Two were firmly opposed to the Canadian leaders' proposal to give shares to the "apostates." According to the constitution, those who are expelled by the majority cannot be given a share. Given the impasse between the Manitoba and United States leaders, the case for and against division was brought to a summit meeting that included the Darius and Lehrer leaders.[3] Here the proposal to divide colonies was also rejected by those leaders. They asserted that Group Two in Manitoba had just reaffirmed allegiance to the constitution yet was now making a proposal that violated that constitution. If an exception were made, what kind of precedent would be set?[4]

As court-appointed receivers pushed for an orderly division as a way to resolve the disputes, and as the position between the two groups at various colonies was increasingly being controlled by the courts, with the judicial determination of the fundamental dispute becoming ever more imminent, it appears that consent, however reluctant, was finally given by the US and Darius and Lehrer leaders to allow the Manitoba Group Two leaders to proceed with the plan to make an exception and allow division in some cases.[5] Negotiations in Manitoba continued for some time. While the senior elder of Group One was away on rest leave, Mike Wollmann and other Group One leaders met with the leaders of Group Two in the offices of the accounting firm of Meyers, Norris and Penny, where they came to an agreement in principle on 9 May 1994.[6] It took another year of negotiations before an agreement between the two groups of Manitoba Hutterites was formalized, on 2 May 1995.[7]

Group One was represented by Michael Wollmann of Spring Hill, Jacob Hofer of Starlite, and Sam Waldner of Decker. Mike Hofer of Sommerfeld took the key role for the Group Two leadership, along with John Hofer of James Valley, Leonard Kleinsasser of Delta, and Levi Gross of Westroc. Some aspects of the negotiation and agreement dealt with disengaging Group Two from the common Schmiedeleut enterprises. While there were some reciprocal benefits, Group One had the most to gain by having Group Two walk away from any claims to common property at the conference level. Thus, subject to conditions and terms that need not concern us here, Group Two colonies were released from interests and obligations related to the Spring Hill hog plant, from Pembina Poultry Packers (then a Hutterite-owned processing plant in Morden), and from the insurance company, the credit company, and so forth. Allowing each of the reaffirmed colonies to sign off from both the potential benefits and liabilities of these enterprises meant that the schism between the two groups was being recognized and formalized.

The most important part of the 2 May 1995 negotiated settlement between the two groups was that they also agreed that various colonies be divided and that all litigation stop. Given that this part of the agreement would be subject to further litigation, I quote the key provisions at length:

> 6. Group I and Group II agree that at the Colonies where problems currently exist there shall be a pro rata division (based on number of people) of

the assets of the Colonies. In the event that members of the respective groups on any Colony are unable to agree at a valuation or resolution of the pro rata split then the matter shall be referred to two groups, each comprising of up to 5 ministers from each of Group I and Group II. [T]hey shall meet and determine the appropriate pro rata split of assets and in the event that there is a dispute that the parties cannot resolve by agreement, then an appraiser appointed by Meyers, Norris, Penny shall be hired with costs borne by each of the Groups of the Colony and the appraiser shall set the values for all of the assets and division shall take place dividing the assets. It there is any dispute as to which asset goes to which group, the matter shall be determined by lot and a lot shall be drawn for any specific asset in dispute. The division of assets both as to value and as to proportion, shall be determined as of the dates hereinafter set forth, for the following colonies:

Rock Lake Colony – May 2, 1995
Huron Colony – May 2, 1995
Cypress Colony – May 1, 1994
Sprucewood Colony – May 2, 1995
Grass River Colony – May 2, 1995
Oak Bluff Colony – the operative date shall be July 1, 1990 for some and staged dates based on the dates parties left.

It is understood and agreed with respect to Huron that Group I shall remove Levi Waldner and Joshua Waldner and their respective families and the pro rata share shall be delivered to a colony of Group I (as designated by Reverend Michael Wollmann of Springhill Colony) in satisfaction of this paragraph, it being understood that the Levi Waldner group shall leave Huron Colony at the same time as the pro rata share of their group is being delivered to the Group I colony designated by Rev. Michael Wollmann.

...

10. Nothing contained herein shall constitute a contravention of the Articles of Association or be construed as granting, conveying, transferring any property or property interest to any individual or deemed to be the giving of a share or shares to any individual.[8]

Six colonies are specifically mentioned in the agreement. Five of these colonies are Group Two colonies; only Oak Bluff is a Group One colony. In other words, if the agreement is limited to the colonies mentioned, the agreement is overwhelmingly geared in favour of Group One, because it is the majority Group Two which is in most cases giving a proportionate share to the Group One minority, rather than expelling them with nothing. In only one case, Oak Bluff, is there a reciprocal duty on behalf of Group One to give a share to the Group Two minority.

The absence of Lakeside on the list of colonies to be divided is glaring. Mike Wollmann of Spring Hill and Jake Hofer of Starlite played a key role in negotiating the 2 May 1995 agreement on behalf of Group One. They were, of course, the overseers and litigants involved in the *Lakeside* case over the last nine years. It is highly unlikely that they would now give a share of Lakeside to the Daniel Hofer group, even though its members were now affiliated with Group Two and not just "renegades." Furthermore, the *Lakeside* case had already been resolved in the sense that, as I noted previously, by the end of 1994 the litigation had ended and the minority had already agreed to leave Lakeside. Nevertheless, there were Group Two leaders who felt that Lakeside should have been split on a pro rata basis just as the other six colonies were.[9]

The last clause of the agreement seems to convey several layers of meaning. At one level it could act as a disclaimer of sorts. As noted above, a Hutterite leader in either camp might argue that under the agreement pro rata shares are being given to those who have left the church, properly so called, but this is unconventional and the agreement to divide colonies should not be seen as a signal or precedent that the traditional rules have changed in any way for other cases. Thus the disclaimer. But at another level the clause might be interpreted as factual, or normative. That is, a Hutterite leader might say that the agreement does not violate the rules. Notice is given here that the pro rata division should not be interpreted as giving any shares to individuals; communal property was not being privatized. The *valuation* may be based on the numbers of individuals leaving, including those who might in other circumstances have been excommunicated, but the property is not going to individuals but to the minority group as a whole, so as to establish a new colony, where the property becomes the common property of the group. In the Huron case, the property is going to an existing Group One colony, rather than to a minority group to establish a new colony. In either case, the division is not a violation of the community of property norms.

Implementing and Failing to Implement the Agreement
The implementation of the agreement to divide colonies took time and involved a lot of controversy. At the colonies where disputes were in the litigation process, battles over the process and values of the assets to be divided ensued.

At Rock Lake and Huron, the court-appointed receiver now had an agreement to divide the colonies, which would lead to the end of the receivership and the litigation. After an independent appraisal of assets remaining at Rock Lake and of those that had been removed to establish Keystone, and the total assets and liabilities were split 72 percent to Group Two and 28 percent to Group One, it became apparent that the value of the assets already taken to start Keystone was greater than the share the group was entitled to. Group One would need to return some of the land and equipment at Keystone and assume some of the debt of Rock Lake Colony.[10] Indeed, the minority group owed the majority group a couple of hundred thousand dollars to implement the pro rata split. After negotiations, in which the majority group at Rock Lake took less than it was entitled to just so the case could be settled, the division of the colony was formalized in a court order and the Rock Lake litigation came to an end.[11] It is, of course, noteworthy that paying for a professional receiver to manage the colony for almost two years, and paying for the legal fees and costs on the motions and appeal proceedings, drained a substantial amount of the assets that were to be divided. In the end, it appears that Rock Lake Colony is doing fine but that Keystone experienced financial problems, as indicated by subsequent litigation brought by creditors.[12]

As for Huron Colony, the agreement contemplated that the small minority group would hardly be able to establish its own colony but that some Group One colony would take the minority group and the pro rata share would be paid to that colony. After an appraisal of Huron Colony assets, it was determined that the minority share amounted to approximately $1.5 million, but given that the colony already had more than $1.5 million in existing debts, it was the opinion of the receiver that the colony could not financially sustain the payment of the share owed to the minority group. The payment to the minority would have to be made over an extended period, or the Group Two colonies would have to provide the financing for Huron Colony to pay the minority group.[13]

The dispute at Huron dragged on for a long time because the Levi Waldner group refused to accept a gradual payment, and Huron was unable to come up with the money given its debt load, and in any event, no Group One colony was identified as being the place to where the minority would move. Finally, the receiver made a motion in court that would have forced the issue, and the receiver also brought new contempt-of-court charges against Levi Waldner, who had returned to Huron Colony, with permission. Once Waldner returned, the receiver yet again discovered another secret bank account opened by Waldner where income that was to go to the Huron's common pot was being held in Waldner's name. Given that Waldner had narrowly avoided being found in contempt last time around, and given Waldner's continuous removal of colony assets and his refusal to cooperate with the receiver, the receiver asked the court to jail Waldner for contempt of court.[14]

Now that the Group One leader of Huron was facing jail, the leadership of Group One took action. An agreement was reached that the Levi Waldner group (consisting of seventeen people) would move to Trileaf Colony. In exchange, the forty-five people at Trileaf Colony who wanted to be part of

Group Two would leave Trileaf, a Group One colony, and move to Huron, a Group Two colony. Pro rata shares of Huron or Trileaf would not be paid to the departing groups, although both groups were allowed to take some equipment from the colony they were leaving. The value of the equipment taken from Huron to Trileaf, and the equipment taken from Trileaf to Huron was approximately the same.

That Group Two was more interested in settling the dispute even at a cost of overall equity is indicated by the fact that in purely economic terms the exchange appears to favour Group One. The large group at Trileaf left the colony to the remaining Group One members without receiving a pro rata share, in exchange for a much smaller group at Huron, who left its colony to Group Two members without receiving a pro rata share.[15] Even more telling, the agreement required that the receiver at Huron pay over $15,000 of colony assets into the trust account of the Baker law firm, which I presume would go to legal fees and costs Levi Waldner had accumulated. Whether fair or not, given the agreement that the Waldner group would leave Huron, the receiver withdrew his motion for contempt, and the court approved the exchange agreement.[16]

Even in the implementation of the agreement, the questionable conduct of Levi Waldner was again manifest. The receiver noted:

> A problem was encountered regarding the unauthorized removal of certain equipment by the Levi Waldner group. The Receiver reviewed with Levi Waldner the items he would be taking as per the settlement agreement. Upon taking an inventory of the equipment following the move, it was determined that additional items were improperly removed. We advised Mr. Waldner that unless the improperly removed items were returned, the $15,192 which was required to be paid to Levi Waldner's solicitor, as per the March 6th Order, would be offset and held in lieu of the equipment improperly removed. Although a few items were returned, the majority were not.[17]

Again rather than pursue a legal case, Group Two Huron members and the receiver agreed to settle the matter with the Waldner group, by taking a loss of about $5,000.[18] Levi Waldner not only found a home at Trileaf, but he was apparently appointed secretary of Trileaf.[19]

There is not much information available to me as to the division of the Cypress, Sprucewood, and Grass River colonies. It will be recalled that there was litigation at Cypress and Sprucewood over the minority group taking title to colony lands. After the 2 May 1995 agreement to divide the colonies in question on a pro rata basis, this litigation was withdrawn.[20] The Group One minority at Cypress received its share to establish Millshof. While at both Rock Lake and Huron the Group Two majority had followed the path of Christian nonresistance in the face of what was thought to be Group One "theft," there is evidence that perhaps the Group Two majority at Cypress was not always fair with the Group One minority.[21] However, at a colony such as Grass River, where the Group One minority had refrained from plundering or litigating, the ultimate division of the colony assets went smoothly.[22] At Sprucewood the division also appears to have taken place without apparent conflict, and the minority left to establish Fairview Colony.

A division took place at at least one colony, even though that colony was not mentioned in the agreement. Several key Group Two leaders spoke highly of the ethics of Group One people at Maple Grove Colony, who gave a fair pro rata share of the colony to Group Two members so that they could establish a new Group Two colony, Twilite.[23] This serves as a good counterexample: Group One people did not always act as if the people in the other group were apostates without communal rights, and enemies to be fought against.

While Maple Grove Colony provides a good example of Group One generosity, Oak Bluff was, and at the time of this writing remains, a sore spot in terms of the implementation of the agreement to divide. After the schism in the church, the dissenters at Oak Bluff decided to leave and establish a Group Two colony. Apparently not one penny of the colony was given to the so-called apostates who left or were expelled. The Oak Bluff Group Two minority objected to this treatment, but they left the colony well before the agreement of May 1995 was made. Many Group Two colonies and several Lehrerleut colonies helped the Oak Bluff group establish its own colony, Prairie Blossom.[24]

As noted previously, Oak Bluff was the only Group One majority colony included in the 2 May 1995 agreement. The leaders of Group One had agreed that a pro rata share of Oak Bluff should go to the Group Two former members to aid them in building their new colony. Yet, despite a continuous series of requests from Group Two leaders to implement the agreement, Oak Bluff never gave a share to the Group Two people, just as Lakeside had not given a share to the Group Two Heartland people. The leaders of Group Two kept pushing for implementation, and they were repeatedly told that the matter would be dealt with.[25] Even the Group One leaders who had negotiated the agreement were unable to get Oak Bluff to implement it.

If Oak Bluff never provides a pro rata share, we may assume that Group Two leaders, if they are to be faithful to Hutterian norms, will not sue to implement the agreement. There is an argument, if I understand it correctly, that some Group One families left Spring Valley Colony, a Group Two colony, without getting a share of Spring Valley. If these families went to Oak Bluff without bringing any assets from their former colony, Oak Bluff might make the argument that it therefore should not have to pay anything for those who left Oak Bluff. Alternatively, the former Oak Bluff people could look to Spring Valley for payment, assuming that Spring Valley is obligated under the agreement or in the circumstances to provide a pro rata share to departing families. But Oak Bluff's failure to pay would be justified as a set-off only if it took in the new members from Spring Valley. If another colony took them in, the failure to live up to the agreement cannot be justified by the argument that another colony is not fulfilling its end of the agreement, assuming of course that the agreement applies to other colonies.

Other Divisions

Whether as an extension of the agreement of 2 May 1995, or outside of the agreement, the two groups were dealing with the conflicts arising from the schism by separating from each other. A dissenting family that was being excommunicated in a Group One colony might find a home in a Group Two colony. There may have been other exchanges of minorities, as happened between Trileaf and Huron. There were also other Group Two colonies where Group One people, sometimes purporting to have management authority, had engaged in "asset grabbing." These colonies also ultimately were divided between Group Two majorities and Group One minorities, which moved on to establish their own colonies. Netley Colony (Group One) was created out of Interlake Colony (Group Two). Oak River (Group One) appears to have been created out of both Deerboine and Holmfield Colonies (Group Two), while Boundary Lane (Group One) is a daughter colony of Plainview Colony (Group Two).

The affiliations with one side or the other sometimes came about in interesting ways. Apparently during the process in which Kamsley Colony was created as a daughter of Oakridge, the women at the colony engaged in a strike against the minister, who was unwilling to affiliate with Group Two. The women refused to make food or come to church services, among other things. In the face of this internal civil disobedience, the minister moved away, and both Oakridge and Kamsley are now Group Two colonies.[26]

In other colony splits subsequent to the schism, the new colony was a Group One colony while the old colony was Group Two. For example, Pineland (Group One) is a colony of Iberville (Group Two), and Ridgeville (Group One) is a colony of Maxwell (Group Two). By the year 2000, the number of Group Two colonies in Manitoba also increased to the point where the Schmiedeleut in Manitoba was split in half (50 50) between Group One and Group Two.

Another Schism: Group One Breaks with the Bruderhof

The senior elder must have been living a nightmare after the stormy meetings at the end of 1992, when a majority indicated that it had lost confidence in his leadership. As I have outlined, the next three years (1993 through

1995) were full of conflicts and controversies surrounding him. Shunning the dissenters had not brought them back into the fold. Instead, they had affiliated with the Darius and the Lehrer, leaving Group One standing outside the wider church. Even though Group One did not initiate the *Rock Lake* or *Huron* litigation, seeking the protection of the court against dissenters by launching and relaunching the *Lakeside* litigation was the cause, in no small measure, for the impending disaster of having judicial decisions that would explode Group One's claim to be the only true Hutterite church. One would have thought that the senior elder, when fighting these battles against Group Two, could at least take comfort in the esteem and warm relationship he enjoyed as the defender of the Bruderhof-Hutterite alliance. As noted previously, the alliance Jacob Kleinsasser had maintained with the Bruderhof was one of the major reasons for the schism. Yet as all the other storms were raging, the relationship between Group One and the Bruderhof became ever more tense and finally was broken completely. To preserve the relationship with the Bruderhof, Group One had allowed itself to be rejected by Group Two and the wider Hutterite church. But then Group One itself rejected the Bruderhof. So in the end, what was the point of it all?

That the divorce between the two groups has happened is undeniable but, as is often the case with a broken marriage, the reasons for the break are not documented for outsiders. The little information available to me must be taken with a grain of salt, as when hearing rumours about someone. Nevertheless, even if the details are lacking, the basic contours of the break may be sketched.

When the leaders of the Lehrer and Darius groups of Hutterites sent a letter to the Bruderhof in 1990 containing their ten-point indictment of the Bruderhof and rejecting the Bruderhof alliance,[27] the Bruderhof decided to hold an East-West conference, in April of 1991. The key speaker at this gathering was Jacob Kleinsasser, who went through each of the ten points and argued against the Darius and Lehrer positions.[28] As head of the Schmiedeleut, Kleinsasser chose to move his group of Hutterites into deeper unity with the Bruderhof, despite the objections of the rest of the Hutterite family. Speculation abounded that Kleinsasser ultimately might be the head of a truly united Bruderhof and Schmiedeleut church where all the communities would be reconstituted into one comprehensive common property regime under the authority of one overseer.[29]

According to one report, however, not long into the Schmiedeleut schism a rift already was occurring in Schmied and Bruderhof relations. In November of 1993 a delegation from the Bruderhof came to Crystal Spring to speak with Kleinsasser and suggest that he place himself "in a state of punishment."[30] After sending the Bruderhof members away, a meeting at Millbrook Colony was called for 11 November 1993. Christoph Arnold, senior elder of the Bruderhof, and about thirty Bruderhof leaders were in attendance. *KIT*

Newsletter, reporting on the meeting, stated that "Christoph and the Woodcrest delegation seemed unhappy with these developments. Christoph said that he was returning to Woodcrest to discuss everything with the brotherhood. Nothing was really concluded at the Millbrook meeting. 'Things just sort of fell apart,' someone said. 'But it does seem that the East is losing confidence in Jake at the same time that Jake can no longer fork over dollars for the East.'"[31]

A more detailed account of the growing tension was provided in an article in the *Mennonite Weekly Review:* "After Kleinsasser's split from the rest of the West, he and Arnold became, in effect, co-elders of a new Hutterite faction. (The rest of the Western Hutterites broke ties with the Bruderhof in 1990.) But as far back as August 1993, Arnold urged that both he and Kleinsasser repent and undergo a period of self-disciple for contributing to the deterioration of relations between East and West. Kleinsasser rejected the idea. 'The word repentance to some of them is like a swear word,' Arnold said."[32]

Mike Wollmann's election as assistant senior elder for Group One may have been another reason for estrangement because it was reported that Christoph Arnold let his name stand as a candidate for assistant senior elder of Group One; he was not elected.[33]

Samuel Kleinsasser, brother of Jacob Kleinsasser, has suggested that another reason for the rift was the encouragement of intermarriage between the Bruderhof and the Hutterites; in many cases these marriages became a source of tension. For example, well-educated Eastern Bruderhof members, imbued with the spiritual ideals and cultural practices of the Eastern group, would marry Hutterites and move to Western Hutterite colonies, believing that their presence would change these colonies for the better, but would soon become disillusioned with how the Hutterites operated. Apparently the Bruderhof in some cases would call these members back East, with Hutterite spouse in tow, without permission of the Western colony.[34] Another report confirmed, and added that there were also problems when these couples lived in the East. For example, one of Jacob Kleinsasser's daughters married Dan Moody, a Bruderhof member. The couple lived in the East, but eventually left.[35] The report states:

> Waldner [a South Dakota minister] said inter-marriages contributed to the break between the East and the West. He mentioned two specific couples who moved to the Bruderhof after trying to live in the West. The result was gossip against the West, he said. "People were forced to elaborate how bad things were in the West," Dan Moody said. "There was a lot of talk against the Hutterites in meetings when they were not present." That eventually led to his leaving the Bruderhof, he said. "I kept hearing a lot of untruths about my father-in-law," Moody said. "There was false witness. I raised a

couple of questions and was excommunicated" ... The Bruderhof has long been an advocate of East-West unity. That has led some on both sides to believe that the East wanted to control the West. Moody, who has connections to both the East and West, but has since distanced himself from the Bruderhof, wrote in 1991: "Uniting implies that the Hutterite colonies would have to give up their traditional understandings" in favor of the Bruderhof style of leadership, which is more hierarchical and centralized.[36]

Another of the many sore spots between the Group One Hutterites and the Bruderhof was the establishment of the Palmgrove Nigerian Bruderhof, which was a joint missionary effort between West and East. After several conflicts, the Bruderhof pulled out its support, and then alleged that the Nigerian leadership would not turn over the communal property to the larger Bruderhof.[37] Unlike the Western Hutterites, where each individual colony holds title to the common property, within the Bruderhof, title to colony property is held by the central organization. An account of the Nigerian controversy includes the following:

Last June (1994), Arnold circulated a letter among the leadership of the West requesting that they stand with the East against Palmgrove. Noting that he supported Kleinsasser in his split from the rest of the Hutterites, he wrote, "Now I expect the same from you." Nevertheless, when Palmgrove approached the West, they responded with material resources and ministers ... In October (1994) in the midst of the Palmgrove developments, Arnold, with his wife, went to Manitoba unannounced for a wedding and to discuss the groups' differences with Kleinsasser. Arnold went to Crystal Spring, Kleinsasser's colony, but was then asked to go to the nearby colony of the Assistant Elder. For Arnold, that amounted to being kicked out of Crystal Spring and was an insult to unity. The East, claiming it had sunk $2.35 million into Palmgrove, in January (1995) brought a lawsuit against Palmgrove to freeze its assets. But a judge in Nigeria recently threw it out because such suits can only be filed against individuals. Arnold said the suit has been withdrawn. "We just wanted to make a point that in Anabaptist history it's wrong for a brother to have private property," he said. Strangely, the lawsuit, filed by the Hutterian Brethren of New York Inc., was filed also on behalf of the West. The West issued a statement opposing the lawsuit.[38]

The bomb that probably finally ended the relationship between the Bruderhof and Group One was launched on 7 January 1995, when Christoph Arnold wrote, on behalf of the members of the Bruderhof, an "Open Letter from the Bruderhof." It was distributed widely and published in *The Plough*, a Bruderhof publication.[39] The contents of the letter had allegedly been discussed and approved by all the Bruderhof colonies. Clearly the Bruderhof did not view itself as in need of spiritual and ethical guidance from the larger Hutterite group so much as it thought of itself as embodying the superior spirituality that might serve as a renewal mechanism for the more "backward" Hutterite church. After reviewing the wonderful joint efforts between East and West since the alliance of 1974, Arnold in the open letter hit the Western Hutterites with a scathing indictment:

> The Hutterian Church has now existed for over 450 years. It has always witnessed to the clear teachings of the New Testament, especially those concerning brotherly love, mutual service, community of goods, nonviolence, sexual purity, and faithfulness in marriage. Unfortunately this witness has been almost completely lost.
>
> In many Hutterite colonies in Canada and the Dakotas, members withhold money and other goods as private property, sometimes working outside the community to earn money for their own personal use. Communal work departments have become independent "kingdoms," and a sense of common work and a common purpose has been lost. There is little or no spiritual leadership, and ministers are no longer true servants of their flock but lord it over them, seeking to increase their personal authority (Mt. 20:25). Young people no longer receive clear guidance and direction from their ministers, teachers, and parents. Many are baptized and enter marriage with consciences burdened by unconfessed sin. Alcoholism is rampant, even among some community leaders. Premarital sex is widespread, and there are illegitimate children.
>
> In other words, the church has lost its salt and has become lukewarm, shallow, and superficial. The right words are still there; the form is still there; but the church has become a lifeless and self-defeating system. The light of Jesus has gone out in many hearts ...
>
> The sharpness of Jesus against sin, especially as emphasized in the Sermon on the Mount, has been completely rejected by modern-day Hutterianism. It has been replaced by a false emphasis on eternal salvation – the attitude that this world is a vale of tears, and we can only hope to find blessedness in the life to come. The rule of Christ is pushed into the distant future, and there is complacency and a general acceptance of sin in the church.[40]

The letter continued along this same theme that the traditional Hutterian church was spiritually and morally dead, and then Arnold made a call for repentance: "We have pleaded many times with the leaders of the Hutterites in Canada and the Dakotas to recognize that we all need to change, and that this change must begin in the leadership of the church. (We should not forget that when Jonah preached repentance to Nineveh, it was the king who was the first to put on sack cloth and ashes; and then God was once more merciful to the people.) Sadly, our pleas have been rejected and deeply resented."[41]

Sometimes we are the most hurt not by statements that are just plain false but by statements that, though grossly exaggerated, have grains of truth to them. This indictment of the Western Hutterites did not sit well with the Western ministers, whether they were Group One or Group Two. It was reported that "Western Hutterites and others deny the East's charges. Michael Waldner, a minister from South Dakota, said some of those things have happened, but that 'allegations to the extent that Christoph writes them' are false. Terry Miller, research director of the Hutterite Studies Centre in Austin, Manitoba, said, 'Of the several hundred Hutterites I've known personally over the last 30 years, the vast majority of them take their Christianity very seriously ... For many thousand of the faithful, the Hutterite way of the 1990s is not a lifeless form.'"[42]

In addition to its pulling out of Nigeria, the rift between East and West may have contributed to the Bruderhof shutting down its attempt to establish a Bruderhof in Germany. The Michaels Bruderhof in Birnbach was established in 1988 with the financial help of the Western Hutterites. However, the group encountered resistance from a faction of local citizens that resulted in long delays in getting approval for communal building projects. Just when these approvals were finally given, the Bruderhof decided to abandon the project, despite large demonstrations from the local community pleading with it to stay.[43] The leadership cited discrimination against the Bruderhof as the reason for leaving, but perhaps the key reason was the schism between East and West. Without the support of the West, the millions of dollars of further investment needed to build up the colony would be difficult to generate.[44]

At the same time that Group One and Group Two were coming to an agreement to end litigation by dividing assets and getting disengaged from each other, Group One was getting disengaged from the Bruderhof. Now another schism was taking place in which refugees were crossing borders; Hutterites particularly were leaving their colonies to join the Bruderhof. A meeting was held in Winnipeg in May 1995 between Bruderhof and Group One leaders to discuss financial matters and disengagement. According to one source, Group One claimed that in the end the Bruderhof owed it nearly $800,000.[45] There apparently was also a colony in Minnesota which, in a repeat of the Forest River conflict that had occurred during the previous Hutterite-Bruderhof romance, had a significant number of members who wanted to leave, or had already left, for the East. Would the assets of this colony (Oakwood, now Haven) be split between Bruderhof and Group One, just like Group One and Group Two were agreeing to divide colonies? According to one report, it was agreed that the colony assets would remain with Group One.[46] Another report suggests, however, that Bruderhof members went to Oakwood and took "several truckloads of furniture and equipment" back to the East.[47]

On 25 October 1995 at a Group One conference, a formal decision to divorce the Bruderhof was agreed upon. The letter sent to the Bruderhof on 16 November 1995, signed by Jacob Kleinsasser and Michael Wollmann and other leaders, included a list of grievances, such as "the different letters you have written and published, spreading propaganda all over the world, labeling the West as unchristian."[48] The issue of money allegedly owed to the West by the East was raised, as was the conflict involving the Nigerian colony and the Bruderhof use of the law courts in an attempt to confiscate property. The indictment of the Bruderhof for its use of law courts, coming as it did from Jacob Kleinsasser and Michael Wollmann, might be viewed as ironic.

It often takes time for former lovers to fully disengage. For a time, the Bruderhof continued to use the term "Hutterian" to describe itself, and the press too continued to refer to the group as a branch of the Hutterites. Eventually, however, the Bruderhof, in compliance with the wishes of the Hutterites, shed any reference to the Hutterite name it had been using for more than twenty years.[49] Even after the divorce, there appears to have been a series of conflicts between the two groups. One day I happened to be listening to a Winnipeg radio talk show. Arnold was the guest, discussing his book on making peace.[50] A lawyer from the Baker firm phoned in and implied that, contrary to its message of peace, the Bruderhof was threatening to bring a copyright lawsuit against Kleinsasser because he had published a second volume of the Hutterian chronicles.[51] The Bruderhof had apparently worked for many years on its own translation and had long announced that its own publication was forthcoming. Arnold, not about to admit to the lawsuit threat on the radio, offered his congratulations on the fine Kleinsasser translation.

As the break between the groups became final, Samuel Kleinsasser from a Group Two perspective wrote:

> Only a short time ago, unity within the Hutterian Church was gambled with, and put to risk by those who admired the Society [Bruderhof], considering it to be a lesser loss to lose Schmiedeleut unity than to lose the friendship of the Society of "Brothers." Earlier, those who spoke evil of the Society were severely church-disciplined. Today, with weather-cock precision, the very ones who classed the Society as above reproach are now the very ones who are speaking against them as being evil, who have cut off all relations with them, have denounced them, and who themselves are now using harsh and malicious language to describe Society behavior.[52]

Postscript on the Bruderhof and Litigation

The issue that interests me, for my limited purpose, is whether the two groups are taking a different position on the use of litigation. Although it appears that Group One did not support the Bruderhof litigation in Nigeria, it is abundantly clear that Group One has engaged in litigation arising from internal disputes. However, after the schism with Group One, the Bruderhof appears to be more likely to resort to litigation, not just in the governmental realm[53] but against individual "apostates" and outside critics. That is, even though Group One was hardly a paragon of virtue on this point, the formal alliance with the Hutterites, deeply rooted in Anabaptist tradition, may have served as a brake on the temptation within the Bruderhof to litigate. Now that the brake is gone, the Bruderhof leadership has demonstrated a willingness to go to law.

The senior elder of the Bruderhof, Johann Christoph Arnold, is the named author of numerous books produced by Plough Publishers, one of the Bruderhof enterprises.[54] Consistent with the Anabaptist emphasis on non-violence and peacemaking, several of his books deal with this theme.[55] After the schism with the Hutterites, the Bruderhof has increased its outreach activism on issues of peace and justice, such as the prison system, the death penalty, going to war, and other acts of exploitation and aggression within society. Arnold travels widely, meeting with an ecumenical assortment of prominent religious, intellectual, and political leaders.[56] No doubt the Bruderhof contains many sincere Anabaptists, but is there an inconsistency between the non-violent, enemy-loving, forgiving community image and the reality of how the Bruderhof leadership deals with those it perceives to be its own enemies?

We are told that instead of agreeing to go to mediation with those who claim to have been abused within the group, or who are denied visitation with family members still in the group, or who have some other issue causing hardship, the Bruderhof leadership launched a series of lawsuits against former members and academic critics.[57] For example, a group called the Children of the Bruderhof, International (COBI) was formed in 1995, similar to the *KIT* network of ex-members, with its newsletters, conferences, and books. COBI established a toll-free phone line, which it advertised in the New York Yellow Pages. People who were thinking about leaving the Bruderhof, or who had recently left or been expelled, could call and receive advice and support in the difficult transition of moving from the shelter of the commune to the outside world. In September of 1995, the Bruderhof filed a civil lawsuit in the federal district court in Albany, New York, alleging a trademark infringement because COBI had used the name "Bruderhof" and "Hutterian" in the advertisement. The lawsuit was settled when COBI agreed not to use "Bruderhof" in its name and the Bruderhof in turn withdrew its demand for a monetary award of damages.[58] In the end, the COBI organization was disbanded.

However, the continued existence of *KIT* served as a counter to the image of harmony, devotion, justice, and peace that the Bruderhof presented to the world. Increasingly, ex-members and academic critics were challenging the Bruderhof image as an idyllic community, not just by posting narratives of their experiences in an obscure newsletter or Internet newsgroup but by participating in media and political forums when issues involving the Bruderhof came up. For example, in 1997, after months of research, including interviews with critics, CBS produced and broadcast a segment of the show *48 Hours* that was highly critical of the Bruderhof. According to one report, the Bruderhof filed a lawsuit against CBS seeking discovery and disclosure of reporters' notes, tapes, and other materials used as sources in the show so as to collect evidence for a defamation lawsuit against CBS and the critics of the Bruderhof. The request for discovery was dismissed in August 1997.[59]

Bruderhof leaders also issued a lawsuit against Ramon Sender, the editor of *KIT Newsletter*, for invasion of privacy and copyright infringement.[60] Sender had published a letter, apparently already in wide circulation, written by Bruderhof leaders and addressed to some Hutterite leaders, calling for a meeting to deal with allegations of child abuse brought by ex-Hutterites now living with the Bruderhof. A few months later the Bruderhof issued another lawsuit, this time against Ramon Sender (KIT), Blair Purcell (spouse of ex-member), and Dr. Julius Rubin (sociologist) for defamation, because of various statements made about the Bruderhof.[61] The claim was for more than $15 million for damaged reputation. When the claim was dismissed at the lower court level on a time-limitations technicality, the Bruderhof appealed but then decided to withdraw both the appeal of the defamation case and the earlier copyright case. Even though the cases were eventually dropped, the demonstrated willingness of the Bruderhof leaders to sue critics might well deter people from risking the publication of their experiences and opinions to avoid the great expense of having to defend themselves in lawsuits.[62]

When the husband of an ex-member started an Internet newsgroup, called alt.support.bruderhof, he received a letter from a law firm in New York acting on behalf of the Bruderhof. The letter advised him that the word "Bruderhof" was protected by trademark and that unless he stopped using the name the law firm would advise the Bruderhof to commence a lawsuit against him.[63] There was also a lengthy battle involving the Bruderhof and Dr. Rubin over both his critical essay[64] and his critical book on the Bruderhof.[65]

More recently it was reported that the air charter company owned by the Bruderhof filed a lawsuit for defamation against Blair Purcell, who had posted an item on the Internet shortly after a family court hearing in New York.[66]

I have made no attempt to research these developments involving the Bruderhof in any depth nor to examine here whether the Bruderhof is justified as a matter of law to bring these cases. My point simply is that if these reports are correct, the Bruderhof leadership in these battles with critics has displayed a willingness to embrace litigation as a weapon. As I have argued, that weapon is ultimately a violent one and thus contradicts the proclaimed pacifism of the group.

The *Concord* and *James Valley* Cases

One of the objectives in making the 2 May 1995 agreement was to end all the litigation that had arisen at various colonies. To a degree, the agreement did result in the ending of lawsuits and also, most significantly, avoided a court determination as to which of the two groups, if not both, were in law entitled to hold common property as members of the Hutterian Brethren Church. Yet new litigation related to the agreement itself broke out, again opening up the possibility of a court determination of the key questions.

The first litigation arose when one of the Group Two colonies did not sign releases in accordance with the agreement. To achieve the disengagement between the two Schmiedeleut groups, Group Two was willing to forgo claims that it might have made for the assets of enterprises that had been created jointly by the Schmiedeleut. However, Samuel Kleinsasser, minister of the Group Two Concord Colony, decided to test the litigiousness of Group One, headed by his brother, Jacob Kleinsasser. Concord Colony had a loan outstanding from H.B. Credit, but it was Samuel's position that the actual value of the share of each Group Two colony in the central pot was greater than the debt that was owed by any one of them to H.B. Credit. Thus, Concord did not sign the release made pursuant to the 2 May 1995 agreement forgoing any further claims for shares in the central church pot, as all the other Group Two colonies did. As predicted, H.B. Credit filed a lawsuit against Concord for the debt owing.[67] Concord did not litigate the matter by filing a statement of defence but simply paid the claim.[68] As far as Concord was concerned, the point as to the litigiousness of Group One had been made.

More to the point of litigating the agreement itself is the lawsuit Keystone Colony (Group One) launched against James Valley Colony (Group Two), alleging that James Valley was bound to give a pro rata share to some families who left James Valley to move to Keystone.[69] Right after the confrontation and vote over the leadership of Jacob Kleinsasser, the minister of James Valley called a meeting of the colony and explained that he had sided with the Joseph Wipf group of ministers. While no vote was taken, "all brothers accepted this decision for now."[70] However, in the spring of 1993, when the issue of approval of fees to lawyers and others to investigate the finances of various Hutterian joint enterprises was brought to the brotherhood meeting at James Valley, it became apparent that two members, Tim and Jonathan Hofer, objected to the investigation. They refused to read or consider the information compiled to that point. Of greater concern to the unity of the colony was the fact that the two men refused to take the Lord's Supper at James Valley because of the split in the church but went instead to a Group One colony. Jonathan's wife went along to the other colony for communion, but Tim's wife stayed home because she had recently given birth.

In May of 1993 at a meeting of the colony members, the two men, even after explanations and discussions, refused to change their minds about the split in the church or their participation at the Lord's Supper at another colony. They were disciplined by the majority. They were still members of the colony, they could still go to church, they could still do their assigned tasks, but they were banned from brotherhood meetings and from having a vote until they were reconciled with the community. In June 1993 James Valley signed the reaffirmation papers and formally became a Group Two colony.

Reconciliation between the majority and the two minority families never was achieved. The tension between the Group One sympathizers and the rest of the colony dragged on for approximately four years. Finally at a meeting of members in the fall of 1997, after hearing from the two men and their wives, the majority group gave the minority group an option: either change your minds and join the majority, or move to a Group One colony. If they moved, James Valley would be prepared to help them relocate by, among other things, paying for a house for the two families.[71]

In November of 1997 the two men informed the James Valley leadership that they were prepared to move to Keystone Colony. They were then told to get a quote for the cost of a duplex. The quote they submitted on 15 December 1997 amounted to $426,600 (land costs were not included and not an issue).[72] To the leaders of James Valley, this amount seemed excessive for construction costs of a duplex to house two Hutterite families; that kind of money would buy one of the finest mansions in Winnipeg. James Valley proposed to pay $225,000 for construction. This was flatly refused by the two men, but as they had already started construction, they asked for assistance to complete the basement. James Valley Colony gave them $25,000. The two families continued to live at James Valley.

In February 1998 at a meeting between leaders of Keystone and James Valley, the leaders of James Valley proposed to put $175,000 into trust at a construction supply company so that the duplex at Keystone could be built and, furthermore, James Valley would pay another $25,000 when the group left that colony. These payments would be made on the condition that the two families immediately leave James Valley for Keystone. In March 1998, James Valley's offer was rejected. Instead, Keystone Colony, as well as, or on behalf of, the two dissenters at James Valley requested a pro rata share of the whole of James Valley Colony according to the agreement of 2 May 1995.

The position of James Valley was that the agreement never was meant to apply to whatever tensions and problems existed at James Valley at the time the agreement was entered into. But even if the agreement might not apply as a matter of law, the issue for James Valley and other colonies is the morality and justice of giving a share to a departing member in this context of a schism in the church. This is not a situation where a Hutterite family leaves for another colony. In the opinion of the James Valley leadership, however, the agreement was not just inapplicable, it was also inappropriate in these circumstances as a matter of Hutterian norms: the rule that a person leaving the colony is not entitled to anything should apply. As to the request for a pro rata share, Rev. John Hofer wrote:

> We have considered your request for a pro rata share with our Brotherhood and have come to the following decision. Our church and biblical doctrine does not allow us to give this share and it is not in our hands to give a share.
>
> Here we refer to the book, *Andreas Ehrenpreis and Hutterite Faith and Practice*, p. 147:
>
> However, in the case of persons who decided to leave the Brotherhood after their indoctrination, probation, and ceremony of initiation, Ehrenpreis contended that for two reasons they no longer had any rights to previous personal possessions: first, they had given their goods of their own free will, never expecting to receive them again; and second, the church was not responsible before God to give them anything. This had been the Hutterian tradition from the earliest days of the movement, and it was explained adequately in the *Great Article Book* ... which in addition to scriptural reasons verified the practice by quoting a common proverb, "for what one gives away in the morning is no longer his in the afternoon."[73]

After noting that nevertheless James Valley continued to stand by its offer to pay $225,000 for aid in housing the families, the minister continued:

> We are basing this assistance again on *Andreas Ehrenpreis and Hutterite Faith and Practice*, p. 147:
>
> On the other hand, the *Great Article Book* made provision for the person who was in the process of "falling away" to receive some aid from the church

if the person "did not act rebelliously; we do not allow him to leave empty-handed, even if he originally brought nothing with him when he joined."[74]

The two men continued to hold the position that they were entitled to a pro rata share, or, more properly, that Keystone as the receiving colony was entitled to it. The two families continued to reside at James Valley, but during the day they worked at Keystone. The two James Valley dissenters and the leaders of Keystone went to the law firm of Duboff, Edwards. This firm with increased frequency was taking on legal matters for Group One colonies that would have previously gone to the Baker law firm. In May of 1998, Paul Edwards wrote to the management of James Valley and requested that, in accordance with the agreement, a panel of Group One and Group Two ministers be appointed to deal with the allocation of pro rata shares for the departing families moving to Keystone.[75] James Valley did not respond to this request. Edwards wrote back in early June 1998, requesting that the dispute be resolved by arbitration if the Group Two leaders were unwilling to appoint a panel as required by the agreement.[76]

James Valley stood firm in its decision, and so on 27 July 1998, Keystone Colony and Tim and Jonathan Hofer filed an application in court.[77] By commencing the claim by way of an application to determine the rights of the parties under the agreement of 2 May 1995, the applicants were evidently attempting to avoid having the case go to trial. Evidence regarding the agreement would be submitted by affidavits, the lawyers would make their arguments to the judge as to the meaning of the agreement, and the court would or would not order that James Valley comply. This would avoid the usual process of a trial, with witnesses in court being examined and cross-examined in an adversarial way. However, at bottom, despite the clear attempt to avoid breaking Hutterian norms, the two men were still members of James Valley, and they were taking their own colony to court in an attempt to get the state to use the power of the sword to force the colony to fulfill an agreement they claimed applied to them. Furthermore, the case illustrates the fact that the Group One leadership was again willing to go to court against Group Two. Here Keystone Colony as a Group One colony was suing James Valley as a Group Two colony. Sam Waldner, minister of Decker Colony and one of the Group One leaders who signed the agreement, submitted an affidavit on behalf of the applicants and argued that James Valley was bound by the agreement of 2 May 1995 to give pro rata shares.[78]

Now that the two men had launched legal proceedings, a formal notice was posted around James Valley Colony and delivered personally to the two men. The notice called for a meeting to be held on 18 September 1998 to consider the expulsion of Jonathan Hofer and Timothy Hofer from membership. Various grounds were listed for expulsion, including in both cases:

"He has commenced legal proceedings in the Court of Queen's Bench against James Valley Hutterian Mutual Corporation and James Valley Colony of Hutterian Brethren contrary to the ways of and religious beliefs of The Hutterian Brethren and The Hutterian Brethren Church according to the interpretation of The Hutterian Brethren Church of the New Testament and without limiting generality of the foregoing contrary to I Corinthians 6."[79] Mirroring the process required by the Supreme Court of Canada in the *Lakeside* case, the two men were invited to attend the meeting and address the charges. At the meeting the two men were expelled from membership. They did not, however, move to Keystone but continued to live at James Valley.

Now that the case was before the courts, the issue as to the application of the agreement needed to be addressed. John Hofer, minister of James Valley, was a prominent Group Two leader. Indeed, he had been centrally involved in the negotiation of the 2 May 1995 agreement to divide colonies on a pro rata basis, and had been one of the four Group Two leaders to sign the agreement. The 2 May agreement did mention six colonies specifically, but as we have seen, other colonies had been divided; some, such as Maplegrove, without the negotiations or interventions of church leaders from either side, but others, such as Interlake, Holmfield, Deerboine, and Plainview, allegedly with reference to the 2 May 1995 agreement.[80] That other colonies had divided did not mean that they did so because of a contractual obligation between Group One and Group Two arising from the agreement. Did the agreement mean that each and every internal dispute related to affiliation was to be resolved by the giving of pro rata shares to those who left as a result of the schism?

On one hand, if the agreement to effect pro rata share separations was intended to apply to only those colonies that were specifically mentioned, the agreement was poorly drafted. The first sentence of clause six of the agreement stated: "Group One and Group Two agree that at the Colonies where problems currently exist there shall be a pro rata division (based on number of people) of the assets of the Colonies."[81] On its face, such a provision standing alone might be interpreted as having a wide scope. Assuming that "problems" means internal dissent over Group One and Group Two affiliations, one could argue that if, at the time of the agreement, at any colony even one person or family wanted to disassociate themselves from the majority group at the colony, that colony should be "divided" so that the one person or family would take a pro rata share to either move to another colony or start a new one. This is not an unreasonable interpretation of the sentence when taken alone. It is noteworthy that the Huron minority essentially involved only two families, and with the James Valley situation we are again dealing with only two families.

On the other hand, there is a good argument that, quite apart from what was subsequently voluntarily done at other colonies, the provision of the agreement should be interpreted narrowly so as to include only the six colonies cited. Given that there was a huge debate about splitting the colonies, and that the provision was agreed to only as a compromise in order to avoid the worse scenario of having nothing in the end for either side to even fight over because colonies were going bankrupt from the costs and malfunction of community life, one might argue that it is reasonable to assume that the agreement was limited to those "problems" where there was a significant stalemate at a colony. The agreement covers those situations where assets were already held by two groups within the same colony, or the management was split, and so forth. Thus, the agreement to pay pro rata shares does not, and was not intended to apply to every situation where a minority leaves a colony to join a colony of the other branch. The schism in the Schmiedeleut affected every colony, and if the agreement was meant to apply broadly to all colonies, the leaders would have made this clear, given what was at stake.

As noted previously, the last clause (10) of the agreement could be used on both sides of the argument in the James Valley case. On one hand, the agreement to provide a pro rata split of assets was not supposed to change the traditional rules in other cases. On the other hand, the two dissenters could claim that they were not asking for an *individual* share. The point of the claim was not to give shares to the two men but to Keystone. In this sense, even though the two men were excommunicated and not entitled to a share, the giving of a pro rata share to Keystone was not unlike what the agreement originally provided for the excommunicated from Huron: the shares would be paid to a Group One receiving colony.

In the end, there was no judicial determination in the case. As to the lawsuit, the Group Two leaders played their own "litigation card," not only claiming that the agreement did not apply but also objecting to the summary application process in that there were contentious issues of material fact that required a trial. On behalf of James Valley, lawyer Sidney Wolchock filed a motion that the applicants be required to commence the action by way of a statement of claim, or in any case that a trial be held on the issues.[82] Thus, although arguments were made as to whether or not the agreement applied in the first place, when the matter came before Mr. Justice Kaufman, he decided that the case should more properly proceed by way of a statement of claim.[83] There was thus no judicial determination on the application or interpretation of the agreement.

The two families departed from James Valley and, having earlier refused to take the $225,000 offered them, they left with nothing but the initial $25,000 given for the basement. At the time of this writing, no further legal proceedings have been brought by Keystone or the two men against James Valley.

The *Tschetter* Case

The agreement between Group One and Group Two leaders in Manitoba to divide at least some colonies on a pro rata basis so as to disengage the two groups from each other does not appear to have ever been accepted as a way of resolving disputes in the American colonies. As we have seen with the *Poinsett* case,[84] if a minority group within a colony in the United States was unwilling to reconcile with the majority group, the only option was for the minority group to leave. Ideally, the minority group would be taken in by a colony where a majority supported its side of the schism, but in any case, the minority would receive no part of the assets of the colony it was departing from. The harshness of the rule seems to be reciprocal. For example, Brentwood Colony is a Group One colony where five families left without assets to join a Group Two colony.[85]

That the courts in the United States will likely refuse to adjudicate the property disputes arising from the schism is illustrated yet again in the more recent case of Tschetter Colony.[86] The facts as taken from the judgment reveal a scenario that is by now familiar. The minister of Tschetter Colony was a supporter of Jacob Kleinsasser, but the majority of the colony was not; the minister refused to baptize, marry, or serve the Lord's Supper to these Group Two supporters. Eventually, however, given the numbers, the minister resigned. Reconciliation between the Group One minority and the Group Two majority was not achieved and thus the Group One members were expelled by vote of the majority. However, they did not leave. As at Lakeside, turf battles broke out, but unlike Lakeside, and setting aside the issue of whether a court would even take the case, the Group Two majority refused to take court action to enforce the church decision of expulsion. Thus, for several years the two sides shunned each other, with the minority group locked out of many colony activities and buildings but still housed and fed by the majority.

After years of tension, the Group One minority brought a legal claim against Group Two, in April of 1998. Part of the claim involved factual allegations that went beyond the foundational determination of whether Group One had been properly expelled, and the consequences of such expulsion if valid. Group One asserted that in the course of the shunning between the two sides, a vehicle purchased by Group One was vandalized, clotheslines belonging to Group One were cut, and Group Two had threatened to cut utilities to Group One houses and, indeed, twice electricity was cut off for a time in houses where there were no children. Most seriously, it was alleged that individuals from Group Two had intentionally driven vehicles toward Group One members in a dangerous and reckless manner so as to endanger the safety of those Group One members. These were all allegations that, as I note below, were never proven in court, but, given the history of Lakeside, it is not difficult to believe that they might be true. When one side refuses to leave a colony after being expelled and the other side refuses to go to court to get the state to throw the minority off the colony, colony life may well descend into war by other means. Of course, we do not know the allegations that might have been brought by Group Two as to the behaviour of Group One.

In the *Tschetter* case, the trial judge, in the process of reviewing an earlier *ex parte* restraining order that had been issued, dismissed the case on the basis that the court did not have jurisdiction over what was essentially a religious dispute.[87] On appeal to the Supreme Court of South Dakota, a majority of the court agreed that the case should be dismissed on jurisdictional grounds.[88] The dispute was over church property, and the issue as to which group, if not both, had rights to the common property could not be decided on neutral principles of law but rather would involve the court in a tangled web of sorting out the religious norms and doctrines of a religious group – in this instance, the Hutterites – something not permitted under the First Amendment of the American constitution. Thus, the dispute would have to be resolved in the church and not in the courts. As to the possibility that some actions in the dispute amounted to torts (civil wrongs recognized by the courts) that crossed the bounds of religious immunity, the majority held that this issue was not properly pleaded. The dissenting judgment, on the other hand, asserted that, while the courts might indeed in the end refuse jurisdiction over the case, this decision was being made prematurely, at least with regard to the possibility that some of the conduct complained of might amount to torts such as trespass or assault, which cross the line of protected religiously motivated conduct.[89]

As had happened earlier with Poinsett Colony, the refusal of the court to get involved meant that the Tschetter minority would have to join the majority or else leave the colony, forfeiting any common property.

Part Six
Concluding Reflections:
The Interaction between Outside
Law and Inside Law

12
Concluding Reflections: Models of Inside Law and Outside Law Interaction

The American courts refused to take jurisdiction to determine the disputes over membership and property that occurred as a result of the schism in the Schmiedeleut. No outside law was imposed on the competing claims that one or the other group was the true church. The Canadian courts in Manitoba, however, entertained in one form or another hundreds of motions, hearings, court orders, trials, and judgments, from *Lakeside* right through to *James Valley*. Yet because of the negotiated settlement to divide property between the two groups and because the second-round *Lakeside* expulsions were said to have predated the reaffirmation process, and because the Daniel Hofer group abandoned its counterclaim because it thought it violated the anti-litigation rule, the Canadian courts never did determine the question of which group was properly the Hutterian Brethren Church for which colony property is entrusted or, alternatively, whether property could be divided between the two groups. In these concluding reflections I wish to comment briefly on this issue of what the outside legal system should do with competing claims for communal property.

But before getting to that topic, there are a couple of themes that I wish to expand on: litigation generally, and the jurisdictional question of whether the courts should be taking these kinds of cases at all. This last issue requires us to look at models of how the outside law and inside law might interact with each other.

Going to Outside Law
In the course of this narrative, we have seen that the traditional inside law against going to outside law has been violated so frequently that there is serious doubt as to whether this norm of inside law exists any longer among the Schmiedeleut. In addition to the two dozen or so Schmiedeleut lawsuits I have outlined in this book, there are also the dozen or so lawsuits brought by the Bruderhof against critics. There is no doubt that outsiders have faced aggressive lawsuits brought against them by Hutterites who claim a breach

of contract or a property right or so on. When Hutterite colonies focused on farming, it was relatively easy for them to maintain a separationist stance within the host society, even in regard to many aspects of outside law. Now that the colonies are moving increasingly into manufacturing, this separationist stance is much harder to maintain, particularly in legal matters. Exclusive partnerships are formed with outsiders to market Hutterite products and protect Hutterite intellectual property. Many transactions are made with suppliers and consumers, giving rise to potential legal liabilities and claims. Like any big business, legal services are an essential part of the operation. One gets the sense that perhaps lawyers and the outside law process of the host society are treated as just another technological tool or system of production that is not viewed from a religious perspective, despite the Anabaptist claim that all of life is under the Lordship of Jesus. Where is the voice of Jesus as it applies to using the latest gadget that increases production? Where is the voice of Jesus when collecting a debt that is owed?

While going to outside law against outsiders may be questioned from a traditional Anabaptist point of view, the greatest violation of traditional inside law is the taking of church disputes to outside law courts, as was repeatedly done in *Lakeside* and subsequent cases. Even though Group One clearly has been the most likely to use the courts, Group Two has not been entirely pure in this matter when the stakes are big enough. Kleinsasser's claim in the first *Lakeside* trial that a person or group can be declared an "apostate" and therefore the lawsuit is no longer against a brother is splitting hairs. The point is that the church is taking ecclesiastical questions of membership and property to a foreign court. This arguably is not only a violation of Anabaptist norms but also places the inside law at risk of outside law interference.

We can certainly understand the impulse to go to court to regain management control over Lakeside, but what in the end was really accomplished in exchange for putting the inside law at risk? Did the outside law courts resolve anything of importance in terms of the actual inside disputes taken to them? I would suggest that the "renegades" at Lakeside did not leave because a court ordered them to. Rather, they abandoned their second-round appeal to the Manitoba Court of Appeal because they were able to leave Lakeside without leaving the church. Indeed, from their point of view, leaving Lakeside was now the way to remain in the church, properly so called. It was not the ruling of the court but the interaction between Group Two leaders and the Lakeside minority that brought closure to the dispute at Lakeside. Similarly, it was not the outside law courts that determined the outcome of the disputes at Oak Bluff, Rock Lake, Huron, and other colonies but the negotiated agreement between Group One and Group Two leaders to separate the disputants and equitably divide communal property. Also recall that the legal hooks the courts used to justify their decisions usually had nothing to do with the substantive dispute. In my view, the ruling in the second *Lakeside* case that there was no need to examine bias because the dissenters were expelled for obviously violating the rule of community of property by failing to give an accounting for their separate communal property pot is a legal hook attached to air, not substance. For that matter, so is the Supreme Court hook that their first expulsion was not valid because they had no formal notice of the cause for the expulsion. Legal hooks can hang judgments that, like doors, either shut out or open to the violence of the state, but they do not resolve disputes. This sort of litigation of ecclesiastical disputes is not dispute resolution at all, even if one side or the other wins a declaration of support from the state-enforced outside law. There are winners and losers, but the underlying issues that divide the parties are not being addressed. What a shame that the real allegations and interests of Daniel Hofer and the senior elder and other leaders were not dealt with fully and openly in front of skilled and neutral mediators or arbitrators within the church but instead the violence of the state was called upon to remove opposition.

The result of going to outside law was that outside law imposed new requirements on the process of inside-law discipline of members. We might affirm that these natural justice requirements are modest and actually good in giving some level of protection to the abuses that may well occur within religious groups. Indeed, we might argue that if the church is going to ask the state for its sword to enforce ecclesiastical judgments, the state has every right to insist on minimum outside law standards of due process before doing so. But then, in my view, a small outside law addition in one case likely leads to a more intrusive rule in the next case, and before long the outside law will be calling the shots. The outside law may start with modest procedural requirements but ultimately move to substantively regulate groups so as to prevent supposed oppression and discrimination when religious groups accept people as members or when they expel or exile members. This would be the end of normative multiplicity, as the outside law would take over. Furthermore, while the outside law may claim that these requirements are procedural and do not interfere with the substantive decisions of ecclesiastical bodies, my view from experience in deconstructing legal judgments is that procedural standards are so flexible that courts can easily make decisions based on whether they like the substantive result or not, and then justify their decisions by procedural rule rhetoric.

In addition to opening the door to outside law control over membership issues, the church destabilized its own community of property regime by going to court. Once again we have judges who express grave concern about the consequences of a community of property regime that gives nothing to expelled members. Perhaps it will only be a matter of time before a court rejects the baptismal contracts made by improvident youths and privatizes some part of communal property by awarding compensation to expelled members?

In my view, the *Lakeside* case should never have been taken to court. This is not to say that the mechanisms of the inside law are always superior as a means of dispute resolution. The unfortunate events that I have outlined in this book raise questions for all Anabaptist groups. If we take non-violence seriously, how do we structure our community relations so as to provide adequate internal processes for dispute resolution? That a senior elder has the discretion of granting an appeal from a majority decision of a colony, and also has the discretion as to what the process of the appeal will be, if granted, seems to me to be quite inadequate and not rooted in any inside law norms based on Scripture. That the senior elder can, on his own authority and without a formal appeal process, demand the exclusion and expulsion of members of a colony is certainly a practice that deserves to be debated within the church. There hardly can be a norm against going to secular courts if adequate procedures for adjudicating disputes within the church have not been set up.

A more adequate dispute resolution process within the church will not ultimately stop a person who loses his or her case in the church from bringing the dispute to court, but we can hope that such cases would be greatly reduced in number.

Finally, if an Anabaptist church is faced with a group that will not obey the ecclesiastical judgments of the church after an adequate internal process, should the church seek the coercion of the state by going to the outside law to enforce the inside law? It is my view that not only will this put the inside law at risk but, from a traditional Anabaptist perspective, such a move to "seek the protection of the state" is an act of unfaithfulness to the sovereignty of God. But then who am I to tell Hutterites what their inside law should be? The inside law of any religious group can change as it is influenced by myriad cultural forces from within and without the group. As outsiders we can hardly object to voluntary changes made by other groups, but we can at least question changes that are brought about by coercive outside law rather than by voluntary assent.

Some concluding reflections on the litigation theme perhaps can be made without reference to religious commitments. My narrative reconstruction of the dispute at Lakeside and subsequent cases as revealed by court records may well strike readers as exceedingly long, tedious, and repetitive. Yet this taxing of patience holds within it a certain lesson about litigation. However expensive litigation is for the parties in terms of filing fees and legal bills, it should be remembered that as taxpayers we pay for the courthouses, judges, clerks, sheriffs, and police whose services are engaged by taking cases to court. We certainly have a stake in considering what social value is being served by this adversarial process that may involve a hundred trips to the courthouse.

We have seen how misleading it is to think of litigation as simply filing or responding to a claim, preparing for trial, and then, if there is no settlement, having a trial, after which a verdict "resolving" the dispute will be forthcoming. Instead of that somewhat limited role for the courts, we have seen how in *Lakeside* the formal system was constantly invoked for many years, with a seemingly never-ending series of motions and hearings and court orders and enforcement processes before trial and between appeals as litigation and turf battles took place. Often it is not the trial that is the important part of litigation but all the ways that the coercion of the state is invoked or defended against through pretrial motions and court orders, supposedly before the legal rights of the parties have even been determined.

Both the patience and resources of the host society were stretched by this dispute as numerous officials of the outside law attempted to "manage" the dispute at Lakeside and at other colonies. Indeed, at Rock Lake and Huron, the court was in effect managing Hutterite colonies so as to keep the peace and allegedly protect creditors pending resolution of the disputes. Whether we see this supervisory function as desirable or not, numerous judges at all levels of courts, aside from a few rhetorical flourishes, spent huge amounts of time and effort on these cases and, despite my regret that the cases were brought at all, I think the Hutterites in both camps were treated with the utmost patience, respect, and dignity by the officials of our law.

And what about the lawyers? Representation of Hutterite clients had been the speciality of the Baker firm for many years. This cannot be said for Donald Douglas, who stood by his clients for close to a decade without being paid and without any assurance that he would ever be paid. But far beyond the issue of payment is the issue of the nature of the work itself; lawyers have to live with and "manage" such prolonged and complex adversarial conflict day in and day out for years. I am quite sure that the Baker lawyers expected Douglas to give up and fold, as many lawyers no doubt would have done. That the dissenters stayed at Lakeside for the length of time necessary to join Group Two is in no small part due to the persistence of their lawyer.

Finally, as we think back on all the competing claims made in the court records as to what happened, we are reminded that the legal history of the dispute is but a fraction of the reality. These last decades of Bruderhof alliance and Schmiedeleut schism are extraordinarily important and momentous events in Hutterite history. While the litigation of the disputes arising from the Schmiedeleut schism might have taken us by surprise, we should not be particularly surprised at the schism itself. Numerous Anabaptist groups have undergone schisms involving people who have separated from each other as a result of disputes between more liberal and more conservative factions. The dynamics of a schism may result in one group becoming more defensively conservative, while the other group becomes even more liberal. But it is also possible that post-schism the more conservative group may well be pulled into more liberal orbits by the continued existence of the more liberal alternative group, and conversely, the more liberal group may be constrained by the conservative influences of the other group. Now that the Bruderhof connection is finished with – and I very much doubt that a new chapter will ever be opened in that regard – perhaps Groups One and Two will discover that nothing much divides them. However, any reunification likely is not possible until a new generation of leaders on both sides is in place.

Models of Interaction Between Outside and Inside Law

One of the key questions not fully addressed in the Canadian cases was whether our courts should take jurisdiction over these disputes in the first place. The obvious reply is that courts should take jurisdiction because, even if the case deals with the territory of inside law, the case falls within the territory of outside law. We are dealing with the interpretation and enforcement of contracts, property rights, corporate charters, and so forth. Recall how in *Rock Lake* and *Huron* the courts had jurisdiction to put a colony into court-supervised receivership as if it were just another commercial corporation. If inside law is translated into outside law categories so as to protect it from outside law attack, the effect is simply to make it more likely that outside law will ultimately have jurisdiction. The Hutterites may live differently from most of us, but they are fully citizens of our country and have the same legal rights and access to our law courts as we do. Having said this, however, I am at least somewhat attracted to the American approach of shutting the courthouse door and leaving the parties to their own devices. Would the outside law be more respectful of inside law by abstaining from providing its sword to any of the parties, just as we have argued reciprocally that the inside law would be safer if church authorities refrained from going to outside law to enforce it? Is it possible for outside law to step aside?

Exploring this option requires us to step back and look at models of how inside and outside law might interact with each other. A fundamental premise of this work is that our society contains within it many legal systems, not just one.[1] Looking at law broadly as an instrument of social control and cultural construction rather than narrowly as official norms backed by state coercion, I have made a distinction throughout this book between inside law – that is, the fundamental norms of a subgroup in society – and outside law – that is, the legal norms of society as a whole expressed through the formal state agencies of legislatures and courts. Old Order Anabaptist religious groups, such as the Hutterites, live within a sectarian or ecclesiastical legal system of norm creation and adjudication that can be distinguished from the Canadian or American civil legal system, which also governs many transactions Hutterites engage in. Other groups within the state, most notably Aboriginal groups, also exhibit a similar capacity to create a normative universe that is operational within some communities and which may be different from the dominant state system. Other associations too may have their own inside law that resists being submerged into a homogenizing formal state system of law.[2]

I want to concentrate here on religious groups, and the extent to which inside law should be respected as a matter of freedom of religion rather than as a matter of multicultural or ethnic rights. Having inside law generated by religion usually adds a dimension of obligation to a higher power, a power greater than the state, rather than just an obligation based on cultural tradition, or personal taste or preference. Religious groups will differ, of course, as to how much of life is covered by inside law, but certainly issues such as church membership and church property disputes will frequently arise in such groups and thus the sorts of considerations that engaged the courts in the *Lakeside* case have resonance far beyond the Hutterite community.

My narrative and exploration of inside law and outside law connects to some degree with a larger debate in a liberal democratic polity about whether subgroups should have some degree of self-determination and autonomy over their own members even if the group denies to its own members individual rights that those members would ordinarily have according to outside law regarding public and private authorities in a liberal society.[3] Can a liberal society accommodate illiberal groups by upholding a conception of collective rights as having a priority over individualistic notions of rights, or must these groups be forced by the power of the outside law to conform to the dominant legal culture based on a homogenizing ideology of individual equality, dignity, and autonomy as defined by the larger society?[4] In a sense, this is just another way of asking whether the outside law should refrain from interfering with the inside law in certain areas of life.

The problem of accommodating religious groups with deeply held different norms may be played out in many areas of the law. But to take the area of anti-discrimination law as just one example, should a religious institution be forced to hire someone who has a religion hostile to that of the group, because to not hire the person would constitute illegal employment discrimination under provincial human rights legislation?[5] Why should a religious group that has norms prohibiting homosexual behaviour be forced by law to accommodate homosexuals?[6] Should religious groups be allowed to have their own inside "discriminatory" norms so long as they are expressed or applied only within the group, but not if the members of the group bring such norms into the public square?[7] Should we use the force of outside law to prohibit the Hutterites in their own society from engaging in our definition of sex discrimination?[8] I could go on, raising many other issues where the basic values contained in the outside law conflicts with the inside law of various religious groups. Can we have spaces in which people live within fundamentally different legal systems in our society, or must we have equality of treatment for every individual in all spheres of life imposed by one formal legal system?

We all have presuppositions that largely govern where we end up in this debate. Recall how Justice Ferg in *Lakeside* affirmed the autonomy of the Hutterites to live by their own norms, whereas Justice O'Sullivan in the Manitoba Court of Appeal painted a picture of a people who needed to be liberated by outside law from a condition of slavery. Mr. Justice O'Sullivan was expressing a classic liberal notion of law as a framework for protecting individual free choice as to the good life, including freedom to dissent and switch religions and even freedom to dissent *within* a religion. On one hand we have the view that outside law should protect people within "oppressive" religious groups, particularly when being exiled from these groups. On the other hand we have the view that our liberal norms, even regarding the terms of exit from a group, should not be imposed because such protections destroy the normative order of the group; such a move is a violation of religious freedom. While modest moves can be made to satisfy one side or the other, in the end these views cannot be reconciled.

The picture of Hutterite life that readers may have drawn from my narrative of colonies in bitter schism is hardly the normal picture of Hutterite life. There may well be many Hutterites who live and move and have their being within a religious structure of community norms that provides to them a joyful and meaningful existence that we on the outside in our perhaps frantic and fractured lives cannot begin to comprehend or appreciate. But at the same time, as noted in a recent book, "[i]f we take them seriously, if we go beyond the captivating nostalgia, Old Orders and their ways are troublesome, even offensive. We are troubled by folks who limit education, restrict occupations, curb personal freedom, and stifle personal achievement and artistic expression. Their pleas for obedience – for yielding to community – appear oppressive, sexist, and suffocating by any stretch of contemporary standards."[9] But are we so confident about the justice of outside law that we will coerce religious groups to adopt our values? Even if we do affirm religious freedom and legal pluralism, these concepts are not absolutes. Where is the boundary where the autonomy of the group must end and the jurisdiction of the state must begin?

When we focus on groups whose identity is primarily religious, we are not dealing with the same claims that might be made by conquered or occupied national or Aboriginal groups that want freedom to establish their own country or at least delegated power of self-government to make and enforce their own laws within a territory or community. Rather, we are dealing with groups that are within the umbrella of the whole, with the benefits and burdens that come from citizenship in the democratic polity, but are at the same time associated by a covenant that differs in material respects from the larger social contract. We are dealing with groups that may want a considerable freedom *within* the state to live by their own norms, norms motivated by religious faith. While limiting the focus to such religious groups, our discussion may nevertheless have relevance to other groups that may also wish to have their inside laws preserved in the face of outside law claims to sovereignty.

As noted previously, the inside law, based on religious beliefs and practices, does not have sheriffs and police officers to use violence to enforce the decisions made. The religious system will have many forms of social incentives and disincentives to uphold inside law and ultimately may utilize the sanction of excommunicating a member and within some groups a level of disassociation (shunning) to put pressure on a person to conform to the decisions of the group and return to the fold or leave. The outside law civil system, on the other hand, has the ability to invoke the violence of the state to uphold the orders of the court. If the state is supposed to have a monopoly on legal violence, any inside law system (but for that of violent criminal groups which ignore the monopoly) will have a degree of weakness insofar as violence cannot be used to enforce inside law. Thus, collaboration with outside law will be necessary if enforcement by such violence is sought. This in effect was what the overseer group at Lakeside was doing when it went to outside law to enforce the inside law on excommunication by the power of the sword.

One last preliminary point is that when we explore options of how the outside law might deal with inside law, the issue really only arises when there is a claimed overlap of subject matter jurisdiction between inside law and outside law within the same community. There may be subject matters or transactions where there is no overlap between the reach of outside law and the claims of inside law, because the outside law simply does not cover the matter. There is a difference between a court refusing jurisdiction over a dispute or an issue in the dispute because the matter is simply outside the existing scope of outside law norms, and a court refusing jurisdiction or using inside law even though the norms of the outside legal system may also be implicated. There is a difference between saying that a church dispute is outside the scope of the outside law and saying that the outside law must give way to the inside law and not cross a particular boundary because it is entering the subject matter or territorial jurisdiction that should be left for the inside law of the church. We are interested in precisely such cases where there is a potential or actual overlap between the norms of outside and inside law, because the dispute may be within the scope of the norms of each legal system.[10] Obviously, when the religious group is more intentional and totalistic about bringing all of life under the umbrella of religion, there may be considerable potential for conflict between the jurisdictional claims of the state and the jurisdictional claims of the church.[11]

The Outside Law Sovereignty Model

One model of interaction between inside law and outside law is that which asserts full sovereignty and superiority of the outside law. Who is going to argue with the superiority of a legal system that claims the legitimacy of the inclusive rule of law and has all the armed enforcers at its disposal? In this centrist model of state law superiority, inside law may be recognized and upheld by the outside law, but only at the mercy of the outside law and to the extent that inside law can be translated into outside law or given some level of recognition by outside law. Inside law norms may be upheld to the extent that they can be poured into existing outside legal categories such as contracts, trusts, and corporate bylaws. Furthermore, subject to very limited *Charter* arguments that I will deal with below, additional outside law requirements may be imposed and inside law inconsistent with outside law may be struck down. The sovereignty of outside law in theory does not necessarily mean that religious communities always change inside law to conform to outside law. So long as members of the community do not run off to outside courts, or so long as outsiders or governmental officials are unaware or unwilling to take matters to outside law, a community might well "hide" from the outside law. It is my premise that the inside law, rather than the outside law, has far greater strength of allegiance within the group because it is the law that expresses the cultural commitments of the faith community. If the outside law is imposed in a way that fundamentally conflicts with the inside law, faithfulness requires disobedience to the outside law, punishment under it, or escape from it by leaving for some other jurisdiction where the outside law is more accommodating.

This model of outside law sovereignty is arguably the model that best describes the historical relationship between ecclesiastical communities and the state in Canada. So long as the outside law reaches the subject matter of the dispute, the outside law has jurisdiction over the dispute. In *Lakeside* the Supreme Court repeated what many Canadian courts have previously stated, namely that the secular courts will not take jurisdiction over a purely religious dispute, but if property rights or civil rights are implicated in the religious dispute, the court will take jurisdiction, and to the extent that it is necessary to judge matters of religion to determine those civil or property rights, the courts will do so.[12] This seems to be just another way of saying that as soon as there is overlap between the inside law and the outside law, the outside law has jurisdiction. The jurisdiction of outside law is as vast as the ever increasing reach of outside law to regulate pretty much everything we do. If there is any territory of sovereignty for inside law, it is simply that little terrain outside law is not interested in covering or has not arrived at yet.

Indeed, the most prominent scholar of religion and the law in Canada has repeatedly emphasized the subservience of religious organizations to the authority of the state and the courts of the state in Canada.[13] The image presented is not the separation of church and state but the subservience of the church to the state, where the church has no independent "sovereign" jurisdiction over members, and where the secular courts have undoubted jurisdiction to deal with ecclesiastical disputes, even if the judges express reluctance to do so. Having reviewed the numerous cases in Canada where courts have taken jurisdiction in disputes involving discipline of clergy or laity or doctrinal disputes leading to church property claims, Professor Margaret Ogilvie states: "If judicial reluctance is not an expression of false modesty in the face of theological claims (of which, in fact few are made in such cases), then the reason for these ritualistic maneuverings is puzzling, since it is trite to state that in a parliamentary system, the sovereign state, through its agent, the courts, enjoys constitutional and legal authority over all within its geographical jurisdiction, including religious organizations and their members."[14]

Rather than religious organizations and groups having a sphere of authority independent from the authority of the state, Ogilvie suggests that the religious organization is clearly submerged under the higher authority of the state and the courts of the state. The courts of the state stand above all ecclesiastical tribunals, and one can always appeal to the higher state courts, which can review the transactions within the ecclesiastical community as to whether the internal law was followed, whether the processes used amounted to procedural fairness, and in some cases whether one group or another has departed from religious doctrine if that determination is necessary to resolve the matter. Thus, as Ogilvie states, "[w]hether a Church in Canada possesses a sophisticated system of courts and laws developed over a millennium, as in the case of the Roman Catholic Church, or simple, informal dispute resolution processes guided only by the rule of Scripture, as in the case of a Mennonite community, from the perspective of the common law, these enjoy no independent or separate jurisdiction over members who do not wish to comply with their orders, and no claims to precedence over the common law courts and law, which is applied to ecclesiastical and secular institutions alike."[15] It is noteworthy that Ogilvie not only presents this subservient model as capturing the reality of the Canadian situation but also appears to be in favour of it. Lawyers who challenge the authority of the courts to hear ecclesiastical disputes are making arguments that are "frivolous and vexatious."[16] While a great deal of the jurisprudence of the courts will involve simply enforcing inside law as contractual terms,[17] occasional court interference with the religious communities' own internal norms and processes does not apparently pose a problem. Ogilvie states: "Interference this may be, but it is a type of interference which ensures that ecclesiastical courts meet standards in keeping with the moral standards typically expressed by religious institutions."[18] In Canada, religious organizations in legal terms are just voluntary associations like sports clubs, stamp collecting societies, or environmental interest groups. According to Ogilvie, "the proper characterization of religious institutions at common law was as voluntary associations. The authority of a religious organization over its members is based on their continuing voluntary membership and mutual consent in contract to the doctrine and discipline of the polity. Since contract is the legal basis for the authority of the polity over its members, the role of the courts when disputes are appealed to them, is to interpret and apply the internal rules according to the general principles for the interpretation of contracts."[19]

We may question Ogilvie as to the desirability of this model of outside law sovereignty, but she is surely correct that this is the dominant approach taken by our courts. For example, there are numerous Canadian cases where the courts have taken jurisdiction over cases involving the discipline or termination of clergy.[20] That ecclesiastical tribunals have been treated by the courts as if they were akin to public authorities is illustrated by the opinion of an Ontario judge who stated in the context of reviewing the discipline of a United Church minister that, "since the Church is a creature of statute of both the federal and provincial legislature and it is common knowledge that it ministers to the spiritual needs of a large segment of the Canadian public[,] it has a sufficient public character that it should be amenable to the process of certiorari."[21]

It is interesting that the leading authority on administrative law in Canada, commenting on the *Lakeside* case, notes and questions the wisdom of the application of outside administrative law principles to decision making that traditionally would be regarded as left to private inside law.[22] Yet there appears to be no movement to shut the courthouse door to litigants who want to review or enforce or overthrow ecclesiastical judgments in Canada. Indeed, there has been a veritable rash of cases dealing with dismissal of clergy or discipline of church members in the last few decades. There is simply no doubt that Canadian courts now take jurisdiction over these cases, which may involve the courts second-guessing the ecclesiastical authorities, not just in regard to procedural matters but even about whether there was sufficient cause to dismiss an employee of the church.[23] As to clergy cases, sometimes the courts have found no liability because the minister sued the wrong party;[24] or effectively resigned rather than was terminated;[25] or agreed to certain limitations to the appointment when he joined the organization;[26] or was treated more than fairly and was not wrongfully terminated.[27] But in other cases the courts have declared the discipline of ministers to be null and void because of failure to follow proper inside process, or lack of natural justice, or lack of cause, and the courts have given damages[28] and have even reinstated the ministers.[29]

When we move from discipline of clergy to discipline of members of an ecclesiastical organization, as in the *Lakeside* case, we see that Canadian courts seem quite willing to jump right in.[30] A judge in British Columbia suggested that the bylaws of a religious society constitute a contract between the society and its members.[31] In Manitoba, Mr. Justice Solomon refused to grant a motion to dismiss a case for want of jurisdiction involving a claim for damages for the so-called wrongful expulsion of a member from the Jehovah Witness Church in Pine Falls. After reviewing older cases suggesting that there was no outside law interest in such cases, Solomon stated: "I think it fair to say that definition of civil rights enforceable in the Courts of law has been extended through the years and today Courts are prepared to grant much more comprehensive remedies to members of voluntary associations."[32]

While courts may interpret and enforce the inside law as it is translated into outside law categories, on a rare occasion the inside law may be deemed unenforceable because the contract itself is purely religious in its terms or the contract is held to be void as a matter of public policy. In one case, the court stated that it could not review the expulsion of a member based on the breach of a contract term in which the church promised that only its members would enjoy a spiritual paradise in the hereafter and not suffer damnation at the time of Armageddon.[33] In 1905 the Ontario Court of Appeal overturned a jury award of damages for wrongful dismissal given to a nun in a religious order who had been dismissed after seventeen years of service.[34] To the degree that the wrongful dismissal claim was based on obligations of the order to look after a person for the rest of his or her life in return for that person's fulfillment of vows of poverty, chastity, and obedience, the court held that such vows, however commendable, were contrary to public policy in terms of restraining marriage, affirming the divestiture of private property, and accepting a kind of slavery to superior orders. The civil courts simply would not enforce such a contract. One may doubt the continued validity of this determination, but it illustrates that inside law may not be recognized by outside law if the court feels that inside law is sufficiently repugnant. Ironically, so long as outside law is not used in substitution, this declaration of repugnancy in some cases actually preserves the inside law from outside law interpretation and potential attack. As we have seen, however, the courts in Canada thus far have consistently upheld the Hutterian communal property regime as a kind of enforceable contract of membership and have resisted claims that such a contract violates public policy. The result of a study of early American cases dealing with communal groups is to the same effect.[35] However, given the existing expressions of judicial regret that I have noted in my review of the Hutterite cases, and the probable movement to ever more individualistic notions of equality that might be expected from new generations of judges, Hutterite authorities who go to outside law to enforce expulsions from property are putting the inside law at a significant risk.

Along with the notion that the outside court has jurisdiction because employment or membership is linked or translated into contract concepts, another jurisdictional hook that allows for outside law jurisdiction over ecclesiastical disputes is potential tort liability. In dealing with a dismissal from a religious order, the Ontario Court of Appeal upheld the liability of church officials for the commission of torts such as false imprisonment, assault, and conspiracy when a nun was dismissed after being wrongfully committed to an insane asylum against her will.[36] Tort claims such as libel, breach of confidence, or interference with economic interests may increasingly lead Canadian courts to regulate church disciplinary matters and, of course, potentially overrule inside law in doing so.[37]

Certainly, there are a large number of Canadian cases in which the courts have taken jurisdiction because the property rights of one group or another to the use of the church was at stake.[38] The incorporation of religious organizations as a more convenient way to hold property and to perhaps limit the personal liability of church officials also means that the religious community cannot hide from the scrutiny of outside law. For example, an Ontario judge made no mention of a problem of jurisdiction when he reviewed the inside law of both a mother church incorporated under federal legislation and a local parish incorporated by provincial legislation, and then overturned the excommunication of a leading member of the board as contrary to the rules of natural justice. He ordered a new election for the board of a parish, supervised by the court.[39] We have also seen how the courts took jurisdiction over the disputes at Rock Lake and Huron by virtue of the provisions contained in corporate legislation. In British Columbia, the courts have been riddled with Sikh disputes to the same extent as the courts in Manitoba have been riddled with Hutterite disputes. There has been violence and turmoil over the control of the temples between so-called moderate and fundamentalist factions. There has been considerable litigation as to which members are entitled to vote, and the fairness of the elections. In the face of violence, the secular courts have issued injunctions, appointed interim executives, supervised elections, and quashed resolutions, while Sikhs have sued each other for defamation and so forth.[40] In these cases the courts refer continuously to the provisions of the *Society Act*,[41] and the specific procedural bylaws of the Sikh societies. While the courts appear to avoid references to the ecclesiastical doctrines and disputes that give rise to the motives to engage in the voting struggles, there is no doubt that the outside law of the state has played a considerable role in the inside struggles of the Sikh community.

While the inside legal system is subject to the sovereignty of the outside legal system, one moderating doctrine is important in the interaction between the two systems. The outside law may overrule the decisions made by inside law and, indeed, may change the norms as to how inside law operates, but there is a kind of deference of jurisdiction that the outside system may grant to the inside system. It is by no means the kind of sovereignty we will soon see in some American cases but a deference to the jurisdiction of the inside process to complete its own determination of the dispute *first*, before the secular legal system intervenes. The secular legal system should be the court of last resort, and a litigant may be denied access to the secular courts if he or she has not exhausted the remedies available in the ecclesiastical realm. For example, in a recent wrongful dismissal suit brought by a priest, the court stated: "I am satisfied, therefore, that before any individual can proceed with an application to the civil courts for redress of a right which he allegedly had against his ecclesiastical superiors that he must first exhaust his remedies within the ecclesiastical realm. Only after he has exhausted his remedies under the Constitution or Laws of his Church can he approach the courts for judicial review of decisions reached by the Church."[42] If a dispute arises in an ecclesiastical setting, even if the dispute involves property or civil rights, a court should not take jurisdiction over that dispute until the internal remedies within the ecclesiastical setting have been exhausted.[43] In another recent case, the court refused to stop the disciplinary process of the church at a point where no formal hearings had even started.[44] While the courts should defer to the completion of the ecclesiastical process, as in the *Lakeside* case, that process is itself subject to the outside law requirement of natural justice. When a priest made a claim for wrongful dismissal, the court dismissed the claim because the priest had not invoked the appeal process set out by canon. However, before directing the priest to the internal process, the court briefly reviewed that process in terms of rights to be heard and the independence of the appeal process from the bishop, and so forth.[45] It would not make sense to close the courthouse door in deference to a process that obviously violated the very requirements a court would ultimately impose when that process was exhausted and the case brought back to court.

There will no doubt be further developments in this trend to insist on the exhaustion of internal remedies. Currently, there is uncertainty as to which cases should be referred back to the inside system. For example, when a priest sued another priest for defamation, the defendant priest argued that the case should be heard in the courts of the church. The statements made by the defendant about the status and behaviour of the plaintiff priest were pervasively a matter of canon law, and that law provided a complete process for the determination of the dispute, including apparently the right to monetary damages, although the church had no power of the state sword to enforce such judgments. Nevertheless, the court rejected the idea that the ecclesiastical courts should be used as a kind of alternative dispute resolution process for a tort claim if the plaintiff objected to the jurisdiction of the ecclesiastical court. Justice Epstein stated: "The fact that the parties are clerics in the Church does not make them less subject to secular law. The Church and all of its members are subject to the jurisdiction of this Court and are subject to secular law."[46] In an earlier case, a rabbi sued another rabbi for defamation. The defendant argued that the statements in issue were riddled with issues of religion and that the plaintiff should bring his case to the ecclesiastical courts. Indeed, the defendant argued that the taking of the case by the secular courts might violate his freedom of religion under the *Charter*. I do not know what happened, because the only report on this case deals with a preliminary matter of the scope of cross-examination on discovery.[47]

In property disputes too there is a possibility that the doctrine of last resort may provide more room for the jurisdiction of the inside law. Even without formal church constitutions and canons giving precise appeal procedures, the parties may acknowledge the authority of 1 Corinthians 6, and a court would be justified in not taking the case if the parties have not attempted to resolve the dispute through a process of mediation within the church.[48] Mandating alternative dispute resolution in the church when one or both of the parties are unwilling to participate can be a recipe for failure but, nevertheless, the requirement to exhaust internal remedies is legitimate. In this context of the sovereignty of the courts over church disputes, we can at least hope that the outside law process will first allow the inside law process to run its course.

Getting back to the basic model of outside law sovereignty, despite it being moderated by the doctrine of last resort, are we attracted to this centrist model of subgroup subservience? In defence it might be said that what is being called outside law is outside only from the perspective of where one is standing. From the perspective of the citizen of the liberal democratic state, it might be said that the law of the state should advance the safety, freedom, and equality of all persons within the state. Members of the religious community are also citizens of the state for whom outside law is another kind of inside law, this time of the broader community of which the group is also a part. In most circumstances, the outside law does not abruptly stop at the gates of a religious commune just because the members of the commune have their own inside law. The members of the commune are also citizens of the state and are entitled to the equal protection of the law. If someone is murdered, or sexually assaulted, or the victim of some other crime, the criminal courts do not refuse jurisdiction over the case because the alleged crimes took place within a church setting. We do not expect that clergy or employees of the church will be immune from liability for sexual abuse nor that religious organizations will be free of vicarious liability for harms perpetrated by their employees or agents. If a member of a church falls down stairs that have not been repaired, or gets electrocuted in the kitchen, the church may have its own norms against members going to outside law, but if the member sues the church for negligence, the outside law courts will not refuse jurisdiction.

Having said that, however, this model provides little security for any inside law, nor does it affirm legal pluralism and robust religious freedom as positive features of our polity rather than cancers that should be removed in the name of one unified law of individual rights and duties that applies equally to every citizen. Inside law is protected only to the extent that the sovereign authority of outside law recognizes it, translates it, and finds it sufficiently consistent with outside law. Inside law does not have some kind of ultimate jurisdiction in some sphere of life.

The Outside Law Abstention Model

I turn now to a very different model of interaction between inside law and outside law. Consider for a moment the idea that the courts might recognize various subject matters as being ecclesiastical, or certain disputes as falling within an ecclesiastical territory as it were, and so allow the inside law to have sovereignty over that territory, even though in theory outside law concepts could also be used to resolve the matter. That is, the outside law would abstain from going into that territory, and it would neither enforce the inside law on behalf of ecclesiastical authorities nor allow the inside law to be challenged by litigants or legislatures attempting to impose outside law concepts. The courts would send the litigants away because the courts would recognize the sovereign jurisdiction of the ecclesiastical community over such matters.

Traditionally this model has been used to some degree in the United States, having arisen from jurisprudence based on both the anti-establishment and free exercise wings of the First Amendment.[49] Recall that in the American cases of *Poinsett*[50] and *Tschetter*,[51] the courts refused to take jurisdiction in the very same types of cases that the Canadian courts were willing to decide. Even though the dispute involved the property rights of Group One and Group Two, the American courts, at least in these two cases, took the position that deciding the property rights would involve deciding a religious dispute between Hutterite factions, and the courts declined to do so.

Beyond a very narrow category of pure belief or worship activities for which the outside law does not care about anyway, we may identify various transactions, relationships, disputes, and activities that are within the sphere of the inside law of the church even when certain outside law concepts, such as torts, property rights, and contracts, are implicated. In theory, a wall of separation could be built around this religious sphere. We might say that the state should not get entangled with church affairs: a boundary separates the church and state, and the outside courts should not step over it. In one case, the fifth circuit Federal Court of Appeal stated the matter in absolutist terms: "Now, the church is a sanctuary, if one exists anywhere, immune from the rule or subjection to the authority of the civil courts, either state or federal, by virtue of the First Amendment."[52] This is fundamentally different from the Canadian ideology.

The idea of giving a degree of sovereignty or autonomy to the legal system of a religious community is one kind of affirmation of legal pluralism. There is also a recognition that the concept of legal federalism could be applied, not only to territorial subdivisions of official governments but to normative communities, with the further recognition that we might grant a degree of sovereignty to communities to live by their own norms in relation to certain subject matters, even if the norms are inconsistent with the norms of the wider community.[53]

The idea of abstaining from hearing disputes falling into a particular sphere is easily stated, but where the courts draw the boundaries of that sphere is controversial. There appears to be a fundamental tension between various models of abstention. For example, a narrower concept of *doctrinal* sovereignty is primarily concerned that a court should abstain only if taking the case will in some way determine or meddle with matters of religious doctrine, whereas a wider *structural* concept of sovereignty is primarily concerned with the autonomy of the church as an institution in governing certain subject matters, even if the dispute is not per se about religious doctrine but simply involves the functioning of the church as an institution.

The abstention approach is immediately encountered in American jurisprudence dealing with the discipline or excommunication of members of religious communities, where many American courts have refused to consider tort claims, or refused to determine if the church followed its own inside law, or refused to apply procedural natural justice to such ecclesiastical matters.[54] When a member of a congregation sued for a declaration that she was still a member because her expulsion was arbitrary and did not follow the proper inside law process of the church, the court sent her away.[55] Even though the church may well have violated its own internal rules, the court refused to grant an injunction to prevent about seventy-five members from being excommunicated from their congregation.[56] It has been said that a secular court does not have the jurisdiction to resolve disputes over who can be a member of a particular church.[57] Courts have no jurisdiction to examine whether a church followed its own ecclesiastical canons in dealing with the discipline of a member.[58] When a bishop and a priest barred certain members from coming to church, a court would not review whether inside law authorized such action.[59] Even though the board of directors might well have been breaking the inside rules in the handling of finances, members of the church could not sue in the secular court because the determination of such matters involved examining an area of ecclesiastical management over which the courts had no jurisdiction.[60] Recently, in dismissing a case involving tort claims associated with church discipline, a Florida Appeal Court asserted that it could not enter the exclusive territory of the ecclesiastical community over such matters.[61] Even when a church was incorporated and alleged infractions of bylaws took place in the excommunication of members, the Oklahoma Supreme Court stated that "[c]ivil courts in this country recognize that they have no ecclesiastical jurisdiction and church disciplinary decisions cannot be reviewed for the purposes of reinstating expelled church members."[62]

Similarly, there are cases where American courts abstain from hearing disputes involving the discipline or termination of clergy, even though the temporal effects of losing employment implicates both contract and property law.[63] Again, some courts have refused to review the matter to see if the church's own internal rules or contracts were breached,[64] or apply standards of due process to the discipline of clergy,[65] or entertain tort claims brought by clergy against the church or church officials.[66] In a claim that church officials defamed a pastoral employee, the Indiana Court of Appeal stated: "[W]hen officials of a religious organization state their reasons for terminating a pastoral employee in ostensibly ecclesiastical terms, the First Amendment effectively prohibits civil tribunals from reviewing these reasons to determine whether the statements are either defamatory or capable of a religious interpretation related to the employee's performance of her duties."[67] Albeit with a narrow majority, the Georgia Court of Appeal refused to entertain a claim that a diocese had breached a contract with a priest that entitled him to a minimum three-year term.[68] The same court rejected jurisdiction to entertain a claim that the dismissal of a minister did not follow the proper inside law of the church in question.[69] It has been said that clergy disputes are at the very core of the sovereign territory of the church in which courts should not meddle.[70]

The American ecclesiastical abstention doctrine is also illustrated in the area of anti-discrimination claims brought against church officials and organizations. Here again, some American courts have given the church a generous degree of sovereignty to be immune from such claims, particularly in regard to clergy or employees with significant religious duties, even where there is no obvious religious motivation for the discrimination.[71]

As I have noted, there are also cases such as *Poinsett* and *Tschetter* where the courts have abstained from taking jurisdiction over church property disputes, because to do so would involve the court in the resolution of an ecclesiastical dispute. Whether the abstention approach will be used in the area of property, however, often relates to the kind of reasons the plaintiff faction gives for why the court should award the property to it or why the court should enforce its wish to have exclusive possession and kick out those who have been excommunicated. It is well established that civil courts in the United States will not adjudicate if the reason is that the defendant faction has departed from religious doctrine and therefore is breaching an express or implied doctrinal trust.[72]

It will be immediately apparent that in its pure form, the abstention doctrine grants sovereignty to inside law but at the same time provides no outside remedy for the enforcement of that inside law against those who are breaking it, whether it be the authorities in charge or members who refuse to obey the authorities. The courts recognize that refusing to take jurisdiction means there will be cases in which religious institutions have treated people unjustly and these people will have no remedy. An Illinois court said: "Church tribunals ought to perform their functions honestly, impartially, and justly, with due regard to their constitutional powers, sound morals and the rights of all who are interested; but, if tyranny, force, fraud, oppression, or corruption prevail, no civil remedy exists for such abuse ... The ordinary courts have no cognizance of the rules of a religious organization ... and cannot consider whether they have been rightly or wrongly applied."[73]

In refusing to take jurisdiction over a matter dealing with the employment of a priest, the California Court of Appeal stated:

> [S]ecular courts will not attempt to right wrongs related to the hiring, firing, discipline or administration of clergy. Implicit in this statement of the rule is the acknowledgment that such wrongs may exist, that they may be severe, and that the administration of the church itself may be inadequate to provide a remedy. The preservation of the free exercise of religion is deemed so important a principle as to overshadow the inequities which may result from its liberal application. In our society, jealous as it is of separation of church and state, one who enters the clergy forfeits the protection of the civil authorities in terms of job rights.[74]

Not surprisingly, the model of giving exclusive jurisdiction to the inside law without lending a sword for its enforcement is only one stream of the American jurisprudence. If we say that the disputants cannot go to civil courts to determine who has the right to control church property, we are conceding that in some cases property may well be controlled by those who according to the inside law of the religious community ought not to be in possession, and when struggles for control involve prolonged tensions, chaos, and even violence, the courts have a hard time justifying abstention. The role of courts to serve society in the peaceful resolution of disputes clashes with the principle that disputes should be solved within the church. Criminal law still applies in assaults between members and retaliatory acts may amount to actionable torts, and so forth, but as to the underlying dispute, the court refuses to get involved. This means that the church itself cannot invoke police power to enforce inside law, and on one level it may be argued that this weakens its effectiveness.

However, removing the resort to outside courts perhaps has the positive effect of preserving inside law from outside law corruption and also providing incentives for inside law to take responsibility to creatively deal with alternative methods of dispute resolution, and to rely on other methods instead of police violence to settle matters. We can only imagine what might have happened if the Canadian courts had refused to intervene when the overseer group at Lakeside first tried to get an injunction to control the Daniel Hofer rebellion at that colony. Perhaps the "renegades" would have taken over Lakeside. But then again, perhaps in the end the schism in the wider Schmiedeleut might not have occurred. It is noteworthy that the abstention approach fits nicely with the Anabaptist inside law against going to outside law. The outside law perfectly agrees and refuses jurisdiction.

Is there any movement in Canada toward an abstention approach? I can find little evidence of it, but a few recent cases signify that there may still be some line between religious inside law and secular outside law which on occasion the courts will not breach. For example, in a recent divorce case, the court refused to enforce an Islamic marriage contract under which a man owed a substantial sum to his ex-wife. The judge concluded that because the nature and extent of the obligation were religious matters, disputes over the obligation should be resolved within the Islamic community and not by a court of law.[75] In another recent case, an Ontario court refused to adjudicate a dispute between an ecclesiastical board of Orthodox Jewish rabbis who grant certification for kosher foods as meeting standards of production set by religious laws, and a producer of kosher food who claimed tort and contract damages because of a denial of that certification.[76] The defendant rabbis had summoned the producer to come to the Jewish court for an adjudication of the dispute, but the producer had refused. The court stated that the essence of the claim was a direct attack on the substance of the religious standards set by the ecclesiastical authorities rather than any issue about the regularity of the process of certification, and thus the court refused to take jurisdiction over what was essentially a religious dispute. Judicial abstentions in Canada have even dealt with church property issues. In a 1983 Ontario case, albeit on a preliminary injunction application, the court refused to find that the rabbi and majority of the congregation, which had agreed to allow mixed seating and also agreed to allow women to take part in the service, had breached the religious trust that the congregation was supposed to be of the Orthodox Jewish faith.[77] No written constitution

or bylaws of the congregation directed the property to be used in a particular way, so the application was dismissed. If the case had gone to trial, there
may well have been a determination as to whether an implied trust existed
and what the content of that trust was, but certainly the judge on the preliminary motion was not interested in getting into such issues. In a statement that might have come out of an American rather than Canadian court,
Callaghan J. stated: "While I recognize that the courts have a role to play
when congregations become dissentient among themselves in relation to
property, contracts, or other civil rights, I am of the view that in the circumstances as presented in this case, the issue is fundamentally an ecclesiastical
issue which must be resolved outside the courts of law. The functions of a
court of law exclude the consideration of such issues. Accordingly, the application will be dismissed."[78] While these are but small seeds with which to
grow a jurisprudential tree, it remains open for the judiciary to change course
and consider seriously whether to develop an abstention model in Canada.

The Outside Law Deference and Neutrality Models

Given the lack of outside law remedy when a robust abstention approach is
taken, American courts, particularly concerning church property disputes,
have developed other models of interaction between the inside and outside
law. One model, called "deference," is related to the sovereignty concerns
of the abstention model. The difference is that while in the abstention model,
the court does not take jurisdiction, in the deference model the court *does*
take jurisdiction, but then defers to the decision of the ecclesiastical authorities as to what the inside law demands. The court enforces this ecclesiastical judgment without reviewing it in terms of conformity with inside or
outside law. Essentially, the court simply enforces the decision of the highest tribunal in a hierarchical church and usually the decision of the majority in a congregational polity. For purposes of our discussion here I will not
go over the strengths and weaknesses of this model.[79] Suffice it to say that
identifying and classifying the church polity and then identifying which
faction has the proper authority to tell the court what to enforce often involves far more judicial scrutiny than the model in its pure form would
allow. One can immediately see, however, that this model is connected to
the abstention approach of not *deciding* religious matters, although it is
enforcing religious decisions. That such an approach has inherent contradic-
tions is obvious. As I have noted in regard to *Lakeside*, we may criticize the
intrusion of the outside law of due process onto Hutterian inside law, but at
the same time, if it is the state that is enforcing such inside law, is it not
appropriate that some measure of outside law justice might well enter into
the picture before the violence of the state can be invoked?

Considerations such as this have led some American courts to adopt a so-
called "neutrality" model of interaction between inside law and outside

law. This model in many respects is similar to the Canadian model of outside law sovereignty. In the neutrality model, courts claim that they can resolve many church disputes by the application of outside law norms that are "neutral" in terms of religion. That is, the court can refer to the secular provisions of contracts and trusts, and inside law documents such as constitutions and bylaws, and procedural canons, and so forth, without any determination of, entanglement with, or interference with religious doctrines or governance. This approach, however, does not allow courts to use religious terms such as doctrinal statements in documents, and this limitation in fact means that the use of the neutrality approach often leads to outcomes that interfere with the inside law.[80] If one is going to resolve a dispute that involves religious issues, it would be far better to attempt to understand the dispute in its full context than to reduce the dispute to a so-called neutral plane where the outcomes may have no relation to the reality of religious inside law.

The Model of Balancing Outside Law and Inside Law

Finally, there is another model, which I call "balancing," in which American courts engage in a constitutional balancing test between the norms of the two legal systems. Should the outside law refrain from displacing the inside law because the inside law is a constitutionally protected part of the free exercise of religion? This is different from abstention, where an area, a territory, a scope of activity, as it were, is declared to be structurally separate and sovereign by virtue of the separation of church and state. In the balancing model there are competing claims to the same territory or area, rather than there being areas that are structurally in one camp or the other. Balancing means that the court may recognize, at least sometimes, that the value of religious freedom to live by inside law outweighs the value that the outside law is trying to achieve by overruling inside law, and thus the outside law should retreat. If, however, the interests of the outside law are compelling enough, the court may apply the outside law even if it contradicts the inside law and violates freedom of religion. This model may have some power to preserve inside law, but it is immediately apparent that unlike structural sovereignty over a subject matter, balancing is a process that involves the changing whims of the judiciary as to what is deemed more important. In any case, balancing is rarely available in the context of Canadian ecclesiastical disputes.

One of the main reasons for the historic difference between the basic Canadian model of *outside* law sovereignty and the various American models of *inside* law sovereignty is the difference between deciding cases within the framework of an entrenched constitution that limits governmental power so as not to infringe on religious freedom or to establish religion through state action, as compared with a framework of parliamentary sovereignty where the reach of the law is constrained only by the common sense of legislatures and courts. Without any need for extensive elaboration, it is obvious that the passing of the *Canadian Charter of Rights and Freedoms*[81] in 1982 ushered in a new era for Canadian jurisprudence, but in terms of the litigation of internal disputes arising in religious organizations or the approach taken to them, it might be said that the *Charter* is irrelevant because it does not apply to the issues of taking jurisdiction over these disputes or to the content of the law when jurisdiction is taken. Thus, at one level, the *Charter* has not changed the basic Canadian model of outside law sovereignty. The *Charter* does not apply to these private disputes nor does it mandate the kind of separation of church and state that would lead the courts to adopt an American model of abstention, or deference, or neutrality or balancing.

It is true that if Canadian legislatures pass laws that restrict the communal ownership of land, or perhaps mandate some kind of compensation for people leaving communal societies, the *Charter* guarantee of freedom of religion and conscience[82] would be invoked in an attempt to strike down the legislation, or to grant exemptions within it, because the legislation violates the freedom of religion of Hutterites. In such a case, the *Charter* would be directly relevant and the balancing of the loss to freedom of religion against the supposed gain of having the legislation would pretty much parallel the American balancing approach. Traditionally, if the outside law burdened or infringed religious belief or practice, the party seeking to impose the outside law would need to prove that the outside law advanced a compelling public interest and, even if there was a compelling interest, it would also need to be established that this public interest could not be advanced in a way that was less restrictive to the operation of the religious inside law. The American cases where the Amish were exempted from certain aspects of the outside educational laws[83] and from certain aspects of the highway safety laws[84] are examples of where the courts have determined that outside law should give way to the inside law. In Canada, *Charter* values have been invoked in some of the governmental cases involving Hutterites.[85]

But suppose that it was not governmental litigation or legislation being dealt with but the common law norms that judges apply and create in the process of deciding disputes between private parties. Suppose that in a *Lakeside* type of case, the judges overruled the inside contract of the Hutterites and ruled that someone should not be bound many years later by the promises they made when joining a religious community and in particular the agreement to have no entitlement to any of the colony property. Further, suppose that the courts ruled that a person was entitled to a compensation package of some kind when leaving or being expelled from a Hutterite colony. If the legislature had passed such a compensation rule, the *Charter* could be invoked to test it, but if the courts create the same rule by way of common law precedent, the *Charter* does not apply in terms of allowing the colony to argue that such a law violates freedom of religion as guaranteed by the *Charter*. It is at least curious that when laws are created by the courts, with the full coercive power of the state backing them, the *Charter* does not necessarily apply, but when the same laws are put into a legislated form, the *Charter* does apply.

The current situation is based on the interpretation the courts have given to section 32 of the *Charter*, which limits its application "to the Parliament and government of Canada" and to the "legislature and government of each province." Thus, it is governmental actors, or those acting under the coercive statutory authority of government, who must conform to the *Charter*, rather than individuals or private entities. Even public universities, at least for some purposes, have been held to be sufficiently independent of government so as to be immune from *Charter* claims.[86] Thus, if ex-members of a colony sue the colony for judicial review of their excommunication, or for compensation, or if ex-members allege that the elders have defamed them, or that there has been an intentional conspiracy to harm them, the lawsuit is not between the government and the Hutterites but between ex-members and the colony. Obviously, the colony, not being a governmental actor, is not burdened with having to treat its own members as if those members had constitutional rights of religion and freedom of conscience as against the colony, but reciprocally it would appear that the colony could not claim a *Charter* right of freedom of religion to defend itself against common law claims brought by ex-members. Even when the lawsuit is between individuals or private entities, if a statute is applied, the statute is an act of government that may be challenged under the *Charter*. However, the Supreme Court of Canada has refused to apply the *Charter* to test common law rules or court orders when the lawsuit is between individuals or private entities.[87] The theory is that to do so would extend the application of the *Charter* beyond the governmental sphere. The coercive acts of the state to enforce the orders of the court are thus attributed not to the court as a part of government but to the private party that has been granted a court order. This is a sleight of hand worth examining, but notice that this conclusion dovetails with the earlier analysis of the difficulty of reconciling Anabaptist pacifism with aggressive litigation. *The courts themselves are suggesting that it is the litigant that is invoking the violence of the state to uphold a "private" legal right, rather than the state being responsible for the coercion.*

While American courts limit the application of the Bill of Rights to the actions of the state and not to private entities, the creation and enforcement of common law rules by the courts has also been held to be state action. Thus, for example, in a private lawsuit for defamation, the Supreme Court still applied the constitution in terms of freedom of expression to set the parameters for the tort of defamation.[88] Even though most cases of internal church disputes in the United States are dealt with by using abstention, deference, or neutrality models, some cases are dealt with using the fourth model of balancing inside law and outside law, because the free exercise of religion is invoked against common law rules when those rules are inconsistent with inside law. In one leading case, the court accepted for the sake of argument that shunning might well amount to an actionable tort associated with causing harm by inflicting emotional distress, hurting reputation, and causing an alienation of affection.[89] But even if shunning did violate the outside law, the court asserted that it would be worse to take away the constitutionally protected freedom of religion of the church to practice shunning, which, in this case, the Jehovah Witnesses believed was mandated by their religion. The court stated:

> We find the practice of shunning not to constitute a sufficient threat to the peace, safety, or morality of the community to warrant state intervention ... The harms suffered by Paul as a result of her shunning ... are clearly not of the type that would justify the imposition of tort liability for religious conduct ... The members of the Church [that] Paul decided to abandon have concluded that they no longer want to associate with her. We hold that they are free to make that choice. The Jehovah's Witnesses' practice of shunning is protected under the First Amendment of the United States Constitution.[90]

In an earlier American case, the court balanced the interests slightly differently when it did not summarily dismiss a shunning case but allowed the case to proceed to trial, at least in regard to providing more evidence that shunning might amount to conduct so harmful that regulating it by tort law would outweigh protecting it as religious conduct.[91] While upholding the constitutional free exercise of religion to discipline and shun members, another court held that the balance shifted in favour of imposing tort liability when a church member voluntarily withdrew from the church before the church discipline took place and requested that her transgressions not be discussed in front of the congregation, and yet the church proceeded to take action anyway as if she were still a member.[92] In an Amish case, the court found liability for the harms of shunning in a context where the member had allegedly been given permission to leave and then was shunned for leaving.[93] My point here is not to canvass all the cases but to illustrate that some liability claims involving church discipline, particularly tort claims, are treated by the American courts as balancing cases under the constitution rather than as abstention cases, and the religious organization or group may argue that such liability interferes with the freedom of religion of the group.

As noted, however, in Canada the *Charter* is not directly relevant. But whether this is a big loss as to the potential for protecting inside law from outside law jurisdiction remains to be seen. While the Canadian courts have denied the direct effect of the *Charter* on such matters as adjudicating disputes in religious groups, the Supreme Court has stated that the common law should be developed in a way that is consistent with *"Charter* values," even in cases involving litigation between private parties.[94] While *Charter* values are more likely to threaten communitarian groups than to protect them, perhaps there is room in Canada for a balancing model as a way of protecting inside law from outside law interference.

However, in my view, one may doubt that any move to use *Charter* values to balance outside law and inside law will do much to protect religious freedom. Why would one think that judges will value religion, particularly high-demand, "intolerant" religions, when they do the balancing against equality and dignity interests of individuals bringing to court their claims packaged in competing *Charter* rights?[95] For example, notice the hostility of one judge to the religious practice of shunning exercised by the Amish:

> But what right is more sacred than that a man shall not have his right to full enjoyment of the natural intercourse with his wife, his children and his brothers interfered with and cut off by fossilized religious doctrines and antiquated literal interpretation of portions of the Bible which make it compulsive upon wife, daughter and brother to literally shun the husband, father and brother because some strange and peculiar sect composed of Low Germans 397 years ago construed portions of the Bible as shown by Art. 16 of the Amish Confession of Faith ... [T]he crude and unnatural conceptions as disclosed ... harmonize better with the views of his Satanic Majesty and his satellites or representatives on earth.[96]

While such overt contempt of religious practices that do not fit into the mainstream is seldom expressed so blatantly, why would one think that modern judges, imbued with rationalistic presumptions, would view religion as anything other than irrational and illiberal superstition? I doubt that the balancing approach would achieve much sovereignty for inside law. The recent repudiation of the compelling interest test by the United States Supreme Court,[97] and the continued controversy and instability in this area,[98] point to the fragile nature of the balancing test model. In Canada freedom of religion is further diluted by equating it with freedom of conscience, which includes non-religious beliefs. Religious belief is no better protected than non-religious beliefs, and religious institutions are voluntary associations no different from recreational clubs.

Far more important than the balancing model are the other American models of abstention, deference, and neutrality, which are grounded in large part on the structural separation of church and state found in the First Amendment. Here, too, it would appear that while such models might be adopted by Canadian courts, nothing in the *Charter* directly compels giving any sort of autonomy to religious communities. It is commonly noted that in Canada we have, and continue to have post-*Charter*, no substantive separation of church and state but active state support for some religions, particularly in the governmental funding of religious schools, and then not even on an equal basis between religions.[99] But just as balancing may be part of *Charter* values, it is predictable that courts will eventually interpret the *Charter* as if it has an anti-establishment clause, except for some sectarian educational guarantees that are anomalous. Scriptural readings and school prayers are struck down even when there is exemption for those who do not wish to participate.[100] Religious education is struck down even when there is an exemption.[101] Prayers at public functions, such as municipal council meetings, are struck down.[102] Critics argue that the thrust of such jurisprudence is not simply equality for different religions in the public sphere but the banishment of religion from the public square.[103] Of course, the boundary between the territory of private religious freedom to be illiberal and the territory of the public square where one must be liberal is contestable.[104] Arguably, the *Charter* has been used far more to free people from unwanted religion than it has been used to protect people in the exercise of their religion.

I am not going to make any arguments here as to how religious belief should be accommodated equally with non-religious belief within the public sphere rather than excluded, but I will say that if Canadian courts are going to increasingly exclude religion from the public square as if the *Charter* had an American-like anti-establishment clause, they ought to at least grant more autonomy to religious organizations to live by their own norms (which bind only their members), as does the American anti-establishment clause. Thus, in the end, the existence of the *Charter* may provide another legal hook if Canadian courts want to move in directions that give more autonomy to inside religious law as compared with the current sovereignty model of outside law. My prediction, however, is that the territory of religious freedom will not expand under the *Charter* but will instead shrink ever smaller as the public sphere of secular liberalism becomes more comprehensive.

Now that these models have been briefly canvassed, we return to the question of how outside law and inside law should interact. Should Canadian courts be so willing to take jurisdiction and decide all the ecclesiastical disputes that keep coming through the courthouse door? Perhaps the litigation of church disputes in the outside secular law courts might be seen as just one way in which the outside sphere provides an equal service to religionists by providing a forum for the authoritative and final settlement of their disputes? Perhaps, instead of a hands-off refusal to intervene, the translation and enforcement of inside law as an outside law contract actually aids religion? But even if jurisdiction is taken, how much deference to the inside law should be given if inside law conflicts fundamentally with the underlying values of the outside law?

My inclination, which by now is apparent, is that our law and legal system should respect group diversity by allowing religious groups the maximum amount of freedom we can tolerate to run their own affairs by their own norms. To tolerate and accommodate them is not the same as affirmatively agreeing with them. Nor would we argue that their normative system should govern anybody other than their members. We are not required to join them. That we can fall back on the theory that people have consented to join the group and are free to leave if they don't like it goes a certain distance to support the limited autonomy of groups to be left alone with their own norms, but I suspect the idea of choice and consent are rather hollow concepts. From an individualistic point of view, the conditions of choice in joining or leaving would require far more options and diversity of opinions than actually exist within a culture that one is born into, socialized to conform to, and in which the costs of leaving may be overwhelming. But nevertheless, we would leave illiberal groups and their inside law alone to the maximum tolerance level.

This is only a starting presumption. The outside law of society at some stage must provide a normative structure of fundamental values regarding bodily integrity, property, and resource allocation as a framework to protect the liberty and welfare of all in society. But there should be compelling evidence indeed of harm done to members of the group before outside law overrules the inside law of a religious group. The harm should be compelling and not merely contestable. When a claim is made that the inside law should be overruled by outside law, that claim should be met with deep skepticism. This is to say that often the dominant legal culture reflected in outside law is dominant simply because it has the power to be dominant, not because it is demonstrably better as a framework for human flourishing than other legal systems subservient to it.

That some groups in society should be given exemptions from generally applicable outside law, or accommodations or preferences from the outside law, raises a red flag for the bull of formal equality that rears up within us. While my modest focus has been on religious groups within a long historical struggle for freedom of religion as a fundamental human right, even in this context, the modern mind asks why religious groups should be treated any differently from other groups. Perhaps the sovereignty model, which treats religious groups as voluntary associations like any other, has the virtue of equality behind it. If we adopt some kind of abstention or deference model based on the separation of church and state, why should religious groups be given this accommodation but not other groups? My limited response at this stage is simply that other groups with a sufficient capacity to generate an inside law in terrain covered by the outside law may well deserve the same treatment. Unless compelling reasons exist for the outside law to step in, why should our law not abstain or defer to the existence of other legal systems in society?

The Outside Law of Church Property

Even though we might give consideration to not taking certain ecclesiastical cases in the first place, we know without a shadow of doubt that Canadian courts thus far have almost always taken jurisdiction over ecclesiastical disputes framed as property disputes. My discussion now assumes this jurisdiction and asks questions about how this jurisdiction should be exercised. So long as the outside law upholds the 1970 Supreme Court of Canada case of *Hofer v. Hofer,*[105] which characterizes Hutterite property as church property, as opposed to commercial property, the Hutterian community of property regime will be safe. The reason for this is that essentially the outside law and inside law conform to each other. Church property in other religious contexts is communal property just as Hutterite property is. There may well be issues as to which group should be entrusted with the benefit of using church property, but generally, church property is not owned by any individual but by a religious association or group and held in trust for the advancement of certain purposes or for the beneficial use of the members of the organization. The title to the property is often in the hands of a nonprofit incorporated society or incorporated trustees who hold that title in trust. Even if the property is held in the name of individual trustees for an unincorporated group, the property is still communal property. A person who is validly expelled from membership has no right to a private share irrespective of how much he or she has given over the years for the purchase and upkeep of the property.

The difficulty, of course, is that the consequence of losing the right to use church property in the Hutterite context is much higher. In most church property disputes, a court may declare that someone or some group can no longer control or use church property. We may well imagine that the very fact that litigation has progressed indicates that the person or group has significant psychic investment in the use of the property and has made significant financial and time contributions to the association. However, contrast this significance with the Hutterite scenario, in which the members of the religious group are prohibited from owning private property and all the land and the agricultural and manufacturing enterprises of the Hutterite colony are church property owned in trust for the benefit of all, and for the individual ownership of none. The Hutterite member will usually live and work at the colony from the cradle to the grave, but unless a gift is bestowed upon his or her voluntary departure or excommunication, the Hutterite is cast into the world with nothing but the skills he or she has to survive on the outside. As seen in my narrative, numerous judges have expressed their displeasure with the rule, even as they have upheld it. To the same effect, if the courts were to award all the assets to Group One or Group Two in the Hutterite context, imagine the significance to the lives of the disputants compared with the usual scenario of awarding sanctuaries or religious schools to one group or the other, where the losing group nevertheless still goes home to their own beds.

Another obvious difficulty is that the more the Hutterite colony operates as a big business enterprise outside the kind of agricultural activities that traditional monastic religious orders might have also engaged in, the more strain there is on the characterization of colony assets as church property. In my view, however inequitable it may seem at times, the courts must continue to refuse to privatize communal property. Any movement by the outside law to grant compensation to departing or expelled individuals would be an assault on the religion of Hutterites, both to the comprehensive nature of the religion and to the communal property doctrine that is fundamental to it. The courts may judicially review expulsions, but the courts must not grant a share of the property or order compensation. And we can be sure that the courts will be under increased pressure in the future to do so. If expelled members sue the colony, the core issue in the end is not the validity of the expulsion. A court may reinstate them, but as we have seen, this is just a temporary victory; the colony can simply turn around and expel them again. The core issue of future lawsuits will be that of departing or expelled members wanting compensation. The courts will be under increased pressure to characterize the colony as a commercial enterprise and not as a religious group, and to perhaps apply concepts of unjust enrichment or draw from family law property concepts to overthrow the religious covenant of not ever owning a share.

I am not here claiming that the inside law of communal property necessarily needs the support of the outside law in the sense that once Hutterites could get a share they would all in mass dissolve their communes. Surely Hutterite religion is not so skin deep that it could not survive the lack of support from outside law. My objection is, more fundamentally, that outside law should not overrule the inside law of the Hutterites. We may be tempted to grant assets as a way of outside law supporting liberal notions of individual autonomy to dissent and exit from illiberal groups. But this sort of support does not simply aid individual dissenters; it significantly attacks those who remain. The common property regime is both drained and destabilized by granting legal rights to assets upon exit or expulsion.

While the courts should resist such an overthrow of inside law, a refusal to privatize communal property does not provide a solution to all the church property disputes that are taken to court. In a schism, the parties are not asking for individual shares but for the court to determine which group has the beneficial right to all the property, or for the communal property to be divided pro rata between two groups that would both preserve it as communal property. As I have repeatedly noted in the narrative, community property is being *awarded* one way or the other, or being *divided*, but it is not being *privatized*. The first issue will always be the difficulty of characterizing the situation. Is the group (or person) simply seeking compensation or a share so as to live in the world, or is the group (or person) claiming that it is the rightful beneficiary to the use of the communal property or that it is in fact still another group of Hutterites, with the potential right to have assets to form a new colony. There may be cases, such as *Lakeside*, where this initial characterization is difficult to make, especially when the excommunicated group is a family clan and not yet formally affiliated with a recognizable sub-branch of the faith in question. While care must be taken to see through false claims of communality, the courts must consider genuine claims that the group is not seeking privatization but is rightfully entitled to beneficial use of communal property because the group is still within the scope of the trust to which the property is dedicated.

A related but different claim from privatization is the kind that to a degree emerged but was not directly dealt with in *Lakeside*, namely a claim by a member that he had been deprived of legitimate beneficial use of the common property and thus should be reimbursed from the collective pot for expenses he faced because of being wrongfully expelled. Just as the colony argued in *Lakeside* that all assets of the dissenters belonged to the colony because the law declared them to be members, so the dissenters could argue that all legitimate debts of the dissenter group were the responsibility of the colony. For example, if people leave a colony after being expelled but a court says years later that in the eyes of the law their expulsion was invalid and therefore these people are reinstated into membership, even temporarily, until the colony does the expulsion properly, will the court now also involve itself in the mess of requiring the colony to pay living expenses of those people for the period when in the eyes of the law they were still members of the colony? There are numerous accounting problems with trying to figure out both legitimate assets and debts that the colony would inherit or have to pay as a result of wrongful expulsion. What is the point of giving a reinstated member money for reimbursement of payments already made when the member was treated as a non-member, when in turn the legal effect of now being a member is that the person has to turn over all assets to the colony? The claim for reimbursement of expenses will make sense only when the person is finally and properly expelled, even though there was a period when the person was still a member yet not receiving the benefits of membership that in law they were entitled to. I doubt that a court should get into the cost-benefit analysis on both sides of the equation. My point here is simply again that this would not be a claim to privatize common property; it would be more like a claim for expenses owed to a supplier, such as a feed company. Property is not taken from the common pot to be used by people when they are no longer members; instead, it is the expenses that were incurred while they were members that are being paid for.

So if there is a claim for the communal property or a portion of it in the context of a schism, rather than a claim for a private share, what basic legal principles do Canadian courts apply? I would start with the notion that a court must find the terms of the trust by which the property is held. If it knows what the scope of the trust is, it can determine which group is within that scope and is therefore the beneficiary of the trust. If one group is out of the scope of the trust, it is entirely free to leave the church, but it cannot claim any benefit of the church property no matter how much money and labour it may have contributed to the church through the years, or even if it holds legal title.

Recall that Justice DeGraves in the second round of *Lakeside* characterized the polity of the Hutterian Brethren Church as essentially congregational. We might take issue with this given the historic power of the senior elder and the larger conference, but even if we concede to a congregational characterization, this does not necessarily mean that a majority wins. A majority wins only if the majority is free to change affiliations or doctrines without any binding trusts to the contrary. If the terms of the trust are indeed simply based on membership in a group as determined by majority vote, which will sometimes be the case, the role of the court is relatively easy: find out who the members are, judicially review the process of voting and the excommunications, and award the property to the majority. But in many cases it is quite irrelevant that one side or the other has excommunicated members, because the terms of the trust are not based on membership by majority vote. Instead, the members must first be in conformity with a confession of faith or must be properly affiliated with a particular higher denomination, and so forth. As Dickson J. noted in the *Interlake* case, the whole Hutterite colony might be entrusted to even one minority faithful member if the vast majority of members were outside the scope of the trust; if all the members abandoned the faith, the colony should be returned to the mother colony or the wider conference.[106]

So the first step is to look for express trusts. We may look for *doctrinal* trusts that bind the group to a particular confession of faith. We may also look for *affiliation* trusts that bind the group to some kind of affiliation with a larger group, even if the polity is congregational. If there are no express trusts, there is a long line of English and Canadian authorities dealing with *implied* doctrinal and affiliation trusts, which I deal with, and criticize elsewhere,[107] and which need not concern us here given that there are express trusts in the Hutterite context. The court will first look for express trusts laid down in the title deeds, the constitution, the bylaws, or the canons of the church in question. Are there provisions as to whether changes can be made and what the process for making those changes are? If the express trust refers to a confession of faith, there may be ambiguities with which a secular court will understandably be loath to deal, given its questionable competence to delve into such matters, but in theory, courts in Canada enforce such express trusts nonetheless, whereas American courts refuse to do so.

Even if the *Articles of Association of Lakeside Hutterite Colony* (similar to the articles at other colonies) allow for excommunication from membership by majority vote, there is a prior express trust that the purpose of the colony is to "worship God according to the religious belief of the Hutterian Brethren Church,"[108] and qualifications that a person must "become a member and communicant of the Hutterian Brethren Church"[109] and that no member can vote at a meeting unless "[h]e conforms to the practices and regulations laid down from time to time by the Schmieden-Leut Group of Hutterian Brethren."[110] Property of the colony can be managed only by a board of managers; the managers must at all times "be members in good standing of the Hutterian Brethren Church."[111] The articles of association cannot be repealed or amended unless such change is in "accordance with the beliefs of the Hutterian Brethren Church."[112] Any member "who shall cease to be a member of the Hutterian Brethren Church shall leave the Colony,"[113] and the colony cannot be dissolved without the consent of the Schmiedeleut group of the Hutterian Brethren Church; any property of the colony upon dissolution remains vested in the Hutterian Brethren Church.[114] All these references to polity and purpose beyond mere majority votes are multiplied when one looks at the higher constitution of the Hutterian Brethren Church that Lakeside Colony signed and affirmed. To mention just one item, both the constitution of 1950 and the new constitution of 1993 import the confession of Peter Riedemann[115] as a doctrinal statement of faith for the church.[116] However, the constitution can be amended by the Board of Managers of the constituted transnational church.[117]

It is obvious that whether the Hutterite polity is congregational or hierarchical, there is nevertheless clear express requirements of both affiliation and doctrinal conformity with a larger group that transcends the particular colony. Thus, the courts may yet face the unpleasant task of giving content to the scope of this trust to determine whether Group One or Group Two, or both, are within it. Suppose that Daniel Hofer and his group had not dropped the counterclaim. Suppose that his group had already been accepted into Group Two. The claim would be that the overseer group at Lakeside might be the majority but in law they were not members any longer in the Hutterian Brethren Church referred to in the articles because they had lost their membership when they sided with the senior elder and refused to reaffirm their membership in the wider church. Thus, Lakeside Colony must be entrusted to the Group Two members. In turn, Group One would likely claim that the reaffirmation process was illegal, that according to inside law the senior elder could not be removed, and so forth. These were the sorts of claims the courts in *Rock Lake* and *Huron* would have had to deal with if the cases had not been settled by the decision to divide assets.

The Canadian courts would be sinking into a swamp of controversy, as they would have to determine essentially religious questions about the power of the senior elder, about which group was properly within the Hutterian Brethren Church, and even if one or another group was violating the confession of faith of Peter Riedemann. The potential for outside law interference with inside law is enormous. This is precisely why the American courts will not look at doctrinal religious trusts, whether express or implied, and refuse to take on such cases or, if they do, will either defer to the decisions of the ecclesiastical authorities or find so-called neutral principles to adjudicate the matter. This is to avoid the problem of secular courts judging religious issues.

In my view, if we focus on the doctrinal trust, Group Two would probably have the stronger claim to be awarded all the assets of a colony even if Group Two members were a minority. However, I doubt that this all-or-nothing approach is necessary or desirable. I have reviewed the details of how courts in Canada have dealt with doctrinal trusts, whether express or implied, in the context of church property disputes, and my conclusion is that our courts have been extremely reluctant to declare that one side or the other is outside the scope of a trust, unless it is just plain obvious that one group has abandoned the faith.[118] My review of the cases has shown that the Canadian courts have a long history of refusing to find breaches of doctrinal trusts and have been quite willing to conclude instead, sometimes over the objections of both factions, that both factions are still within the scope of the trust.[119] Neither side can exclude the other on the basis of breach of doctrinal trusts. We may well assume that a Canadian court could find that both Group One and Group Two are doctrinally within the Hutterian Brethren Church. As an outsider, you could visit any colony in Manitoba and not know which of the two groups it belonged to unless you had substantial background knowledge with which to detect the subtle clues. While we might argue that Group Two is departing from traditional Hutterite doctrine in bringing lawsuits against its own brethren, do we really think the Canadian courts are going to determine and add up the fundamentals of the faith and decide that Group One has 100 of them while Group Two has 101, or vice versa? Plainly, the two groups are still Hutterites in their identity and religious practice, even if they have been bitterly divided over certain issues. I doubt that a court would or should exclude one group or another from community property on the basis of the general doctrinal trusts.

The enforcement of affiliation trusts, express or implied, as the basis for allocating property entitlements is more likely, however.[120] Here again it is arguable that the Group Two faction at a colony in schism would have a strong claim to be entrusted with all the assets, even if Group Two was a minority. The Hutterian Brethren Church, that is, the highest level union of the three Leuts, has recognized and accepted that Group Two is the legitimate successor to the Schmiedeleut and is the group that is part of the body that the colony is supposed to be affiliated with, namely the Hutterian Brethren Church. But even with the express affiliation trust, a court might find that both groups are within the scope of the trust by accepting the argument that "Hutterian Brethren Church" is a concept wider than the church as constituted by those who have signed the new constitution. The Group One Schmiedeleut conference also has a constitution that claims it is the Hutterian Brethren Church. Furthermore, one may seriously doubt that any court would want to set a precedent that proclaims in effect that half of the Hutterite colonies in Manitoba, namely all the Group One colonies, must be given over to the other half, namely Group Two Hutterites. While litigation was indeed brought by Group One loyalists at particular colonies that were in schism, I doubt that either group would desire a judicial remedy that legally sent half the Hutterites in Manitoba out into the streets with but the shirts on their back. Courts are no longer blind to consequences in the name of fidelity to absolutist legal principles.

One option that seems to be supported by Justice DeGraves in the second-round *Lakeside* decision is the idea that a majority will win all the property of the colony irrespective of whether that majority is Group One or Group Two. But this does not appeal to me unless there are no trusts at stake, and I think there are clearly both affiliation and doctrinal trusts here. Thus, the logic of a judicial determination that both Group Two and Group One are sufficiently within the trust means that a minority group in a schism at a colony simply cannot be deprived of the beneficial use of church property by being excommunicated by the majority. I do not think the sword of the state in one case should be invoked to drive a minority group from church property and then in another case have the court rule in favour of the same group simply because it is the majority. The court should not force the two groups to remain with each other against their will, but it should divide church assets rather than awarding the property to one side or the other. The courts do have the option to muddle through the religious controversy and award the property all or nothing to one side, but by now it is obvious that I think the courts should support precisely the same kind of pro rata division of assets that the Hutterites themselves agreed to so as to bring an end to the litigation.[121] This does not violate the rule of community property, and while the courts have indeed meddled in religious matters sufficiently to dismiss the claim that either side is the only true church, at least the court has not determined that issue by taking sides in what is essentially a religious dispute.

Postscript

After this book was written in draft form, there was news of further litigation. A lawsuit has been filed on behalf of Waldheim Colony, a Group One colony not far from Lakeside.[122] According to the report, the colony majority is suing to get the power of the state to evict twenty "dissident" members. As earlier, Michael Radcliffe is acting for the colony, and Donald Douglas is acting for the so-called dissident group. Here we go again.

Additionally, there has been litigation involving Ponderosa Colony in Southern Alberta, where at least seven members who had been expelled by the majority sued the colony.[123] As in *Hofer v. Hofer,* the colony has counterclaimed for an injunction to remove expelled members from the colony if they have not already left. There has already been a preliminary judgment by Mr. Justice Hembroff of the Alberta Court of Queen's Bench applying the *Lakeside* case to reinstate one member who was expelled without the formalities of the natural justice requirements.[124] But as we saw in *Lakeside,* reinstatement by court order is not much more than buying time. Of greater interest to us, should the case go to trial, is how the courts will deal with claims by ex-members and their families for compensation after they have been properly expelled.

Appendix
Male Genealogy of Lakeside Families[1]

The Joseph Hofer Clan (almost all overseer-obedient)

I. **Rev. Joseph Hofer** – 1907-98. Married **Anna Wipf** in 1929 and had four sons and nine daughters. The extended families of the four sons constitute the Joseph Hofer clan at Lakeside. The sons are:

1. **Joseph Hofer** (called "**K.O.**") – b. 1932. Married **Elisabeth Gross** in 1954 and had five sons and three daughters. He "left" or was expelled from the colony for significant periods. The five sons, all of whom established families, with numerous children, at Lakeside, are:

    1(a). **Joseph Hofer** (called "**K.O. Jr.**") – b. 1956.

    1(b). **Isaak Hofer** – b. 1959.

    1(c). **Garry Hofer** – b. 1960.

    1(d). **Willy Hofer** – b. 1962.

    1(e). **Tommy Hofer** – b. 1963.

    K.O. Jr. was rarely mentioned in the court record, if at all, as a combatant in the dispute, but the other four are mentioned frequently.

2. **Joshua Hofer (Sr.)** – b. 1933. Married **Katie Hofer** in 1956 and had five sons and five daughters. Two sons died tragically in their youth. The remaining three sons at Lakeside are:

    2(a). **Rev. Joshua Hofer (Jr.)** – b. 1959.

    2(b). **Sammy Hofer** – b. 1963.

    2(c). **Kenneth Hofer** – b. 1965.

During the time of the dispute and litigation, the two younger men were not married but have since established families at Lakeside. Joshua Hofer Jr. was the key inside leader of the colony during the period of the dispute and is now minister and head of the colony. His brother Sammy is the secretary of Lakeside, the second most powerful position at the colony.

3. **Benjamin Hofer** – b. 1935. Married **Sarah Waldner** in 1956 and had nine sons and three daughters. The sons are:

    3(a). **Benny Hofer** – b. 1957.

    3(b). **Mike Hofer** – b. 1958. At the time of the dispute, Mike was married to Rachel Hofer (b. 1962), a daughter of Rev. Paul Hofer of the "renegade group."

    3(c). **Joe Hofer** – b. 1960.

    3(d). **Arnold Hofer** – b. 1961.

    3(e). **Leonard Hofer** – b. 1965. Leonard joined the "renegades" and after leaving the colony for a time, returned, married, and became a member of the colony that had previously sued him as a dissenter.

    3(f). **Hardy Hofer** – b. 1969.

    3(g). **Ernest Hofer** – b. 1971.

    3(h). **Peter Hofer** – b. 1973.

    3(i). **Zacky Hofer** – b. 1975.

During the period of the dispute, most of the younger sons were unmarried teenagers. Several of the older men in this family were not married either. The sons of Ben do not appear to have played as significant a role as the sons of K.O. and Joshua Sr. in the conflict between the two groups. The four youngest have all married and are establishing families at Lakeside.

4. **Paul Hofer** (called **"Paul K."**) – b. 1941. Married **Katie Gross** in 1962 and had one son and three daughters. Paul K. left or was expelled for most of the period of this dispute but toward the end joined the "renegades," as did his son:

    4(a). **Paul Hofer** (called **Paul Wayne**) – b. 1971.

The families of Paul K. and Paul Wayne are now at Heartland Colony.

The Daniel Hofer Clan (the "renegade" group)

I. **Daniel Hofer (Sr.)** – b. 1936. His parents were **John Hofer** and **Katharina (Wollman)**, who moved from Lakeside to Cypress to Homewood and had eight sons and three daughters. Daniel and his brother Paul remained at Lakeside, while their brothers moved to Cypress and then Homewood. Daniel married **Sarah Wipf** (daughter of the then minister of Lakeside) in 1959 and had six sons and four daughters. The sons are:

1. **Daniel Hofer (Jr.)** – b. 1959. Married **Josie Hofer** (a daughter of Ben) and had four children as at 1992. As at 2000, Daniel was secretary of Heartland Colony and had seven children.

2. **David Hofer** (twin brother to Daniel Jr.) – b. 1959. Married to **Kathleen Hofer** (a daughter of Paul K.) and had four children as at 1992. As at 2000, David was farm boss of Heartland Colony and had several more children.

3. **Larry Hofer** – b. 1961. Baptized member of Lakeside but not married during the period of the dispute. He subsequently married, had children, and became minister and head of Heartland Colony.

4. **Jacob Hofer** – b. 1970. Injured during one of the events of violence on Lakeside Colony and did not return to either Lakeside or Heartland.

5. **Conrad Hofer** – b. 1972.

6. **Roland Hofer** – b. 1974.

The younger sons have established families at Heartland Colony. The oldest daughter, Linda (b. 1963) was married and absent from Lakeside for the period of the dispute. The three younger daughters, **Bertha** (b. 1964), **Susie** (b. 1967), and **Rita** (b. 1968), were married once Heartland was established.

II. **Rev. Paul Hofer (Sr.)** – b. 1937. Slightly younger brother of Daniel. He married **Rachel Wipf** (daughter of then minister of Lakeside) in 1960. They had six sons and two daughters. Before the schism, Paul was the second minister at Lakeside. The sons are:

1. **Paul Hofer Jr.** – b. 1963. Left the colony for a time and was not a baptized member. In 1991 he married one of Paul K.'s daughters. He became a baptized member of Heartland, with six children, as at 2000.

2. **John (Gerald) Hofer** – b. 1967.

3. **Nathan Hofer** – b. 1969.

4. **George Hofer** – b. 1971.

5. **Steve Hofer** – b. 1973.

6. **Jerold Hofer** – b. 1975.

All six sons, with families, are now living at Heartland. Only the youngest was not married as of 2000.

Notes

Acknowledgments

1 Samuel Kleinsasser, *Community and Ethics* (1998) [unpublished, on file with author].
2 Alvin J. Esau, "Communal Property and Freedom of Religion: *Lakeside Colony of Hutterian Brethren v. Hofer*," in John McLaren and Harold Coward, eds., *Religious Conscience, the State, and the Law* (Albany: State University of New York, 1999) at 97-116.
3 Alvin J. Esau, "Law and Property: The Establishment and Preservation of Hutterite Communalism in North America: 1870-1925," in John McLaren, Nancy Wright, and A.R. Buck, eds. *Despotic Dominion: Property Rights in British Settler Societies* (Vancouver: UBC Press, 2004).

Introduction

1 The judicial decisions for the first round of litigation are *Lakeside Colony v. Hofer*, [1992] 3 S.C.R. 165, reversing (1991), 77 D.L.R. (4th) 202 (Man. C.A.), and (1989), 63 D.L.R. (4th) 473 (Man. Q.B.). For the second round of litigation, see *Lakeside Colony v. Hofer* (1994), 93 Man. R. (2d) 161 (Man. Q.B.).
2 *Hofer v. Hofer*, [1970] S.C.R. 958, affirming (1967), 65 D.L.R. (2d) 607 (Man. C.A.), affirming (1966), 59 D.L.R. (2d) 723 (Man. Q.B.).
3 For a more detailed overview of the law related to church property disputes, see Alvin J. Esau, "The Judicial Resolution of Church Property Disputes: Canadian and American Models" (2003) 40 Alta. L. Rev. 767-816.
4 I deal with some aspects of this in a case study of *Schroen v. Steinbach Bible College* in Alvin J. Esau, "Islands of Exclusivity": Religious Organizations and Employment Discrimination" (2000) 33 U.B.C. L. Rev. 719-827.

Chapter 1: The Hutterites

1 I have found the following six sources, listed by date of publication, to be particularly helpful: Victor Peters, *All Things Common: The Hutterian Way of Life* (New York: Harper and Row, 1971); John A. Hostetler, *Hutterite Society* (Baltimore: Johns Hopkins University Press, 1974); Karl A. Peter, *The Dynamics of Hutterite Society: An Analytical Approach* (Edmonton: University of Alberta Press, 1987); John Hofer, *The History of the Hutterites*, rev. ed. (Altona, MB: Friesen and Sons, 1988); Samuel Hofer, *The Hutterites: Lives and Images of a Communal People* (Saskatoon: Hofer Publishers, 1998); Donald B. Kraybill and Carl F. Bowman, *On the Backroad to Heaven: Old Order Hutterites, Mennonites, Amish and Brethren* (Baltimore: Johns Hopkins University Press, 2001).
2 Guy F. Hershberger, ed., *The Recovery of the Anabaptist Vision* (Scottdale, PA: Mennonite Publishing House, 1957). I am aware that the original Anabaptist movement included competing visions. See, for example, the collection of essays in "The Anabaptist Vision: Historical Perspectives" Conrad Grebel Review 12:3 (1994); James Stayer, *Anabaptists and the Sword* (Lawrence, KS: Coronado Press, 1972); and James Stayer, *The German Peasant's War and Anabaptist Community of Goods* (Montreal: McGill-Queen's University Press, 1991).

3 Much of the early history of the Hutterites has been preserved in sixteenth-, seventeenth-, and eighteenth-century Hutterite chronicles. These have been gathered together and translated into English. See *The Chronicle of the Hutterian Brethren, Volume I* (Rifton, NY: Plough Publishing, 1987). This work, referred to as "The Great Chronicle," contains approximately eight hundred pages of Hutterian writing to 1665. "The Small Chronicle," written by Johannes Waldner, continues the story to 1802. Until recently, this masterful work was available in German only. See A.J.F. Zieglschmid, ed., *Klein-Geschichtsbuch der Hutterischen Bruder* (Philadelphia: Carl Schurx Foundation, 1947). It has now been translated into English and published by Crystal Spring Colony, which is led by Senior Elder Jacob Kleinsasser, a key figure in this narrative involving the *Lakeside* case and the schism of the Schmiedeleut. See Hutterian Brethren of Crystal Spring Colony, eds., *The Chronicle of the Hutterian Brethren, Volume II* (Altona, MB: Friesen Printers, 1998).

4 See Robert Friedmann, *Hutterite Studies* (Goshen, IN: Mennonite Historical Society, 1961) at 83-85.

5 A recent translation by John J. Friesen is *Peter Riedemann's Hutterite Confession of Faith* (Waterloo, ON: Herald Press, 1999). An earlier translation is Peter Rideman, *Confession of Faith* (Rifton, NY: Plough Publishing, 1970). The *Confession* was originally published in 1545.

6 See L. Gross, *The Golden Years of the Hutterites* (Scottdale, PA: Herald Press, 1980).

7 See Wes Harrison, *Andreas Ehrenpreis and Hutterite Faith and Practice* (Kitchener, ON: Pandora Press, 1997).

8 See Rod A. Janzen, *The Prairie People: Forgotten Anabaptists* (Hanover, NH: University Press of New England, 1999).

9 Based on counting colonies and averaging about one hundred people per colony. Some colonies are larger, of course, and more recent ones have smaller populations. A helpful source is the annual phonebook published by the James Valley Colony, which lists the colonies and phone numbers for all three Leuts. See *James Valley Switchboard Address Book 2000* (Elie, MB: James Valley Colony, 2000). A similar source is the *Riverview Directory* (Saskatoon: Riverview Colony). Huntington notes that in 1995 the Hutterites had a population of approximately 36,000 living in about 390 colonies. See Gertrude E. Huntington, "Living in the Ark: Four Centuries of Hutterite Faith and Community," in Donald E. Pitzer, ed., *America's Communal Utopias* (Chapel Hill, NC: University of North Carolina Press, 1997) 319 at 320.

10 See John Ryan, *The Agricultural Economy of Manitoba Hutterite Colonies* (Toronto: McClelland and Stewart, 1977).

11 Hostetler, *supra* note 1 at 126.

12 *Ibid.* at 127.

13 *Ibid.* at 129.

14 *Ibid.*

15 See Douglas E. Sanders, "The Hutterites: A Case Study in Minority Rights" (1964) 42 Can. Bar. Rev. 225; David Flint, *The Hutterites: A Study in Prejudice* (Toronto: Oxford University Press, 1975); and, especially, William Janzen, *Limits on Liberty: The Experience of Mennonite, Hutterite, and Doukhobor Communities in Canada* (Toronto: University of Toronto Press, 1990).

16 On file with author. In response to the schism in the Schmiedeleut, a new constitution was passed in 1993.

17 *Act to Incorporate the Hutterian Brethren Church*, S.C. 1951, c. 77.

18 Ruth E. Baum, *The Ethnohistory of Law: The Hutterite Case* (PhD thesis, State University of New York, 1977) [unpublished]. On file with author.

19 See Donald B. Kraybill, *The Riddle of Amish Culture* (Baltimore: Johns Hopkins University Press, 1989).

20 See Ryan, *supra* note 10.

21 See Janzen, *supra* note 15, c. 2 and 3 re Mennonite and Doukhobor land reserves.

22 See James Urry, *None But the Saints: The Transformation of Mennonite Life in Russia, 1789-1889* (Winnipeg: Hyperian Press, 1989).

23 Over six thousand Mennonites left Manitoba for Latin America in the 1920s because of the failure of the Manitoba government to accommodate their desire for private schools. See

Janzen, *supra* note 15, c. 5. See also Adolph Ens, *Subjects or Citizens? The Mennonite Experience in Canada, 1870-1925* (Ottawa: University of Ottawa Press, 1994).

24 One of the disagreements between the traditional Hutterites and the Arnoldleut, a group that is examined in the next chapter, is that the Arnoldleut let their children go to public high school off the colony, as well as to college and university.

25 *Deerfield Hutterian Association v. Ipswich Board of Education* (1979), 468 F.Supp. 1219 (U.S.D. S.D./N.D.).

26 See Karl A. Peter, *supra* note 1, c. 3.

27 For an account of some of the controversy surrounding evangelical movements within the Hutterian community, see Rod Janzen, *Terry Miller: The Pacifist Politician: From Hutterite Colony to State Capital* (Freeman, SD: Pine Hill Press, 1986). Also see Caroline Hartse, *On the Colony: Social and Religious Change Among Contemporary Hutterites* (PhD diss., University of New Mexico, 1993).

28 See Karl A. Peter, *supra* note 1, c. 2.

Chapter 2: The Bruderhof

1 Historical details of the Bruderhof movement are provided in Yaacov Oved, *The Witness of the Brothers: A History of the Bruderhof* (New Brunswick: Transaction Publishers, 1996), and Benjamin Zablocki, *The Joyful Community*, rev. ed., 1980 (Chicago: University of Chicago Press, 1971).

2 Correspondence from the 1930-31 period and an account of Dr. Arnold's North American trip from his diaries are found in Eberhard Arnold, *Brothers Unite* (Rifton, NY: Plough Publishing, 1988).

3 *Ibid.* "Letter of Arnold," 24 June 1930, at 68.

4 *Ibid.* "Letter of Arnold," 15 July 1930, at 73.

5 *Ibid.* "Letter of Arnold," 1932, at 313.

6 *Ibid.* "Letter of Arnold," 1 December 1930, at 176-77.

7 *Ibid.* "Letter of Arnold," at 187.

8 Oved, *supra* note 1 at 62.

9 Oved, *supra* note 1 at 85, 110, 175 notes that the Cotswold farm in England was purchased with the help of Quakers, and that the move to Paraguay was aided by Quaker financing, as was the establishment of American colonies. The Hutterites did make a major gift to the Bruderhof in 1949, however, as noted by Oved at 190-91.

10 See Elizabeth Bohlken-Zumpe, *Torches Extinguished* (San Francisco: Carrier Pigeon Press, 1993) at 28.

11 *Ibid.* at 21, 37.

12 Zablocki, *supra* note 1.

13 Bohlken-Zumpe, *supra* note 10 at 30-31 outlines an earlier "crisis" in 1936, just after the death of Eberhard Arnold, when the Arnold sons and the wife of Eberhard had to be dealt with in terms of their demands for special leadership considerations within the community.

14 Roger Allain, *The Community That Failed* (San Francisco: Carrier Pigeon Press, 1992) at 165-66.

15 Bohlken-Zumpe, *supra* note 10 at 146-47.

16 Allain, *supra* note 14 at 193.

17 Merrill Mow, *Torches Rekindled* (Rifton, NY: Plough Publishing, 1989) at 123.

18 Bohlken-Zumpe, *supra* note 10 at 120.

19 John A. Hostetler, *Hutterite Society* (Baltimore: Johns Hopkins University Press, 1974) at 281.

20 Zablocki, *supra* note 1.

21 *Ibid.* at 62.

22 Gerald Renner, "Bruderhof Leader Defends Close-Knit Community Against Outside Critics" *Hartford Courant* (12 November 1995).

23 Laurie O'Neill, "Governed by Love, a Commune Thrives" *New York Times* (14 December 1980).

24 Richard Weizel, "A Simple Life of Tradition, Hard Work and Peace" *New York Times* (30 August 1992), sec. 12 at 1.

25 Ruth Baer-Lambach, *A Daughter of the Flock* (Ramat Efal, Israel: Yad Tabenkin, 1992) at 28, as translated from Hebrew by Oved, *supra* note 1 at 194.

26 Mow, *supra* note 17.
27 Letter from Senior Elder Peter Hofer, 6 September 1955. Reprinted in *KIT Newsletter* 6, 1 (January 1994).
28 See Hostetler, *supra* note 19 at 282.
29 The letter is translated and reprinted in Bohlken-Zumpe, *supra* note 10 at 260-62.
30 Allain, *supra* note 14 at 315-16.
31 *Ibid.* at 322.
32 Julius H. Rubin, *The Other Side of Joy: Religious Melancholy Among the Bruderhof* (New York: Oxford University Press, 2000) at 121.
33 Mow, *supra* note 17 at 21.
34 Oved, *supra* note 1 at 247.
35 *Ibid.* at 248-49.
36 See, for example, some of the writings of Rev. Samuel Kleinsasser, a brother of Rev. Jacob Kleinsasser. In particular, Samuel Kleinsasser, "Our Broken Relationship with the Society of Brothers," reprinted in *KIT Newsletter* 6, 7 (July 1994), and Samuel Kleinsasser, *Community and Ethics* (1998) [unpublished, on file with author].
37 Wilma Derksen, "Bruderhof and Kleinsasser Hutterites Part Company" *Mennonite Reporter* (3 April 1995), 3.
38 Richard Weizel, "A Simple Life of Tradition, Hard Work and Peace" *New York Times* (30 August 1992), sec. 13 at 1.
39 John Milgrom, "Communal Hutterites Become Jet Sect" *Middletown Times Herald-Record* (31 March 1996). See also Rifton Aviation web page at <www.riftonaviation.com>, accessed 7 January 2001.
40 Lucy Bloomfield, "Belief That Stays the Course" *Guardian* (29 September 1992).
41 Ari Goldman, "Hutterites Put Sharing to the Test" *New York Times* (14 June 1988): B1. See also Daniel Hatch, "Living the Faith the Hutterian Way" *New York Times* (14 August 1988), sec. 12 at 1.
42 Judith Gaines, "Where Strict 'Communism' Works" *Chicago Tribune* (22 March 1989), Tempo sec. at 1.
43 John A. Hostetler, "Expelled Bruderhofer Members Speak Out," undated draft article available at Peregrine Foundation <www.perefound.org/archives.html>, accessed 6 January 2001.
44 Andres Tapia and Rudy Carrasco, "A Christian Community Makes Waves, Not War: Pacifist Bruderhofers Do Not Shy Away from Controversy," reprinted in *KIT Newsletter* 8, 3 (March 1996), as excerpts from *Christianity Today*, 1995, volume and page not provided.
45 Timothy Miller, "Stress and Conflict in an International Religious Movement: The Case of the Bruderhof," 1993, Peregrine Foundation <www.perefound.org/archives.html>, accessed 6 January 2001.
46 See Ramon Sender Barayon, "The Heart Will Find a Way: Creating a Network of Reunion," *Communities Magazine* 88 (Fall 1995).
47 See <www.perefound.org>. An estimated one thousand people have left the Bruderhof community. The Bruderhof too has its own official web pages. See <www.bruderhof.com>, and for various Bruderhof publications see <www.plough.com>.
48 Hostetler, *supra* note 43.
49 See Allain, *supra* note 14, Bohlken-Zumpe, *supra* note 10, Nadine Moonje Pleil, *Free from Bondage* (San Francisco: Carrier Pigeon Press, 1994); Belinda Manley, *Through Streets Broad and Narrow* (San Francisco: Carrier Pigeon Press, 1996); Miriam Arnold Holmes, *Cast Out in the World* (San Francisco: Carrier Pigeon Press, 1997).
50 Pleil, *ibid.* at 134.
51 *Ibid.* at 189-91.
52 *Ibid.* at 295-308.
53 *Ibid.* at 361.
54 As outlined in Rubin, *supra* note 32 at 178-79.

Chapter 3: The Inside Law against Going to Outside Law
1 As to original diversity, see Harry Loewen, "Church and State in the Anabaptist-Mennonite Tradition: Christ versus Caesar?" in Ross Bender and Alan Sell, eds., *Baptism, Peace and the*

State in the Reformed and Mennonite Traditions (Waterloo: Wilfred Laurier University Press, 1991), 145-65. As to the dominant model, see Guy F. Hershberger, ed., *The Recovery of the Anabaptist Vision* (Scottdale, PA: Herald Press, 1957).

2 This use of "Sunday and Monday" comes from Frank H. Epp, *The Glory and the Shame* (Winnipeg: Canadian Mennonite Publishing Association, 1969) at 25.

3 "Schleitheim Confession (Anabaptist, 1527)," Mennonite Historical Society of Canada, *Canadian Mennonite Encylopedia Online*, 2000, <www.mhsc.ca/encyclopedia>, accessed 6 January 2001. This version of the confession is taken from John Howard Yoder, *The Legacy of Michael Sattler* (Scottdale, PA: Herald Press, 1979).

4 *Ibid.*

5 See 1 Corinthians 6:1-11.

6 P.J. Klassen, *The Economics of Anabaptism* (Ann Arbor, MI: University Microfilms International, 1962) at 154, n. 1.

7 Claus-Peter Clasen, *Anabaptism: A Social History* (Ithaca, NY: Cornell University Press, 1972) at 179-80.

8 For an overview of more activist Anabaptism see Leo Driedger and Donald B. Kraybill, *Mennonite Peacemaking: From Quietism to Activism* (Scottdale, PA: Herald Press, 1994).

9 David M. Smolin, "A House Divided? Anabaptist and Lutheran Perspectives on the Sword" (1997) 47 J. Legal Educ. 28 at 34.

10 See, for example, John Howard Yoder, *The Politics of Jesus* (Grand Rapids, MI: Eerdmans, 1992).

11 From Article 22, "Peace, Justice, and Nonresistance," *Confession of Faith in a Mennonite Perspective* (Scottdale, PA: Herald Press, 1995). This confession was adopted jointly in 1995 by the Mennonite Church (MC) and the General Conference Mennonite Church (GC), the two largest Mennonite groups in North America. These two groups merged in 2001.

12 There are a variety of competing paradigms for the new activist models. See John R. Burkholder and Barbara Gingerich, eds., *Mennonite Peace Theology: A Panorama of Types* (Akron, OH: Mennonite Central Committee, 1991). See also J.R. Burkholder, "Mennonite Peace Theology: Reconnaissance and Exploration," (1992) 10 *Conrad Grebel Review* 259.

13 On restorative justice in the area of criminal law and procedure, see Howard Zehr, *Changing Lenses* (Scottdale, PA: Herald Press, 1990).

14 For example, one might argue that while many prisoners could be released, a few are so obviously dangerous that the violence of the state must be used to keep them in custody.

15 Article 23, "The Church's Relation to Government and Society," *supra* note 11.

16 The literature on the shortcomings and need for reform of the civil justice system is voluminous. Recent Canadian examples include *Report of the Canadian Bar Association Task Force on Systems of Civil Justice* (Ottawa: Canadian Bar Association, 1996); *Ontario Civil Justice Review: Supplement and Final Report* (Toronto: Ontario Civil Justice Review, 1996); Ontario Law Reform Commission, *Rethinking Civil Justice: Research Studies for the Civil Justice Review* (Toronto: Ontario Law Reform Commission, 1996); *Manitoba Civil Justice Review Task Force Report* (Winnipeg: Department of Justice, 1996). For an American perspective, see Larry Kramer, ed., *Reforming the Civil Justice System* (New York: New York University Press, 1996); American Bar Association, *An Agenda for Justice* (Chicago: American Bar Association, 1996); *ABA Blueprint for Improving the Civil Justice System* (Chicago: American Bar Association, 1992).

17 There is a vast literature on alternative dispute resolution. Recent Canadian examples include A.J. Pirie, *Alternative Dispute Resolution* (Toronto: Irwin Law, 2000); G. Chornenki and C. Hart, *Bypass Court: A Dispute Resolution Handbook* (Toronto: Butterworths, 1996); The 1997 Isaac Pitblado Lectures, *Dispute Resolution: Systems in Transition* (Winnipeg: Law Society of Manitoba, 1997); Alberta Law Reform Institute, *Dispute Resolution: A Directory of Methods, Projects and Resources* (Edmonton: Alberta Law Reform Institute, 1990). A leading American reference is S. Goldberg, F. Sander, and N. Rogers, *Dispute Resolution,* 3rd ed. (New York: Aspen, 1999).

18 See Robert Cover, "Violence and the Word" (1986) 95 Yale L.J. 1601. For a broader treatment of other forms of coercion beyond physical violence see Grant Lamond, "The Coerciveness of Law" (2000) 20 Oxford J. Legal Stud. 39.

19 Classic criticisms of the adversary process include Marvin Frankel, *Partisan Justice* (New York: Hill and Wang, 1980) and Anne Strick, *Injustice for All* (New York: Putman, 1977).

20 Joseph G. Allegretti, *The Lawyer's Calling: Christian Faith and Legal Practice* (New York: Paulist Press, 1996).
21 *Ibid.*, c. 6, "Lawyers and Litigation," at 81-95.
22 John 18:37.
23 All quotations are from the Revised Standard Version.
24 Peter Riedemann, *Confession of Faith*, trans. and edited by John J. Friesen (Waterloo: Herald Press, 1999) at 138-39.
25 Andreas Ehrenpreis, *Sendbrief*, 1647. For an abridged English translation see Robert Friedmann, *Brotherly Community: The Highest Command of Love* (Rifton, NY: Plough Publishing, 1978).
26 A discussion of this issue is provided in Wes Harrison, *Andreas Ehrenpreis and Hutterite Faith and Practice* (Kitchener, ON: Pandora Press, 1997) at 160-61.
27 *Ibid.* at 161.
28 Hutterian Brethren of Crystal Spring Colony, eds., *The Chronicle of the Hutterian Brethren, Volume II* (Altona, MB: Friesen Printers, 1998), 586-87.
29 The following account is based on the two *Chronicles. The Chronicle of the Hutterian Brethren, Volume I* (Rifton, NY: Plough Publishing, 1987) at 724-31, and *supra* note 28 at 214-26.
30 *Supra* note 28 at 215.
31 *Ibid.*
32 *Ibid.* at 216.
33 *Ibid.*
34 *Ibid.* at 219.
35 *Ibid.*
36 *Ibid.* Details of these matters are provided at 220-25.
37 *Ibid.* Details of the *Kuhr* case are found at 340-41.
38 *Ibid.* at 341.
39 *Ibid.*
40 *Ibid.* Details of Kuhr's resolute triumph over adversity are provided at 342-45, 354-55, 359-60, 407-9.
41 The two other major branches of the Mennonite side of the Anabaptist tree apparently did not formulate statements on the issue to the degree that the Mennonite Church did. A trip to both the Archives of the Mennonite Brethren Church at Concord College (MB) and the Archives at Canadian Mennonite Bible College (CMBC) turned up little on the topic of litigation. There was a General Conference Mennonite Church (GC) study conference on "The Church and Its Witness in Society" in Winnipeg in 1959, where Mennonite lawyer John J. Enns presented "Concerns Related to Legal Problems and Involvements." Enns, who later became a provincial court judge, affirmed that the traditional position of Mennonites was to not resort to the law courts for settlement of disputes. While agreeing with this principle in general, he noted circumstances where it should not apply. For example, when special funds to compensate victims had been set up by the government, but required court action to access. On the MB side, there is a 1985 unpublished paper by R.M. Baerg, "The Christian and Litigations." This paper focuses on disputes between Christians and the 1 Corinthians 6 passage. As to the smaller branch of Old Order Mennonites, it is often asserted that this group still has an absolutist position against litigation. See, for example, Donald B. Kraybill and Carl F. Bowman, *On the Backroad to Heaven* (Baltimore: Johns Hopkins University Press, 2001) at 72 and 81, where it is submitted that the Mennonite Ordnung specifically forbids hiring lawyers even to *defend* oneself in a court trial.
42 See Alvin J. Esau, "Mennonites and Litigation," 2000, available at my home page under selected writings at <www.umanitoba.ca/faculties/law/faculty/esau>.
43 The unpublished papers and discussion summaries for "Conference on Nonresistance and Political Responsibility," Peace Problems Committee, 1956, found in the Canadian Mennonite University Library, Winnipeg.
44 Guy F. Hershberger, "Litigation in Mennonite History," *ibid.* at 32. This summary of the Mennonite position on litigation is also contained in an article on "Litigation" by Hershberger in the *Mennonite Encyclopedia* (Scottdale, PA: Herald Press, 1956). Subsequently, Hershberger restated his position in his influential book *The Way of the Cross in Human Relations* (Scottdale, PA: Herald Press, 1958) at 317-21.

45 In the first half of the twentieth century, lawyers with Mennonite backgrounds would usually leave the church: "Mennonite lawyer" was an oxymoron. However, Samuel Wenger, who received his law degree in 1937, was an exception in that he was not only a lawyer but also a faithful member of the Mennonite Church denomination. See "Mennonites and Professionalism: Beginnings in Lancaster" *Mennonite Historical Bulletin* 44:4 (1983) 1, which gives an overview of Wenger's career and views. Note too that in the more liberal GC church group, Maxwell H. Kratz practised law from the beginning of the century and continued to be a leading figure in the church, as noted in Paul Toews, *Mennonites in American Society 1930-1970* (Scottdale, PA: Herald Press, 1996) at 23. In contrast, all the lawyers of Mennonite background in Western Canada during the period that Kratz and Wenger were called to the bar left the Mennonite Church. It would be a later generation of lawyers who would venture to call themselves both a lawyer and a Mennonite. See Harold Dick, *Lawyers of Mennonite Background in Western Canada Before the Second World War* (Winnipeg: Legal Research Institute, 1992).

46 Wenger's comments were expanded on in Samuel S. Wenger, "Mennonites and the Law" (February 1958) *Christian Living* 6 at 33.

47 The unpublished background papers for "Consultation on Litigation Problems" are found in the Canadian Mennonite University Library, Winnipeg.

48 "The Christian and Litigation, Statement of Findings Adopted at Consultation," found in the John Howard Yoder Collection, "Litigation, 1939-1984," Hist. Mss. 1-48, Box 23, Archives of the Mennonite Church, Goshen, IN.

49 "Litigation and the Use of the Law" *Gospel Herald* 56, 23 (11 June 1963) at 498-99, 509-10.

50 See "Task Force on Litigation," Official Files of the Mennonite Church General Board, Collection, I-6-5, Archives of the Mennonite Church, Goshen College. [Henceforth *Task Force Files*.] Most of these items are also found in the John H. Yoder collection, "Litigation, 1939-1984," Hist. Mss. 1-48, Box 23, Archives of the Mennonite Church, Goshen, IN.

51 J.R. Burkholder, "Litigation: Mennonite Church Teaching and Its Scriptural Background." *Task Force Files*.

52 *The Use of the Law* (Scottdale, PA: Mennonite Publishing House, 1982). The statement was adopted by the Mennonite General Assembly in Bowling Green, Ohio, August 1981.

53 Driedger and Kraybill, *supra* note 8.

54 "Resume," *supra* note 52 at 3.

55 *Ibid.* at 11-12.

56 Of course, the other side of the coin is that the potential threat of negative publicity allows the "unscrupulous" plaintiff to leverage monetary awards from large entities that would rather settle the case than defend against such lawsuits.

57 This distinction is problematic in that so-called private civil litigation still involves governmental action because courts, though having independence from other branches of government, are nevertheless a part of the formal governing structure of society, and furthermore, civil adjudication often involves public-governmental functions such as the creation of judge-made law through precedent.

Chapter 4: Hutterite Litigation before *Lakeside*

1 For a more detailed survey of the Hutterite cases see Alvin J. Esau, "Hutterite Litigation," 1997, available at my home page under *Selected Writings* at <www.umanitoba.ca/faculties/law/faculty/esau>. There may well be more cases, since only a small portion of the litigation that is commenced is ultimately reported by way of published judicial decisions. Most cases are settled before a trial is held, while other cases may go to trial but the judicial reasons for the decision may remain unreported at that level. Historically, most reported decisions involve the judicial opinions at the appeal court level. Given the existence of an electronic database for superior court files covering the last few decades in Manitoba, I am able to identify a few of these recent cases from my home province even though they did not result in a published judicial decision.

2 *State ex rel. Chamberlain v. Hutterische Bruder Gemeinde* (1922), 191 N.W. 635 (S.D. Sup. Ct.); reversing in part the harshest dicta of the unreported trial decision but still removing the right of Hutterite colonies to incorporate as religious corporations.

3 *State of South Dakota ex rel. W.G. Dunker, State's Attorney of Spink County v. Spink Hutterian Brethren* (1958), 90 N.W.2d 365 (S.D. Sup. Ct.).

4 *Appeal of Hutterische Bruder Gemeinde* (1925), 1. B.T.A. 1208 (U.S.B.T.A.); *Hutterishe Church v. The United States* (1928), 64 Ct. Cl. 672 (U.S. Ct. Cl.).

5 *Hutterische Bruder Gemeinde v. Commissioner of IRS* (1928), 14 B.T.A. 771 (U.S.B.T.A.). Hutterite appeal successful. See also *Kleinsasser v. United States* (1983), 707 F.2d 1024 (U.S. Ct. App., 9th Cir.) affirming (1981), 522 F.Supp. 460 (U.S.D.). Hutterite claim to tax credit denied.

6 *Re Cloverleaf Colony* (1990), 114 B.R. 1010 (U.S. Bankruptcy Ct., S.D.).

7 *Deerfield Hutterian Association v. Ipswich Board of Education* (1978), 444 F.Supp. 159 (U.S.D. S.D./N.D.).

8 *Deerfield Hutterian Association v. Ipswich Board of Education* (1979), 468 F.Supp. 1219 (U.S.D. S.D./N.D.).

9 *Barickman Hutterian Mutual Corp. v. Nault,* [1939] S.C.R. 223 (S.C.C.), reversing [1938] 1 W.W.R. 777. (Man. C.A.).

10 *Wipf v. The Queen,* [1976] C.T.C. 57 (S.C.C.), affirming [1975] F.C. 162 (Fed. C.A.) reversing *Hofer, Tschetter, Wipf, Wurtz v. M.N.R.* (1973), 73 D.T.C. 5558 (F.C.T.D.), affirming [1972] C.T.C. 2275; 72 D.T.C. 1248 (T.R.B.).

11 For more detail on the tax litigation see William Janzen, *Limits on Liberty: The Experience of Mennonite, Hutterite, and Doukhobor Communities in Canada* (Toronto: University of Toronto Press, 1990) at 272-85.

12 *Hutterian Brethren Church of Wilson v. The Queen,* [1980] C.T.C. 1 (Fed. C.A.) affirming [1979] D.T.C. 5052 (F.C.T.D.).

13 In *Hutterian Brethren Church of Morinville v. Royal Bank,* [1979] 5 W.W.R. 214 (Alta. C.A.) the court held that it did not violate due process for the bank to comply with a demand from the federal tax department to remit the alleged amount of money due for tax from the colony account while the colony was appealing the assessment. The Hutterites attempted to appeal to the Supreme Court of Canada but leave was denied (1979), 17 A.R. 360. In *Alberta v. MNR and Hutterian Brethren Church of Smoky Lake* (1980), 22 A.R. 317 (Alta. C.A.), on the other hand, the court held that the federal tax department could not garnishee certain term deposit certificates of Hutterite colonies held in provincial government treasury branches. The result hinged on technical interpretations of the obligations of the bank under the terms of the certificate. Recently, in *Mayfair Colony Farms v. M.N.R.,* [1996] M.J. No. 488 (Man. C.A.), affirming the order of Mr. Justice Wright, Man. Q.B., *Case File CI95-01-92682,* a colony was successful in appealing the seizure of a vehicle that had been impounded after being used by some members of the colony without authorization for illegal importation of cigarettes and liquor. Finally, note *Midland Hutterian Brethren v. Canada,* [2000] F.C.J. No. 2098 (Fed. C.A.) reversing [1999] T.C.J. No. 136 (T.C.C.) where a colony was successful in appeal of denial of input tax credits on the cost of materials to make work clothes.

14 For detailed treatment see Douglas E. Sanders, "The Hutterites: A Case Study in Minority Rights" (1964) 42 Can. Bar. Rev. 225; David Flint, *The Hutterites: A Study in Prejudice* (Toronto: Oxford University Press, 1975); and Janzen, *supra* note 11 at 60-84.

15 See *Walter v. A.G. of Alberta,* [1969] S.C.R. 383, affirming (1966), 60 D.L.R. (2d) (Alta. C.A.), affirming (1965), 54 D.L.R. (2d) 750 (Alta. S.C.). Earlier litigation was dismissed on a jurisdictional point. See *Re Hatch and East Cardston Hutterian Colony,* [1949] W.W.R. 900 (Alta. Dist. Ct.). The only successful litigation involved the procedure for approval of a particular colony purchase of adjacent land, but this was within the framework of the restrictive legislation, rather than a challenge to it. See *Re Communal Property Act* (1967), 60 W.W.R. 559 (Alta. Dist. Ct.).

16 See *R. v. Vanguard Hutterian Brethren,* [1979] 6 W.W.R. 335 (Sask. Dist. Ct.) nullifying a municipal bylaw restricting buildings to single-family dwellings. Earlier decisions on this matter dealt with evidential issues. See (1979), 97 D.L.R (3d) 86 (Sask. C.A.), reversing [1979] 3 W.W.R. 248 (Sask. Q.B.). Also see *Hutterian Brethren Church of Eagle Creek v. Eagle Creek Rural Municipality,* [1983] 2 W.W.R. 438 (Sask. C.A.), where the majority invoked the *Canadian Charter of Rights and Freedoms* against the municipal denial of development permits for a Hutterite colony. After approvals were given, the municipality appealed once

more and again the Saskatchewan Court of Appeal upheld the Hutterite development. See (1984), 35 Sask. R. 293 (C.A.).

17 *Hutterian Brethren Church of Starland v. Municipal District of Starland* (1991), 6 M.P.L.R. (2d) 67 (Alta. C.A.); (1993), 9 Alta. L.R. (3d) 1 (Alta. C.A.); (1994), 149 A.R. 288 (Alta. C.A.). See also *Starland No. 47 Municipal District v. Hutterian Brethren Church of Starland* (1996), 182 A.R. 373 (Alta. Q.B.).

18 *South Interlake Planning Dist. v. Prairie Blossom Holding*, Man. Q.B., *Case File 97-01-03127*. Another case involving land use was settled. See *Rural Municipality of Portage v. Norquay Colony*, Man. C.A., *Case File AI97-30-03282*.

19 Hutterites made submissions to the Public Utility Board for compensation for loss of colony lands in *Calgary Power v. Hutterian Brethren of Pincher Creek* (1961), 35 W.W.R. 227 (Alta. P.U.B.). Hutterites were successful in defending an appeal from the Surface Rights Board fixing compensation for the taking of two well sites and roadways. See *Paloma Petroleum v. Hutterian Brethren Church of Smoky Lake* (1987), A.R. (2d) 288 (C.A.). Also see *Little Bow Hutterian Brethren v. Alberta*, [1999] A.J. No. 530 (Alta. C.A.) re pending appeal arising from expropriation.

20 *Re Gallagher* (1981), 11 Sask. R. 215 (Sask. Dist. Ct.) deals with the characterization of members of Hutterite colonies and their voting rights in rural municipal elections.

21 *R. v. Hofer*, Man. Q.B., *Case File 88-01-05311*.

22 *R. v. Hofer*, [1977] 4 W.W.R. 64 (Man. Co. Ct.); *R. v. Hofer*, Man. Q.B., *Case File 88-01-04370*.

23 The scandal was reported widely. For example, Jeffrey Jones, "Sexual Assault Scandal Rocks Canadian Hutterites" *Reuters AAP Overseas News Wire* (23 May 1998); Peter Beaumont, "Prairie Sect 'Abused Children'" *Guardian Observer* (24 May 1998), 19; Alanna Mitchell, "Hutterite Communities Rocked by Sex Charges" *Globe and Mail* (30 May 1998).

24 Brock Ketcham, "Whistle-Blowing Hutterite Teen Brave, Officer Says" *Calgary Herald* (21 November 1998) at A3.

25 Alanna Mitchell, "Hutterite Farmer Jailed for Abusing His Daughter" *Globe and Mail* (18 July 1998).

26 "Hutterite Jailed for Sex Assault" *Montreal-Gazette* (5 September 1998), A13.

27 "Hutterites Convicted of Sex Abuse" *Christian Week* (4 August 1998), 5.

28 Daryl Slade, "Colony 'Embarrassed' by Sex Charges, Lawyer Says" *Calgary Herald* (16 June 1998), A4, stating that Hugh Sommerville is acting as a friend of the court in advising the colony but not representing any of the men individually because the colony will not allow such legal representation. See also Brock Ketcham, "'They Have Taken This Matter Very, Very Seriously' Legal Advisor Says" *National Post* (21 November 1998), A9, quoting lawyer Hugh Somerville, legal advisor for the colonies. Also see report that lawyer Dennis Abbott acted in sentencing hearing, according to "Hutterite Youth Pleads Guilty" *Ottawa Citizen* (31 October 1998), A3.

29 For example, in virtually every essay in Donald B. Kraybill, ed., *The Amish and the State* (Baltimore: Johns Hopkins University Press, 1993), we are told that the Amish do not use litigation.

30 For a more comprehensive survey of Amish cases see Alvin J. Esau, "The Amish and Litigation," 1998, available at my home page under *Selected Writings* at <www.umanitoba.ca/faculties/law/faculty/esau>. For background reading on Amish society generally see John A. Hostetler, *Amish Society*, 3rd ed. (Baltimore: Johns Hopkins University Press, 1993) and Donald B. Kraybill, *The Riddle of Amish Culture* (Baltimore: Johns Hopkins University Press, 1989). See also John A. Hostetler, "The Amish and the Law: A Religious Minority and Its Legal Encounters" (1984) 41 Wash. & Lee L. Rev. 33; Wayne Fisher, *The Amish in Court* (New York: Vantage Press, 1996); Albert N. Keim, ed., *Compulsory Education and the Amish: The Right Not to Be Modern* (Boston: Beacon Press, 1975); Ted Regehr, "Relations Between the Old Order Amish and the State in Canada" (1995) 69 Mennonite Q. Rev. 151-77.

31 For a more comprehensive survey of Mennonite cases see Alvin J. Esau, "Mennonites and Litigation," 2000, available at my home page under *Selected Writings* at <www.umanitoba.ca/faculties/law/faculty/esau>.

32 In Canada, the Mennonite Central Committee retained lawyers to represent some dairy farmers, including some Amish, who were reluctant to go to court over the issue of electric

cooling systems for milk and Sunday milk pickup schedules. See also *Janssen v. Ontario Milk Marketing Board* (1990), 13 C.H.R.R. D/397 (Ont. Bd. of Inq.).

33 Again, it is important to bear in mind that there may be more cases that were never reported.

34 *Shearer v. Hutterische Bruder Gemeinde* (1912), 134 N.W. 63 (S.D. Sup. Ct.).

35 *King v. Hutterische Bruder Gemeinde* (1913), 143 N.W. 902 (S.D. Sup. Ct.).

36 A couple of unreported cases are noted briefly in Ruth E. Baum, *The Ethnohistory of Law: The Hutterite Case* (PhD thesis, State University of New York, 1977) [unpublished] at 234-35. These are *Cobel v. Hutterishe Gemeinde* (1918) in which plaintiffs were awarded title, and *Harris v. Hutterishe Gemeinde* (1918) re validity of purported contract for sale of land without authorization of all voting members of the colony. According to Baum, this case was dismissed.

37 *Stablein v. Hutterishe Gemeinde* (1920), 177 N.W. 810 (S.D. Sup. Ct.) ordering new trial, and then successful appeal of second trial in (1922), 189 N.W. 312 (S.D. Sup. Ct.).

38 *Blinn v. Hutterishe Society of Wolf Creek* (1920), 194 P. 140 (Mont. Sup. Ct.).

39 *Waggoner v. Glacier Colony of Hutterites* (1957), 312 P.2d 117 and (1953), 258 P.2d 1162 (Mont. Sup. Ct.).

40 *Wyatt v. School District* (1966), 148 Mont. 83, 417 P.2d 221 (Mont. Sup. Ct.).

41 *Cuka v. Jamesville Hutterian Mutual Society* (1980), 294 N.W.2d 419 (S.D. Sup. Ct.).

42 *Grindheim v. Safeco Insurance Co.* (1995), 908 F.Supp. 794 (U.S.D. Mont.).

43 Based on a manual search through *Western Weekly Reports* from 1918 to present and through available provincial law reports in Alberta, Saskatchewan, and Manitoba.

44 See, for example, *D.S. Scott Transport v. Hutterian Brethren of Milford,* [1969] S.J. No. 130 (Sask. Q.B.); *Waterman v. Waldner and West Raley Colony,* [1975] A.J. No. 245 (Alta. S.C.); *Tomlinson v. Wurtz and Deerboine Colony and Pine Creek Colony* (1982), 16 Man. R. (2d) 145 (Q.B.); *Lauder v. Wollman and Hutterian Brethren Church of Leask* (1984), 31 Sask. R. 105 (Q.B.); *Taylor v. Hofer and Waterton Hutterian Brethren,* [1986] 67 A.R. 279 (Alta. Q.B.), affirmed by (1987), 50 Alta. L.R. (2d) 260 (Alta. C.A.); *Mathison v. Hofer and Airport Colony,* [1984] 3 W.W.R. 343 (Man. Q.B.); *Baer v. Hofer and New Rosedale Colony,* [1990] M.J. No. 557 (Q.B.), [1991] 73 Man. R. (2d) 145 (Man. C.A.); *Johannesson v. Mandel and South Bend Colony* (1994), A.R. 53 (Q.B.). Results of a search of the court files in Manitoba indicate a large number of cases like this that never went to trial.

45 See, for example, *Hudson v. Riverside Colony* (1981), 5 Man. R. (2d) 304 (Man. Q.B.) reversed in part by (1981), 114 D.L.R. (3d) 352 (Man. C.A.) re liability for escaping fire; *Fingas v. Summerfeld Colony* (1981), 5 M.R. (2d) 373 (Man. Co. Ct.) re liability for drifting chemicals while crop spraying.

46 For example, claim against colony in contract and for unjust enrichment: *East-Man. Feeds v. Cypress Colony Farms* (1993), 87 Man. R. (2d) 250 (Man. Q.B.). Claim against colony and other parties for sale of infected hogs: *Modern Livestock v. Elgersma* (1989), Alta. L.R. (2d) 392 (Q.B.).

47 Based on search in 2000 of Manitoba Small Claims, Queen's Bench, and Court of Appeal files since about 1984.

48 *Michael Waldner and others, as trustees for the Hutterische Society and Church v. Blachnik* (1937), 65 S.D. 449, 274 N.W. 837 (S.D. Sup. Ct.).

49 *Hutterian Brethren of Wolf Creek as a Church of Sterling, Alberta v. Hass* (1953), 116 F.Supp. 37 (U.S.D. Mont.).

50 The contemporary list of Dariusleut colonies mentions that Deerfield Colony in Montana was established in 1947 as a daughter colony of Wolf Creek, Alberta. See *James Valley Switchboard Address Book* (Elie, MB: James Valley Colony, 2000).

51 As reported in Vance Joseph Youmans, *The Plough and the Pen: Paul S. Gross and the Establishment of the Spokane Hutterian Brethren* (Boone, NC: Parkway Publishers, 1995) at 78-80.

52 *Ibid.* at 80. When Paul S. Gross, one of the most prominent Hutterite leaders of his generation, died recently, the lawsuit was again mentioned in press clippings. For example, Dan Hansen, "Hutterite Leader Dies" and "Hutterites Bury a Legend" *Spokesman-Review* (11 and 12 April 1998).

53 *Hofer v. W. M. Scott Livestock Company* (1972), 201 N.W.2d 410 (N.D. Sup. Ct.).

54 *Warden Hutterian Brethren v. Washington Trust Bank and Seattle-First National Bank* (1996), WL 325722 (Wash. C.A.).
55 *Hutterian Brethren of Red Willow v. Bradshaw,* [1962] S.J. No. 119 (Sask. Q.B.).
56 *Hutterian Brethren Church of Hillcrest v. Willms and Crossmount Farm Co. Ltd.* (1982), 18 Sask. R. 180 (Q.B).
57 *Hutterian Brethren Church of Standoff Colony v. Child* (1988), 62 Alta. L.R. (2d) 36 (C.A.), re fire spread to colony land from burning vehicle, and *Barickman Colony Farms v. Western Canadian Agritrade,* [2000] M.J. No. 488 (Q.B.) re liability for fire loss of pig barn. Note separate action brought against Hutterian Brethren Mutual in *Western Canadian Agritrade v. H.B. Mutual,* Man. Q.B., *Case File CI95-01-92423.*
58 *New Rosedale Colony v. Carlson Feeds,* Man. Q.B., *Case File CI83-01-011151.*
59 *Designated Genetics v. H.B. Mutual Insurance and Ranger Insurance Brokers,* Man. Q.B., *Case File CI96-01-97288.*
60 *Waldner v. Barkman Concrete,* Statement of Claim, 6 June 1989, Man. Q.B., *Case File 89-01-38907.*
61 Notice of Discontinuance, 27 July 1989.
62 *Iberville Window and Door Manufacturing v. Collyer,* Man. Q.B., *Case File CI00-01-17475;* Counterclaim brought in *Ridley Inc. v. Rainbow Colony,* Man. Q.B., *Case File CI99-01-14994; Riverside Colony v. Managro Harvestore,* Man. Q.B., *Case File 98-01-06164; Suncrest Colony v. Man. Coop Honey,* Man. Q.B., *Case File 97-01-04209; Riverbend Holding Co. v. McLaren Farms,* Man. Q.B., *Case File 97-01-03312; Prairie Blossom v. Darrin Steward,* Man. Q.B., *Case File 96-01-98447; Suncrest Colony v. Friesen,* Man. Q.B., *Case File 90-01-49203; New Haven Colony v. Richard Rex,* Man. Q.B., *Case File 89-01-42611; Sturgeon Creek Colony v. Richard Rex,* Man. Q.B., *Case File 89-01-42610; Suncrest Colony v. Friesen,* Man. Q.B., *Case File 88-01-30215; Iberville Manufacturing v. Lauzon,* Man. Q.B., *Case File 87-01-23102; Forest River Colony v. East-Man Feeds,* Man. Q.B., *Case File 85-01-000065.*
63 *Hofer v. Waldner,* [1921] 1 W.W.R. 177 (Alta. S.C. (T.D.)).
64 As found in John A. Hostetler, *Hutterite Society* (Baltimore: Johns Hopkins University Press, 1974) at 368.
65 Fold-out pages at the back of John Hofer, *The History of the Hutterites,* rev. ed. (Altona, MB: Friesen and Sons, 1988).
66 *Supra* note 63 at 179.
67 *Ibid.* at 182.
68 *Ibid.* at 183.
69 *Ibid.*
70 *James Valley Switchboard Address Book* (Elie, MB: James Valley Colony, 2000).
71 Hofer, *supra* note 65.
72 Hostetler, *supra* note 64 at 368-69.
73 Rod A. Janzen, *The Prairie People: Forgotten Anabaptists* (Hanover, NH: University Press of New England, 1999) at 170-71.
74 As noted in a case dealing with the process of winding up a corporate farm that at one stage had been the Felger Hutterite Colony. See *Hutterian Brethren of Lethbridge v. Felger Farming Co.,* [1984] A.J. No. 289 (Alta. Q.B.).
75 Michael Holzach, *The Forgotten People* (Sioux Falls, SD: Ex Machina Publishing, 1993). Originally published in 1980 in German as *Das Vergessene Volk: Ein Jahr bei den deutschen Hutteren in Kanada.*
76 *Ibid.* at 182-83.
77 *Walter's Estate v. Walter* (1986), 75 A.R. 330 (Alta. C.A.). See also on a preliminary issue of notice of winding up and issues to be addressed at trial, *Hutterian Brethren of Lethbridge v. Felger Farming Co., supra* note 74.
78 Minutes of the Hutterian Brethren Church, Exhibit 142, *Lakeside Trial 1.* On file with author.
79 *Supra* note 77.
80 Article 44, *Constitution of the Hutterian Brethren Church and Rules as to Community of Property,* 1 August 1950. On file with author.
81 Article 44, *Constitution of the Hutterian Brethren Church and Rules as to Community of Property,* 21 July 1993. On file with author.

82 *Hofer v. Bon Homme Hutterian Brethren* (1961), 109 N.W.2d 258 (S.D. Sup. Ct.).
83 *Benjamin Hofer, John Hofer, Joseph Hofer and David Hofer v. Zacharias Hofer, Jacob Hofer and Jacob S. Hofer, as Trustees of the Interlake Colony* (1966), 59 D.L.R. (2d) 723 (Man. Q.B.). Only a portion of Dickson's judgment was reported. The whole judgment in the form of thirty-three single-spaced typescript was reproduced by the plaintiffs at the subsequent *Lakeside* case. On file with author.
84 *Hofer v. Hofer* (1967), 65 D.L.R. (2d) 607 (Man. C.A.).
85 *Hofer v. Hofer*, [1970] S.C.R. 958, (1970), 73 W.W.R. 644 (S.C.C.).
86 *Supra* note 83, unpublished portion of Dickson J. opinion. Typescript at 13.
87 *Ibid.* at 15.
88 *Supra* note 83 (unpublished portion), at 3, 8, and published report 733.
89 Article 39, *Articles of Association of Interlake Colony*, May 1961. On file with author. [Henceforth *Interlake Articles.*]
90 Article 3, *Interlake Articles.*
91 *General Assembly of Free Church of Scotland v. Lord Overton*, [1904] A.C. 515 (H.L.).
92 *Schnorr's Appeal* (1870), 67 Pa. St. R. 138 at 146.
93 Article 37, *Interlake Articles.*
94 *Supra* note 83 at 730.
95 *Ibid.* at 17 (unpublished portion).
96 *Supra* note 63.
97 For example, Articles 30, 31, 32, 38. *Interlake Articles.*
98 *Supra* note 83 at 736.
99 *Supra* note 84.
100 *Ibid.* at 620.
101 *Supra* note 85.
102 *Ibid.* at 657.
103 *Ibid.* at 658.
104 *Ibid.* at 648.
105 *Ibid.* at 664.
106 *Ibid.* at 671.
107 As reported by Hostetler, *supra* note 64 at 278.
108 Brian Dickson, "The Role and Function of Judges" (1980) 14 L. Soc'y Gaz. 138 at 152-54; 171-72; 188-89 at 189.
109 Kevin Martin, "Hutterite Suit Off to Trial" *Calgary Sun* (30 April 1999).
110 *Canada v. Stahl*, [1999] A.J. No. 460 (Alta. Q.B.).

Chapter 5: Daniel Hofer, Hog Feeders, and Excommunication

1 An excellent source of information on Hutterite genealogy and history in the Elie region of Manitoba to 1984 is John S. Hofer (James Valley Colony), "The Hutterian Brethren," in *Treasures of Time: The Rural Municipality of Cartier 1914-1984* (Altona, MB: Friesen Printers, 1985) at 649-770. Particularly useful to this study is the list of family members at Lakeside from 1946 to 1984.
2 It would appear that Broad Valley, a daughter colony of Lakeside, also has had difficulties, at least financially, judging by the at least fifteen lawsuits launched by unpaid creditors over the years to collect money owing. A search of the court records since 1984 indicates that no other colony in Manitoba was sued more often by creditors. Indeed, out of the approximately one hundred colonies in Manitoba, there are only two or three where lawsuits indicate some pattern of financial difficulty. There is, however, as we will see, a blizzard of recent litigation related to the conflicts within the Schmiedeleut.
3 Noted by Samuel Kleinsasser, *Community and Ethics* (1998) [unpublished, on file with author] at 190.
4 See Minutes of Meeting, Exhibit 19, of first trial of *Lakeside Colony v. Hofer* at 2065. The exhibits are found in volumes 11 and 12 of the *Case on Appeal to the S.C.C.*, Court File 22382, a twelve-volume collection of the transcript of the trial and selected exhibits. [Henceforth *Case on Appeal.*] The transcripts of the first trial are also available in the Provincial Archives of Manitoba, Case 524/89. For purposes of reference, I am using the Supreme Court of Canada materials.

5   Interview with Daniel and Paul Hofer, Heartland Colony, 25 July 2000. Interview with Mike Hofer, Sommerfeld Colony, 1 August 2000.
6   Testimony of Michael Wollmann, *Case on Appeal* at 1353.
7   According to testimony of Jacob Hofer, *ibid.* at 797.
8   *Lakeside v. Hofer* (1989), 63 D.L.R. (4th) 473 at 479 (Man. Q.B.).
9   Testimony of Jake Hofer, *Case on Appeal* at 809.
10 As to the population in 1984, see Hofer, *supra* note 1 at 765-67. The number of people in 1987 was given by Joshua Hofer Jr. on cross-examination on an affidavit, 21 December 1987. Some transcripts from the discovery and a host of notices of motion, affidavits, and court orders in the case are found in the voluminous court file of *Wollmann v. Hofer*, Man. Q.B., *Case File CI87-01-17996.* [Henceforth *Case File.*]
11 Testimony of Daniel Hofer, *Case on Appeal* at 1391-95, and testimony of Paul Hofer, *Case on Appeal* at 1686-89.
12 Rev. James Hofer moved from James Valley in 1991 to become the minister of the new daughter colony, Starlite, established by James Valley.
13 Exhibit 28, *Case on Appeal* at 2098.
14 Daniel Hofer had a long list of decisions made by the overseers that were allegedly upsetting to the ordinary members. See Examination for Discovery of Daniel Hofer, 19 October 1987, at 240. *Case File.*
15 Testimony of Daniel Hofer on cross-examination, *Case on Appeal* at 1495.
16 Testimony of Daniel Hofer on examination in chief, *ibid.* at 1394.
17 Written comments from Michael Radcliffe to Alvin J. Esau, 5 September 2001, at 3. [Henceforth *Radcliffe Comments.*]
18 Exhibit 75, *Case on Appeal* at 2170. My emphasis.
19 Exhibit 76, *ibid.* at 2171.
20 Exhibit 77, *ibid.* at 2176.
21 Exhibit 78, *ibid.* at 2177.
22 Testimony of Daniel Hofer, *ibid.* at 1405-8.
23 Exhibit 79, *ibid.* at 2178.
24 Exhibit 81, *ibid.* at 2182.
25 Testimony of Daniel Hofer, *ibid.* at 1408.
26 Exhibit 85, *ibid.* at 2189.
27 Exhibit 86, *ibid.* at 2191.
28 Exhibit 90, *ibid.* at 2197.
29 Exhibit 89, *ibid.* at 2195.
30 Exhibit 90, *ibid.* at 2197. Emphasis in original.
31 Exhibit 91, *ibid.* at 2198.
32 Exhibit 92, *ibid.* at 2200.
33 Exhibit 93, *ibid.* at 2201.
34 *Ibid.*
35 Exhibit 95, *ibid. at* 2203.
36 Exhibit 96, *ibid. at* 2205.
37 Exhibit 101, *ibid.* at 2230.
38 Exhibit 160, *ibid.* at 2378. The statement of claim filed against Grand Colony is found in Queen's Bench File *CI86-01-14834.*
39 Exhibit 161, *Case on Appeal* at 2379.
40 I. Donald Gibb, *Summary of Transactions Involving Rosedale Hutterian Brethren, Inc.; Mike Waldner, Millbrook Hutterian Brethren, Inc.; and Jacob Kleinsasser, Crystal Spring Colony Farms, Ltd. (From 1982 to the Present)* (31 May 1992) [unpublished, on file with author and supplied to me by Prof. B. Bass]. I will deal with the impact of this manuscript in the discussion of the second round of the Lakeside litigation.
41 As noted in *Radcliffe Comments* at 3.
42 Testimony of Jacob Kleinsasser on cross-examination, *Case on Appeal* at 573, 577.
43 From the Crystal Spring School web page <www.escape.ca/~css/business.htm>, accessed 14 August 2002.
44 Testimony of Jacob Hofer, *Case on Appeal* at 818. I do not know if the spelling of the firm is correct.

45 Testimony of Daniel Hofer, *ibid.* at 1398.
46 Exhibit 103, *ibid.* at 2236.
47 Exhibit 105, *ibid.* at 2239.
48 Exhibit 106, *ibid.* at 2240.
49 Exhibit 107, *ibid.* at 2241.
50 Exhibit 110, *ibid.* at 2244.
51 Exhibit 114, *ibid.* at 2251.
52 Exhibit 113, *ibid.* at 2249.
53 Testimony of Mike Wollmann, *ibid.* at 1219.
54 Testimony of Daniel Hofer on examination for discovery, Transcript at 117. *Case File.*
55 As admitted by Jacob Kleinsasser on cross-examination, *Case on Appeal* at 559-65.
56 Testimony of Jacob Kleinsasser on cross-examination, *ibid.* at 565.
57 Testimony of Michael Wollmann, *ibid.* at 1185.
58 Testimony of Mike Wollmann on cross-examination, *ibid.* at 1291-95.
59 Exhibit 116, *ibid.* at 2254.
60 Exhibits 118-26, *ibid.* at 2257-73.
61 Testimony of Joshua Hofer Jr. on cross-examination, *ibid.* at 1126-27.
62 *Ibid.* at 1126; and evidence of Paul Hofer at 1696-1702.
63 Testimony of Jacob Hofer on cross-examination, *ibid.* at 899, 900, 910.
64 Testimony of Jacob Hofer, *ibid.* at 834.
65 Exhibit 127, *ibid.* at 2274.
66 Exhibit 166, *ibid.* at 2387.
67 Exhibit 30, *ibid.* at 2100.
68 Testimony of Michael Wollmann on cross-examination, *ibid.* at 1360-62.
69 Exhibit 168, *ibid.* at 2388.
70 Exhibit 20, *ibid.* at 2068.
71 *Ibid.*
72 Testimony of Mike Wollmann, *ibid.* at 1229-31.
73 Testimony of Jacob Hofer, *ibid.* at 841.
74 Testimony of Daniel Hofer on examination for discovery, Transcript at 282. *Case File.*
75 *Supra* note 69. My emphasis. The emphasized portion appears to have been written into the minutes after they were first prepared.
76 *Supra* note 70.
77 Testimony of Jacob Hofer, *Case on Appeal* at 842.
78 *Ibid.* at 844-45.
79 Testimony of Mike Wollmann, *ibid.* at 1237-38.
80 As admitted by Jacob Hofer on cross-examination, *ibid.* at 987.
81 Testimony of Jacob Hofer, *ibid.* at 846. My emphasis.
82 Testimony of Jacob Kleinsasser on cross-examination, *ibid.* at 612.
83 As to the colony functioning normally for the ten days from 21 to 31 January 1987, see testimony of Joshua Hofer Jr., *ibid.* at 1083.
84 Testimony of Daniel Hofer, *ibid.* at 1437.
85 *Supra* note 69.
86 *Supra* note 70.
87 Testimony of Joshua Hofer Jr., *Case on Appeal* at 1141.
88 Exhibit 21, *ibid.* at 2076.
89 Testimony of Mike Wollmann, *ibid.* at 1243, 1245; testimony of Jacob Kleinsasser at 613.
90 Testimony of Mike Wollmann, *ibid.* at 1242; testimony of Jake Hofer at 860.
91 As noted in *Radcliffe Comments* at 6.
92 Testimony of Jacob Kleinsasser, *Case on Appeal* at 348-49.
93 Exhibit 29, *ibid.* at 2099.
94 *Supra* note 88.
95 Testimony of Daniel Hofer, *Case on Appeal* at 1439.
96 Testimony of Daniel Hofer on cross-examination, *ibid.* at 1606.
97 Testimony of Daniel Hofer on examination for discovery, Transcript at 295-96. *Case File.*
98 Exhibit 32, *Case on Appeal* at 2102.

99   Testimony of Daniel Hofer on cross-examination, *ibid.* at 1610.
100 Testimony of Michael Wollmann, *ibid.* at 1256.
101 Affirmation of Jacob Hofer, 23 February 1987. *Case File.*
102 *Supra* note 88.
103 Testimony of Jacob Kleinsasser, *Case on Appeal* at 303.
104 Jacob Kleinsasser admitted on cross-examination that he was involved in the decision to sue. *Ibid.* at 627, 636.

Chapter 6: Going to Court
1   Notices to Vacate, Exhibits 35, 36, 37, of first trial of *Lakeside Colony v. Hofer* at 2105-9. The exhibits are found in volumes 11 and 12 of the *Case on Appeal to the S.C.C.*, Court File 22382. [Henceforth *Case on Appeal.*]
2   Exhibit 39, *ibid.* at 2112.
3   Exhibit 55, *ibid.* at 2129.
4   Statement of Claim as amended from time to time, *ibid.* at 1.
5   Notice of Motion and Affirmation of Jacob Hofer, 25 February 1987, *Wollmann v. Hofer,* Man. Q.B., *Case File CI87-01-17996.* [Henceforth *Case File.*]
6   Order of Mr. Justice Wright, 6 March 1987. *Case File.*
7   Exhibit 41, *Case on Appeal* at 2114.
8   Exhibits 42, 45, 47, *ibid.* at 2115, 2118, 2120.
9   Testimony of Joshua Hofer Jr., *ibid.* at 1085. Also see Affirmation of Jacob Hofer, 4 March 1987, in *Case File.*
10 Notice of Motion, 6 March 1987, *Case File.*
11 Exhibit 46, *Case on Appeal* at 2119.
12 Testimony of Jacob Kleinsasser, *ibid.* at 309.
13 Court Order, 16 March 1987. *Case File.*
14 *Ibid.*
15 Testimony of Michael Wollmann, *Case on Appeal* at 1263-64 and on cross-examination at 1304.
16 Affirmation of Jacob Hofer, 20 March 1987. *Case File.*
17 Notice of Motion, 24 March 1987. *Case File.*
18 Second Notice of Motion, 24 March 1987. *Case File.*
19 Affirmation of Daniel Hofer, 2 September 1988 at 2-3. *Case File.* The number affiliated with the dissenting group at that time was stated to be thirty-seven people out of the approximately seventy-five people at the colony.
20 Amended Statement of Claim, *Case on Appeal* at 1.
21 Exhibit 23, *ibid.* at 2082.
22 *Ibid.*
23 *Ibid.*
24 Affirmation of Daniel Hofer, 25 March 1987, at 9-10. *Case File.*
25 Court Orders of Mr. Justice Dureault on 1 and 2 April 1987. *Case File.*
26 Statement of Defence and Counterclaim as amended from time to time, *Case on Appeal* at 10.
27 *An Act to Incorporate the Hutterian Brethren Church,* S.C. 1951, c. 77.
28 *Supra* note 26.
29 Statement of Defence to Counterclaim, *Case on Appeal* at 22.
30 Notice of Motion, 2 May 1988. *Case File.*
31 Exhibit 51, *Case on Appeal* at 2125.
32 Exhibit 52, *ibid.* at 2126.
33 Affirmation of Daniel Hofer, 21 June 1988. *Case File.*
34 Exhibit 53, *Case on Appeal* at 2127.
35 Statement of Donald Douglas to the court, *ibid.* at 648-51.
36 Exhibit 70, *ibid.* at 2158.
37 Testimony of Daniel Hofer on redirect, *ibid.* at 1652-53.
38 Order of Justice Simonsen, 9 September 1988. *Case File.*
39 *Lakeside Colony of Hutterian Brethren v. Hofer,* [1988] M.J. No. 576 (Man. C.A.).

40 Testimony of Daniel Hofer, *Case on Appeal* at 1458.
41 See Affirmation of Jacob Hofer, 17 June 1987. *Case File.*
42 *Ibid.* at 4.
43 Notice of Motion, 17 June 1987. *Case File.*
44 Notice of Motion and Affirmation of Daniel Hofer, 29 June 1987. *Case File.*
45 Court Orders of 29 April and 4 May 1988. *Case File.*
46 R.S.M. 1987, D12.
47 Municipal documents attached to Affirmation of Jacob Hofer, 19 April 1998. *Case File.*
48 See Order of Clean Environment Commission, 30 March 1988, attached to Affirmation of Daniel Hofer, 4 May 1988. *Case File.*
49 Affirmation of Daniel Hofer, 4 May 1988. *Case File.*
50 Orders of Mr. Justice Scollin, 4 and 26 May 1988. *Case File.*
51 Exhibit 24, *Case on Appeal* at 2087.
52 Exhibit 68, *ibid.* at 2156.
53 Statement of Claim, 21 July 1988 in *Wollmann v. Hofer, Case 88-01-30823* in Man. Q.B. [Henceforth *Case File 88-01-30823.*]
54 Affidavit of Attempted Service, 2 August 1988. *Case File 88-01-30823.*
55 Affidavit of Daniel Orlikow, 30 August 1988. *Case File 88-01-30823.*
56 Court Order, 3 August 1988. *Case File 88-01-30823.*
57 Affirmation of Joshua Hofer Sr., 24 August 1988. *Case File 88-01-30823.*
58 Affirmation of Paul Hofer Sr., 2 September 1988, *Case File 88-01-30823.*
59 Court Order, 6 September 1988. *Case File 88-01-30823.*
60 Notice of Motion, 5 May 1989. *Case File 88-01-30823.* Notice of Motion, 5 May 1989. *Case File.*
61 Affirmation of Joshua Hofer Sr., 19 April 1989, at 8. *Case File.*
62 Affirmation of Daniel Hofer, 4 May 1989. *Case File 88-01-30823.*
63 Order of Mr. Justice Scollin, 5 May 1989. *Case File.*
64 Affirmation of John Hofer, 7 November 1987, *Case File.*
65 Notice of Motion, 9 November 1987. *Case File.*
66 Testimony of William Hofer, preliminary hearing, in the criminal case of *R. v. Hofer,* Transcript at 17. *Case File 88-01-05671.*
67 Affirmation of Joshua Hofer, 27 November 1987. *Case File.*
68 Testimony of Paul Hofer Jr., preliminary inquiry, *Case File 88-01-05591.*
69 Testimony of Tommy Hofer, preliminary inquiry, *ibid.*
70 Affirmation of Joshua Hofer Sr., 21 April 1988, at 3. *Case File.*
71 Affirmation of Daniel Hofer, 9 May 1988. *Case File.*
72 Affirmation of Jacob Hofer, 19 April 1998, at 4. *Case File.* In the overseer camp, there were two charges of assault and two charges of mischief laid against Gary Hofer, two charges of assault against Joseph Hofer, and one charge of intercepting communications against Ken Hofer. In the dissenter camp, there was a charge of assault against Larry Hofer, a charge of assault against Paul Hofer Jr., a charge of theft against Paul Wayne Hofer, a charge of breach of restraining order against Larry Hofer and also against Daniel Hofer Jr.
73 Affirmation of Daniel Hofer, 29 April 1988. *Case File.*
74 Notice of Motion, 19 April 1988. *Case File.*
75 Notice of Motion, 9 March 1988. *Case File.*
76 Affirmation of Jacob Hofer, 19 April 1998, at 3. *Case File.*
77 Court Orders, Mr. Justice Scollin, 29 April and 4 May 1988. *Case File.*
78 Affirmation of Paul Hofer, 9 May 1988. *Case File.*
79 Affirmation of Isaac Hofer, 10 May 1988, at 4-6. *Case File.*
80 See *R. v. Hofer and Hofer, Case File 88-01-04468 and 69.* See also Kevin Rollason, "Hutterite Fined $150 for Assault" *Winnipeg Free Press,* referring to incidence on 5 May 1988.
81 List attached to the Affirmation of Joshua Hofer Jr., 20 April 1989. *Case File.*
82 Letter from Crown Attorney L.H. Kee to Michael Radcliffe, 1 March 1989, attached to Affirmation of Joshua Hofer Jr., 20 April 1989. *Case File.*
83 Affirmation of Joshua Hofer Sr., 19 April 1989. *Case File.*
84 Affirmation of Daniel Hofer Sr., 4 May 1989. *Case File.*

85   Twelve-volume *Case on Appeal to the Supreme Court of Canada,* Court File 22382.

86   As reported in the *Canadian Press Newswire.* There was daily coverage of the trial. See *Canadian Press Newswire,* 20 June through 13 July 1989.

87   Statement of Murray, *Case on Appeal* at 65.

88   *Ibid.* at 68.

89   Victor Peters, *All Things Common: The Hutterian Way of Life* (Minneapolis: University of Minnesota, 1965). The fieldwork for the book was done in the 1950s.

90   Testimony of Dr. Peters, *Case on Appeal* at 97.

91   Testimony of Dr. Peters, *ibid.* at 104.

92   *Ibid.* at 121-22.

93   *Ibid.* at 147-48.

94   Testimony of Rev. Arnold, *ibid.* at 183.

95   Exhibit 133, *ibid.* at 2295.

96   Testimony of Rev. Arnold, *ibid.* at 205-9.

97   Evidence of Rev. Arnold on cross-examination, *ibid.* at 217-22.

98   *Ibid.* at 222.

99   *Ibid.* at 222-23.

100 Testimony of Jacob Kleinsasser, *ibid.* at 355-60.

101 Testimony of Jacob Kleinsasser on cross-examination, *ibid.* at 628.

102 *Ibid.* at 630-31.

103 *Ibid.* at 717-18.

104 *Hofer v. Hofer* (1970), 73 W.W.R. 644 (S.C.C.).

105 *Canadian Press Newswire,* 21 June 1989.

106 *Canadian Press Newswire,* 22 June 1989. Repeated in story on 23 June 1989.

107 Terry Weber quoting Michael Radcliffe, "Judge Reserves Expulsion Ruling" *Winnipeg Free Press* (14 July 1989) at 12.

108 *Canadian Press Newswire,* 11 July 1989.

109 *The Chronicle of the Hutterian Brethren, Volume I* (Rifton, NY: Plough Publishing, 1987).

110 *Ibid.* at 103-4.

111 *Case on Appeal* at 382-85.

112 Testimony of Mike Wollmann on cross-examination, *ibid.* at 1333-34. Interpolation is in official transcript.

113 For example, Wilma Derksen, "Hutterite Conflicts Exposed in Court" *Mennonite Reporter* (10 July 1989) at 1.

114 Harold Jantz, "Hutterite Trial Tests the Fabric of Communal Vision" *Christian Week* (8 August 1989).

115 James R. Coggins, "Hutterites Find Revolutionary Faith Hard to Live in Good Times" *Mennonite Reporter* (29 August 1989).

116 *Case on Appeal* at 1779.

117 *Lakeside Colony v. Hofer* (1989), 63 D.L.R. (4th) 473 at 481.

118 *Canadian Press Newswire,* 12 July 1989.

119 *Canadian Press Newswire,* 13 July 1989.

120 *Lakeside Colony of Hutterian Brethren v. Hofer* (1989), 63 D.L.R. (4th) 473 (Man. Q.B.).

121 *Ibid.* at 481.

122 *Ibid.* at 482-83.

123 *Ibid.* at 484.

124 *Ibid.*

125 *Ibid.* at 482.

126 *Articles of Association of Lakeside, Case on Appeal,* at 1996.

127 *Constitution of the Hutterian Brethren Church and Rules as to Community of Property,* 1950, *Case on Appeal* at 2023.

128 *Supra* note 120 at 477.

129 *Ibid.* at 486.

130 *Ibid.* at 487.

131 *Ibid.* at 488.

132 Bill of Costs. *Case File.*

133 Aldo Santin, "Hutterites' Rule Upheld" *Winnipeg Free Press* (1 November 1989) at 8.

134 *Business Wire News*, 7 November 1989.

135 *Canadian Press Newswire*, 1 November 1989.

136 Wilma Derksen, "Give Final Arguments" *Mennonite Reporter* (31 July 1989).

Chapter 7: Lakeside under Appeal

1 Notice of Appeal, available in Provincial Archives of Manitoba, File 524/89. [Henceforth *Appeal Case 524/89.*]

2 Affirmation of Josh Hofer Jr., 17 January 1990. *Case File.*

3 Affirmation of Daniel Hofer, 19 January 1990. *Case File.*

4 *Supra* note 2.

5 Order of Mr. Justice Ferg, 12 February 1990. *Case File.*

6 Affirmation of Daniel Hofer, 22 February 1990. *Case File.* Affirmation of Ken Hofer, 14 February 1990. *Case File.*

7 Notice of Motion, 20 February 1990. *Case File.*

8 See "Colony Fails Again to Expel Renegade" *Winnipeg Free Press* (28 February 1990) at 10.

9 Order of Mr. Justice DeGraves, 2 March 1990. *Case File.*

10 Affirmation of Josh Hofer Jr., 30 March 1990. *Case File.*

11 *Factum of the Appellant* (Defendants), filed, 8 May 1990, *Appeal Case File 524/89.*

12 *Ibid.* at 59.

13 *Ibid.* at 51.

14 *Factum of the Respondents (Plaintiffs)* at 18. *Appeal Case File 524/89.*

15 Terry Weber, "Expulsion Battle Tearing Colony Apart" *Winnipeg Free Press* (25 May 1990) at 15.

16 Affirmation of Josh Hofer Jr., 18 June 1990. *Case File.*

17 Court Order, 20 June 1990. *Case File.*

18 Notice of Motion, 26 July 1990. *Case File.*

19 Affirmation of Joshua Hofer Sr., 25 July 1990. *Case File.*

20 *Ibid.* at 4.

21 Affirmation of Daniel Hofer, 26 July 1990. *Case File.*

22 Unreported reasons for decision, Mr. Justice DeGraves, 23 July 1990, as certified and corrected on 26 July 1990. *Case File.*

23 *Ibid.*

24 Notice of Appeal, Man. C.A., *Case File AI90-30-00324.* For some reason, this court pocket is currently empty of all documentation.

25 Affirmation of Daniel Hofer Jr., 16 October 1990. *Case File.*

26 Affirmation of Isaac Hofer, 11 October 1990, at 5-6. *Case File.*

27 *Supra* note 25 at 5-6.

28 *Ibid.* at 7.

29 Affirmation of William Hofer, 11 October 1990. *Case File.*

30 Notice of Motion, 16 October 1990. *Case File.*

31 Notice of Motion, 17 October 1990. *Case File.*

32 Order of Mr. Justice Morse, 18 October 1990. *Case File.*

33 Order of Mr. Justice Ferg, 6 December 1990. *Case File.*

34 Notice of Intention to Act in Person, 21 November 1990. *Case File.*

35 Affirmation of Joshua Hofer Sr., and Notice of Motion, 5 December 1990. *Case File.*

36 Order of Mr. Justice Ferg, 19 December 1990. *Case File.*

37 *Ibid.* at 3.

38 Notice of Appeal, 21 December 1990. Man. C.A., *Case File AI90-30-00469.*

39 Order of Mr. Justice Huband, 28 December 1990. *Ibid.*

40 *Lakeside Colony v. Hofer* (1991), 77 D.L.R. (4th) 202 (Man. C.A.).

41 *Ibid.* at 214-18.

42 *Ibid.* at 218.

43 *Ibid.* at 219.

44 *Ibid.* at 211-14.

45 *Ibid.* at 236.

46 *Ibid.* at 230.

47 *Ibid.* at 231.

48 *Ibid.* at 233.
49 *Ibid.* at 227-28.
50 *Ibid.* at 235.
51 *Ibid.*
52 Nick Martin, "Maverick Vows to Remain" *Winnipeg Free Press* (10 February 1991) at 1.
53 Notice of Motion, and Affirmation of Josh Hofer, 29 January 1991. *Case File.*
54 Notice of Motion, 29 January 1991. *Appeal Case File 524/89.*
55 Order of Mr. Justice Twaddle, 31 January 1991. *Appeal Case File* 524/89.
56 *Ibid.*
57 Terry Weber, "Renegade Hutterites' Expulsion Put on Hold" *Winnipeg Free Press* (1 February 1991) at 2.
58 Affirmation of Josh Hofer Sr., 27 August 1991. *Appeal Case File 524/89.*
59 Affirmation of Josh Hofer Jr., 27 August 1991. *Appeal Case File 524/89.*
60 Affirmation of Daniel Hofer Sr., 29 August 1991. *Appeal Case File 524/89.*
61 Order of Mr. Justice Ferg, 19 December 1990. *Case File.*
62 Affirmation of Josh Hofer Sr., 22 December 1990. *Case File.*
63 Order of Mr. Justice Ferg, 7 February 1991. *Case File.*
64 "Hofer Equipment Towed from Colony," *Winnipeg Free Press* (10 February 1991) at 4.
65 Notice of Appeal, 20 February 1991. Man. C.A., *Case File AI90-30-00070.*
66 Affirmation of Josh Hofer Jr., 25 February 1991. *Appeal Case File AI90-30-00070.*
67 Affirmation of Daniel Hofer Sr., 20 February 1991. *Ibid.*
68 Order of Mr. Justice Twaddle, 28 February 1991. *Ibid.*
69 Notice of Motion, 7 March 1991. *Case File.*
70 Affidavit of William R. Murray, 7 March 1991. *Case File.*
71 Donna Carreiro, "Trouble in the Colony" *Winnipeg Sun* (14 March 1991) at 3.
72 Notice of Motion, Daniel Hofer Sr., 13 March 1991. *Case File.*
73 Affirmation of Josh Hofer Jr., 18 March 1991. *Case File.*
74 Affirmation of Daniel Hofer Sr., 22 March 1991. *Case File.*
75 *Canadian Press Newswire,* 31 March 1991.
76 *Daniel Hofer v. Wally Stratochuk,* Manitoba Small Claims, *Case File 91-01-27678.*
77 *Paul Hofer v. Wally Stratochuk,* Manitoba Small Claims, *Case File 91-01-27679.*
78 Notice of Motion and Affirmation, Daniel Hofer, 15 April 1991. *Case File.*
79 Terry Weber, "Court Refuses Bid to Bar Judge from Hofer Case" *Winnipeg Free Press* (23 April 1991) at 8.
80 See Nick Martin, "Wreckers Cry Foul over Hutterite Firm" *Winnipeg Free Press* (date lost by author).
81 *South Interlake Planning District Board v. Block and Hofer,* Statement of Claim, Manitoba Queen's Bench, *Case File 91-01-54765.*
82 Affidavit of Thor Sigurdson, 22 May 1991. *Ibid.*
83 Order of Mr. Justice Kroft, 30 May 1991. *Ibid.* Also found at [1991] M.J. No. 335.
84 Order of Mr. Justice Hanssen, 26 June 1991. *Ibid.*
85 Affidavit of Reeve R. John Miller, 30 October 1991. *Ibid.*
86 Affidavit of Brian Savage, 24 October 1991. *Ibid.*
87 As to service of documents, see Affidavit of Service of Thor Sigurdson, 18 December 1991. As to foul language, see Affidavit of Brian Savage, 24 October 1991. *Ibid.*
88 *South Lake Interlake Planning District Board v. Block and Hofer* (1992), 80 Man. R. (2d) 168 at 171-72 (Q.B.).
88 Correspondence of Brian Savage, 11 July 1992. *Case File 91-01-54765.*
90 Affirmation of Daniel Hofer, 2 September 1992. *Ibid.*
91 Notice of Motion, 12 August 1992. *Ibid.*
92 Order of Mr. Justice Kroft, 3 September 1992. *Ibid.*
93 Affirmation of Kenneth Hofer, 5 March 1992. *Case File.*
94 *Ibid.*
95 Affirmation of Josh Hofer Sr., 17 July 1992. *Case File.*
96 Order of Mr. Justice Wright, 22 July 1992. *Case File.*
97 *Lakeside Colony v. Hofer* (1992), 97 D.L.R. (4th) 17; [1992] 3 S.C.R. 165; 142 N.R. 241; [1993] 1 W.W.R. 113; 81 Man. R. (2d) 1; 30 W.A.C. 1.

98 *Supra* note 40.
99 *Lakeside v. Hofer* (1992), 97 D.L.R. (4th) 17 at 20 (S.C.C.).
100 *Ibid.*
101 *Ibid.* at 21.
102 S.C. 1951, c. 77.
103 Exhibit 3, *Case on Appeal* at 2023.
104 Article 6, *ibid.*
105 Articles 20, 23, *ibid.*
106 Article 46, *ibid.*
107 Article 39, *Articles of Association of Lakeside Colony of Hutterian Brethren*, 12 November 1971. *Case on Appeal* at 1996.
108 Article 12, *ibid.* My emphasis.
109 *Supra* note 99 at 32.
110 *Ibid.* at 33.
111 *Supra* note 102.
112 *Supra* note 99 at 31.
113 *Ibid.* at 35.
114 *Ibid.* at 61.
115 *Ibid.* at 36.
116 *Ibid.* at 36.
117 *Ibid.* at 55.
118 *Ibid.* at 56.
119 *Ibid.*
120 *Ibid.* at 55.
121 *Ibid.* at 59, 60, 62.
122 *Ibid.* at 37.
123 Bill to Lakeside, 30 November 1992, attached to Affidavit of Donald Douglas, 26 September 1994. *Case File.*
124 "Hutterite Expulsions Unfair, Supreme Court of Canada Rules" *Canadian Press Newswire* (29 October 1992).
125 Paul Samyn, "Rebel Hutterites Vindicated" *Winnipeg Free Press* (30 October 1992).

Chapter 8: Lakeside and the Schism within the Schmiedeleut

1 Douglas letter, *Agreed Documents* in second trial of *Wollmann v. Hofer*, Man. Q.B. at 23-24. On file with author. [Henceforth *Agreed Documents*.] The author was present at the counsel table with Donald Douglas at the second-round trial but took no formal part in the proceedings.
2 *Agreed Documents* at 25.
3 *Lakeside Colony v. Hofer* (1992), 97 D.L.R. (4th) 17 at 58 (S.C.C.).
4 Hofer letter, *Agreed Documents*, at 29-31.
5 Exhibit 4, in trial of *Wollmann v. Hofer*, Man. Q.B. On file with author.
6 Exhibit 17, in trial of *Wollmann v. Hofer*, Man. Q.B. On file with author.
7 *Ibid.*
8 Minutes, *Agreed Documents*, at 33-35.
9 Exhibits 7-10, at trial of *Wollmann v. Hofer*. Man. Q.B. On file with author.
10 Gibb's manuscript is entitled "Summary of Transactions Involving Rosedale Hutterian Brethren, Inc.; Mike Waldner, Millbrook Hutterian Brethren, Inc.; and Jacob Kleinsasser, Crystal Spring Colony Farms, Ltd. (From 1982 to the Present)." On file with author. [Henceforth *Gibb Manuscript.*]
11 For example, in Manitoba, see *Crystal Spring Colony Farms v. Consumers Savings Bank*, Man. Q.B., *Case File 84-01-02502*; and *H.B. Enterprises v. Leslie and Don Edel and Valley Agro Services*, Man. Q.B., *Case File 85-01-07666*.
12 Covering letter, *Gibb Manuscript* at 2 and 6.
13 Letter from Radcliffe to Esau, 7 August 2001, at 1. [Henceforth *Radcliffe Comments.*]
14 Pretrial memorandum, on behalf of Edel and Valley Agro, 13 June 1989, in *H.B. Enterprises v. Leslie and Don Edel and Valley Agro Services*, Man. Q.B., *Case File 85-01-07666*. [Henceforth *Edel Case File.*]

15 *Gibb Manuscript*, Exhibit 2.
16 *Gibb Manuscript* at 13.
17 *Gibb Manuscript*, Exhibit 3.
18 *Ibid.*, Exhibit 4.
19 *Ibid.*, Exhibits 5 and 6.
20 *Gibb Manuscript* at 18.
21 *Ibid.* at 20.
22 *Ibid.* at 4.
23 *Radcliffe Comments* at 12.
24 *Gibb Manuscript*, Exhibit 13.
25 Examination for Discovery of Mike Waldner, 20 October 1986, at 24. *Edel Case File.*
26 *Gibb Manuscript*, Exhibit 25.
27 *Supra* note 25 at 80.
28 *Gibb Manuscript* at 8.
29 *Radcliffe Comments* at 12.
30 *Gibb Manuscript* at 15.
31 *Ibid.* Appendix 5, List of Investments.
32 *Ibid.* at 18.
33 See, for example, *People v. Alfred Deleo* (1992), 585 N.Y.S.2d 629 (App. Div.) Appeal of con-
    viction for forgery, perjury, and grand larceny. Appeal denied.
34 As he admitted in *Supra* note 25 at 148.
35 See, for example, *Rosedale Hutterian Brethren v. Harold Cornell* (1987), 521 N.Y.S.2d 10. Ap-
    peal from summary judgment denied.
36 *Gibb Manuscript* at 9.
37 *Ibid.* Appendix 3, Cast of Characters, at 5.
38 *Supra* note 25 at 22.
39 *Gibb Manuscript* at 30.
40 *Ibid.* at 37.
41 *Ibid.* at 30.
42 *Supra* note 25 at 24.
43 *Ibid.* at 43.
44 *Gibb Manuscript* at 33.
45 *Ibid.* at 24.
46 *Crystal Spring Colony Farms v. Consumer Savings Bank*, Man. Q.B., *Case File 84-01-02502.*
47 Statement of Claim and Notice of Motion, 24 September 1984. *Ibid.*
48 *Gibb Manuscript* at 25.
49 For a detailed account see *Gibb Manuscript* at 47-51.
50 Gibb lists nine lawsuits in Appendix 7.
51 *Supra* note 14.
52 Statement of Claim, 8 November 1985. *Edel Case File.*
53 Statement of Defence and Counterclaim, 23 December 1985. *Edel Case File.*
54 The case was not formally concluded until a notice of discontinuance was filed on 21
    August 1996. *Edel Case File.*
55 Minutes of Settlement, 21 August 1991. *Edel Case File.*
56 Documents in the file were sealed as recently as 8 February 1999. Notation in *Edel Case File.*
57 *Supra* note 55 at 4-5.
58 Affidavit of Leslie Edel, 20 October 1993. *Edel Case File.*
59 *Valley Agro Services Ltd., Leslie Edel and Donald Edel v. H.B. Enterprises Ltd. and Jacob Kleinsasser,*
    Man. Q.B., *Case File CI93-01-75461.* [Henceforth *Edel Case File 2.*]
60 Statement of Claim, Notice of Motion, 22 October 1993. *Edel Case File 2.*
61 Statement of Defence, 30 November 1994, and Affirmation of Jacob Kleinsasser, 24 January
    1995. *Edel Case File 2.*
62 Notice of Motion, Motions Brief, 13 June 1995. *Edel Case File 2.*
63 Affidavit of Leslie Edel, 12 June 1995. *Edel Case File 2.*
64 Order of Justice Duval, 25 August 1995. *Edel Case File.*
65 *Gibb Manuscript* at 45.

66 *Ibid.* at 57.
67 As first mentioned to me about a decade ago by Professor Bass, Faculty of Law, University of Manitoba.
68 For an extended account of what he considered the misuse of shunning and church discipline by the senior elder and other Group One leaders, see Samuel Kleinsasser, *Community and Ethics* (1998) [unpublished, on file with author].
69 Minutes of Meeting, at Hodgeville Colony, Saskatchewan, 17 July 1980. On file with author.
70 Minutes of Meeting, Bernard, Manitoba, 9 August 1978. On file with author.
71 Minutes of Meeting, Parkland, Alberta, 28 July 1982. On file with author.
72 Minutes of Meeting, Milltown, Manitoba, 17 July 1984. On file with author.
73 Minutes of Meeting, Bernard, Manitoba, 8 October 1987. On file with author.
74 Minutes of Meeting, Lakeside, Alberta, 16 August 1989. On file with author.
75 Letter of 11 December 1990. On file with author.
76 *Ibid.*
77 Minutes of Meeting, Clearview, Alberta, 17 July 1991. On file with author.
78 Brian Preston, "Jacob's Ladder" *Saturday Night* (April 1992) 30.
79 *Ibid.* at 34.
80 After the schism, Pine Creek became a Group Two colony.
81 *Radcliffe Comments* at 13.
82 Preston, *supra* note 78 at 76.
83 After the schism, Rainbow is still a colony hot spot and not yet clearly associated with either Group One or Group Two. Interview with Mike Hofer, Group Two leader, 1 August 2000. No legal action was ever taken against Rainbow Colony.
84 *Supra* note 78 at 77.
85 *Ibid.* at 38.
86 See Affirmation of Jacob T. Maendel, 23 September 1991, in *Jake Maendel v. Jacob Maendel,* Man. Q.B., *Case File CI91-01-56943.* [Henceforth *Oak Bluff Case File.*]
87 Examination of Jake H. Maendel, 30 September 1991, at 58. *Oak Bluff Case File.*
88 Based on information in the *Oak Bluff Case File.*
89 Kleinsasser, *supra* note 68 at 108.
90 *Ibid.* at 109.
91 See Stevens Wild, "Colony Children Victims: Lawyer" *Winnipeg Free Press* (12 September 1991) at 2; Terry Weber "Hutterite Factions Joust over School" *Winnipeg Free Press* (13 September 1991) at 12; Zena Olijnyk, "You Must Make Peace, Judge Tells Hutterites" *Winnipeg Free Press* (10 October 1991).
92 Statement of Claim, 21 August 1991. *Oak Bluff Case File.*
93 Notice of Motion, 29 August 1991. *Oak Bluff Case File.*
94 Affirmation of minister, Jacob T. Maendel, 4 September 1991. Affirmation of German schoolteacher, Joseph Waldner, 10 September 1991. *Oak Bluff Case File.*
95 Affirmations of dissenters, 22 September 1991. *Oak Bluff Case File.*
96 Olijnyk, *supra* note 91.
97 Transcript of examination, 30 September 1991, at 8-9. *Oak Bluff Case File.*
98 Affirmation of Jacob T. Maendel, 23 September 1991. *Oak Bluff Case File.*
99 Responding Parties Brief, 10 September 1992, at 4. *Oak Bluff Case File.*
100 Notice of Motion, and various affirmations, 28 August 1992. *Oak Bluff Case File.*
101 Order of Mr. Justice DeGraves, 6 October 1992. *Oak Bluff Case File.*
102 Kevin Rollason, "Hutterite Colony Ordered to Return Classroom Trailer" *Winnipeg Free Press* (1992) (day and month unknown).
103 Untranslated letters dated 20 and 26 August 1992. On file with author.
104 Translated version, Exhibit 58, at trial of *Wollmann v. Hofer.* [Henceforth *Lakeside Trial 2.*]
105 *Ibid.*
106 Testimony of Leonard Kleinsasser, minister of Delta Colony. Author's Notes, Book Three at 43. *Lakeside Trial 2.* While I rely on my notes, there is a transcript of the second trial available in the Court of Appeal files at the provincial Archives. See Man. C.A., *Case File AI94-30-01810.*

107 *Ibid.* at 46.
108 As best I can determine from the untranslated letter of Joseph Wipf, 19 November 1992. On file with author.
109 Letter of Darius and Lehrer elders, 1 December 1992. On file with author.
110 *Ibid.* The term "Vetter" is a common Hutterian expression of respect for an elder.
111 Fax from Woodcrest, 28 November 1992. On file with author.
112 Testimony of Leonard Kleinsasser, Author's Notes, Book Three at 47. *Lakeside Trial 2.*
113 Exhibit 28, *Lakeside Trial 2.*
114 Testimony of Leonard Kleinsasser, Author's Notes, Book Three at 48. *Lakeside Trial 2.*
115 *Ibid.* at 50-52.
116 Minutes of Meeting, Exhibit 23, *Lakeside Trial 2.*
117 Testimony of Leonard Kleinsasser, Author's Notes, Book Three at 52. *Lakeside Trial 2.*
118 See "Hutterite Majority in Manitoba Rejects Kleinsasser Leadership" *Mennonite Reporter* (28 December 1992) at 3.
119 Testimony of Wollmann, Author's Notes, Book One at 46. *Lakeside Trial 2.*
120 Testimony of Hofer, Author's Notes, Book Two at 29. *Lakeside Trial 2.*
121 Minutes of Meeting, Exhibit E, *Lakeside Trial 2.*
122 Minutes of Meeting, Exhibit 23, *Lakeside Trial 2.*
123 Exhibit 29, *Lakeside Trial 2.*
124 Reply from Woodcrest, 14 December 1992. On file with author.
125 Wilma Derksen, "Majority of Hutterite Colonies Rally Around New Constitution" *Mennonite Reporter* (1 November 1993) at 3.
126 See Samuel Kleinsasser, "An Open Letter to the Hutterian Church," fifty-eight-page manuscript plus approximately twenty-page addendum, on file with author.
127 Letter of Bishop Jacob Kleinsasser, 29 April 1993, as found between pages 162 and 163 of Samuel Kleinsasser, *supra* note 68.
128 Samuel Kleinsasser, *ibid.* at 145.
129 Interview with Mike Hofer, Group Two leader, 1 August 2000.
130 An account of this is provided in Aiden Enns, "Hutterites Take Steps to Divide" *Mennonite Reporter* (19 April 1993) at 3.
131 *Ibid.*
132 Events as recounted by Mike Hofer, Sommerfeld Colony. Interview with author, 1 August 2000.
133 See Sidney Wolchock, "Legal Matters and Documents," on file with author. This report was given to the author by Prof. Burton Bass.
134 That Wolchock came up with the process was confirmed by Mike Hofer in interview with author, 1 August 2000.
135 Letter of Rev. John Wipf, president and senior elder of the Hutterian Brethren Church, Parkland Colony, 7 April 1993. On file with author.
136 Minutes of Meeting of 9 June 1993, Exhibit 39, *Lakeside Trial 2.*
137 Reaffirmation, Exhibit 30, *Lakeside Trial 2.*
138 Radcliffe letter of 25 June 1993, Exhibit 43, *Lakeside Trial 2.*
139 Reported in Minutes of Meeting of the Managers of the Hutterian Brethren Church, 21 July 1993. Exhibit D, *Lakeside Trial 2.*
140 *Radcliffe Comments* at 14.
141 These numbers taken from *James Valley Switchboard Address Book, 2000*, which lists all the colonies, and from a list of Group Two colonies provided by Mike Hofer, 1 August 2000. On file with author.
142 Exhibit C, *Lakeside Trial 2.*
143 *Constitution of the Hutterian Brethren Church and Rules as to Community of Property*, Macleod Dixon. Dated effective 21 July 1993. Exhibit 41, *Lakeside Trial 2.*
144 Minutes of Meetings of 13 July 1993, Exhibit 44, *Lakeside Trial 2.*
145 Radcliffe letter, Exhibit 45, *Lakeside Trial 2.* Also correspondence from Philip Matkin of Macleod Dixon as to the representations by the Baker Radcliffe firm is found in the *Precision Feeds v. Rock Lake*, Man. Q.B., *Case File CI93-01-75639.*
146 Minutes of Meeting, Exhibit 46, *Lakeside Trial 2.*

147 *Ibid.* at 6.
148 For example, Letter of Radcliffe to Mr. Ernst, Minister of Consumer and Corporate Affairs, 14 September 1994. On file with author.
149 Exhibit 20, *Lakeside Trial 2.*
150 Letters Patent, 27 June 1996.
151 Supplementary Letters Patent, 20 June 2000. On file with author.
152 *Ibid.*
153 1993 Constitution, *supra* note 142. Definitions, Article 1.
154 *Ibid.*, Article 7.
155 *Ibid.*, Article 22.
156 Article 6 of *1950 Constitution.*
157 *Ibid.*, Article 8.
158 *Ibid.*, Article 21.
159 Article 24 of *1950 Constitution.*
160 *Ibid.*, Article 46.

Chapter 9: Litigating Again at Lakeside

1 Hofer letter, Exhibit 18, *Lakeside Trial 2.*
2 Hofer letter of 27 January 1993, *Agreed Documents*, at 37-38, *Lakeside Trial 2.*
3 Hofer letter, on file with author.
4 *Michael Wollmann, Jacob Hofer and Joshua Hofer, in their representative capacity for and on behalf of Lakeside Colony of Hutterian Brethren, Lakeside Holding Co. Ltd. and Lakeside Colony Ltd. v. Daniel Hofer Sr., Daniel Hofer Jr., David Hofer and Paul Hofer Sr.* Statement of Claim, 29 April 1993. Man. Q.B., *Case File CI93-01-71212.* [Henceforth *Case File 2.*]
5 *Michael Wollmann, Jacob Hofer and Joshua Hofer, in their representative capacity for and on behalf of Lakeside Colony of Hutterian Brethren, Lakeside Holding Co. Ltd. and Lakeside Colony Ltd. v. Leonard Hofer, Paul Wayne Hofer, and Paul K. Hofer.* Man. Q.B., *Case File CI93-01-71213.* [Henceforth *Case File 93-71213.*]
6 Letter from Michael Radcliffe to Donald Douglas responding to questions from the examination of Joshua Hofer, 10 June 1993. *Case File 2.*
7 *R. v. Joseph Hofer*, Man. Q.B., *Case File 88-01-04370.*
8 *Administrative Facilities v. Hutterian Brethren Church and Lakeside Colony of Hutterian Brethren,* Statement of Claim, 17 May 1993. Man. Q.B., *Case File CI-93-01-71650.*
9 Notice of Motion, 29 April 1993. *Case File 93-71213.*
10 As indicated by Joshua Hofer Jr. on cross-examination on an affidavit, 26 May 1993. *Case File 93-71213.*
11 Order of Mr. Justice Smith. *Case File 93-71213.*
12 Statement of Defence, 10 May 1993, p. 6. *Case File 93-71213.*
13 Notice of Motion and Affidavit, 13 May 1993. *Case File 93-71213.*
14 Affirmation of Joshua Hofer Jr., 19 May 1993. *Case File 93-71213.*
15 These facts are related by Joshua Hofer Jr. on cross-examination on an affidavit, 26 May 1993. *Case File 2.* Josh disputed that the trailer had no running water, because there was an underground water tank that he claimed Paul Hofer Jr. could fill. Obviously, the colony was not going to fill the tank for him.
16 Order of Mr. Justice Oliphant. *Case File 93-71213.*
17 Joshua Hofer Jr. on cross-examination on an affidavit, 26 May 1993, *Case File 93-71213.*
18 Affirmation of Josh Hofer Sr., 4 May 1993. *Case File 2.*
19 *Ibid.* at 3-4.
20 Notice of Motion, 20 May 1993. *Case File 2.*
21 Letter of Douglas. Exhibit 1, *Agreed Documents*, p. 39. *Lakeside Trial 2.*
22 Notice of Motion, 2 June 1993. *Case File 2.*
23 *Lakeside Colony of Hutterian Brethren v. Hofer* (1993), 87 M.R. (2d) 216 (Man. Q.B.).
24 Receiving Order, 18 June 1993. *Case File 2.*
25 *Supra* note 23 at para. 5. My emphasis.
26 Notice of Appeal, 5 July 1993. *Case File 2* and *Lakeside Colony of Hetterian Brethren v. Hofer,* Man. C.A., *Case File 93-30-01319.*

27   Letter of Douglas. 8 June 1993. *Agreed Documents,* p. 41.
28   For example, Group Two leaders would be concerned with willingness to submit to the collective will and nonviolence.
29   Author's Notes, Book Three at 62.
30   *Ibid.* at 64.
31   *Ibid.* at 66.
32   Exhibit 64, *Lakeside Trial 2.*
33   Letter of John Hofer, Exhibit 65, *Lakeside Trial 2.*
34   *Administrative Facilities Ltd. v. Hutterian Brethren Church,* Notice of Discontinuance, 19 July 1993. *Case File CI93-01-71650.*
35   Letter of Taylor to Hofer, 23 July 1993. On file with author.
36   *Ibid.*
37   Letters of Mr. Taylor, 23 July and 6 August 1993, Exhibits 66 and 67, *Lakeside Trial 2.*
38   Letter of Mr. Taylor to Daniel Hofer, 6 August 1993. On file with author.
39   Letter of Daniel Hofer to Taylor, 5 August 1993, Exhibit 68, *Lakeside Trial 2.*
40   *Administrative Facilities Ltd. v. Hutterian Brethren Church,* Statement of Defence, 3 September 1993. *Case File CI-93-01-71650.*
41   Statement of Defence and Counterclaim, 20 October 1993. *Case File 2.*
42   *Ibid.* at 6.
43   *Ibid.* at 10.
44   Author's Notes, Book One at 24. *Lakeside Trial 2.*
45   *Ibid.* at 36, 37.
46   *Ibid.* at 39.
47   *Ibid.* at 43.
48   *Ibid.* at 22.
49   *Ibid.* at 48.
50   *Ibid.* at 49.
51   Testimony of Jacob Hofer, Author's Notes, Book Two at 22. *Lakeside Trial 2.*
52   *Ibid.* at 25.
53   *Ibid.* at 63.
54   *Ibid.* at 79-81.
55   *Ibid.* at 113.
56   *Ibid.* at 99.
57   Exhibit 63, *Lakeside Trial 2.*
58   Author's Notes, Book Three at 102-5. *Lakeside Trial 2.*
59   *Ibid.* at 111.
60   *Ibid.* at 123.
61   Peter Riedemann, *Confession of Faith* (Rifton, NY: Plough Publishing, 1970) at 112-14. *Confession* was originally published in 1545.
62   Author's Notes, Book Five at 1. *Lakeside Trial 2.*
63   *Ibid.* at 7.
64   *Ibid.* at 12.
65   Articles of Association, Exhibit 1, *Lakeside Trial 1.*
66   Author's Notes, Book Five at 18. *Lakeside Trial 2.*
67   *Lakeside Colony of Hutterian Brethren v. Hofer* (1994), 93 Man. R. (2d) 161 (Man. Q.B.).
68   *Ibid.* at 171.
69   *Ibid.* at 173.
70   *Ibid.* at 174.
71   *Ibid.*
72   *Ibid.* at 176.
73   *Ibid.* at 164.
74   *Ibid.* at 176.
75   Plaintiffs Submission, 25 April 1994. *Case File 2.*
76   *Lakeside Colony v. Hofer* (1994), 98 Man. R. (2d) 81 (Man. Q.B.).
77   Order of Mr. Justice DeGraves, 13 May 1994. *Case File 2.*
78   Notice of Appeal, 24 June 1994. Man. C.A., *Case File AI94-30-01810.*

79 Notice of Cross-Appeal, 27 June 1994. *Case File 2*.
80 Assessment Certificate, 31 August 1994. *Case File 1*.
81 Notice of Motion, 13 September 1994. *Case File 1*.
82 Affirmation of Joshua Hofer Jr., 21 September 1994. *Case File 1*.

Chapter 10: Litigating at Rock Lake, Huron, Cypress, Sprucewood, Poinsett, and Leaving Lakeside

1 One account of the Rock Lake conflict is found in Samuel Kleinsasser, *Community and Ethics* (1998) [unpublished, on file with author] at 163-72.
2 Confirmation of Meetings of 24 June and 6 July 1993 attached to Affirmation of Ben Hofer, 12 November 1993, in *Precision Feeds Limited v. Rock Lake Colony Ltd.*, Man. Q.B., *Case File CI93-01-75639*. [Henceforth *Rock Lake Case File*.]
3 First Report of the Receiver/Manager, 23 March 1994, at 5. *Rock Lake Case File*.
4 *The Corporations Act*, R.S.M. 1987, c. C223.
5 *Ibid.*, section 234(3).
6 Notice of Application and Affirmation of Peter Vis, 4 November 1993. *Rock Lake Case File*.
7 Affirmation of Ben Hofer, 12 November 1993. *Rock Lake Case File*.
8 Affirmation of Sam Hofer, 14 January 1994. *Rock Lake Case File*.
9 Affirmation of David Hofer, 16 November 1993. *Rock Lake Case File*.
10 Affirmation, *supra* note 6.
11 *Precision Feeds v. Rock Lake Colony* (1994), 93 Man. R. (2d) 1 at 4. (Man. Q.B.).
12 *Ibid.* at 7.
13 Affirmation of Ben Hofer, 10 January 1994. *Rock Lake Case File*.
14 Court Order, 11 January 1994. *Rock Lake Case File*.
15 Notice of Motion, 21 January 1994. *Rock Lake Case File*.
16 Notice of Motion, 21 January 1994. *Rock Lake Case File*.
17 For example, Interpleader Notice of Motion by Westburne Industry, 6 January 1994. *Rock Lake Case File*.
18 *Precision Feeds Ltd. v. Rock Lake Colony Ltd.* (1994), 93 Man. R. (2d) 10 (Q.B.).
19 Court Order, 8 February 1994. *Rock Lake Case File*.
20 *Supra* note 18 at 12.
21 Notice of Motion, 14 February 1994. *Rock Lake Case File*.
22 Notice of Appeal, 16 February 1994. Man. C.A., *Case File AI94-30-01641*.
23 *Precision Feeds v. Rock Lake Colony*, (1994), 93 Man. R. (2d) 13 (Q.B.).
24 *Ibid.* at 18.
25 *Precision Feeds v. Rock Lake Colony* (1994), 92 Man. R. (2d) 292 (Man. C.A.).
26 *Supra* note 3 at 4.
27 Affirmation of Sam Hofer, 2 August 1994. *Rock Lake Case File*.
28 Affirmation of Ike Hofer, 2 August 1994. *Rock Lake Case File*.
29 Order of the Court, 4 August 1994. *Rock Lake Case File*.
30 *Precision Feeds v. Rock Lake*, [1994] M.J. No. 450 (Man. Q.B).
31 *Ibid.* at 1.
32 Proposal to the Members of Rock Lake Colony, 12 October 1994, Appendix 4 to the Report of the Receiver/Manager, 20 December 1994. *Rock Lake Case File*.
33 Notice of Motion, 16 November 1994. *Rock Lake Case File*.
34 Affidavit of A.R. Holmes, 16 November 1994. *Rock Lake Case File*.
35 Affirmation of Sam Hofer, 16 November 1994. *Rock Lake Case File*.
36 *Precision Feeds Ltd. v. Rock Lake Colony*, [1994] M.J. No. 703 (Q.B.).
37 Notice of Appeal, 17 February 1995, *Precision Feeds v. Sam Hofer*, Man. C.A., *Case File AI95-30-02137*.
38 Factum of Appellant, 24 March 1995. *Case File AI95-30-02137*.
39 Statement of Claim, 14 April 1994, in *Royal Bank of Canada v. Huron Colony Farms Ltd.*, Man. Q.B., *Case File CI94-01-79789*. [Henceforth *Huron Case File*.] The Royal Bank also brought a separate action to appoint a receiver pursuant to the *Family Farm Protection Act*. See Man. Q.B., *Case File CI94-01-79735*.
40 Affirmation of Levi Waldner, 21 April 1994. *Huron Case File*.

41 Kleinsasser, *supra* note 1 at 173.
42 Minutes of Meetings of Huron Colony, 25 May and 3 September 1993. *Huron Case File.*
43 Notice of Special Meeting, Appendix D to Affirmation of Dave Waldner, 26 April 1994. *Huron Case File.*
44 According to Report of Interim Receiver/Manager, A.R. Holmes, 31 May 1994, at 1. *Huron Case File.*
45 Affirmation of Dave Waldner, 26 April 1994, at 4. *Huron Case File.*
46 Court Order, 15 April 1994. *Huron Case File.*
47 Notice of Appeal, 29 April 1994. Man. C.A., *Case File AI-94-01-79789.* This appeal was dropped after the case was settled.
48 Court Order, 22 April 1994. *Huron Case File.*
49 Report of Receiver, 12 December 1994, at 3. *Huron Case File.*
50 Affidavit of A. Russell Holmes, 12 December 1994. *Huron Case File.*
51 Report of Receiver/Manager, 15 August 1994. *Huron Case File.*
52 As reported in *ibid.* at 2.
53 Court Order, 19 December 1994. *Huron Case File.*
54 Affidavit of Holmes, and Order of Court, 30 January 1995. *Huron Case File.*
55 Affidavit of Holmes, 7 March 1995. *Huron Case File.*
56 Affirmation of Levi Waldner, 20 March 1995. *Huron Case File.*
57 Court Order, 23 March 1995. *Huron Case File.*
58 Report of Receiver/Manager, 20 December 1994, at 6-7. *Huron Case File.*
59 *Joseph Hofer, as President of Cypress Colony v. Paul Wollmann Sr., Paul Wollmann Jr., George Wollmann and MIBIDA Inc.,* Man. Q.B., *Case File CI94-01-85797. Joseph Wollmann as President of Sprucewood Colony v. David Wollmann, Thomas Wollmann and MINTO Holdings Co.,* Man. Q.B., *Case File CI95-01-87332.*
60 A tentative agreement in principle to divide some colonies between the two groups was reached on 9 May 1994. On file with author.
61 Statement of Defence, 14 March 1995, *Hofer v. Wollmann, supra* note 59.
62 I have not attempted to research the American court registries as to case files but have searched only for those cases that have resulted in reported judicial decisions.
63 See Kleinsasser, *supra* note 1 at 195-97.
64 *Wollman v. Poinsett Hutterian Brethren and Clarmont Hutterian Brethren* (1994), 844 F.Supp. 539 (U.S.D. S.D.).
65 See Trautmann, "Judge Refuses to Hear ...," *[Sioux Falls] Argus Leader* (2 February 1994).
66 *Supra* note 64 at 542-43.
67 As reported by Trautmann, *supra* note 65.
68 For example, interview with Samuel Kleinsasser, 14 December 1998. Interview with Mike Hofer, 1 August 2000.
69 *Hutterian Brethren Mutual v. Delta Colony,* Man. Q.B., *Case File CI95-01-87510. Hutterian Brethren Mutual v. Hidden Valley Colony,* Man. Q.B., *Case File C95-01-87511.* The statement of claim in both cases was filed on 15 February 1995 and discontinued on 11 March 1996.
70 Hofer letter, Exhibit 17, *Lakeside Trial 2.* On file with author.
71 Genesis 26:19-22.
72 Visit to Heartland Colony, 25 July 2000.
73 As outlined by Kleinsasser, *supra* note 1 at 192-93.
74 According to Rev. John Hofer, James Valley Colony, in interview with author, 27 July 2000.
75 Interview with Daniel and Paul Hofer, 25 July 2000. Also interview with Rev. Samuel Kleinsasser of Concord Colony, 14 December 1998.
76 On 15 December 1994 the Block land was transferred to the Daniel Hofer group, which then mortgaged the land. By spring the property was more cluttered with scrap than it had been in 1992. It would appear that Daniel Hofer, even after moving to Heartland, was using the Block land as a base for the demolition work of the colony. The municipality brought a motion that Daniel Hofer Sr. be found in contempt of court but, in early 1996, Daniel Hofer Sr. consented to an order by the court that he remove all extraneous structures and vehicles and items of metal, lumber, and concrete from the Block land, or the items could

be seized and sold. Order of Justice Steel, 12 February 1996, Man. Q.B., *Case File 91-01-54765*.

77 Process explained by Rev. John Hofer, James Valley Colony. Interview with author, 27 July 2000.

78 As at 25 July 2000. These figures may not be exact.

79 No one I talked to could remember just when the final deadline was.

80 Letter of Donald Douglas, 8 November 1994. *Lakeside Case File 1*.

81 Notice of Discontinuance, 24 November 1994. *Case File AI94-30-01810*.

82 Notice of Discontinuance, *Case File CI93-01-71650*.

83 Notice of Discontinuance, 2 December 1994. *Case File CI93-01-71213*.

84 The senior patriarch, Rev. Joseph Hofer, died in 1998.

85 Interview with Joshua Hofer Jr., Lakeside Colony, 27 July 2000. The overseer and powerful Kleinsasser loyalist leader, Mike Wollmann of Spring Hill Colony, died in 1999.

86 Kleinsasser, *supra* note 1 at 75.

87 Interview with Rev. Josh Hofer Jr., *supra* note 85.

88 *Ibid.*

Chapter 11: Agreeing to Divide Assets, Further Schism, and Yet More Litigation

1 Samuel Kleinsasser, *Community and Ethics* (1998) [unpublished, on file with author] at 151.

2 *Ibid.* at 152-56.

3 *Ibid.* at 156.

4 *Ibid.* at 160.

5 *Ibid.* at 172.

6 Agreement in Principle, 9 May 1994. On file with author.

7 Agreement of 2 May 1995. This agreement is now a part of the public record attached to the decision of Mr. Justice Kaufman in *Keystone Colony of Hutterian Brethren v. James Valley Colony*, 25 February 1999, [1999] M.J. No. 91 (Q.B.). The *James Valley* decision is also reported at (1995), 135 Man. R. (2d) 130, but without the agreement attached. The agreement is also included in an appendix to the Report of the Receiver, 15 September 1995, in the *Rock Lake Case File*, and as an appendix to the Report of the Receiver, 5 February 1996, in the *Huron Case File*.

8 *Ibid.*

9 Interview with John Hofer, 27 July 2000. See also Kleinsasser, *supra* note 1 at 193-94.

10 Report of the Receiver, 15 September 1995, at 2. *Rock Lake Case File*.

11 Court Order, 12 October 1995. *Rock Lake Case File*.

12 For example, *Unifeed v. Keystone Colony*, Man. Q.B., *Case File CI00-01-16480*. Keystone is sued for almost half a million dollars and the creditor receives garnishment orders on proceeds of sales of hogs and other commodities of colony.

13 Report of Receiver, 15 September 1995, and 5 February 1996. *Huron Case File*.

14 Notice of Motion, 20 February 1996. *Huron Case File*.

15 The member exchange agreement between Trileaf and Huron is attached to the order of the court, 6 March 1996, approving the agreement. *Huron Case File*.

16 Court Order, 6 March 1996. *Huron Case File*.

17 Final Report of the Receiver, 7 November 1996. *Huron Case File*.

18 *Ibid.* at 2.

19 According to Samuel Kleinsasser, *supra* note 1 at 178.

20 Notice of Discontinuance, 26 March 1996, in *Wollmann v. Wollmann* (Sprucewood), *Case File CI95-01-87332*. Notice of Discontinuance, 2 July 1996, *Hofer v. Wollmann* (Cypress), *Case File CI94-01-85797*.

21 Interview with Mike Hofer, Sommerfeld Colony, 1 August 2000.

22 Kleinsasser, *supra* note 1 at 177.

23 Interview with Mike Hofer, Sommerfeld Colony, 1 August 2000.

24 Kleinsasser, *supra* note 1 at 186.

25 *Ibid.*

26 Interview with Mike Hofer, Sommerfeld Colony, 1 August 2000.

27 Letter of 11 December 1990. On file with author.

28 The conference remarks were published in a fifty-three-page booklet by Plough Publishing and the comments of Kleinsasser are also summarized in Michael Cole Barnett, *The Bruderhof and the Hutterites in Historical Context* (PhD diss., Southwestern Baptist Theological Seminary, 1994) at 223-37.

29 As noted by Barnett, who interviewed many Bruderhof leaders. *Ibid.* at 237.

30 *KIT Newsletter* 5:12 (December 1993).

31 *Ibid.*

32 Rich Preheim, "Hutterites Break Along East-West Lines" *Mennonite Weekly Review* (15 June 1995). Reprinted in *KIT Newsletter* 7:7 (July 1995).

33 *KIT Newsletter* 6:8-9 (August-September 1994).

34 Kleinsasser, *supra* note 1 at 150.

35 *Supra* note 32.

36 *Ibid.*

37 *KIT Newsletter* 7:4 (April 1995).

38 *Supra* note 32.

39 *The Plough,* Winter 1995. Before all references to Hutterites were removed, the letter was also available on the Bruderhof web pages. The letter is reproduced in Barnett, *supra* note 28 at 267-72.

40 *Ibid.*

41 *Ibid.*

42 *Supra* note 32.

43 *KIT Newsletter* 7:4 (April 1995).

44 Arthur Allen, "Hutterites Are Shaking the Dust of German Village Off Their Feet" *Charleston Gazette* (4 March 1995).

45 *KIT Newsletter* 7:8-9 (August-September 1995).

46 *Ibid.*

47 Wayne and Betty Chesley, "The Bruderhof Communities, Some Experiences and Observations" (December 1996). Available at <http://w3.ime.net/~wchesley/bruderhof/>, accessed 26 October 2000.

48 As excerpted in *KIT Newsletter* 8:2 (February 1996).

49 Maria Harding, "Local Bruderhofs Split from Hutterites" *Kingston Daily Freeman* (23 February 1997).

50 Peter Warren on CJOB, 30 September 1998.

51 Hutterian Brethren of Crystal Spring Colony, eds., *The Chronicle of the Hutterian Brethren, Volume II* (Alton, MB: Friesen Printers, 1998).

52 Kleinsasser, *supra* note 1 at 53.

53 For example, the Bruderhof Foundation took legal action in court asserting First Amendment rights of children to demonstrate outside a prison. "Bruderhof Children Prevail" *The Plough Online* (18 August 1997). Also, as to tax assessment, see *Hutterian Brethren in New York, Inc., Now Known as Bruderhof Communities of New York, Inc. v. Town of Hunter* (1999), 695 N.Y.S.2d 500 (Super. Ct. Greene County, N.Y.).

54 See <www.plough.com>, accessed 24 October 2000.

55 For example, Johann Christoph Arnold, *Seventy Times Seven: The Power of Forgiveness* (Farmington, PA: Plough Publishers, 1997); Johann Christoph Arnold, *Seeking Peace: Notes and Conversations Along the Way* (Farmington, PA: Plough Publishers, 1998); and Johann Christoph Arnold, *Why Forgive?* (Farmington, PA: Plough Publishers, 2000).

56 For example, Arnold has met with Catholic cardinals and with the Pope. See Johann Christoph Arnold, "Meeting Brother John Paul II," *The Plough* 46 (November-December 1995). He has also travelled to Cuba and met with Fidel Castro.

57 Letter from Bruderhof Leaders Rejecting Mediation by Mennonite Conciliation Service, 12 March 1997. *KIT Newsletter* 9:4 (April 1997).

58 *KIT Newsletter* 8:7 (July 1996).

59 Julius H. Rubin, "Contested Narratives: A Case Study of the Conflict Between a New Religious Movement and Its Critics" (paper presented at the annual meeting for the Society of the Scientific Study of Religion, November 1999). Available at <www.perefound.org>, accessed 25 October 2000.

60 *Bruderhof v. The Peregrine Foundation and Ramon Sender*, U.S. District Court, New York, 19 March 1997, reprinted in *KIT Newsletter* 9:4 (April 1997).

61 *Bruderhof Communities of New York, Inc. and Christian Domar v. The Peregrine Foundation, Ramon Sender, Julius Rubin and Blair Purcell*, July 1997. Available at <www.perefound.com>, accessed 24 October 2000. See also Paul Brooks, "Bruderhof Suit Targets Newsletter" *Times Herald-Record* (10 September 1997).

62 See, for example, opinion of lawyer Barnabas Johnson on the Internet newsgroup <alt.support.bruderhof>, 5 November 1997.

63 Letter to Mr. Peters from Cooper and Dunham law firm, 16 June 1997. Posted on the Internet newsgroup at alt.support.bruderhof.

64 Julius H. Rubin, "The Other Side of Joy: Harmful Religion in an Anabaptist Community," in L. Osborn and A. Hacker, eds., *Harmful Religion: Studies in Religious Abuse* (Lincoln, UK: Society for Promoting Christian Knowledge, 1997), c. 5.

65 Julius H. Rubin, *The Other Side of Joy: Religious Melancholy Among the Bruderhof* (New York: Oxford University Press, 2000).

66 *Rifton Aviation v. Blair Purcell*, U.S.D., Baltimore, MD, reprinted in *KIT Newsletter* 12:8-9 (August-September 2000). See also Peter Geier, "Gaithersburg Man Crosses the Bruderhof" *Daily Record* (31 August 2000).

67 Statement of Claim, 10 March 1997, *H.B. Credit v. Concord Colony*, Man. Q.B., *Case File CI97-01-01535.*

68 See Notice of Discontinuance, 3 April 1998. *Ibid.*

69 *Keystone Colony of Hutterian Brethren, Timothy Hofer and Jonathan Hofer v. James Valley Colony of Hutterian Brethren*, Man. Q.B., *Case File CI98-01-08845.* [Henceforth *James Valley Case File.*]

70 Notation as to "Tim and Jonty," attached to Affirmation of John Hofer, 12 September 1998. *James Valley Case File.*

71 Affirmation of Tim Hofer, 25 June 1998. *James Valley Case File.*

72 Attached as Appendix C to Affirmation. *Ibid.*

73 Letter from James Valley Colony, 26 March 1998. Attached to the Affirmation of John Hofer, 15 September 1998. *James Valley Case File.*

74 *Ibid.*

75 Letter of Paul Edwards, 20 May 1998. Attached to Affirmation of Tim Hofer, 25 June 1998. *James Valley Case File.*

76 Letter of Paul Edwards, 2 June 1998. *James Valley Case File.*

77 Notice of Application. *James Valley Case File.*

78 Affidavit of Samuel Waldner, 20 July 1998. *James Valley Case File.*

79 Notice attached to Affidavit of John Hofer, 15 September 1999. *James Valley Case File.*

80 Position taken by Samuel Waldner, minister of Decker Colony, in Affirmation of 20 July 1998. *James Valley Case File.*

81 *Supra* note 7.

82 Notice of Motion, 20 November 1998. *James Valley Case File.*

83 *Keystone Colony v. James Valley*, [1999] M.J. No. 91. Man. Q.B. Reported (1999), 35 Man. R. (2d) 130.

84 *Wollman v. Poinsett Hutterian Brethren and Clarmont Hutterian Brethren* (1994), 844 F.Supp. 539 (U.S.D. S.D.).

85 Interview with Mike Hofer, 1 August 2000.

86 *Decker v. Tschetter Hutterian Brethren* (1999), 594 N.W.2d 357 (S.D. Sup. Ct.).

87 *Ibid.* at 362.

88 Majority judgment of Gilbertson J. with Miller C.J. and Konenkamp J. concurring, *ibid.* at 358.

89 Dissenting judgment of Sabers J. with Amundson J. concurring, *ibid.* at 366.

Chapter 12: Concluding Reflections

1 The literature dealing with legal pluralism is vast. Noteworthy are articles published in the *Journal of Legal Pluralism*. See, for example, Marc Galanter, "Justice in Many Rooms: Courts, Private Ordering and Indigenous Law" (1981) 19 J. Legal Pluralism 1; and John Griffiths,

"What Is Legal Pluralism?" (1986) 24 J. Legal Pluralism 1. Some legal pluralist literature deals with the critical questions of how the formal laws and legal systems of colonial and post-colonial powers did or did not make room for the pre-existing laws and legal systems (often called customary law) of the groups colonized. See M.B. Hooker, *Legal Pluralism: An Introduction to Colonial and Neo-Colonial Laws* (Oxford: Oxford University Press, 1975). Other legal pluralist literature has moved to the recognition that all societies have multiple associations of semi-autonomous fields of legal ordering and that there are complex interactions between these systems. For a good bibliography and overview see Sally Engle Merry, "Legal Pluralism" (1988) 22 Law & Soc'y Rev. 869. Canadian references include Harry Arthurs, *Without the Law: Administrative Justice and Legal Pluralism in Mid 19th-Century England* (Toronto: University of Toronto Press, 1985); Peter Fitzpatrick, "Law and Societies" (1984) 22 Osgoode Hall L.J. 115; Rod Macdonald, "Metaphors of Multiplicity: Civil Society, Regimes and Legal Pluralism" (1998) 15 Ariz. J. Int'l & Comp. L. 69.

2 To take just one example, see W. Weyrauch and M. Bell, "Autonomous Lawmaking: The Case of the 'Gypsies'" (1993) 103 Yale L.J. 323.

3 The literature is vast. A bibliography is provided by Linda Cardinal, "Collective Rights in Canada: A Critical and Bibliographical Study" (2000-2001) 12 N.J.C.L. 165. See also a special symposium on collective rights edited by Michael McDonald in (1991) 4 Can. J.L. & Jur. One prominent Canadian theorist is Will Kymlicka, *Liberalism, Community and Culture* (Oxford: Clarendon Press, 1989); *Multicultural Citizenship: A Liberal Theory of Minority Rights* (Oxford: Clarendon Press, 1995); *Finding Our Way, Ethnocultural Relations in Canada* (Toronto: Oxford University Press, 1998). See also a collection of essays edited by Will Kymlicka, *The Rights of Minority Cultures* (New York: Oxford University Press, 1995); and Will Kymlicka and Wayne Norman, eds., *Citizenship in Diverse Societies* (Oxford: Oxford University Press, 2000). See also Eric Metcalfe, "Illiberal Citizenship? A Critique of Will Kymlicka's Liberal Theory of Minority Rights" (1996-97) 22 Queen's L.J. 167; Brian Walker, "Plural Cultures, Contested Territories: A Critique of Kymlicka" (1997) 30 Can. J. Poli. Sci. 211. Another theorist of significant importance to the debate is Charles Taylor, *Multiculturalism and "The Politics of Recognition"* (Princeton, NJ: Princeton University Press, 1992). See also John Gray, *Two Faces of Liberalism* (New York: New Press, 2000). Also see Mark D. Rosen, "The Outer Limits of Community Self-Governance in Residential Associations, Municipalities, and Indian Country: A Liberal Theory" (1998) 84 Va. L. Rev. 1053; Mark D. Rosen "'Illiberal' Societal Cultures, Liberalism, and American Constitutionalism" (2002) 12 J. Contemp. Legal Issues 803.

4 A recent symposium on liberalism and illiberal groups is found in (2002) 12 J. Contemp. Legal Issues 625-938.

5 For an argument that groups, whether religious or not, should be free to hire only those who covenant with them as to the social contract of the group, see Alvin J. Esau, "Islands of Exclusivity: Religious Organizations and Employment Discrimination" (2000) 33 U.B.C. L. Rev. 719-827.

6 A Catholic school is forced by law to accommodate a homosexual student wanting to bring his partner to the school prom in *Hall v. Powers* (2002) 213 D.L.R. (4th) 308 (Ont. S.C.).

7 See, for example, *Trinity Western University v. B.C. College of Teachers*, [2001] S.C.C. 31.

8 Regarding the issue of gender equality within illiberal groups, see, for example, Ayelet Shachar, "Reshaping the Multicultural Model: Group Accommodation and Individual Rights" (1998) 8 Windsor Rev. Legal Soc. Issues 83.

9 Donald B. Kraybill and Carl F. Bowman, *On the Backroad to Heaven: Old Order Hutterites, Mennonites, Amish and Brethren* (Baltimore: Johns Hopkins University Press, 2001) at 277.

10 Even if the outside law does not cover a subject matter that is covered by inside law, it should not be forgotten that outside law as a whole may exert a heavy symbolic influence on the development of inside law.

11 For a thoughtful examination of this topic see Ryan Rempel, *Anabaptist Relations with the State: Forms for the Coexistence of Sovereignties* (LL.M. thesis, University of Toronto, 1998). An interesting examination of Mormon efforts to operate their own court system with

broad jurisdictional powers is found in Edwin B. Firmage and Richard C. Mangrum, *Zion in the Courts: A Legal History of the Church of Jesus Christ of Latter-Day Saints 1830-1902* (Urban, IL: University of Illinois Press, 1988).

12 *Lakeside v. Hofer* (1992), 97 D.L.R. (4th) 17 at 20 (S.C.C.).

13 M.H. Ogilvie, *Religious Institutions and the Law in Canada* (Toronto: Carswell, 1996).

14 M.H. Ogilvie, "Ecclesiastical Law – Jurisdiction of Civil Courts – Status of Clergy: *McCaw v. United Church of Canada*," (1992) 71 Can. Bar Rev. 597 at 601.

15 M.H. Ogilvie, "Canadian Civil Court Intervention in the Exercise of Ecclesiastical Jurisdiction" (1997) 31 Stud. Canon. 49 at 50.

16 *Supra* note 14 at 602.

17 See, for example, Mr. Justice B.H. McPherson, "The Church as Consensual Compact, Trust or Corporation," (2000) A.L.J. 159.

18 *Supra* note 15 at 65.

19 *Ibid.* at 61.

20 Older cases include *Bishop of Columbia v. Cridge* (1874), 1 B.C.R. 5 (S.C.); *Halliwell v. The Incorporated Synod of the Diocese of Ontario* (1884), 7 O.R. 67 (Ont. Ch.); *Ex. Parte Currie* (1886), 26 N.B.R. 403 (C.A.); *Ex. Parte Currie* (1889), 28 N.B.R. 475 (C.A.); *Ex Parte Little* (1895), 33 N.B.R. 210 (C.A.); *Ash v. Methodist Church* (1901), S.C.R. 497; *Orr v. Brown*, [1932] 2 W.W.R. 626 (B.C.C.A.); *Chawrink v. Sabulak*, [1938] O.J. No. 121 (C.A.). Newer cases are cited below.

21 Justice Rosenberg in *Lindenburger v. United Church* (1985), 10 O.A.C. 191 (Ont. Div. Ct.) at 193.

22 David Mullan, "Administrative Law at the Margins," in Michael Taggart, ed., *The Province of Administrative Law* (Oxford: Hart Publishing, 1997) at 134. See also Janet McLean, "Intermediate Associations and the State," in Taggart at 160.

23 For example, in *Smith and Kneebone v. Worldwide Church of God* (1980), 39 N.S.R. (2d) 430 (S.C.) the court found sufficient cause re disobedience of higher church authority re minister Kneebone, but insufficient cause to dismiss minister Smith who was awarded eight months' salary in lieu of notice.

24 *Teale v. United Church at Woodlawn*, [1979] N.S.J. No. 23 (C.A.) re should have sued United Church of Canada. *Zec v. St. Archangel*, [1999] O.J. No. 2573 (S.C.) re should have sued diocese and bishop rather than the local parish.

25 *Lindenberger v. United Church* (1987), 20 O.A.C. 381 (C.A.), affirming (1985), 10 O.A.C. 191 (Ont. Div. Ct.).

26 *Lewery v. Governing Council of Salvation Army* (1993), 104 D.L.R. (4th) 449 (N.B.C.A), affirming [1992] N.B.J. No. 756 (Q.B.), appeal to Supreme Court of Canada denied (1994), 107 D.L.R. (4th) vii.

27 *Brewer v. Diocese of Ottawa*, [1996] O.J. No. 634 (C.J.). This case also deals with the legal status of Anglican priests in terms of whether they are employees or office holders. However, it may be read simply for the proposition that absent an agreement to the contrary, the canons of the church constitute the employment contract. This is not unlike the implication found in *Lewery, ibid.*, that a minister, no less than a member, may agree to certain limitations when joining the organization that may amount to less benefits than would be afforded by the common law in other employment settings.

28 *Belding v. Calton Baptist Church*, [1995] O.J. No. 2843 (C.J.).

29 *McCaw v. United Church* (1991), 82 D.L.R. (4th) 289 (Ont. C.A.), reversing in part (1988), 64 O.R. (2d) 513 (H.C.); *Davis and Hobbs v. United Church* (1992), 92 D.L.R. (4th) 678 (Ont. Gen. Div.). In another case, a court reversed a decision of Presbytery to remove a minister for violation of the sexual abuse policy, at least pending an appeal process within the church. See *Frogley v. Ottawa Presbytery* (1995), 16 C.C.E.L. (2d) 249 (Ont. C.J.).

30 See *Tully v. Farrell* (1876), 23 Gr. 49 (Ont. Ch.); *Johnstone v. St. Andrew's Church* (1877), 1 S.C.R. 235 (S.C.C.); *Zawidoski v. Ruthenian Greek Catholic Parish*, [1937] 2 D.L.R. 509 (Man. K.B.); *Patillo v. Cummings* (1915), 24 D.L.R. 775 (N.S.S.C.); *Cohen v. Hazen Avenue Synagogue* (1920), 47 N.B.R. 400 (S.C.); *Wetmon v. Bayne*, [1928] 1 W.W.R. 519 (Alta. C.A.); *Routledge v. Johnston*, [1968] O.J. No. 309 (H.C.); *Mott-Trille v. Steed and Jehovah's Witnesses* (1996), 27 O.R. (3d) 486 (Gen. Div.).

31 *Canadian Temple Cathedral of the Universal Christian Apostolic Church* (1971), 21 D.L.R. (3d) 193 at 199 (B.C.S.C.).
32 *Christensen v. Bodner* (1975), 65 D.L.R. (3d) 549 at 552 (Man. Q.B.).
33 *Zebroski v. Jehovah's Witnesses* (1988), 87 A.R. 229 (C.A.), reversing in part (1986), 71 A.R. 259 (Q.B.), leave to appeal to S.C.C. denied (1989), 94 A.R. 320.
34 *Archer v. Sacred Heart of Jesus* (1905), 9 O.L.R. 474 (C.A.).
35 Carol Weisbrod, *The Boundaries of Utopia* (New York: Pantheon Books, 1980).
36 *Basil v. Spratt and Sisters of Charity* (1918), 45 D.L.R. 555 (Ont. C.A.).
37 In *Zebrowski, supra* note 33, the court held that the tort claims were brought too late and thus statute barred. A tort claim arising from Mennonite shunning was successful in *Heinrichs v. Wiens* (1916), 31 D.L.R. 94 (Sask. S.C.), but cast in doubt in Manitoba in *Toews v. Isaac* (1931), 39 Man. R. 436 (C.A.).
38 I deal with these cases in Alvin J. Esau, "The Judicial Resolution of Church Property Disputes: Canadian and American Models" (2003) 40 Alta. L. Rev. 767-816.
39 *Doder v. Radojkovic,* [1987] O.J. No. 497 (H.C.).
40 Recent cases include *Gill v. Dhillon,* [1997] B.C.J. No. 384 (C.A.), affirming *Dhillon v. Khalsa Diwan Society* (1997), 32 B.C.L.R. (3d) 248 (S.C.); *Bagri v. Sikh Cultural Society,* [1997] B.C.J. No. 1770 (S.C.); *Gill v. Guru Gurobind Singh Temple Assn.,* [1997] B.C.J. No. 2071 (S.C.); *Singh v. Gill,* [1998] B.C.J. No. 805; *Pannu v. Khalsa Diwan Society,* [1998] B.C.J. No. 1613; *Gill v. Bhandal* (1998), 165 D.L.R. (4th) 151 (S.C.); *Hara v. Khalsa Diwan Society – New Westminster,* [1998] B.C.J. No. 2928 (S.C.) and [1998] B.C.J. No. 1495 (S.C.); *Sohi v. Khalsa Diwan Society,* [1999] B.C.J. No. 1299 (S.C.); *Khalsa Diwan Society of Abbotsford v. Sidhu,* [2000] B.C.J. No. 600 and [2000] B.C.J. No. 568 (S.C.); *Korotana v. Guru Gobind Singh Temple Assn.,* [2000] B.C.J. No. 628 (S.C.); *Gill v. Bhandal,* [1999] B.C.J. No. 3115 (S.C.); *Bal v. Kular,* [2000] B.C.J. No. 1941 (S.C.).
41 *Society Act,* R.S.B.C. c. 433.
42 *Zec v. St. Archangel Michael Association,* [1999] O.J. 2573 (Ont. Sup. Ct.) at para. 14.
43 If the church is going to argue that the claim should be dismissed because internal remedies have not been exhausted, the church must provide evidence of the availability of internal processes, which it did not do in a wrongful dismissal claim made by a priest in *Royer v. Ukrainian Catholic Corp. of Western Canada,* [2000] A.J. No. 601 (Alta. Q.B.).
44 *Thompson, Elmhirst, and Symons v. United Church* (1994), Ont. Div. Ct. as reported in (1996) 2 J. Church L. Assoc. Canada 127.
45 *Pederson v. Fulton* (1994), 111 D.L.R. (4th) 367 (Ont. Gen. Div.).
46 *Gruner v. McCormuck,* [2000] O.J. No. 789 (C.J.).
47 *Berg v. Schochet,* [1995] O.J. No. 2983 (C.J.).
48 Given that the synod of the Christian Reform Church of North America had passed a rule that property disputes resulting from congregational schisms should be resolved by a 1 Corinthians 6 process, the court did not take jurisdiction because that route had not been exhausted. See *Breukelman v. Heida,* [1992] O.J. 2604 (Ont. Gen. Div.).
49 The First Amendment of the US Constitution provides that "Congress shall make no law respecting an establishment of religion, or prohibiting the free exercise thereof." This provision has been made applicable to the states as well by being incorporated into the 14th Amendment. See *Cantwell v. Connecticut* (1940), 310 U.S. 296.
50 *Wollman v. Poinsett Hutterian Brethren* (1994), 844 F.Supp. 539 (U.S.D. S.D.).
51 *Decker v. Tschetter Hutterian Brethren* (1999), 594 N.W.2d 357 (S.D. Sup. Ct.).
52 *Simpson v. Wells Lamont* (1974), 494 F.2d 490 at 492 (5th Cir. C.A.).
53 One of the seminal articles on the value of structural autonomy for religious groups is D. Laycock, "Towards a General Theory of the Religion Clauses: The Case of Labor Relations and the Right to Church Autonomy" (1981) 81 Colum. L. Rev. 1373. See also Carl Esbeck, "The Establishment Clause as a Structural Restraint on Governmental Power" (1998) 84 Iowa L. Rev. 1; C. Weisbrod, "Emblems of Federalism" (1992) 25 U. Mich. J.L. Ref. 795; Ira C. Lupu and Robert Tuttle, "The Distinctive Place of Religious Entities in Our Constitutional Order" (2002) 47 Vill. L. Rev. 37.
54 In *Klagsbrun v. Va'ad Harabonim of Greater Monsey* (1999), F.Supp.2d 732 (D.N.J.), the court refused jurisdiction over a case of defamation brought against orthodox Jewish rabbis who

had published their conclusions about the plaintiff's behaviour after he refused to obey the *Beis Din* (Jewish court). In *Grunwald v. Bornfreund* (1988), 696 F.Supp. 838 (N.Y.) the court held that it did not have subject jurisdiction over a threatened excommunication by a Jewish court. In *Fein v. Fein* (1994), 610 N.Y.S.2d 1002 the court refused to either enforce or annul an arbitration decision submitted to a Jewish court.

55 *Burgess v. Rock Creek Baptist Church* (1990), 734 F.Supp. 30 (D.D.C.). Also *Nunn v. Black* (1981), 506 F.Supp. 444 (D.C. Va.).

56 *Alexander v. Shiloh Baptist Church* (1990), 592 N.E.2d 918 (Ohio Com. Pl.).

57 See also *O'Conner v. Diocese of Honolulu* (1994), 885 P.2d 361 (Hawaii Sup. Ct.); *Korean Presbyterian Church v. Lee* (1994), 880 P.2d 565 (Wash. App.). To the same effect re expulsion from religious school, see *Gaston v. Diocese of Allentown* (1998), 712 A.2d 757 (Pa. Super. Ct.).

58 *Gundlach v. Swain* (1996), WL 24748 (E.D. Pa.). The same matter was also dealt with by the state courts in the same way. See *Gundlach v. Laister* (1993), 625 A.2d 706, and *In re St. Clement's Church* (1996), 687 A.2d 11 (Pa. Commonwealth). The court refused jurisdiction to review church discipline in *Williams v. Gleason* (2000), 26 S.W.3d 54 (Tex. C.A.).

59 *Krebs v. Keating* (1997), W.L. 1070589 (Va. Cir. Ct.).

60 *Kelsey v. Ray* (1998), 719 A.2d 1248 (D.C.).

61 *Kond v. Mudryk* (2000), 769 So.2d 1073 at 1076 (Fla. C.A.), quoting from *Partin v. Tucker* (1937), 172 So. 89 (Fla.).

62 *Fowler v. Bailey* (1992), 844 P.2d 141 (Ok. Sup. Ct.).

63 For example, in *O'Conner Hosp. v. Superior Court* (1987), 240 Cal. Rptr. 766 (Cal. C.A.) the court refused to entertain a claim for wrongful dismissal of a priest hired by a Catholic hospital as a chaplain even though there was strong evidence that the dismissal violated the notice provision of the contract of employment. Within some territory of church-related employment, the church is simply immune from liability in the civil courts for civil wrongs that might be alleged to have occurred in the course of the hiring and firing of clergy. Also *Natal v. Christian and Missionary Alliance* (1989), 878 F.2d 1575 (Pu. Rico C.A.); *United Methodist Church v. White* (1990), 571 A.2d 790 (D.C. C.A.); *Patterson v. Southwestern Baptist Theological Seminary* (1993), 858 S.W.2d 602 (Tex. C.A.).

64 *Kral v. Sisters of the Third Order* (1984), 746 F.2d 450 (C.A.); *Lewis v. Seventh Day Adventists Lake Region Conference* (1992), 978 F.2d 940 (D.C. Mich.); *Jay v. Christian Methodist Episcopal Church* (2000), S.E.2d 369 (Ga. C.A.); *Kleppinger v. Anglican Catholic Church* (1998), 715 A.2d 1033 (N.J. Super. Ct.).

65 *Green v. United Pentecostal Church* (1995), 899 S.W.2d 28 (Tex. C.A.).

66 *Higgens v. Maher* (1989), 258 Cal Rptr. 757. (Cal. C.A.); *Farley v. Wisconsin Evangelical Lutheran Synod* (1993), 821 F.Supp. 1286 (D.C. Minn.); *Yaggie v. Indiana-Kentucky Synod* (1995), 64 F.3d 664 (Ky. C.A.); *Downs v. Roman Catholic Archbishop of Baltimore* (1996), 683 A.2d 808 (Md. C.A.); *Tran v. Fiorenza* (1996), 934 S.W.2d 740 (Tex. C.A.)

67 *Brazauskas v. Fort Wayne-South Bend Diocese* (1999), 714 N.E.2d 253 (Ind. C.A.).

68 *McDonnell v. Episcopal Diocese of Georgia* (1989), 381 S.E.2d 126 (Ga. C.A.).

69 *Bledsoe v. Morningside Baptist Church of Atlanta* (1998), 501 S.E.2d 292 (Ga. C.A.).

70 *Gabriel v. Immanuel Evangelical Lutheran Church* (1994), 640 N.E.2d 681 (Ill. C.A.); *Singleton v. Christ the Servant Evangelical Lutheran Church* (1996), 541 N.W.2d 606 (Minn. C.A.); *Bell v. Presbyterian Church* (1997), 126 F.3d 328 (C.A.).

71 *McLure v. Salvation Army* (1972), 460 F.2d 553 (5th Cir.), cert. denied (1972), 409 U.S. 896; *Sanchez v. Catholic Foreign Soc. of America* (1999), 82 F.Supp.2d 1338 (Fla. D.C.); *Geraci v. Eckankar* (1995), 526 N.W.2d 391 (Minn. C.A.). For a more complete analysis of American cases see Esau, *supra* note 5 at 814-24.

72 For an overview of the American cases, see Esau, *supra* note 38.

73 *Fussell v. Hail* (1908), 84 N.E. 42 (Ill. Sup. Ct.).

74 *Higgins v. Maher* (1989), 258 Cal. Rptr. 757 at 760-61 (Cal. C.A.).

75 *Kaddoura v. Hammoud*, [1998] O.J. No. 5054 (C.J.). There is also an earlier ruling from the Manitoba Court of Appeal refusing to force a husband to grant a Jewish bill of divorcement to his wife who had been granted a divorce in the secular courts. See *Morris v. Morris,* [1974] 2 W.W.R. 193 (Man. C.A.).

76 *Levitts Kosher Foods v. Levin* (1999), 45 O.R. (3d) 147 (S.C.).

77 *Cohen v. First Narayav Congregation*, [1983] O.J. No. 499 (H.C.).

78 *Ibid.* at para. 11.

79 For a good overview see Kent Greenawalt, "Hands Off! Civil Court Involvement in Conflicts Over Religious Property" (1998) Colum. L. Rev. 1843.

80 See Esau, *supra* note 38.

81 *Canadian Charter of Rights and Freedoms*, Part I of the *Constitution Act, 1982*, being Schedule B to the *Canada Act 1982* (U.K.), 1982, c. 11. [Henceforth *Charter.*]

82 Section 2 of the *Charter* provides that "everyone has the following fundamental freedoms: (a) freedom of conscience and religion. Section 15 provides that "every individual is equal before and under the law and has the right to equal protection and equal benefit of the law without discrimination and, in particular, without discrimination based on race, national or ethnic origin, colour, *religion*, sex, age, or mental disability" [my emphasis]. Section 1 however says that the rights and freedoms are "subject only to such reasonable limits prescribed by law as can be demonstrably justified in a free and democratic society."

83 *Wisconsin v. Yoder* (1972), 406 U.S. 205.

84 See, for example, *Michigan v. Swartzentruber* (1988), 429 N.W.2d 225 (C.A.); *Minnesota v. Hershberger* (1990), 462 N.W.2d 393 (Sup. Ct.); and *Wisconsin v. Miller* (1995), 538 N.W.2d 573 (C.A.).

85 *Hutterian Brethren Church of Eagle Creek v. Eagle Creek Rural Municipality*, [1983] 2 W.W.R. 438 (Sask. C.A.).

86 *McKinney v. University of Guelph*, [1990] 3 S.C.R. 229.

87 *RWDSU v. Dolphin Delivery*, [1986] 2 S.C.R. 573. In *Thomas v. Norris*, [1992] 2 C.N.L.R. 139 (B.C.S.C.) an action was brought for false imprisonment, assault, and battery because the plaintiff had been forcefully grabbed and initiated into the spirit dance without his consent. The defendants did not claim freedom of religion under the *Charter*, but they did claim that the spirit dance was an existing Aboriginal right. The court held that the *Charter* did not apply to possible defences to the tort claims between private individuals.

88 *New York Times v. Sullivan* (1963), 376 U.S. 254.

89 *Paul v. Watchtower Society* (1987), 819 F.2d 875 (9th Cir.), cert. denied, (1987) 484 U.S. 926.

90 *Ibid.* at 883 (9th Cir.).

91 *Bear v. Reformed Mennonite Church* (1975), 341 A.2d 105 (Pa. Sup. Ct.). To the same effect in a case involving the possible tort of interference with business relations when a dentist was expelled from a church, see *Lide v. Miller* (1978), 573 S.W.2d 614 (Tex. C.A.).

92 *Guinn v. Church of Christ* (1989), 775 P.2d 766 (Ok. Sup. Ct.). In a subsequent case where church officials revealed embarrassing information during the process of expulsion the court upheld the freedom of religion of the church against tort claims where the plaintiffs had not voluntarily withdrawn from the church before the process of discipline took place. See *Hadnot v. Shaw* (1992), 826 P.2d 978 (Ok. Sup. Ct.). More recently, the Michigan Supreme Court held that withdrawal of membership alone is not definitive on the factual issue as to whether the plaintiff has withdrawn consent to actions by the church which might otherwise amount to an actionable wrong. See *Smith v. Calvary Christian Church* (2000), 614 N.W.2d 590 (Mich. Sup. Ct.) holding that the plaintiff continued to be involved in the church despite his purported resignation of membership and, thus, his original consent to be bound by the discipline of the group continued. However, in a case involving a claim for breach of confidence brought by an expelled bishop who allegedly was promised confidentiality about his confession of having an extramarital affair but then had the information disclosed in the process of expulsion, the appeal court remanded the case back to the trial level for the application of a balancing test on the facts. See *Snyder v. Evangelical Orthodox Church* (1989), 264 Cal. Rptr. 640 (Cal. C.A.).

93 *Ginerich v. Swartzentruber* (1919), 22 Ohio N.P. (N.S.) 1.

94 *Dolphin Delivery*, *supra* note 87; *Dagenais v. C.B.C.*, [1994] 3 S.C.R. 835; *Hill v. Church of Scientology*, [1995] 2 S.C.R. 1130.

95 Although for an interesting and refreshing argument for the secular value of protecting religious faith as a mode of belief, see T. Macklem, "Faith as a Secular Value" (2000) 45 McGill L.J. 1.

96 *Supra* note 93 at 10.

97 *Employment Division v. Smith* (1990), 494 U.S. 872.
98 The *Religious Freedom Restoration Act of 1993* which was passed to restore the test was declared in some respects to be unconstitutional in *City of Boerne v. Flores* (1997), 521 U.S. 507. However, many state courts continue to utilize a compelling interest test under religious freedom provisions of state constitutions.
99 *Re Bill 30* [1987] 1 S.C.R. 1148; *Adler v. Ontario,* [1996] 3 S.C.R. 609.
100 *Zylberberg v. Sudbury Board of Education* (1988), 65 O.R. (2d) 641 (C.A.).
101 *C.C.L.A. v. Ontario* (1990), 71 O.R. (2d) 341 (C.A.).
102 *Freitag v. Town of Penetanguishene* (1999), 179 D.L.R. (4th) 150 (Ont. C.A.).
103 For an overview of Canadian jurisprudence see Ogilvie, "The Unbearable Lightness of Charter Canada" (2002) 3 J. Church L. Assoc. Canada 201; Shannon Smithey, "Religious Freedom and Equality Concerns under the Canadian Charter" (2001) 34 Can. J. Poli. Sci. 85; Janet Epp Buckingham, "Caesar and God: Limits to Religious Freedom in Canada and South Africa" (2001) 15 Sup. Ct. L. Rev. (2d) 461; David M. Brown, "Freedom from or Freedom for? Religion as a Case Study in Defining the Content of Charter Rights" (2000) 33 U.B.C. L. Rev. 551; Paul Horwitz, "The Sources and Limits of Freedom of Religion in a Liberal Democracy: Section 2(a) and Beyond" (1996) 54 U.T.Fac. L. Rev. 1.
104 See, for example, Bruce MacDougall, "A Respectful Distance: Appellate Courts Consider Religious Motivation of Public Figures in Homosexual Equality Discourse – The Cases of *Chamberlain* and *Trinity Western University*" (2002) 35 U.B.C. L. Rev. 511-538; Benjamin Berger, "The Limits of Belief: Freedom of Religion, Secularism and the Liberal State" (2002) 17 C.J.L.S. 39.
105 [1970] S.C.R. 958.
106 *Hofer v. Hofer* (1966), 59 D.L.R. (2d) 723 (Man. Q.B.).
107 *Supra* note 38. Also see M.H. Ogilvie, "Church Property Disputes: Some Organizing Principles" (1992) 42 U.T.L.J. 377.
108 *Articles of Association of Lakeside Hutterite Colony,* clause 2. On file with author.
109 *Ibid.,* clause 3.
110 *Ibid.,* clause 12.
111 *Ibid.,* clause 13.
112 *Ibid.,* clause 44.
113 *Ibid.,* clause 39.
114 *Ibid.,* clauses 36 and 37.
115 A recent translation by John J. Friesen is Peter Riedemann, *Hutterite Confession of Faith* (Waterloo: Herald Press, 1999).
116 *Constitution of the Hutterian Brethren Church and Rules as to Community of Property* (21 July 1993), Preamble. The same in both new and old versions.
117 *Ibid.,* clause 49 in both new and old versions.
118 *Supra* note 38. It was obvious in *Hofer supra* note 105 that the plaintiffs had switched religions. It was also obvious in another Manitoba case dealing with a switch from the Icelandic Evangelical Lutheran to the Unitarian Church. See *Anderson v. Gislason* (1920), 30 M.R. 536 (C.A.).
119 See *Dorland v. Jones* (1886), 14 S.C.R. 39; *Itter v. Howe* (1896), 23 O.A.R. 256 (Ont. C.A.); *Wodell v. Potter,* [1930] 1 D.L.R. 726; [1930] 2 D.L.R. 449 (Ont. C.A.); *Cohen v. First Narayav Congregation,* [1983] O.J. No. 499 (H.C.); *Chong v. Lee* (1981), 29 B.C.L.R. 13 (S.C.).
120 Numerous Canadian cases are based on the determination of implied or express affiliation trusts. See, for example, *Zacklynski v. Pulushie,* [1908] A.C. 65 (P.C.); *The King v. Kapj* (1905), 9 C.C.C. 186 (Man. K.B.); *Huegli v. Pauli* (1912), 4 D.L.R, 319 (Ont. H.C.); *Stein v. Hauser* (1913), 15 D.L.R. 223 (Sask. S.C.); *Forler v. Brenner,* [1922] Ont. W.N. 249; *Henning v. Trautman,* [1926] 2 D.L.R. 280 (Alta. S.C.); *Brendszij v. Hajdij,* [1926] 2 D.L.R. 626 (Man. Q.B.); *Balkou v. Gouleff* (1989), 68 O.R. (2d) 574 (C.A.); *United Church of Canada v. Anderson* (1991), 2 O.R. (3d) 304 (Gen. Div.); *Edmonton Korean Baptist Church v. Kim* (1996), 189 A.R. 156 (Q.B.).
121 The idea of dividing property between factions who are still within the scope of the trust has some judicial support. See *Buma v. Sikkema,* [1993] O.J. No. 2356 (Gen. Div.), appealed on other grounds [1994] O.J. No. 2791 (C.A.). See also subsequent litigation, *Mount Hamilton Christian Reformed Church v. Sikkema,* [1995] O.J. No. 1568 (Gen. Div.).

122 Mike McIntyre, "Hutterites Want Rebels Out of Colony" *Winnipeg Free Press* (19 September 2001).
123 Some background to the dispute is provided by Dawn Walton, "Family Feud Lifts Veil on Private World of Hutterite Colony" *Globe and Mail* (20 January 2003) at A1 and A4.
124 *Waldner v. Ponderosa Hutterian Brethren,* [2003] A.J. No. 6 (Q.B.).

Appendix: Male Genealogy of Lakeside Families
  1 Some of this information is taken from John S. Hofer, "The Hutterian Brethren," in *Treasures of Time: The Rural Municipality of Cartier 1914-1984* (Altona, MB: Friesen Printers, 1985). Other information comes from the court records or from interviews.

Index

Printed and bound in Canada by Friesens

Set in Stone by Artegraphica Design Co. Ltd.

Copy editor: Judy Phillips

Proofreader: Alison Cairns

Indexer: Patricia Buchanan